Canadian Guide to Uniform Legal Citation

9th Edition

Manuel canadien de la référence juridique

9e édition

THOMSON REUTERS®

A cataloguing record for this publication is available from Library and Archives Canada.

ISBN 978-0-7798-8581-7 (bound) – 978-0-7798-8582-4 (pbk)

THOMSON REUTERS CANADA, A DIVISION OF THOMSON REUTERS CANADA LIMITED

One Corporate Plaza
2075 Kennedy Road
Toronto, Ontario
M1T 3V4

Customer Support
1-416-609-3800 (Toronto & International)
1-800-387-5164 (Toll Free Canada & U.S.)
Fax 1-416-298-5082 (Toronto)
Fax 1-877-750-9041 (Toll Free Canada Only)
Email CustomerSupport.LegalTaxCanada@TR.com

Acknowledgements / Remerciements

Jakub Adamski
Laura Alford
Nigah Awj
Justice Ian Binnie
Laura Buckingham
Connie Budaci
Laura Cárdenas
Cathy Costa-Faria
Sophie Doyle
Éléna Sophie Drouin
Bonnie Fish
Michel Fraysse
Mark Gannage
Patrick Garon-Sayegh
Raphaël Grenier-Benoit
George Gretton
Justice Patrick Healy
Maegan Hough
A. Max Jarvie
Barhilla Jesse-Buadoo
Amy Kaufman
Rob Kligman
Robert Leckey
Nicole Léger
Neva Lyn-Kew
Jonathan Mooney
Elizabeth Moore
Juge Yves-Marie Morissette
Donal Nolan
Emma Noradounkian
Adrian Pel
Lana Rackovic
Giorgio Resta
Sadri Saieb
Svetlana Samochkine
Kerry Sloan
Angela Swan
Lukas Heckendorn Urscheler
Ivo Vogel
Elizabeth Wells
Lisa-Marie Williams
Victoria Woo

SUMMARY TABLE OF CONTENTS / TABLE DES MATIÈRES ABRÉGÉE

English

French

Appendices / Annexes

A Word from the Editor

For more than thirty years, the McGill Law Journal has contributed to the development of legal citation through its *Guide*. We have always presented our work as a pan-Canadian landmark on the subject. In the English version of the title, the term "uniform" generates many debates and it does not constitute a disregard on our part. We have created a work that reflects Canadian reality as no other legal reference manual has done. We are constantly fighting to preserve its bilingualism, and with each edition we strive to establish standards that take into account the particularities of different cultures and the different types of legal sources in Canada.

The two main objectives that have guided us in the preparation of this ninth edition are conciseness and accessibility. While these two characteristics usually go hand in hand, at times, we had to make difficult decisions in order to reconcile them. In the name of accessibility, we kept many details that brevity commanded us to reduce. It was monastic work to determine the elements to be retained and withdrawn, but each of the decisions we made was studied at length and debated with experts. Notably, we agreed to eliminate several tables of examples and to delete bulleted lists. A legal reference manual should not resemble a scientific protocol, but rather should contain general and coherent rules and principles so that all sources, however unique, can be cited.

If civil and common law sources have always been represented in a balanced way in our *Guide*, Indigenous law sources have generally been neglected. In this edition, we have included rules for referencing Indigenous constitutional documents and intergovernmental documents (treaties and land claim agreements), not counting the new examples of Indigenous law disseminated in the existing sections. However, in preparation for the upcoming edition, we plan to conduct extensive consultations with practitioners and scholars in this area in order to broaden the scope of Indigenous sources covered by this *Guide*.

In editing this work, we have dedicated a large effort toward making the citation rules accessible with regard to electronic sources. The *Guide* is published on a quadrennial basis, therefore, it is essential that each edition is consistently updates online references. While electronic documents are often ephemeral and informal, they are nonetheless very accessible and increasingly used by Canadian jurists. There are now many Internet link archiving systems, which address both the problem of broken links and endless addresses. Like the *Bluebook*, the *Guide* now encourages reference to permanent links whenever a website needs to be identified.

Our reconfiguration of the hierarchy of jurisprudential sources also gives online databases greater status. It is pointless to deny that a large number of users of the *Guide* do not use printed versions of jurisprudential sources; they consult decisions on CanLII, LexisNexis or Westlaw, and then choose the printed collections from those listed on these electronic services to include in their reference. Under this ninth edition, versions found on online databases have the same status as any unofficial collection. Indeed, it would have been absurd to discourage the use of a service like CanLII, which is all at once free, reliable and accessible.

Thanks to the many orchestrated changes in this edition, we are confident that the *Guide* will continue to be at the forefront of legal reference. In December 2017, the Quebec Society for Legal Information (SOQUIJ) set up an electronic citation help tool that automatically records legal references in accordance with the Guide's standards. In April 2018, Hein Online also introduced a system that provides legal references according to the standards of the *Guide* for all documents in its database. These are two examples that demonstrate the scope of the *Guide* and its presence in the world of online legal research.

When we initiated this ninth edition, we had a plethora of ambitious projects in mind and established long lists of improvements to be made. The support of many experts has been instrumental in advancing these many projects. We have therefore included for the first time a list of acknowledgments to account for the invaluable contribution of each expert who made this edition possible. The contribution of the Citations Editor, 2018-2019, Barhilla Jesse-Buadoo, who finalized this work, should also be highlighted.

It is unthinkable to achieve perfection in an undertaking that is constantly evolving and that is why other editions will follow. The key is to be able to keep up to date on a regular basis and improve some sections in each edition. We have a great need for the opinions of members of the legal community and their support to perfect our *Guide*. Therefore, please send us your comments and suggestions to the following address:

McGill Law Review
3644 Peel Street
Montreal, Quebec H3A 1W9
Canada

Tel: 514-398-7397
Fax: 514-398-7360
http://lawjournal.mcgill.ca
journal.law@mcgill.ca

Nicolas Labbé-Corbin
Editor of the Reference Manual, 2017-2018

Foreword by the Honourable Ian Binnie

This ninth edition of the *Canadian Guide to Uniform Legal Citation* is a welcome update to a very serious and practical work. Lawyers and judges are always seeking legitimacy for their views from prior authorities. While this observation is self evidently true for the common law, the judgments of the Quebec courts are replete with citations of cases decided under the *Civil Code* or other statute. Reliance on precedents and authorities puts a high premium on accurate citation. Readers cannot be expected to verify what they cannot quickly and efficiently locate.

Amassing wide-ranging and meticulous research embracing Canada's multi-juridical and bilingual traditions was (and continues to be) a monumental undertaking. The topic is deceptively straightforward for beneath the surface the ground sometimes shifts. There are numerous examples of conventions shifting over time. While this *Guide* carefully explains the proper usage of references like *supra*, the Supreme Court has banished this word from its reports. The use of a dead language is not to be encouraged, apparently. Equally, while the Supreme Court used to strenuously avoid the use of footnotes even where supplementary information in a footnote may have been helpful, footnotes now appear in judgments with reasonable frequency, and their use varies greatly from judge to judge. There is room for idiosyncrasy. Some appellate judges eschew references to "the court below" on the basis that such elitist language conveys an unwarranted pretension to personal superiority. These are sensitivities that do not (and need not) find their way into the *Guide*.

The editors are quite right to insist on the desirability of citing the official reports (e.g. the *Supreme Court Reporter* series), where available, over the private services (e.g. the *Dominion Law Reports*) as this increases the accessibility of legal information to all readers. Furthermore, for a variety of reasons, citing from internet versions of sources can be problematic. For example, references to paragraph numbers in the online version of the SCRs from the 1990s or earlier are wrong because in that era, the paragraphs in Supreme Court judgments were not numbered. Thus, a pinpoint was referenced to the page, not the paragraph. However, the *Guide* in its commitment to detail and accuracy requires, whenever possible, citing the pinpoint to the paragraph. Moreover, in the case of official federal reports, the two official language versions are printed side by side. Both versions are equally authoritative, and some judges like to resolve an alleged ambiguity in one version by cross referencing it with the other version. Therefore, a citation that only references the DLR, WWR, or an online version of a judgment where a text is otherwise available in a bilingual format is to rightly be discouraged per the dictates of the *Guide*.

The present work is also helpful because, beyond the basics-such as the use of round versus square brackets-many of us are unfamiliar with the intricate "rules" governing proper legal citation. We cannot apply what we do not know. Certainly, many of us would not know the proper way to cite a "Tweet" (but within the confines of this book, the lawyer practicing due diligence will find the answer in section 6.19.5.1.2). By way of further example, the editors articulate gradations in the meaning of references that lawyers may otherwise perceive only dimly, such as the distinctions between "see", "see especially", "see e.g." and "see also", until they read the explanation in section 1.3.6. Now, armed with the guidance laid out in these pages, the legal community is better equipped to join the effort towards uniformity.

The Faculty of Law at McGill University is in an ideal position to provide guidance on such a multi-juridical and bilingual project because its scholarship spans the civil, common, and Indigenous legal systems of Canada. Moreover, as illustrated by this ninth edition of the *Guide*, the Faculty is also blessed with student editors of great initiative and industry. We continue to be in their debt.

The Honourable Ian Binnie CC QC
Former Justice at the Supreme Court of Canada
May 2018

Foreword by the Honourable Patrick Healy

The suggestion for a guide to legal citation was originally considered by the Editorial Board of the McGill Law Journal in 1981. The first edition was published in 1986 and new editions have since appeared almost every four years. With each edition, including this ninth edition, there have been significant modifications and improvements. The quality of the *Guide* is reflected in the wide range of publications and institutions that use it. These include most legal journals in Canada, various courts and other institutions.

The publication of the *Guide* filled a gap in Canada. Citation in legal writing was previously marked by inconsistency in form and substance. It was common to find inconsistency within a single text, among texts in a single publication, and among various publications. There were various books available that were typically concerned with methods of legal research, some of which included materials concerned with citation. But there was no consensus on the principles or forms of citations. Today there are various styles and models that are used in academic writing, by courts and other institutions, and by practitioners in Canada. This variety of styles and practices will remain and, for this reason, it is not easy to speak comfortably of binding, let alone uniform, rules of citation. None of these has established the influence of the *Guide* published by the *McGill Law Journal*. Widespread adoption of the *Guide* has enhanced the measure of consistency and discipline in legal citation in Canada.

A guide to citation is a specialised form of style manual but not one that lends itself to aesthetic elegance. Its aims are to promote the efficient communication of information, typically in technical references that justifies or explains the corresponding text. Citations in a text bear some resemblance to the relation between evidence and a thesis or argument. Legal citation is functional but vital to effective communication in the same manner as evidence supports a thesis. Any citation must be understood as an integral part of the text it serves. It should be in the text only if it merits a place and only to the extent that is necessary to make the text as a whole effective as the communication of its intended meaning.

On the principle that brevity is a virtue, citations must nevertheless be complete, accurate, and consistent. These characteristics cannot justify a claim or an ambition to a uniform style or practice of citation. This is amply demonstrated not only in the array of various models in Canada, and elsewhere, but in the noisy polemical debates in the United States concerning the merits of various guides.[1] At

1 See Susie Salmon, "Shedding the Uniform: Beyond a 'Uniform System of Citation' to a More Efficient Fit" (2016) 99:3 Marq L Rev 763; Fred R Shapiro & Julie Graves Krishnaswami, "The Secret History of the Bluebook" (2016) 100:4 Minn L Rev 1563; Richard A Posner, "The Bluebook Blues" (2011) 120:4 Yale LJ 850; Richard A Posner, "Goodbye to the Bluebook" (1986) 53:4 U Chicago L Rev 1343.

best guides can provide advice and conventions for consistent practice without claiming the authority of orthodox dogma.

This ninth edition once again shows great effort to maintain the currency and timeliness of the *Guide*. Apart from its bilingual character, the materials show close attention to French and other issues of citation in continental, national, and international jurisdictions. The editors have also made continuing efforts to simplify the style of citations, as in the reduction of periods, commas, and other cosmetic blemishes, but even here there might be room for further simplification. Perhaps the most recent feature in the *Guide* is the attention to materials available on the internet and other electronic media. With only little exaggeration, it is possible to find in the keyboard of many devices several national libraries and the accumulation of legal materials over centuries.

The shift from print to other sources of information is radical, of course, and far surpasses in magnitude the revolution of moveable print. It might be asked whether this shift will also lead to radical changes in the practice of citation. For example, the *Guide* maintains its position in favour of parallel citations for cases and many other forms of information. Print has not fallen into desuetude but serious consideration might well be given to a recommendation that favours neutral citations to the exclusion of parallel citations. Many lament the passing of hours in institutions called libraries in the reassuring company of objects of art known widely as books. Notwithstanding this nostalgia, the steady march of information technology has eroded the lumpish pleasure derived from the tactile manipulation of quires of paper stitched in a binding. The routine practices of research and writing have diminished the significance of paper sources and it might be argued in a near future that a neutral citation should be preferred, without need for parallel citations, for any available source. Such a shift would significantly enhance simplicity, brevity, and easy access.

The editors of the McGill Law Journal will continue through successive editions to ensure that the *Canadian Guide to Uniform Legal Citation* will keep pace with the dizzying changes in information and the demands for effective citation. For this ninth edition they deserve the warmest congratulations of the Canadian legal community for welcome, and necessary, guidance.

The Honourable Patrick Healy
Quebec Court of Appeal
May 2018

Foreword by Mtre Daniel Boyer

Citations are essential components of legal writing as we lead others, and others lead us, to legislation, jurisprudence, and secondary materials. All jurists must deploy and decipher references, and the protocols in this ninth edition of the *Canadian Guide to Uniform Legal Citation* present methods and formats to make the use of this indispensable informational apparatus easier and more comprehensive.

Citations can never be right or wrong in a judicial sense, but they can be accurate or inaccurate as they fulfil their task of leading researchers-effortlessly and efficiently-to the proper legal sources. This is proven by the frustrations inaccurate and incomplete citations cause when they lead us to seek erroneous information.

Citation is not a matter of *elegantia juris* and remains a predominantly formal exercise. Whereas consistency is vital to proper citation, homogeneity is not and citation practice often requires critical reflection. In his brilliant and witty book on the fundamental elements of academic writing, the Italian semiotician and novelist Umberto Eco thus sums up the purpose and function of citation:

> These guidelines are of the utmost importance, and you must have the patience to become familiar with them. You will realize that they are primarily functional guidelines, because they allow you and your reader to identify the exact book to which you are referring. But they are also rules, so to speak, of erudite etiquette. Their observance reveals a scholar who is familiar with the discipline, and their violation betrays the academic parvenu, and sometimes casts a shadow of discredit on an otherwise rigorous work. These rules of etiquette matter, and they should not be disparaged as a formalist's weakness. [. . .] [B]efore you can declare that it is unnecessary to italicize a book's title, you must first know that this is in fact the convention, and you must understand the reasons for this convention.[1]

Citation protocols have their critics, be they pragmatic, academic, or even conceptual. Debates on the form, content, and access of citation guides appear nowhere close to being settled. Nonetheless, development, if not progress, in citation continues thanks to an acceptance of Eco's "reasons for the convention." The ever-evolving form and content of legal sources and, of course, legal writing's extensive reliance on intertextuality, is the *raison d'être* of this volume.

Most, if not all, citation rules deploy abbreviations and part of becoming a fully-fledged legal scholar implies acquiring a fluency in their use. Just as any baseball fan knows that a "K" is a strike or any Mozart fan knows that "K" stands for the

---

[1] Umberto Eco, How to Write a Thesis, translated by Caterina Mongiat Farina and Geoff Farina (Cambridge, Mass: MIT Press, 2015) at 62.

Köchel catalogue, an accomplished jurist knows that "KB" is the King's Bench. Legal abbreviations have been with us since the days of Emperor Justinian who, notwithstanding his monumental achievement in guiding the Law's codification, failed to eradicate legal abbreviations despite having banned their usage in the *Corpus Juris Civilis*: "We order that the text of this codex shall not be written with deceptive symbols (*siglorum captiones*) and puzzling abbreviations (compendiosa aenigmata) [...] but they must be made intelligible by the ordinary sequence of letters."[2] The Emperor went on to stipulate punitive measures for those who "should dare to write Our laws in obscure symbols (siglorum obscuritates)."[3] Yet, as anyone familiar with legal texts knows, not even the Emperor could stop the growth of abbreviations in legal publications. Thanks to the rules and tables laid out in the *Guide*, both writers and readers can decipher and use abbreviations effectively.

Citation protocols reflect various jurisdictions' originality and can be characterized as deeply comparative despite the lack of grand theories buttressing them. As one can see at section 7.5.2 of the *Guide*, French decisions are cited with the court's name first and the name of the reporter (or the periodical) second, followed by the exact date of the decision; names of the parties are usually omitted, unlike the Common Law citation practice. What would a legal semiotician say of the continental emphasis on the court, versus the common law stress on the parties, despite the reliance of the principle of *stare decisis* on courts and dates?

Despite my long-standing involvement with the *Guide*, I have never succumbed to either citation fetishism or citation fundamentalism. I am happy to have borne witness to the *Guide*'s evolution from a rigid formalism to a clearer style and structure that increases access to legal knowledge, while consistently holding firm on fuzzy citation.

Mtre Daniel Boyer
Faculty advisor to the
Canadian Guide to Uniform Legal Citation
May 2018

---

[2] Cod 1.17.1 s 13 (Bruce W Frier, ed, *The Codex of Justinian: A New Annotated Translation, with Parallel Latin and Greek Text Based on a Translation by Justice Fred H Blume* (Cambridge: Cambridge University Press, 2016).

[3] *Ibid*, 1.17.2 s 22.

TABLE OF CONTENTS

1 General Rules E-3

1 GENERAL RULES

The rules in this *Guide* apply only to **footnote citations**, **in-text citations**, and **bibliographies**. They do not apply to the main text or textual footnotes (i.e., sentences and clauses that exist outside the confines of the citation); a style guide, such as the *Chicago Manual of Style*, should be used for issues arising in these areas.

Use the rules from the English section when writing in English, even if the source being referred to is in another language. Use the French rules only when writing in French. If a rule states that parentheses ( ) must be used, do not replace them with brackets [ ] and vice versa. The **bold, coloured font** has been used to make some examples in this *Guide* explicit.

1.1 BIBLIOGRAPHIES / TABLES OF AUTHORITIES

Divide bibliographies and tables of authorities into the following sections: **Legislation**, **Jurisprudence**, and **Secondary Materials**. If a source does not fit into a defined section, a residual section entitled **Other Materials** may be used. When appropriate, divide the Legislation and Jurisprudence sections into subsections (e.g., **Legislation: Canada**; **Legislation: France**; **Jurisprudence: Foreign**; etc.). It may also be useful to divide the **Secondary Material** section into subsections (e.g., **Secondary Material: Articles**; **Secondary Material: Monographs**).

Within each section, **list the entries in alphabetical order**. Sort legislation by title, jurisprudence by style of cause, and secondary materials by the author's family name.

If a citation directly follows a citation to another work by the same author, replace the author's names with a 3-em dash (i.e., three em dashes in a row, see the "Wampum at Niagara" example, above).

For secondary material included in a bibliography, **the author's family name appears first** to facilitate the classification in alphabetical order. Depending on cultural conventions, a family name may appear before, after, or in-between given names. If the family name normally appears first (e.g., **Wang Sheng Chang**), do not place a comma after it. If the given name normally appears first, place a comma after the surname (e.g., **Smith, Graham JH**). In the service of accuracy and respect for the source, present the author's name as it appears on the title page of the source publication, including any initials, even if this leads to different versions of his or her name in a subsequent reference to that author's work.

If there is more than one author for a reference, write the given name before the surname for every author except the first one (e.g., **Baudouin, Jean-Louis & Pierre-Gabriel Jobin**). If there is a work by a single author and a work by that same author and others (e.g., **Baudouin** and **Baudouin & Jobin**), cite the one with a single author first.

Insert a **hanging indent** of 0.63 cm (1/4 inch) before each citation. Indent all the lines except for the first one.

LEGISLATION

Anti-terrorism Act, SC 2001, c 41.
Aggregate Resources Act, RSO 1990, c A.8.
National Arts Council Act (Cap 193A, 1992 Rev Ed Sing).
Tobacco Product Control Act, RSC 1985, c 14 (4th Supp).

JURISPRUDENCE

Delgamuukw v British Columbia, [1997] 3 SCR 1010, 153 DLR (4th) 193.
Kendle v Melsom, [1998] HCA 13.
Létourneau c Laflèche Auto Ltée, [1986] RJQ 1956 (Sup Ct).
Nova Scotia (Workers' Compensation Board) v Martin, 2003 SCC 54.

SECONDARY MATERIAL: MONOGRAPHS

Bakan, Joel *et al*, *Canadian Constitutional Law*, 3rd ed (Toronto: Edmont Montgomery, 2003).

Baudouin, Jean-Louis & Pierre-Gabriel Jobin, *Les obligations*, 5th ed (Cowansville, QC: Yvon Blais, 1998).

Christians, Allison, Samuel A Donaldson & Philip F Postlewaite, *United States International Taxation*, 2nd ed (New Providence, NJ: LexisNexis, 2011).

Macklem, Patrick, *Indigenous Difference and the Constitution of Canada* (Toronto: University of Toronto Press, 2001).

Nadeau, Alain-Robert, *Vie privée et droits fondamentaux* (Cowansville, QC: Yvon Blais, 2000).

Smith, Graham JH, *Internet Law and Regulation*, 3rd ed (London, UK: Sweet & Maxwell, 2002).

SECONDARY MATERIAL: ARTICLES

Borrows, John, "With or Without You: First Nations Law (in Canada)" (1996) 41 McGill LJ 629.

———, "Wampum at Niagara: The Royal Proclamation, Canadian Legal History, and Self-Government" in Michael Asch, ed, *Aboriginal and Treaty Rights in Canada: Essays on Law, Equity, and Respect for Difference* (Vancouver: UBC Press, 1997) 155.

Deleury, E, "Naissance et mort de la personne ou les confrontations de la médecine et du droit" (1976) 17 C de D 265.

Wang Sheng Chang, "Combination of Arbitration with Conciliation and Remittance of Awards: With Special Reference to the Asia-Oceana Region" (2002) 19 J Intl Arb 51.

1.2 IN-TEXT REFERENCES: MEMORANDUM AND FACTUM

In legal writing, the standard rule is to use footnotes; however, in memoranda and facta, citations should be included **in the main text**.

1.2.1 Memorandum

Include the reference immediately after the text, in parentheses.

The first time a reference is used, follow the usual rules for footnotes. If a reference is repeated later in the text, include a short form after the first citation (see *Hill*). If a reference is not repeated, do not include a short form (see *Robitaille*).

After the first time a reference is used, use only the short form and include a pinpoint reference if appropriate (e.g., ***Hill* at para 195**).

In addition to the requirement of an "actionable wrong" independent of the breach sued upon, punitive damages will only be awarded "where the defendant's misconduct is so malicious, oppressive, and high-handed that it offends the court's sense of decency" (***Hill v Church of Scientology of Toronto*, [1995] 2 SCR 1130 at para 196, 184 NR 1, Cory J [*Hill*]**). Such behaviour has included defamation (***ibid***), failure to provide medical care (***Robitaille v Vancouver Hockey Club Ltd*, 124 DLR (3d) 228, [1981] 3 WWR 481 (BCCA)**), and exceptionally abusive behaviour by an insurance company (***Whiten v Pilot Insurance Co*, 2002 SCC 18 [*Whiten*]**).

Since the primary vehicle of punishment is the criminal law, punitive damages should be scarcely used (***ibid* at para 69**). It is also important to underline that there cannot be joint and several responsibility for punitive damages because they arise from the misconduct of the particular defendant against whom they are awarded (***Hill* at para 195**).

1.2.2 Factum

Paragraphs must be numbered. These numbers normally begin at the "Facts" section.

Provide a short form for every source cited.

Place the short form in parentheses immediately after the relevant text.

Write the complete reference **at the end of each paragraph**. Indent from both margins and use a smaller font size. Organize the references **in the order in which they appear in the paragraph text**. Start a new line after each reference. Do not use a semicolon.

Write the short form, used in the paragraph text, in brackets after the **first** citation of each source. Subsequent references need only use the short form with ***supra*** (section 1.4.3), which guides the reader to the appropriate paragraph (e.g., ***Whiten, supra* para 5 at para 69**). Do not use ***ibid*** (section 1.4.2) in a factum.

Include relevant pinpoints in the order that they are referenced in the paragraph text (e.g., ***Whiten v Pilot Insurance*, 2002 SCC 18 at paras 69, 101**).

5. In addition to the requirement of an "actionable wrong" independent of the breach sued upon, punitive damages will only be awarded "where the defendant's misconduct is so malicious, oppressive and high-handed that it offends the court's sense of decency" (*Hill*). Such behaviour has included defamation (*Hill*), failing to provide medical care (*Robitaille*), and exceptionally abusive behaviour by an insurance company (*Whiten*)

Hill v Church of Scientology of Toronto, [1995] 2 SCR 1130 at paras 196, 62–64, 184 NR 1, Cory J [_Hill_].

Robitaille v Vancouver Hockey Club Ltd, 124 DLR (3d) 228, [1981] 3 WWR 481(BCCA) [_Robitaille_ cited to DLR].

Whiten v Pilot Insurance Co, 2002 SCC 18 [_Whiten_].

6. Since the primary vehicle of punishment is the criminal law, punitive damages should be scarcely used (*Whiten*). It is also important to underline that there cannot be joint and several responsibility for punitive damages because they arise from the misconduct of the particular defendant against whom they are awarded (*Hill*).

Whiten, supra para 5 at para 69.

Hill, supra para 5 at para 195.

1.3 FOOTNOTES: RULES

In legal writing, the two most common forms of footnotes are textual footnotes and citation footnotes. **Textual footnotes** contain peripheral information that is relevant but would detract from the thrust of the argument if placed in the main text. **Citation footnotes** are used to indicate the source from which an argument or quotation has been drawn. Both textual and citation information can occur within a single footnote.

1.3.1 When to Footnote

Footnotes are required under the following circumstances: (1) at the first reference to the source; (2) at every subsequent quotation from the source; and (3) at every subsequent reference or allusion to a particular passage in the source. The full citation should be provided in the first footnote referring to a source.

1.3.2 How to Indicate a Footnote in the Text

In legal writing, footnotes are indicated by superscripted numbers. Roman numerals and special characters such as *, †, and ‡ are not normally used (the traditional exception being the use of * to indicate the author's biographical information at the beginning of an article).

Generally, place the footnote number at the end of the sentence, after the punctuation.[1] Note the contrast with the applicable rule for French footnote indications, where the footnote number precedes the punctuation. When referring to a word, place the footnote number[2] directly after the word, wherever it occurs in the sentence. When quoting a source, place the footnote number "after the quotation marks"[2] and, "where applicable, the punctuation."[3]

1.3.3 Where Footnotes Appear

Place footnotes on the same page as the text to which they refer (if possible). Set footnotes in a **smaller font** with a **horizontal line** separating them from the body of the text.

1.3.4 When to Combine Footnotes

Never place more than one footnote number at any given point in the main text. Instead, combine the supporting citations into one footnote. **Separate different citations in a footnote with a semicolon,** and end the entire footnote with a period.

Where the result is not confusing, citations to multiple sources may be combined into a single footnote at the end of a sentence or paragraph. Avoid combining footnotes that cite quotations from different sources.

> [3] Martin Loughlin, "The Functionalist Style in Public Law" (2005) 55 UTLJ 361; Martin Loughlin, *Public Law and Political Theory* (Oxford: Clarendon Press, 1992).

1.3.5 Citation of Non-English Sources

When writing in English, use the English citation rules regardless of the language of the source, with the exception of the **title of the source**: keep the title in its original language and follow that language's rules for capitalization and punctuation. For all other elements of the citation, follow the English rules.

> [1] Sylvio Normand, *Introduction au droit des biens* (Montreal: Wilson & Lafleur, 2000) at 40.
> [2] *Loi n° 94-653 du 29 juillet 1994*, JO, 30 July 1994, (1994 2e sem) Gaz Pal Lég 576.

1.3.6 Introductory Signals

An introductory signal indicates the logical relationship between the cited source and the proposition stated in the main text. The default rule is to **put an introductory signal in all cases**:

> ... the name of the corporation shall be set out in the articles of incorporation.[1]
> [1] See *Canada Business Corporations Act*, RSC 1985, c C-44, s 6(1).

There are **two exceptions**:

1) Where the footnote refers to a source which is directly quoted in the main text.

> ... "the fruits of the investigation which are in the possession of counsel for the Crown are not the property of the Crown for use in securing a conviction but the property of the public to be used to ensure that justice is done."[1] ...
> [1] *R v Stinchcombe*, [1991] 3 SCR 326 at 333, 1991 CanLII 45.

2) Where the title of the source appears for the first time in the main text and the footnote only provides the other elements of the citation.

In *R v Stinchcombe*[1], the court held that...
[1] [1991] 3 SCR 326 at 333, 1991 CanLII 45 (SCC).

An introductory signal relates to every citation included in the sentence. In the following example, the signal **see** relates to the two books cited before the period and **see also** to the last book cited.

See Madeleine Cantin Cumyn, *L'administration du bien d'autrui* (Cowansville, QC: Yvon Blais, 2000) at nos 24-51; Emmanuel Gaillard, *Le pouvoir en droit privé* (Paris: Economica, 1985) at 150-55. **See also** Paul Roubier, *Droits subjectifs et situations juridiques* (Paris: Dalloz, 1963) at 186-87.

Italicize ***cf*** and ***contra*** only; **e.g.** remains in Roman font. Do not put a punctuation mark between the introductory signal and the source cited (even with **e.g.**). While not exhaustive, the following table presents the standard introductory signals.

See	The source cited **directly supports** the proposition.
See also	The source cited **provides added support** for the proposition, but is not the most authoritative or is not directly on point.
But see	The source cited **is in partial disagreement** with the proposition, but does not directly contradict it.
See e.g.	*Exempli gratia*, literally "for example". The source cited **is one of several that support** the proposition given, but the other supporting sources are not cited.
See generally	The source cited **supports and provides background information** relevant to the proposition. Explanatory parenthetical remarks are recommended (see section 1.3.7).
See especially	The source cited **is the strongest of several that support** the proposition. Use only when listing the best of many possible sources.
Cf	*Confer*, literally "compare". The source cited supports a different proposition, but one that is **sufficiently analogous so as to lend support** to the proposition. Explanatory parenthetical remarks are recommended (see section 1.3.7).
Contra	The source cited **directly contradicts** the proposition.

1.3.7 Parenthetical Information Within Footnotes

Where it is helpful to clarify how the cited source supports the in-text proposition, provide a **brief description or quotation of not more than one sentence** in parentheses following the citation. A pinpoint reference must follow any quotation in parentheses.

Begin the parenthetical information with a lower case letter. If the citation begins with a capital letter, change it to lower case in bracket.

[1] *Roncarelli v Duplessis*, [1959] SCR 121, 16 DLR (2d) 689, Rand J **(discretionary decisions must be based on "considerations pertinent to the object of the administration" at 140)**; *Oakwood Development Ltd v St François Xavier (Municipality)*, [1985] 2 SCR 164, 20 DLR (4th) 641, Wilson J [*Oakwood* cited to SCR] **("[t]he failure of an administrative decision-maker to take into account a highly relevant consideration is just as erroneous as the improper importation of an extraneous consideration" at 174).**

Parenthetical information refers to the source immediately preceding it. Therefore, in the example below, the parenthetical information would be placed immediately before **aff'd** if it were meant to refer only to the court of appeal decision.

[2] See *Lawson v Wellesley Hospital* (1975), 9 OR (2d) 677, 61 DLR (3d) 445, aff'd [1978] 1 SCR 893, 76 DLR (3d) 688 [*Lawson*] **(duty of hospital to protect patient)**; *Stewart v Extendicare*, [1986] 4 WWR 559, 38 CCLT 67 (Sask QB) [*Stewart*] **(duty of nursing home to protect resident).**

1.4 PRIOR AND SUBSEQUENT REFERENCES TO A CITATION

Indicate the full citation only the first time a source appears. Subsequent references refer back to this initial citation.

1.4.1 Establishing a Short Form

1.4.1.1 General Rules

Do not create a short title if there is no further reference to the source in the work. If the title of a source is short (around three words or less), the full title may be used in all subsequent references (see note 10). If the title of a source is longer, create a short title for subsequent references.

Place the short title in brackets directly after the citation but before any parenthetical information (see *Stewart* in section 1.3.7) and case history (see section 3.11). Do not italicize the brackets.

Always italicize the short title for cases or legislation (e.g., ***Charter***). Abbreviations of codes such as **CCQ** are not considered short forms, and thus should not be italicized.

In subsequent footnotes, use the appropriate cross-referencing signals (***supra***, ***ibid***) and, where appropriate, the short title to direct the reader back to the footnote containing the full citation (see note 5).

[1] *Kadlak v Nunavut (Minister of Sustainable Development)*, 2001 NUCJ 1 [***Kadlak***].
[5] *Kadlak*, *supra* note 1 at para 15.
[7] *R v W (R)*, [1992] 2 SCR 122 at para 1, 74 CCC (3d) 134.
[10] *R v W (R)*, *supra* note 7 at para 3.
[14] James E Ryan, "The Supreme Court and Voluntary Integration" (2007) 121 Harv L Rev 131.
[40] **Ryan**, *supra* note 14 at 132.

1.4.1.2 Legislation

If a statute has an **official short title**, use only this short title in the initial citation. If the short title is brief, it may also be used in subsequent references.

> [1] ***Museums Act***, SC 1990, c 3.

If a statute has **no official short title**, or if the official short title is too long for subsequent references, create a distinctive short title and indicate it in brackets at the end of the citation.

> [2] *Nordion and Theratronics Divestiture Authorization Act*, SC 1990, c 4 [***Nordion Act***].
> [3] *Canadian Charter of Rights and Freedoms*, Part I of the *Constitution Act, 1982*, being Schedule B to the *Canada Act 1982* (UK), 1982, c 11 [***Charter***].
> [4] *Charter of the French Language*, CQLR c C-11 [***Bill 101***].

Well-recognized abbreviations may also be used.

> [5] *Canada Business Corporations Act*, RSC 1985, c C-44) [***CBCA***].

1.4.1.3 Cases

Create a short form by choosing **one of the parties' surnames or a distinctive part of the style of cause**.

> *PPL Corp v Commissioner of Internal Revenue*, 569 US ___, 133 S Ct 1897 (2013) [***PPL***].

If appropriate, you may use other elements to identify the case:

1) A more widely known style of cause from a lower court.

> *Quebec (AG) v A*, 2013 SCC 5 [***Eric v Lola***].

2) The name of a ship in admiralty cases.

> *Overseas Tankship (UK) Ltd v Miller Steamship Co* (1966), [1967] 1 AC 617 at 625, [1966] 2 All ER 709 [***Wagon Mound No 2***].

3) The name of the drug in pharmaceutical patent litigation.

> *Apotex v Pfizer*, 2009 FCA 8 [***Viagra***].

To eliminate confusion when there are multiple cases with the same name, use the date of the decision for clarity. Note that the date is in Roman type.

> *R v Morgentaler*, [1993] 3 SCR 462, 1993 CanLII 158 [***Morgentaler* 1993**].

To distinguish decisions from the same case at different court levels, use the abbreviations found in **Appendix B-2**. Note that the court abbreviation is in Roman type.

> [13] *Pappajohn v R*, [1980] 2 SCR 120, 1980 CanLII 13 [***Pappajohn* SCC**].
> [14] *R v Pappajohn* (1978), 45 CCC (2d) 67, [1979] 1 WWR 562 (BCCA) [***Pappajohn* CA**].

If the initial citation includes more than one source, but contains no pinpoint reference, indicate the reporter to which subsequent pinpoint references will be made by including

cited to followed by the abbreviation of the reporter. If there is a pinpoint reference in the initial citation, do not include **cited to**. Make all further pinpoint references to the same source. For cases with a **neutral citation**, do not indicate the reporter to which subsequent references are directed. The paragraph numbers are determined by the court and are uniform across all reporters.

> [2] *R v Van der Peet*, [1996] 2 SCR 507, 1996 CanLII 216 [***Van der Peet* cited to SCR**].
> [3] *R v Ruzic*, 2001 SCC 24 at para 2 [*Ruzic*].

1.4.1.4 Secondary Materials

Do not create a short form at the end of the first reference to the source. Only **use the author's surname** in subsequent references to the source.

> [2] John Humphrey, *No Distant Millennium: The International Law of Human Rights* (Paris: UNESCO, 1989).
> [12] **Humphrey**, *supra* note 2 at 25.

If citing two or more authors with the same last name, include an initial for each, or several if appropriate.

> [7] Stephen A Smith, "Duties, Liabilities, and Damages" (2012) 125:7 Harv L Rev 1727.
> [9] Lionel Smith, "The Province of the Law of Restitution" (1992) 71:4 Can Bar Rev 672.
> [20] **S Smith**, *supra* note 7 at 1731.
> [27] **L Smith**, *supra* note 9 at 675.

If **more than one work by a particular author is cited**, create a short form consisting of the author's name and a shortened form of the title of the work. In the short form of the title, maintain the same formatting as the full title-italics for books and quotation marks for articles.

> [3] G Blaine Baker, "The Province of Post-Confederation Rights" (1995) 45 UTLJ 77 **[Baker, "Post-Confederation Rights"]**.
> [14] **Baker, "Post-Confederation Rights"**, *supra* note 3 at 86.

If there are **two or more essays from the same collection**, apply the same rules to create a short form for the collection, and then use that form in the first citation of each additional essay. The short form rules found in this section should be applied normally to the subsequent references of any essay from that collection.

> [13] Rebecca Veinott, "Child Custody and Divorce: A Nova Scotia Study, 1866-1910" in Philip Girard & Jim Phillips, eds, *Essays in the History of Canadian Law*, vol 3 (Toronto: University of Toronto Press, 1990) 273.
> [86] Kimberley Smith Maynard, "Divorce in Nova Scotia, 1750-1890" in **Girard & Phillips**, *supra* note 13, 232 at 239.
> [91] **Maynard**, *supra* note 86 at 243.

1.4.2 *Ibid*

Ibid is an abbreviation of the Latin word *ibidem*, meaning "in the same place". Use *ibid* to direct the reader to the **immediately preceding reference**. Do not provide the number of the footnote in which the preceding reference appears.

Ibid may be used **after a full citation** (see note 2), **after a *supra*** (see note 4) or even **after another *ibid*** (see note 5). For clarity, if there is more than one reference in the previous footnote, use *supra* rather than *ibid* (see note 3).

An *ibid* used without a pinpoint reference refers to the same pinpoint as in the previous footnote (see note 5). To cite the source as a whole, where the previous reference includes a pinpoint, use ***supra*** (see note 6).

To refer to the previous source within the same footnote, use *ibid* in parentheses (see note 98).

[1] See *Canada Labour Relations Board v Halifax Longshoremen's Association, Local 269*, [1983] 1 SCR 245, 144 DLR (3d) 1 [*HLA* cited to SCR].
[2] *Ibid* at 260. See also *Fraser v Canada (Public Service Staff Relations Board)*, [1985] 2 SCR 455 at 463, 23 DLR (4th) 122 [*Fraser*]; *Heustis v New Brunswick Electric Power Commission*, [1979] 2 SCR 768, 98 DLR (3d) 622 [*Heustis* cited to SCR].
[3] *Heustis*, *supra* note 2 at 775.
[4] *Ibid* at 780–82.
[5] *Ibid*.
[6] *Heustis*, *supra* note 2.
[98] For a more detailed analysis, see *Union des employés de service, Local 298 v Bibeault*, [1988] 2 SCR 1048, 95 NR 161 [*Bibeault* cited to SCR]. The Court cited a "patently unreasonable" standard of review (*ibid* at 1084–85).

1.4.3 *Supra*

Supra is the Latin word for "above". Use the short form in combination with *supra* to refer to the **footnote containing the original, full citation**. Do not use *supra* to refer to either an *ibid* or another *supra*.

Unlike *ibid*, *supra* always refers to the source alone and never implies reference to a pinpoint. Accordingly, reiterate the pinpoint even if the *supra* cites to the same passage as the original reference (see note 57).

If the source is clearly identified in the main text, it is unnecessary to re-identify that source in the footnote (see note 58).

To refer to both a previous footnote and the main text to which that footnote relates, use *supra* note # **and accompanying text** (see note 60). To refer only to the main text (rather than a footnote), use **above** rather than *supra* (section 1.4.4).

[1] *MacMillan Bloedel Ltd v British Columbia (AG)* (1996), 22 BCLR (3d) 137 at 147, 30 WCB (2d) 446 (CA) [*MacMillan*]; *Towne Cinema Theatres Ltd v R*, [1985] 1 SCR 494 at 501, 18 DLR (4th) 1 [*Towne Cinema*].

[2] *MacMillan*, ***supra*** note 1.
[57] *Towne Cinema*, ***supra*** note 1 at 501.
[58] ***Supra*** note 1 at 140.
[60] See also *Faraggi*, *supra* note 24 **and accompanying text.**

1.4.4 Above and Below

Use the words **above** and **below** to direct the reader to **a portion of the main text** and not to the footnotes.

See Part III-A, ***above***, for more on this topic.
Further discussion of this case will be found at 164–70, ***below***.

If there are no easily identifiable section or paragraph markers, or if the final pagination of the text is unclear at the time of writing, use the formulation **see the text accompanying note** #.

For further analysis of the holding in *Oakes*, **see the text accompanying note 41.**

1.5 PINPOINTS

	page	paragraph	section	article	footnote	number
singular	*Ibid* at 512.	*Ibid* at **para** 6.	*Ibid*, **s** 4(1).	*Ibid*, **art** 1457.	*Ibid* at 512, **n** 139.	*Ibid* at **no** 45.
plural	*Ibid* at 512–14.	*Ibid* at **paras** 6, 12.	*Ibid*, **ss** 4(1), 6(2)(*b*)(i)–(ii).	*Ibid*, **arts** 1457–69.	*Ibid* at 512, **nn** 139, 142–46.	*Ibid* at **nos** 45–47.

Use a pinpoint to cite to a specific portion of the text. Reference should be made, where possible, to paragraphs, sections, articles, footnotes, numbers, or any other division that is more precise than the page number. If there is no such divisions in the source, then refer to the page. For divisions that are not included in the table above, include **at**, the appropriate division, and the number (e.g. **at note 7/3**)

Separate **non-consecutive pinpoints** by a **comma**, and **consecutive pinpoints** by an **en dash** (–), not a **hyphen** (-). Retain at least the two last digits following the en dash (e.g., **159–60**).

If the page indexing system contains hyphens (e.g., **70.1-3, 70.1-4** etc.) or any other system that would otherwise be confusing to the reader when coupled with en dashes, prefer "**to**" when citing to a range of pages (e.g., **70.1-3 to 70.1-5**).

It is generally preferable to cite to a specific number or range, but to indicate a **general area**, place **ff** (the abbreviation of the Latin word "*folio*" or "*folium*", used to indicate "and following") immediately after the number (e.g., see paras **69ff**). Note that the divisions referred to are in the plural when **ff** is used (paras, ss, arts, nn, nos).

Do not abbreviate unnumbered elements (e.g., **Preamble**, **Schedule**, **Appendix**, **Preliminary Provision**, etc.) in a pinpoint.

1.6 ONLINE RESOURCES

A website is a collection of pages published on a server and accessible via the Internet. This does not include online databases, which will be dealt with in the appropriate sections relating to the various sources. Websites have the advantage of being accessible to all, but have the drawback of presenting temporary content and of not always having an official status. The only instances where it is possible to refer only to an Internet version of a source are when it is an official version, the only existing version, or the only reasonably accessible version. See the specific rules for online resources for every type of sources. See especially section 6.19.1 for websites.

1.6.1 Archiving of Internet Sources

To remedy the ephemeral nature of online content and to prevent link rot, refer to an archived URL in addition to the original URL. Place the archived URL in brackets at the end of the citation. The Perma system is strongly recommended (see the examples in section 1.6.2).

If the original URL is long and unwieldy, and an archived URL is included, indicate only the root original URL of the website.

1.6.2 Parallel Citations to Online Resources

If the content of a website exists in another format, refer first to the other format. It is nonetheless encouraged to mention the website as an additional reference because it is generally easier to access. Add the URL after the traditional citation. For the traditional citation, use the appropriate sections relating to the relevant type of sources.

Traditional citation, | online: | <URL> | [archived URL].

Henry Samuel, "March for Girl Set Alight After Marriage Refusal", *The Daily Telegraph* (28 November 2005), online: <www.telegraph.co.uk> [perma.cc/HC6D-K9M9].

Kahikino Noa Dettweiler, "Racial Classification or Cultural Identification?: The Gathering Rights Jurisprudence of Two Twentieth Century Hawaiian Supreme Court Justices" (2005) 6:1 Asian Pac L & Pol'y J 5, online: <www.hawaii.edu/aplpj> [perma.cc/8EYU-FMGV].

Jean Teillet, *Metis Law in Canada* (Vancouver: Pape Salter Teillet, 2013), online: <www.pstlaw.ca/resources/Metis-Law-in-Canada-2013.pdf> [perma.cc/TT3D-R42Z].

1.6.3 Digital Object Identifier

A digital object identifier (DOI) is a permanent, unique resource locator used to identify documents online, independent of their online location(s) at any given time. Documents assigned a DOI can be retrieved by entering the identifier into a search tool that recognizes and/or resolves them. Where a DOI is available for a given document, append the DOI to the end of the traditional citation.

Traditional citation | DOI: | <digital object identifier>.

> Sir Daniel Bethlehem, "The Secret Life of International Law" (2012) 1:1 Cambridge J of Intl & Comp L 23, DOI: <10.7574/cjicl.01.01.1>.

1.7 CITING SOURCES THAT QUOTE OR REPRINT THE ORIGINAL SOURCE

It is always preferable to cite directly to an original source. If an original source is quoted in another work (the citing source), consult the original work in order to verify the context and accuracy of the reference.

1.7.1 Obscure Original Source

The original source may sometimes be **difficult to find** or may have been **destroyed**. In such exceptional circumstances, it may be necessary to cite to the original source as presented in a citing source. Provide as much information on the original work as possible, followed by **cited in** and the citation to the citing source.

> *Papers Relating to the Commission appointed to enquire into the state and condition of the Indians of the North-West Coast of British Columbia*, British Columbia Sessional Papers, 1888 at 432–33, **cited in** Hamar Foster, "Honouring the Queen's Flag: A Legal and Historical Perspective on the Nisga'a Treaty" (1998) 120 BC Studies 11 at 13.

In certain cases, the original version of a document fully reprinted in a collection (e.g., collections reprinting debates, letters, treaties or manuscripts) is **only available in archives**. Provide a complete citation to the original work, followed by **reprinted in** and the citation to the citing source. Do not refer to books reprinting excerpts from original sources that are readily available (e.g., textbooks).

> George R to Governor Arthur Phillip, Royal Instruction, 25 April 1787 (27 Geo III), **reprinted in** *Historical Documents of New South Wales*, vol 1, part 2 (Sydney: Government Printer, 1892–1901) 67.

1.7.2 Emphasis on the Citing Source

To highlight the fact that a work is referring to the original material (for example, when the secondary work is more eminent or trustworthy) include the citation to the citing source, followed by **citing** and the citation to the original source.

Canada (Citizenship and Immigration) v Khosa, 2009 SCC 12 at para 38, **citing** Pierre-André Côté, *Interprétation des lois,* 3rd ed (Cowansville, QC: Yvon Blais, 1999) at 91, n 123.

1.8 GENERAL RULES FOR QUOTATIONS

These rules apply to both main text and footnotes.

1.8.1 Positioning of Quotations

Place short quotations of **four lines or fewer** in quotation marks and incorporate them directly into the text. Indent from both margins and single space quotations of **more than four lines**. Do not use quotation marks. Legislative provisions may be indented even if they are fewer than four lines long.

This principle, which has existed since 1929, is based on a dynamic conception of the constitution as **"a living tree capable of growth and expansion."**[1]

Justice LeBel, writing for the Court, invoked the scenario that Justice Dickson (as he then was) used in *Perka* to explain the concept:

> **By way of illustration in *Perka*, Dickson J. evoked the situation of a lost alpinist who, on the point of freezing to death, breaks into a remote mountain cabin. The alpinist confronts a painful dilemma: freeze to death or commit a criminal offence. Yet as Dickson J pointed out at p 249, the alpinist's choice to break the law "is no true choice at all; it is remorselessly compelled by normal human instincts", here of self-preservation.**[2]

The *Civil Code of Quebec* begins in a peculiar way, introducing two legal concepts that are meaningless to the common citizen. Article 1 reads as following:

> **Every human being possesses juridical personality and has the full enjoyment of civil rights.**[3]

1.8.2 Format of Quotations

Spelling, capitalization, and internal punctuation in a quotation must be **exactly the same as in the original source**; any changes and additions must be clearly indicated in brackets. If the sentence becomes incorrect in terms of grammar or punctuation, make the proper adjustments in brackets (for example, change a lower case letter to an upper case letter). Use an ellipsis (. . .) to indicate the omission of a passage from the quoted material. An ellipsis at the beginning or the end of the quoted material is usually unnecessary. Use an ellipsis at the extremities of a quotation only where the sentence is deliberately left grammatically incomplete.

Where the original source contains an error, **enclose the correction in square brackets, replacing the erroneous word or phrase**. Refrain from using [*sic*], except to draw attention to the original error or to keep the quotation unaltered.

In-text

It was clear from this moment that "**[t]**he centre . . . of American jurisprudence had changed."[32]

"**[A]** mixed question of fact and law" must be appealable.[42]

Text may be emphasized by using italics and placing **[emphasis added]** at the end of the citation. If the text was emphasized in the original copy, place **[emphasis in original]** at the end of the citation. If there are footnotes in the original text that are not reproduced in the quotation, place **[footnotes omitted]** at the end of the citation. (Note that the placement of such expressions after the citation in the footnote is contrary to the rule applicable in French.) Place these expressions after the establishment of a short form.

Footnotes

[31] *Norris*, *supra* note 21 **[emphasis added]**.

[32] *Kadlak v Nunavut (Minister of Sustainable Development)*, 2001 NUCJ 1 at para 32 [*Kadlak*] **[emphasis in original]**.

[77] Lamontagne, *supra* note 65 at 109 **[footnotes omitted]**.

1.8.3 Quoting a Source in Another Language

If at all possible, use an English version of a source when writing in English and a French version when writing in French. Every Canadian jurisdiction passes statutes in English. If quoting in another language, a translation may be provided, but is not required. Clearly indicate any translation in the footnote and identify the translator. If the work is translated by a professional, indicate the translator's name (see section 6.2.2.4.1). If you, the author, translated the work, include **[translated by author]**.

[1] Jacques Ghestin & Gilles Goubeaux, *Traité de droit civil: Introduction générale*, 4th ed (Paris: Librairie générale de droit et de jurisprudence, 1994) at para 669 **[translated by author]**.

1.9 WRITING IN A FOREIGN LANGUAGE

The *Guide* is a Canadian work and applies to texts written in the country's two official languages. However, it is possible to adapt these rules to any other language, inspired by the English **or** the French section. The guidelines are **uniformity**, **clarity** and **facility of retracing a source** for the reader. The following guidelines are examples of adaptation rules.

Translate expressions such as "see", "cited in", "reprinted in", "emphasis added", and "with reference to", but keep the Latin expressions as they are. Follow the **form** rules, such as the order of elements and the structure of the document. Follow the **punctuation** rules of the language in which the text is written. If needed, consult grammar and usage guides. Make sure that the form of the punctuation marks remains consistent throughout the text.

For **legislation and jurisprudence**, follow the Canadian general forms, or adapt the forms presented in Foreign Sources (section 7). Use the statute volume and jurisdiction abbreviations as presented in the legislation's official document. Include the court and jurisdiction. For **jurisprudential sources**, follow the hierarchy of sources. Always keep the audience in mind and verify that the information is accessible to the reader. Use the abbreviation of the reporter as presented in the source, and always include the court and jurisdiction.

2 Legislation....E-21

Legislation

2 LEGISLATION

2.1 STATUTES

2.1.1 General Form

Title, | statute volume | jurisdiction | year, | chapter, | other indexing elements, | (session or supplement), | pinpoint.

Criminal Code, RSC 1985, c C-46, s 745.

Do not include a space between the statute volume and the jurisdiction.

If the statute reference includes session or supplement information, omit the comma that normally follows the immediately preceding element.

Income Tax Act, RSC 1985, c 1 (5th Supp), s 18(1)(m)(iv)(c).

Notwithstanding their quasi-constitutional status, the *Quebec Charter* and the *Canadian Bill of Rights* follows the rules provided in this section.

Charter of Human Rights and Freedoms, CQLR c C-12, s 10.
Canadian Bill of Rights, SC 1960, c 44, s 2.

When referring to Indigenous legislative documents, include basic, critical information, so that readers can track the source. If the document title is not in English or French, provide a description in parentheses or a translation in square brackets. Do not italicize such additional information. It is not necessary to translate names of Indigenous nations.

Akwesasne Tekaia'torehthà:ke Kaianerénhsera [Akwesasne Court Law], Kaiahnehronshera Iehiontakwa [Law Registry] No 2016-01, (2016), enacted pursuant to Mohawk Council Resolution 2015/2016-332, online (pdf): *Mohawk Council of Akwesasne* <webdev.akwesasne.ca> [perma.cc/9MW6-VXTZ].

Tk'emlúps te Secwépemc Property Transfer Tax Law, 2017, s 4, online (pdf): *Tk'emlúps* <tkemlups.ca> [perma.cc/BV5R-5LW3].

2.1.2 Point in Time Citations

When citing to a particular point in time, and the standard citation form is inadequate, use **as it appeared on [day month year]** or **as it appeared on [month year]** to clarify the point in time cited to.

Income Tax Act, RSC 1985, c 1 (5th Supp), s 20(1)(c) **as it appeared on 12 October 2012.**

2.1.3 Sources

In the following order, find legislation in (1) the appropriate jurisdiction's official electronic versions. If the official version is not available online, refer to (2) the printed revised or re-enacted statutes. As a last resort, refer to (3) annual volumes. Refer to annual volumes only if the statute was enacted since the last revision was published or if the relevant section of the statute has been added or amended since the revision date.

To find the official electronic versions, consult the table below, which provides the most relevant website on which legislation enacted by a given jurisdiction can be found. Many jurisdictions do not have an official electronic version of their statutes. The websites marked with an asterisk (*) refer to an unofficial version of the legislation. Official electronic versions are cited in the same manner as print sources; a URL reference is only required when referring to an unofficial version.

Jurisdiction	**Website**
Canada	lois-laws.justice.gc.ca/eng
Alberta	www.qp.alberta.ca/Laws_Online.cfm
British Columbia	www.bclaws.ca*
Manitoba	web2.gov.mb.ca/laws*
New Brunswick	www2.gnb.ca/content/gnb/en/departments/attorney_general/acts_regula-tions.html
Newfoundland & Labrador	www.assembly.nl.ca/legislation
Northwest Territories	www.justice.gov.nt.ca/en/legislation*
Nova Scotia	nslegislature.ca/legc
Nunavut	www.nunavutlegislation.ca
Ontario	www.ontario.ca/laws
Prince Edward Island	www.princeedwardisland.ca/en/legislation/all*
Quebec	legisquebec.gouv.qc.ca/en/home
Saskatchewan	www.publications.gov.sk.ca/freelaw*
Yukon	www.gov.yk.ca/legislation*

Nunavut: For statutes enacted specifically for Nunavut by the Northwest Territories prior to 1 April 1999, provide the standard citation followed by **as enacted for Nunavut, pursuant to the *Nunavut Act*, SC 1993, c 28**.

> *Nunavut Judicial System Implementation Act*, SNWT 1998, c 34, as enacted for Nunavut, pursuant to the *Nunavut Act*, SC 1993, c 28.

Many Northwest Territories statutes are applied, mutatis mutandis, to Nunavut via section 29 of the federal Nunavut Act, SC 1993, c 28. When applicable, provide the standard citation followed by "**as duplicated for Nunavut by s 29 of the Nunavut Act, SC 1993, c 28.**"

Legislation

Official Languages Act, RSNWT 1998, c O-1, as duplicated for Nunavut by s 29 of the *Nunavut Act*, SC 1993, c 28.

Quebec: Quebec maintains the Compilation of Quebec Laws and Regulations (**CQLR**), an **official, updated compilation** of its laws in force, available online. Statutes cited to this database use CQLR instead of the usual SQ or RSQ designation. Note that the Q for the jurisdiction is exceptionally in the middle of the statute volume (C**Q**LR). The database is constantly updated and is undated; accordingly, do not provide a date when citing to the CQLR.

Securities Act, **CQLR** c V-1.1, s 9.

Official **historical versions of legislation**, dating back until 1969, are available online at <www3.publicationsduquebec.gouv.qc.ca/loisreglements/loisannuelles.fr.html>. When citing historical versions, use the **RSQ** or **SQ** designation. At present, the years 1977-1995 are only available in French.

An Act Respecting the caisses d'entraide économique, **RSQ** c C-3, s 1.

2.1.4 Title

Provide the **official short title**, which is usually found in the first section of the statute. If no official short title is provided, use the title found at the head of the statute. Include **The** only if it forms part of the title (as indicated in the official short title or at the head of the statute). If the title of the statute is provided in the main text, do not repeat it in the citation.

Italicize the title of the statute and place a non-italicized comma after the title. If the year is included as part of the title of the statute, ensure that it appears in italics (e.g., ***Income War Tax Act, 1917***). Add the year after the jurisdiction even if the year is part of the title.

Follow the capitalization of words in the title as set out in the statute. Many English titles of Quebec statutes follow French capitalization rules. Do *not* capitalize letters in these titles to conform to English language capitalization rules.

Civil Marriage Act, SC 2005, c 41.
Reciprocal Enforcement of Maintenance Orders Act, SY 1980, c 25, s 5(2).
Income War Tax Act, 1917, SC 1917, c 28.

NB: The statutes of the following jurisdictions are adopted in both English and French: Canada, Manitoba, New Brunswick, Ontario, Quebec, Nunavut, Northwest Territories, and Yukon. However, statutes adopted prior to a certain date may exist only in English.

2.1.5 Revised Statutes and Annual Volumes

Both **Revised Statutes** and **Re-enacted Statutes** are abbreviated to **RS**. For citations to annual volumes, abbreviate **Statutes** to **S**. Use **S** for Statutes (and not **O** for Ordinances) when referring to any volume, past or present, of Northwest Territories or Yukon legislation.

Children's Law Reform Act, **RSO** 1990, c C.12.

Agricultural Land Commission Act, SBC 2002, c 36.

If a statute cannot be found in the current Revised Statutes, do not assume that it does not exist or that it is no longer relevant. For example, the *York University Act, 1965*, SO 1965, c 143, is still in force, despite not being included in a revision. Some jurisdictions, such as Ontario, list these statutes in a Table of Unconsolidated Statutes.

2.1.6 Loose-leafs

Loose-leafs are consolidations of legislation that are continually updated; accordingly, a citation to a loose-leaf service does not contain a date as it is assumed to be to the most recent version of the referenced statute (if greater clarity with respect to the date of the legislation is needed, use Point in Time Citation, section 2.1.2). With the advent of online consolidations, loose-leafs are generally falling out of use and authors should avoid referring to them when another official version is available somewhere else.

The provinces of Manitoba and Nova Scotia publish an official loose-leaf compilation, whereas some jurisdictions, like Alberta, publish an unofficial consolidation. The Nova Scotia loose-leafs do not have any special catalogue identifiers and should accordingly be cited in the same manner as revised statutes and annual volumes (see section 2.1.5).

Manitoba, which does not have an official online legislative database, maintains a loose-leaf service entitled the *Continuing Consolidation of the Statutes of Manitoba* (**CCSM**); this publication, however, should be used only as an optional parallel source, with the main citation being to either the revised statutes or the annual volumes. Do not place a comma between the name of the volume and the chapter number.

Retirement Plan Beneficiaries Act, SM 1992, c 31, **CCSM c R138**, s 14.

Quebec discontinued its loose-leaf updates to the RSQ in 2010 when the service was superseded by the Compilation of Quebec Laws and Regulations.

2.1.7 Jurisdiction

Place the jurisdiction immediately after the statute volume.

Proceeds of Crime (Money Laundering) and Terrorist Financing Act, **SC** 2000, c 17.
Workers Compensation Act, **SPEI** 1994, c 67.

See the column Statutes and Gazettes in **Appendix A-1** for Jurisdiction abbreviations.

2.1.8 Year, Session, and Supplement

Place the year after the jurisdiction, followed by a comma. If a session or regnal year follows the year, place the comma after the session or regnal year. Omit the year when citing the Compilation of Quebec Laws and Regulations (CQLR), or the loose-leaf edition of the statutes of Manitoba (CCSM), as these sources are continually updated and do not contain a date of publication. If greater accuracy with respect to the date is needed, use Point in Time citation (section 2.1.2).

Animal Protection Act, RSA **2000**, c A-41.

When a **session spans more than one year**, write the full date span of the volume (e.g., **1980–81**).

Government Organization Act, 1983, SC **1980–81–82–83**, c 167.

If a **statute volume is divided into several sessions** with independent chapter numbering, place the number of the session (**1st**, **2nd**, **3rd** or **4th**) and the abbreviation **Sess** in parentheses following the year.

An Act to amend the Business Licence Act, SNWT **1985 (3rd Sess)**, c 1.

Refer to the **supplement** for acts and amendments that were passed during the year in which the *Revised Statutes* were issued, but that were not included in the revision. For example, the 1985 RSC was not proclaimed in force until late 1988; accordingly the statutes from 1985–1988 were reprinted to bring them within the ambit of the newly revised statutes (First Supplement = 1985 Acts; Second Supplement = 1986 Acts; Third Supplement = 1987 Acts; Fourth Supplement = 1988 Acts; Fifth Supplement = *Income Tax Act*). Place the supplement number and the abbreviation **Supp** in parentheses after the chapter.

Customs Act, RSC 1985, c 1 **(2nd Supp)**.

For federal statutes enacted before 1867, and for provincial statutes enacted before the province entered Confederation, give the **regnal year** in parentheses following the calendar year. Otherwise give the calendar year and not the regnal year.

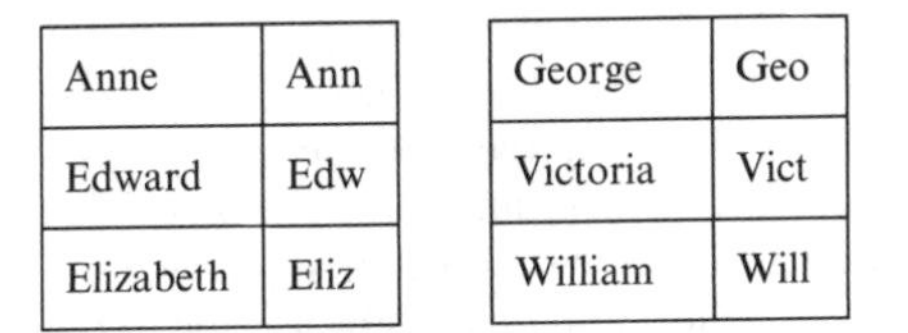

Anne	Ann
Edward	Edw
Elizabeth	Eliz

George	Geo
Victoria	Vict
William	Will

An Act respecting the Civilization and Enfranchisement of certain Indians, S Prov C 1859 **(22 Vict)**, c 9.

2.1.9 Chapter

Abbreviate chapter to **c** and write the chapter designation exactly as shown in the statute volume, **including dashes and periods**.

Holocaust Memorial Day Act, SBC 2000 **c 3**.
An Act respecting acupuncture, CQLR **c A-5.1**.

Between 1934 and 1975–76, statutes in Newfoundland's annual volumes are designated by number. Abbreviate **Number** to **No**.

Child Welfare Act, 1972, SN 1972 **No 37**.

2.1.10 Pinpoint

To cite a specific section of a statute, place a comma after the chapter and then indicate the relevant section or sections. Abbreviate **section** to s and **sections** to ss in the footnotes, but always write the full word in the text. Do not insert **at**.

> *Environmental Protection and Enhancement Act*, RSA 2000, c E-12, **ss** 2, 38-42, 84.

Indicate further subdivisions (e.g., subsections, paragraphs, subparagraphs) as they appear in the legislation. Use parentheses to separate each subdivision even if there are no parentheses in the official version of the statute. Note that the abbreviation remains s or ss even in such cases.

> *Legal Profession Act*, 1990, SS 1990, c L-10.1, **ss 4(1), 6(2)(b)(i)-(ii), 9.**

Cite an unnumbered or unlettered subdivision like a paragraph, abbreviated as **para** in the singular and **paras** in the plural.

> *Charter of the French Language*, CQLR c C-11, Preamble, **para 3**.

For more general information on pinpoints, see section 1.5.

2.1.11 Amendments, Repeals, and Re-enactments

Citations are presumed to be to the statute **as amended on the date of publication** of the author's text.

> *Crown Liability and Proceedings Act*, RSC 1985, c C-50.

Indicate that the statute has been amended only if it is relevant to the point being discussed in the text. When indicating an amendment, cite the original statute first, followed by **as amended by** and the citation for the amending statute. Indicate the title of the second statute only if it is different from the title of the first statute, or if it is not included in the title of the first statute cited.

> *Emergency Measures Act*, SM 1987, c 11, **as amended by SM 1997, c 28**. *Municipal Government Act*, RSA 2000, c M-26, s 694(4), **as amended by *Municipal Government Amendment Act*, SA 2003, c 43, s 4**.

When an act has been **repealed**, always indicate the repeal in the citation (**as repealed by**).

> *Family Benefits Act*, RSO 1990, c F.2, **as repealed by *Social Assistance Reform Act, 1997*, SO 1997, c 25, s 4(1)**.

Use **amending** when referring specifically to a statute that amends an earlier statute, and use **repealing** when citing a statute that repeals an earlier statute.

> *An Act to Amend the Labour Standards Act*, SNWT 1999, c 18, **amending RSNWT 1988, c L-1**.
>
> *An Act respecting the James Bay Native Development Corporation*, CQLR c S-9.1, **repealing *An Act to incorporate the James Bay Native Development Corporation*, SQ 1978, c 96**.

If a statute or part of a statute was repealed and another substituted, cite the original statute first, followed by **as re-enacted by** and the citation for the new replacement section. Use this term only if the repealed and substitute provisions are found in the same section.

2.1.12 Appendices

For statutes that appear in an appendix, always provide the official citation first, followed by the citation to the appendix. Introduce the appendix reference with the phrase **reprinted in**. Indicate the statute revision or volume to which the appendix is attached, followed by a comma and the appendix number. Write the appendix number in Roman numerals.

> *Canadian Bill of Rights*, SC 1960, c 44, **reprinted in** RSC 1985, **Appendix III**.

2.1.13 Statutes Within Statutes

Refer first to the title of the statute within the statute. Indicate the relevant part of the containing act and its full citation, introduced by a comma and **being**. Place pinpoint references to section numbers before the citation to the containing act.

> *Enterprise Cape Breton Corporation Act*, s 25, **being** Part II of the *Government Organization Act, Atlantic Canada, 1987*, RSC 1985, c 41 (4th Supp).

2.2 CONSTITUTIONAL STATUTES

Many constitutional statutes were enacted under different names than those used today; use the **new title**. Consult the Schedule to the *Constitution Act, 1982* to determine the new title of the statute. If appropriate, provide the old title in parentheses at the end of the citation. If necessary, include a citation to **Appendix II of RSC 1985** after the official citation. Most Canadian constitutional statutes are reprinted in Appendix II.

Note that pinpoint references to the *Canadian Charter* and the *Constitution Act, 1982* are immediately after the title. For any other constitutional statutes, place pinpoint references after the chapter number.

When referring to Indigenous constitutional documents, include basic, critical information, so that readers can track the source. If the document title is not in English or French, provide a description in parentheses or a translation in square brackets. Do not italicize such additional information.

Constitution Acts:

> *Constitution Act, 1867* (UK), 30 & 31 Vict, c 3, s 91, reprinted in RSC 1985, Appendix II, No 5.
>
> *Constitution Act, 1982*, s 35, being Schedule B to the Canada Act 1982 (UK), 1982, c 11.

Canadian Charter:

> *Canadian Charter of Rights and Freedoms*, s 7, Part I of the *Constitution Act, 1982*, being Schedule B to the *Canada Act 1982* (UK), 1982, c 11.

Legislation

Indigenous Constitutions:

Nipissing Gichi-Naaknigewin (Nipissing First Nation Constitution), (2014).
Nunatsiavut Constitution Act, CIL 31-12-2012 N-3, online (pdf): <www.nunatsiavut.com/wp-content/uploads/2015/07/CIL-31-12-2012-N-3-Nunatsiavut-Constitiution-Act.pdf> [perma.cc/ZC35-89XB].

2.3 CODES

Do not use full citation form when referring to Canadian codes. Use the abbreviations below. Note that the full titles are in italics, whereas the abbreviations are in Roman type.

Title	Abbreviation
Civil Code of Québec	CCQ
Civil Code of Québec (1980)	CCQ (1980)
Civil Code of Lower Canada	CCLC
Code of Civil Procedure	CCP
Code of Penal Procedure	CPP

To cite another Canadian code, follow the general form of section 2.1.1 for the first reference, and create a short form, if needed, for subsequent citations. To refer to the former Code of Civil Procedure, place the year of adoption **(1965)** in parentheses after the abbreviation.

Art 477 CCP **(1965)**.

The provisions of Quebec codes are **articles**, not **sections**. Abbreviate article to **art** and articles to **arts**.

Arts 1457-58 CCQ.

To cite the Minister's Comments on the Civil Code of Quebec, see section 4.2.1. To cite an annotated code, see the last example in section 6.2.1.

2.4 BILLS

Number, | *title*, | session, | legislature, | jurisdiction, | year, | pinpoint | (additional information).

For the number, add **C-** before bills originating in the House of Commons and **S-** before bills originating in the Senate.

Use the long title of the bill. Italicize the title and follow the bill's capitalization. If referring to a provincial bill, include the jurisdiction. Do not provide the regnal year.

The subdivisions of a bill are **clauses**, abbreviated to **cl** and **cls** for plural. Include additional information as needed (e.g., the date of first reading or the state that the bill has reached at the time of writing). Place the information in parentheses at the end of the citation. If the chapter number of the bill is known, include the **future statute citation** after the date of assent as additional information (e.g., **(assented to 10 November 2004), SQ 2004, c 23**).

Canada

Bill C-26, *An Act to establish the Canada Border Services Agency*, 1st Sess, 38th Parl, 2005, cl 5(1)(e) (as passed by the House of Commons 13 June 2005).

Bill S-3, *An Act to amend the Energy Efficiency Act*, 2nd Sess, 40th Parl, 2009, cl 5 (first reading 29 January 2009).

Provinces and territories

Bill 59, *An Act to amend the Civil Code as regards marriage*, 1st Sess, 37th Leg, Quebec, 2004 (assented to 10 November 2004), SQ 2004, c 23.

2.5 REGULATIONS

The table below provides information on the appropriate form when referring to regulations based on the jurisdiction from which they originate. Not all the jurisdictions publish revised versions of their regulations (here the word "revised" should be understood as meaning "revised", "consolidated", or "re-enacted"). In the form column, the word "year" is marked with an asterisk (*) to indicate that only the last two digits must be used. Also, note that the year for revised regulations is the year of revision.

Jurisdiction		**Form**	**Example**
Canada	Revised	*Title*, **CRC**, chapter, pinpoint (year).	*Migratory Birds Regulations*, CRC, c 1035, s 4 (1978).
	Unrevised	**SOR**/year-number, pinpoint.	SOR/2000-111, s 4.
Alberta		**Alta Reg** number/year, pinpoint.	Alta Reg 184/2001, s 2.
British Columbia		**BC Reg** number/year, pinpoint.	BC Reg 362/2000, s 6.
Manitoba	Revised	**Man Reg** number/year*R, pinpoint.	Man Reg 468/88R, s 2.
	Unrevised	**Man Reg** number/year, pinpoint.	Man Reg 155/2001, s 3.
New Brunswick		**NB Reg** year-number, pinpoint.	NB Reg 2000-8, s 11.
Newfoundland	Revised	**CNR** number/year*, pinpoint.	CNR 331/78, s 7.
	Unrevised	**Nfld Reg** number/year*, pinpoint.	Nfld Reg 78/99, s 4.

Jurisdiction		Form	Example
Newfoundland and Labrador	Revised	**CNLR** number/year*, pinpoint.	CNLR 1151/96, s 6.
	Unrevised	**NLR** number/year*, pinpoint.	NLR 08/02, s 2.
Northwest Territories	Revised	**RRNWT** year, chapter, pinpoint.	RRNWT 1990, c E-27, s 16.
	Unrevised	**NWT Reg** number-year*, pinpoint.	NWT Reg 253-77, s 3.
Nova Scotia		**NS Reg** number/year, pinpoint.	NS Reg 24/2000, s 8.
Nunavut		**Nu Reg** number-year*, pinpoint.	Nu Reg 045-99, s 2.
Ontario	Revised	**RRO** year, Reg number, pinpoint.	RRO 1990, Reg 1015, s 3.
	Unrevised	**O Reg** number/year*, pinpoint.	O Reg 426/00, s 2.
Prince Edward Island		**PEI Reg EC**year-number, pinpoint.	PEI Reg EC1999-598, s 3.
Quebec	Revised	**CQLR** chapter, rule number, pinpoint.	CQLR c C-11, r 9, s 10.
	Unrevised	**OC** number-year*, date, *Gazette* citation, pinpoint.	OC 868-97, 2 July 1997, (1997) GOQ II 3692, s 2.
Saskatchewan	Revised	**RRS** chapter, Reg number, pinpoint.	RRS c C-50-2, Reg 21, s 6.
	Unrevised	**Sask Reg** number/year, pinpoint.	Sask Reg 67/2001, s 3.
Yukon		**YOIC** year/number, pinpoint.	YOIC 2000/130, s 9.

Include the title of the regulations (mandatory) when referring to Consolidated Regulations of Canada. However, it is always recommended to include the title in italics at the beginning of the citation, followed by a comma.

Canada: Find federal regulations promulgated after the Consolidation in Part II of the ***Canada Gazette***. Do not include a direct citation to the *Gazette*. For regulations starting from the year 2000, include the four digits of the year. For years up until 1999, use exceptionally the last two digits even if there is no asterisk in the table.

> *Offset of Taxes by a Refund or a Rebate (GST/HST) Regulations*, SOR/**91**-49, s 4.

Newfoundland: All references to Newfoundland were retroactively amended to Newfoundland and Labrador. Only use the Newfoundland section of the table above for regulations repealed before 6 December 2001. Use the Newfoundland and Labrador section for other regulations.

Quebec: To cite the *Gazette officielle du Québec*, see section 2.6.1.

The table below provides the meaning of the abbreviations used in this section. For jurisdiction abbreviations, refer to the regulations column of **Appendix A-1**.

Abbreviation	Meaning	Abbreviation	Meaning
CRC	Consolidated Regulations of Canada	RR	Revised Regulations
SOR	Statutory Orders and Regulations	EC	Executive Council
Reg/R	Regulation(s)	OC/OIC	Orders in Council
CNR	Consolidated Newfoundland Regulation	GOQ	*Gazette officielle du Québec*
CNLR	Consolidated Newfoundland and Labrador Regulation	CQLR	Compilation of Quebec Laws and Regulations

2.6 OTHER INFORMATION PUBLISHED IN *GAZETTES*

2.6.1 General Form

Title (person or body), | (year) | *Gazette* abbreviation | part of *Gazette*, | page | (additional information).

Indicate the title of the item if appropriate. If the item is numbered in some way, include the number with the title, as it appears in the *Gazette*. Include the statutory instrument number (SI) if there is one. Include the name of the person or body concerned by a notice in parentheses after the title (optional).

The *Gazette* abbreviation is generally composed of the jurisdiction abbreviation followed with **Gaz**. See the Gazette column of the table in **Appendix A-1** for the jurisdiction abbreviation. Note that exceptionally the Gazette abbreviation in Quebec is **GOQ** for *Gazette officielle du Québec*.

Indicate the part of the *Gazette* following the abbreviation. If the *Gazette* is **not published in parts**, add a comma after the abbreviation and cite the page number (e.g., **GOQ, 74**).Include additional information, such as the name of the statute under which an order in council is made.

Ministerial Order 36/91, (1991) A Gaz I, 1609.
Notice (City of Abbotsford), (2004) C Gaz I, 2520.
OC 309/2001, (2001) A Gaz I, 1752 (*Provincial Parks Act*).

NB: The PDF of the *Canada Gazette* has been official since 1 April 2003 at <www.gazette.gc.ca>.

2.6.2 Orders in Council

An Order in Council is an instrument issued by the executive, which implements a government decision (such as the creation of a regulation).

2.6.2.1 *Federal*

Title, | PC year-number **or** SI/year-number | *Gazette* citation | (additional information).

Include the title in italics, if applicable. Include the **Privy Council** (**PC**) number or the statutory instrument (**SI**) number, if there is one. Provide additional information, such as the title of the act under which the order in council is made, if necessary.

> PC 1997-627, (1997) C Gaz II, 1381.
>
> *Withdrawal from Disposal Order (North Slave Region NWT)*, SI/97-42, (1997) C Gaz II, 1338.

2.6.2.2 *Provincial and Territorial*

Title, | Order in Council number, | *Gazette* citation | (additional information).

Include the title of the instrument if available. For the Order in Council number, use the abbreviation for **Order in Council** and the number as it appears in the relevant *Gazette* (this may include the year or the last two digits of the year). Provide additional information, such as the title of the act under which the order in council is made, if necessary.

> OIC 1989/19, (1989) Y Gaz II, 57.
>
> *Town of Paradise Order*, OC 99-529, (1999) N Gaz II, 451 (*Municipalities Act*).
>
> *Regulation respecting the lifting of the suspension and the application of section 41.1 of the* Act respecting labour standards for certain employees, OIC 570-93, (1993) GOQ II, 2607.

2.6.3 Proclamations and Royal Instructions

Citation of law that entered into force **or** issuer of proclamation or instruction, | type of document, | date, | SI/year-number, | *Gazette* or other citation.

For the type of document, use the words **Proclamation** or **Royal Instruction** if it is appropriate in the context. Include the date, followed by the *Gazette* or other citation. To cite the federal proclamations dating from 1972, include the statutory instrument (**SI**) number.

> *Sex Offender Information Registration Act*, SC 2004, c 10, proclaimed in force 15 December 2004, SI/2004-157, (2004) C Gaz II, 2021.
>
> Proclamation, 1 April 1991, (1991) S Gaz I, 1174.
>
> George R, Proclamation, 7 October 1763 (3 Geo III), reprinted in RSC 1985, App II, No 1.

George R to Governor Arthur Phillip, Royal Instruction, 25 April 1787 (27 Geo III), reprinted in *Historical Documents of New South Wales*, vol 1, part 2 (Sydney: Government Printer, 1892-1901) 67.

2.7 MUNICIPAL BY-LAWS

Municipality,	by-law **or** revised by-law	number,	*title*	(date),	pinpoint.

Provide the full title if no short title is available.

Unrevised

City of Whitehorse, by-law No 97-42, *Zoning By-law* (11 May 1998), s 1.

Revised

City of Montreal, revised by-law C S-0.1.1, *By-law Concerning Collection Services*, s 5.

2.8 RULES OF COURT

Jurisdiction,	issuing body,	*title*,	indexing number,	additional indexing information,	pinpoint.

Rules of court are procedural regulations governing judiciary and administrative bodies. Include the jurisdiction and issuing body unless it is part of the title of the rules. See the column of postal abbreviations in **Appendix A-1**. Do not indicate **Canada** for the rules of the Supreme Court of Canada or the Federal Court. Abbreviate **rule** as **r**. To cite to the Quebec ***Code of Civil Procedure*** or ***Code of Penal Procedure***, see section 2.3.

Federal Court Immigration Rules, r 18.
Commission québécoise des libérations conditionnelles, *Règles de pratique*, r 10(4).
AB, *Rules of Court*, AR 124/2010, vol 1, r 10.50.

2.9 SECURITIES COMMISSIONS

Title,	commission	document	bulletin citation	(date),	pinpoint.

Cite securities national instruments, national policies and other documents to **provincial securities commissions**. Abbreviate **National Policy** as **NP** and **National Instrument** as **NI**. For amendments, proposed rules, staff notices, requests for comments, and other commission documents, cite to the **securities commission bulletin** or similar publication, if available.

Mutual Reliance Review System for Exemptive Relief Applications, OSC NP 12-201, (2005) 28 OSCB 7166.

Proposed Amendments to Multilateral Instrument 52-109 Certification of Disclosure in Issuers' Annual and Interim Filings and Companion Policy 52-109CP, MSC Notice 2005-19 (1 April 2005).

CSA Notice — Amendments to NI 31-101 National Registration System and NP 31-201 National Registration System, OSC6 CSA Notice, (2006) 29 OSCB 3955 at 3956.

3 Jurisprudence E-37

3 JURISPRUDENCE

3.1 SOURCES

Hierarchy of sources:

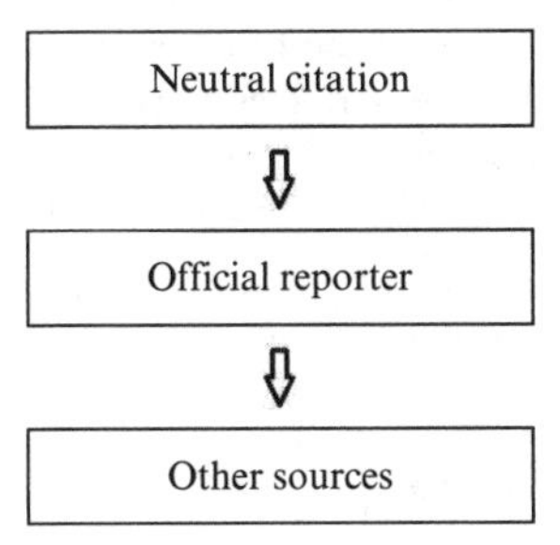

Providing the reader with at least two sources (main citation and parallel citation) is strongly recommended in absence of neutral citation. Citing to several sources provides greater ease of access to the referenced decision. In conjunction with the hierarchy of sources, parallel citation allows for the communication of added relevance that a decision's appearance in a highly regarded or practice-specific reporter (e.g., DLR, CCC, Admin LR, etc.) may provide.

The main citation should be the higher source available in the hierarchy and the parallel citation should be the second higher source available. **Before citing less authoritative sources, make sure that more authoritative sources are not available**.

Where available, the neutral citation should always be the main citation. As a general rule, a parallel citation is unnecessary where reference is made to a neutral citation. Include a parallel citation only where there are no court-assigned paragraph numbers.

In absence of neutral citation or if a parallel citation is nonetheless needed, provide the official reporter for national jurisdictions if it is available

If none of the above is available, provide other sources, which comprise online databases and unofficial reporters. This *Guide* has established a hierarchy within the category of other sources. Online databases that are readily accessible and unofficial reporters that are owned by almost every law library and that provide complete decisions are to be preferred. In **Appendix C-2**, those sources to be preferred are marked with an asterisk (*).

3.2 GENERAL FORM

Style of cause, | main citation | pinpoint, | parallel citation | [*short form*].

> *Fisher v Fisher*, 2008 ONCA 11 at paras 52-59 [*Fisher*].
> *Gordon v Goertz*, [1996] 2 SCR 27 at para 13, 134 DLR (4th) 321 [*Gordon*].

Further sections will clarify each of the elements required in this general form. Note that other elements not mentioned above should be provided in specific cases (year of the decision, jurisdiction, court, judge, history of case, etc.). Refer to the following sections to include these elements.

3.3 STYLE OF CAUSE

The style of cause is a shorter version of the title, referring to a decision informally. **When the style of cause is provided by the reporter, keep it as it is**. If the decision does not indicate the style of cause, follow the supplementary rules indicated in sections 3.3.1 to 3.3.18, below. If the style of cause is indicated in the text, do not repeat it in the footnote.

Italicize both the names of the parties and the ***v*** or ***c*** that separates their names. The use of ***v*** and ***c*** in the style of cause indicates the language of the decision. If the decision of the tribunal is in English, use ***v***.

Pacific Developments Ltd ***v*** *Calgary (City of)*

If the decision of the tribunal is in French, use ***c***.

Traverse Trois-Pistoles Escoumins Ltée ***c*** *Quebec (Commission des Transports)*

If the decision is bilingual, use ***v*** if you are writing in English.

Committee for the Equal Treatment of Asbestos Minority Shareholders ***v*** *Ontario (Securities Commission)*

When the style of cause includes terms normally appearing italicized, they should appear in roman type (reverse italics). This applies, for example, to a ship sued *in rem* (e.g., *Porter v The* **Pinafore**). As indicated above, this rule does not apply to ***v*** and ***c***.

3.3.1 Names of Parties

Use **surnames**; omit given names or first initials.

Toneguzzo-Norvell v ***Savein***
Best v ***Best***

Where more than one person is on either side of the action, use only the first person's name and refrain from using **et al** to indicate multiple parties.

Capitalize the first letter of a party name and the first letter of all words, other than prepositions, conjunctions, and words in procedural phrases (e.g., ***in re***, ***ex rel***). Translate into English descriptions words such as **city** but do not translate words forming part of the name of a party, such as **University**, and abbreviations such as **Ltd** or **LLP**. Do not include **The**, **Le**, **La**, **L'**, or **Les** as the first word of a party name, even if it is part of a company name. Include these words if they are part of the name of an object proceeded against *in rem* (such as aircraft or ships: ***The Mihalis Angelos***).

3.3.2 Person Represented by Guardian or Tutor

Phrases such as ***(Guardian ad litem of)*** or ***(Litigation guardian of)*** appear in parentheses after the name of the represented person.

*Williams **(Guardian ad litem of)** v Canadian National Railway*
*Dobson **(Litigation guardian of)** v Dobson*

3.3.3 Names of Companies and Partnerships

It is important to identify business entities as such. Accordingly, always include **Co, Corp, Inc, Ltd, ltée, Limited, srl, LLP**. Do not translate these identifying words or abbreviations. Include given names and initials that form part of a company or firm name. Also include the names of all partners in a partnership. When a company has a bilingual name, use the name of the company in the language of the decision. If the decision is bilingual, use the name of the company in the language in which you are writing.

*Sloan v **Union Oil Co of Canada Ltd***
*Metson v **RW de Wolfe Ltd***
*Prowse Chowne **LLP** v Northey*
*National Party of Canada v Canadian Broadcasting **Corp***
***Shell Canada Ltd** v Canada*
*Wickberg v **Shatsky & Shatsky***

3.3.4 Countries, Federal Units, Provinces, and Municipalities

Use the **common name of a country**, not its formal name or abbreviation.

United States v Burns

Omit **Province of, State of, People of**, or any other similar identifiers.

*Mercier v **Alberta** (AG)*

Include identifiers such as **City of, County of, District of**, or **Township of** in parentheses.

*Bay Colony Ltd v Wasaga Beach **(Town of)***
*Markle v Toronto **(City of)***
*Toronto Dominion Bank v **Alfred (Township of)***

3.3.5 Wills and Estates

Do not use the names of executors only the name of the estate.

*Kipling v **Kohinsky Estate***

The term **Re** should precede the name of the estate if no plaintiff or defendant is included in the style of cause.

Re Eurig Estate

However, always follow the style of cause provided by a reporter, even if the **Re** is placed differently.

Lipton Estate (Re).

3.3.6 Bankruptcies and Receiverships

Use the name of the bankruptcy or company in receivership followed by **Trustee of, Receiver of,** or **Liquidator of** in parentheses.

*Chablis Textiles (**Trustee of**) v London Life Insurance*
*Confederation Trust Co (**Liquidator of**) v Donovan*

3.3.7 Statute Titles

When the jurisdiction cannot be discerned from the name of the statute, it should be indicated in parentheses afterwards.

Re Canadian Labour Code
Reference Re Fisheries Act (Canada)

3.3.8 The Crown

Use **R** to refer to the Crown. It should also replace expressions such as **The Queen, Regina, The Crown,** or **The Queen in Right of**.

R v Blondin

3.3.9 Government Entities

Include the name of the jurisdiction that the government entity represents. Place the name of the government body (such as an agency, commission, or department) in parentheses after the name of the jurisdiction. Do not repeat the name of the jurisdiction in the parenthetical information.

*Susan Shoe Industries Ltd v Ontario (**Employment Standards Officer**)*

Abbreviate the **Minister of National Revenue** to MNR, the **Deputy Minister of National Revenue** to Deputy MNR, and **Attorney General** to AG.

Schreiber v Canada (AG)
Buckman v MNR

Do not include the name of an individual representing a government body.

*Canada (**Combines Investigation Branch, Director of Investigation and Research**) v Southam*

3.3.10 Crown Corporations

Do not include the name of the jurisdiction before the name of the Crown corporation.

Westaim Corp v Royal Canadian Mint

3.3.11 Municipal Boards and Bodies

Indicate the name of the municipal board or body after the jurisdiction.

Johnson v Sarnia (City of) Commissioners of Police

3.3.12 School Boards

Omit such terms as **Board of Education**, **Board of Trustees**, or **Governors of**. Include only the name of the institution.

Prince Albert Rural School Division No 56 v Teachers of Saskatchewan

3.3.13 Unions

Do not abbreviate union names, as such abbreviations vary widely.

Canadian Autoworkers Union, Local 576 v Bradco Construction Ltd

3.3.14 Social Welfare Agencies

Include the name of the community where the aid agency is based unless it forms part of the name of the agency.

Doe v Metropolitan Toronto Child and Family Services
EP v Winnipeg (Director of Child and Family Services)

3.3.15 Parties' Names that are Undisclosed

If the names of the parties are not disclosed in the case, use initials where available, or the title and numerical description provided by the reporter.

Droit de la famille - 1544
M v H

3.3.16 If The Case Is Known Under Two Names — The *Sub Nom* Rule

Sub nom is the abbreviated version of *sub nomine*, which is Latin for "under the name of". Use the style of cause **provided in the most** authoritative **source** (see the hierarchy of sources at section 3.1). If a **parallel citation refers to the parties by different names**, enclose this style of cause in parentheses introduced by the phrase ***sub nom***. Place the parentheses immediately before the citation for the reporter using those names.

Reference Re Resolution to Amend the Constitution, [1981] 1 SCR 753, (***sub nom Reference Re Amendment of the Constitution of Canada (Nos 1, 2 and 3)***) 125 DLR (3d) 1.

3.3.17 One Party Acting for Someone Else — The *Ex Rel* Rule

Ex rel is the abbreviated version of *ex relatione*, which is Latin for "upon relation or information". Where a third party enters the suit to act on behalf of one of the parties, note this by using the phrase ***ex rel***.

Ryel v Quebec (AG) ***ex rel*** *Société immobilière du Québec*

3.3.18 Procedural Phrases and Constitutional References

Use ***Reference Re*** for constitutional cases only.

Reference Re Firearms Act

In all other cases, use ***Re*** alone before the subject. Shorten ***In re***, **In the matter of**, and ***Dans l'affaire de*** to ***Re***.

Re Gray

Write ***Ex parte*** in full. The expression indicates that the named party is the one that has brought the action.

Ex parte James: Re Condon

3.4 YEAR OF DECISION

When a decision has a **neutral citation** or when **the year of decision is the same as the year in the main citation**, do not write the year after the style of cause.

Cadbury Schweppes v FBI Foods Ltd, [1999] 1 SCR 142, 59 BCLR (3d) 1.

If **the year is not indicated in the main citation**, provide the year of decision in parentheses after the style of cause. This is the case even if the year of decision is the same as the year in the parallel citation. Do not italicize the year.

R v Borden **(1993)**, 24 CR (4th) 184, 1993 CarswellNS 18 (WL Can) (NSCA).

If **the year in the main citation and the year of decision are different**, provide the year of decision in parentheses after the style of cause in addition to the year in the main citation.

Joyal c Hpital du Christ-Roi **(1996)**, [1997] RJQ 38, 1996 CarswellQue 1062 (WL Can) (CA).

3.5 NEUTRAL CITATION

The number of the neutral citation emanates from the court itself; **never create a neutral citation** when an official one is unavailable. Each Canadian court and a growing number of administrative tribunals have adopted the neutral citation. The date of its implementation for each entity is available at **Appendix B-3**.

The neutral citation can be used to identify a particular case independently from the reporter or electronic database in which it is published. For more information, see section 3.2.2 ("Neutral Citation") of the Canadian Citation Committee's *The Preparation Citation and Distribution of Canadian Decisions* at <lexum.com/ccc-ccr/preparation/en>.

> *R v Senko*, 2004 ABQB 60 at para 12.
> *Ordre des arpenteurs-géomètres du Québec c Tremblay*, 2001 QCTP 24 at para 18, n 14.

The jurisdiction and level of court are indicated in a neutral citation. It is not necessary to include supplementary abbreviations of jurisdictions and courts. Some databases provide citations that resemble neutral citations (e.g., Quicklaw's SCJ or OJ). Use these identifiers only when citing to that database's source, and not in lieu of an official neutral citation.

When writing for foreign audiences or when citing foreign jurisprudence, it may be appropriate to include the country's neutral three letter **ISO-3166-1 alpha-3** reference code before the neutral citation (e.g., ***R v Law*, CAN 2002 SCC 10**). Other codes include **GBR** for the United Kingdom, **FRA** for France, **AUS** for Australia, **NZL** for New Zealand and **ZAF** for South Africa.

3.5.1 Year

The neutral citation begins with the year in which the decision was rendered by the court.

3.5.2 Tribunal Identifier

The tribunal identifier is assigned by the court and can be up to eight characters in length. It is composed of two elements. The prefix is the jurisdiction. With the exception of the Northwest Territories, the provincial and territorial identifiers begin with a prefix of **two characters**. See the column of neutral citation in **Appendix A-1**.

The usual acronym of the tribunal or court follows this prefix. Omit the reintroduction of any letters representing the jurisdiction (e.g., the "Tribunal des professions du Québec" is **QCTP** and not **QCTPQ**).

Federal tribunals and courts do not follow the prefix rule described above (e.g., Supreme Court of Canada = **SCC**). See **Appendix B-3** for a complete list of Neutral Citation Abbreviations.

3.5.3 Decision Number

The sequence number is assigned by the court. This number reverts to "1" on 1 January of every year.

3.6 PINPOINT

3.6.1 General Form

Place the pinpoint reference **after the main citation**. Always refer to **paragraphs** if there is a neutral citation or official paragraph number (i.e., determined by the court and uniform across all reporters). If there is no neutral citation or official paragraph number, refer to a page number or a paragraph and indicate the cited reporter (section 3.6.2). Begin a page or paragraph pinpoint with **at**. Do not place a comma before **at** and do not use **p** to indicate the page number. Cite paragraphs by using **para** or **paras**. Cite to footnotes using **n** (see *Ordre des arpenteurs-géomètres*). Include the corresponding paragraph number for ease of reference, and separate the paragraph and footnote indications by a comma. For general rules regarding pinpoint, see section 1.5

> *R v Proulx*, 2000 SCC 5 **at para 27**.
> *Vriend v Alberta (AG)*, [1998] 1 SCR 493 **at 532–34**, 156 DLR (4th) 385.
> *Ordre des arpenteurs-géomètres du Québec c Tremblay*, 2001 QCTP 24 **at para 18, n 14**.

3.6.2 Cited Reporter

The page and paragraph numbering often differ from one reporter to the other in the absence of neutral citation. The reader must know to which reporter the pinpoint references cite. Cite the pinpoint reference to the **most official reporter, mentioned first** (as required by the hierarchy of sources at section 3.1). For every subsequent pinpoint, cite to the same reporter. If subsequently citing to pinpoints, add **cited to** after the short title, followed by the abbreviation of the reporter. No **cited to** is necessary when not subsequently referring to pinpoints or if the first citation contains a pinpoint.

> *Delgamuukw v British Columbia*, 79 DLR (4th) 185, [1991] 3 WWR 97 (BCSC) [*Delgamuukw* **cited to DLR**].

Do not specify the source of the pinpoint in the subsequent references if there is a pinpoint reference the first time a case is mentioned. It is implied that the subsequent references will follow the same model and cite to the same reporter.

> *Université du Québec à Trois-Rivières v Larocque*, [1993] 1 SCR 471 **at 473**, 101 DLR (4th) 494 [*Larocque*].

Do not specify the source of the pinpoint when there is a neutral citation with numbered paragraphs. In this case, the paragraph numbers are set by the court and not by the individual publishers.

> *R v Sharpe*, **2007 BCCA 191** [*Sharpe*].

3.7 PRINTED REPORTER

3.7.1 Year of Reporter

Reporters are published either in volumes organized by year of publication (e.g., SCR, RJQ) or in volumes numbered in series (e.g., DLR, CCC). If the reporter volumes are numbered by **year of publication**, enclose the year in brackets.

> **[2003]** RJQ 89

Some reporters organized by year of publication publish **several volumes per year** (e.g., SCR). Indicate the year in brackets followed by the volume number.

> **[1998] 2** SCR 217

If the reporter volumes are numbered in **series**, no year is needed to identify the reporter volume (but remember to include the year in the style of cause if not otherwise indicated in the citation; see section 3.4). Note that, by convention, reporters use **2d** and **3d** for "second" and "third" respectively.

> **214** NSR (2d) 295

Note that **some reporters have changed their mode of organization**. The *Supreme Court Reports* were organized by volume from 1877–1923 (e.g., **27 SCR**). Then, from 1923–1974, they were organized by year (e.g., **[1950] SCR**). Since 1975, they have been organized by year with several volumes per year (e.g., **[1982] 2 SCR**). Prior to 1974, the *Ontario Reports* were organized by year of publication (e.g., **[1973] OR**). Since 1974, they have been published in a numbered series (e.g., **20 OR**).

3.7.2 Reporter

Abbreviate the name of the reporter according to the list in **Appendix C**.

3.7.2.1 Official Reporters

Official reporters apply to federal jurisdictions and are published by the Queen's Printer. Whenever there is a discrepancy between two versions of the same case, the version in the official reporter takes precedence.

3.7.2.2 Unofficial Reporters

The category of unofficial reporters comprises all the printed reporters that are not official; note that this *Guide* does not maintain the distinction between semi-official and unofficial reporters. See **Appendix C-2** for a non-exhaustive list of unofficial reporters. We strongly recommend that you use the listed reporters that are marked with an asterisk (*). They have been selected in accordance with the following guidelines: (1) reporters that are **most readily available** are preferred to more obscure reporters, (2) **general** reporters are preferred to specific reporters, and (3) reporters covering a **large geographic area** are preferred to reporters covering a smaller geographic area.

If a choice is to be made (for example between several recommended unofficial reporters), the aforementioned guidelines should be applied to select the most appropriate reporter. Keep in mind the intended readership. If writing for a specialized audience, citing to a practice specific reporter may be more appropriate.

3.7.3 Series

If the reporter has been published in more than one series, indicate the series in parentheses, between the reporter abbreviation and the first page of the judgment. Do not put the series number in superscript (e.g. **(4th)** and not **(4th)**).

34 BCLR **(4th)** 62 (CA)

Note that, by tradition, reporters use **2d** and **3d** for "second" and "third" respectively.

214 NSR **(2d)** 295

Abbreviate **New Series** or *Nouvelle série* to **NS**.

29 CELR **(NS)** 117 (FCTD)

3.7.4 First Page

Indicate the number of the first page of the decision after the reporter.

[1998] 2 SCR **217**.

3.8 ONLINE DATABASE SERVICES

Online database services provide access to jurisprudence and their content can be referred to either as a main citation or a parallel citation. They have the same status as unofficial reporters in the hierarchy of sources (see section 3.1). Abbreviations for the various services (e.g. **CanLII, QL, WL Can**) can be found in **Appendix E**, but the identifiers of the individual databases within the services (e.g. **CanLII, SCJ, CarswellOnt**) are found in **Appendix C-2** with printed reports. We strongly recommend reference to database identifiers marked with an asterisk (*). As not all services are accessible everywhere and/or free of charge, keep in mind the intended readership when referring to an online database. Do not cite online database services which the majority of readers cannot access.

Do not refer to a URL when citing an online database. Use only the identifier provided by the database below the style of cause. Do not confuse it with printed reporters. In the following example, the reference to the *Supreme Court Reports* is the main citation and **1993 CanLII 151** is the parallel citation to the online database CanLII.

Caisse populaire de Maniwaki v Giroux, [1993] 1 SCR 282, **1993 CanLII 151**.

If the identity of the online database service referred to is not obvious from the database identifier or if the service provides no identifier for the judgment, write the name of the online database in parentheses (using abbreviations found in **Appendix E**).

Almad Investments Ltd v Mister Leonard Holding Ltd, 1996 CarswellOnt 4402 **(WL Can)** at para 3 (Ont Ct J (Gen Div)).

Include the paragraph number for the pinpoint reference. Do not cite the page numbers reproduced in the online source, as these are specific to the service used and can vary in different forms (e.g. PDF, txt, html). If the paragraphs are not numbered, avoid main citation to the online database.

Abitibi-Consolidated Inc v Doughan, EYB 2008-139174 (Référence) **at para 23** (Qc Sup Ct).

Use the rules of section 3.4 when the year is not provided in the identifier.

Desputeaux c éditions Chouette **(2001)**, AZ-50085400 (SOQUIJ) at para 19 (Qc CA).

3.8.1 CanLII

The **Canadian Legal Information Institute** (CanLII) is a freely accessible online database available on <canlii.org>. To ensure accessibility by all readers, CanLII should be preferred over commercial services. CanLII identifiers usually consist of the year, followed by **CanLII** and the serial number of the document. Where a neutral citation is available, the identifier consists of the neutral citation followed by **(CanLII)**. In this case, provide only the neutral citation without reference to the online database.

1993 CanLII 2848 2016 CanLII 96404

3.8.2 LexisNexis Quicklaw

LexisNexis Quicklaw is a commercial online database service that provides access to Canadian jurisprudence, as well as other legal sources, such as legislation and secondary sources. Database identifiers usually consist of the year, the court or jurisdiction abbreviation followed by **J** for Judgments (e.g. **SCJ**, for Supreme Court Judgments), and the serial number of the document. For judgments that are only available in French, the J for "Jugements" may appear before the court or jurisdiction abbreviation (e.g. **JQ**, for "Jugements du Québec"). The year is in square brackets and the number is introduced by **No** for decisions rendered in English or **no** for decisions rendered in French.

[2001] SCJ No 1 [1995] OJ No 4335
[1995] FCJ No 206 [2001] JQ no 1510

3.8.3 Westlaw Canada

WestlawNext Canada is a commercial online database service that provides access to Canadian jurisprudence, as well as other legal sources, such as legislation and secondary sources. Database identifiers usually consist of the year, the word **Carswell** followed without space by the jurisdiction abbreviation, and the serial number of the document.

1995 CarswellOnt 88 1985 CarswellNat 145
2001 CarswellSask 4 1990 CarswellYukon 4

3.8.4 SOQUIJ

The **Société québécoise d'information juridique** (SOQUIJ) is an online database service that provides access to jurisprudence from Quebec and federal courts, as well as legislation, secondary sources, and court registry records. Individual case identifiers usually consist of **AZ-** followed without space by the serial number of the document. The year of the decision is never indicated.

AZ-50085400 AZ-5016965

3.8.5 La Référence

La Référence is an online database service that provides access to jurisprudence from Quebec and federal courts, as well as legislation and many secondary sources published by Éditions Yvon Blais. Individual case identifiers usually consist of **EYB** followed by the year, and the serial number of the document.

EYB 1993-84186 EYB 2011-191663

3.9 JURISDICTION AND COURT

The jurisdiction and court should be indicated if there is **no neutral citation** (which indicates both jurisdiction and court level); and if this **information is not evident** from the title of the reporter. Indicate the jurisdiction and court in parentheses, following the parallel citation. There is no space in an abbreviation consisting solely of upper case letters. Leave a space when an abbreviation consists of both upper case letters and lower case letters (e.g. **BCCA**; **Ont Div Ct**; **NS Co Ct**; **Alta QB**).

If the court is bilingual, use English abbreviations. If the court renders judgments only in French, use the French abbreviations. Use the abbreviations for the jurisdictions found in **Appendix A-1** and the court abbreviations in **Appendix B**.

Taylor v Law Society of Prince Edward Island (1992), 97 DLR (4th) 427 **(PEISC (AD))**.

Ballard v Ballard (2001), 201 Nfld & PEIR 352 **(Nfld SC (TD))**.

O'Brien v Centre de location Simplex ltée (1993), 132 NBR (2d) 179 **(CA)**.

Boisjoli c Goebel (1981), [1982] **CS** 1 **(Qc)**.

Dobson (Litigation Guardian of) v Dobson, [1999] 2 **SCR** 753.

Jurisprudence

3.10 JUDGE

If relevant, a reference to the name of the judge may be included. Add **dissenting** if it is a dissenting opinion. Do not insert a comma between the name of the judge and the office. Where the entire bench (and not a select panel) heard the case, the term **en banc** may be used.

R v Sharpe, 2001 SCC 2 at para 24, **McLachlin CJC**.

Gosselin c Québec (PG), [1999] RJQ 1033 (CA), **Robert JA, dissenting**.
R v Wholesale Travel Group Inc, [1991] 3 SCR 154, 84 DLR (4th) 161, **en banc**.

Office abbreviations:

CJC	Chief Justice of Canada
CJA	Chief Justice of Appeal
CJ	Chief Justice, Chief Judge
JA	Justice of Appeal, Judge of Appeals Court
JJA	Justices of Appeal, Judges of Appeals Court
J	Justice, Judge
JJ	Justices, Judges
LJ	Lord Justice
LJJ	Lord Justices
Mag	Magistrate

3.11 HISTORY OF CASE

3.11.1 Prior History

Cite the prior history of the case as the last element of the citation if it is relevant to the argument. Separate different decisions with a comma. Abbreviate affirming to **aff'g**.

Law v Canada (Minister of Employment and Immigration), [1999] 1 SCR 497, **aff'g** (1996), 135 DLR (4th) 293 (FCA).

Abbreviate reversing to **rev'g**.

Wilson & Lafleur ltée c *Société québécoise d'information juridique*, [2000] RJQ 1086 (CA), **rev'g** [1998] RJQ 2489 (Sup Ct).

Both **aff'g** and **rev'g** refer to the first citation. In *Tsiaprailis*, the Supreme Court affirmed the Court of Appeal, and upheld the reversal of the Tax Court of Canada decision by the Court of Appeal.

Tsiaprailis v Canada, 2005 SCC 8, **aff'g** 2003 FCA 136, **rev'g** [2002] 1 CTC 2858, [2002] DTC 1563 (TCC [General Procedure]).

If the decision is affirming or reversing the prior decision on grounds other than those being discussed, use **aff'g on other grounds** or **rev'g on other grounds**. If the decision is affirming or reversing the prior decision only in part, use **aff'g in part** or **rev'g in part.**

3.11.2 Subsequent History

Cite the subsequent history of the case if it was subsequently appealed to other courts. Place the subsequent history of the case as the last element of the citation. Separate different decisions with a comma. Abbreviate affirmed to **aff'd** and reversed to **rev'd**.

> *R v Paice* (2003), [2004] 5 WWR 621 (CA), **aff'd** 2005 SCC 22.

If the decision was affirmed or reversed on grounds other than those being discussed, use **aff'd on other grounds** or **rev'd on other grounds**. If the decision was affirmed or reversed only in part, use **aff'd in part** or **rev'd in part**.

> *Ontario English Catholic Teachers' Association v Ontario (AG)* (1998), 162 DLR (4th) 257 (Ont Ct J (Gen Div)), **rev'd in part** (1999), 172 DLR (4th) 193 (Ont CA), **rev'd** 2001 SCC 15.

Both **aff'd** and **rev'd** refer to the first citation. In *Ontario English Catholic Teachers' Association*, the Supreme Court agreed with the Court of Appeal that the judgment of the Ontario Court of Justice, General Division, should be reversed; the Supreme Court did not reverse the decision of the Ontario Court of Appeal.

3.11.3 Prior and Subsequent History

Apply the rules for prior and subsequent history listed above. All affirming and reversing decisions refer back to the first citation. Include only the style of cause in the first citation, unless it changes on appeal.

> *Ardoch Algonquin First Nation v Ontario* (1997), 148 DLR (4th) 126 (Ont CA), **rev'g** [1997] 1 CNLR 66 (Ont Ct J (Gen Div)), **aff'd** 2000 SCC 37.

In *Ardoch*, the Ontario Court of Appeal reversed a decision by the lower court; the reversal was later affirmed by the Supreme Court of Canada.

> *Canada v Canderel Ltd*, [1995] 2 FC 232 (CA), **rev'g** [1994] 1 CTC 2336 (TCC), **rev'd** [1998] 1 SCR 147.

In *Canderel Ltd*, the Federal Court of Appeal reversed the decision of the Tax Court of Canada, but the Federal Court of Appeal was in turn reversed by the Supreme Court of Canada (i.e., the Supreme Court of Canada upheld the Tax Court's decision).

Place prior history before subsequent history.

3.11.4 Leave to Appeal

Citation of the decision for which leave to appeal is requested, | court, | citation of the decision as to the appeal.

The **Supreme Court of Canada** decisions on leave to appeal are available on CanLII, Lexum, Westlaw Canada, and Quicklaw, as well as at the beginning of the SCR. Pre-2005 decisions are only listed at the beginning of the SCR. Decisions on leave to appeal to a **court of appeal** are sometimes available in printed reporters and online databases. Include the citation of the decision for which leave to appeal is requested.

> *White Resource Management Ltd v Durish* (1992), 131 AR 273 (CA), leave to appeal to SCC **requested**.

Indicate the court to which the appeal is requested. If available, indicate whether leave was granted or refused and include the citation for that decision.

> *Westec Aerospace v Raytheon Aircraft* (1999), 173 DLR (4th) 498 (BCCA), leave to appeal to SCC **granted**, [2000] 1 SCR xxii.
> *Procter & Gamble Pharmaceuticals Canada Inc v Canada (Minister of Health)*, 2004 FCA 393, leave to appeal to SCC **refused**, 30714 (21 April 2005).

Indicate if it was an appeal as of right.

> *Whiten v Pilot Insurance* (1996), 132 DLR (4th) 568 (Ont Ct J (Gen Div)), **appeal as of right** to the CA.

Provide either the printed reporter reference (see *Westec Aerospace*) or the docket number (followed by the date in parentheses; see *Procter & Gamble*). Certain applications for leave are published. In this case, cite using the normal rules for decisions, and include the result (i.e., **leave to appeal to [court] granted, or leave to appeal to [court] refused**).

> *R v Gallagher*, 2013 ABCA 269, **leave to appeal to Alta CA refused**.

Leave Decision Availability by Jurisdiction		
Supreme Court	Leave decisions are available on CanLII, Lexum, Westlaw Canada and Quicklaw, as well as at the beginning of the SCR.	
Federal Court of Appeal	Leave decisions are not currently listed online.	
Alberta	Certain leave decisions are given a standard neutral citation and are available via the court's website.	www.albertacourts.ca
British Columbia	Certain leave decisions are given a standard neutral citation and are available via the court's website.	www.courts.gov.bc.ca
Manitoba	Certain leave decisions are given a standard neutral citation and are available via CanLII.	
New Brunswick	Certain leave decisions dating back until 2010 are listed in the Rulings on Motions.	www.gnb.ca/cour/03COA1/motions-e.asp
Newfoundland and Labrador	Leave decisions are not currently listed online.	

Northwest Territories	Certain leave decisions are available on the Department of Justice's website.	decisia.lexum.com/nwtcourts-courstno/en/nav.do
Nova Scotia	Certain leave decisions are given a standard neutral citation and are available via the court's website.	decisions.courts.ns.ca/site/nsc/en/nav.do
Nunavut	Certain leave decisions are available on the Department of Justice's website.	www.justice.gov.nt.ca/CourtLibrary/library_decisions.shtml
Ontario	Motions for leave to appeal dating back to 2002 are listed with their docket number.	www.ontariocourts.ca/coa/en/leave/
Prince Edward Island	Certain leave decisions are given a standard neutral citation and are available via the court's website.	www.gov.pe.ca/courts/supreme/reasons.php3
Quebec	Certain leave decisions are given a standard neutral citation and are available via a provincial database.	citoyens.soquij.qc.ca
Saskatchewan	Certain leave decisions are given a standard neutral citation and are available via CanLII or a provincial database (which links to CanLII) .	www.lawsociety.sk.ca/library/public-resources/court-of-appeal-judgments.aspx
Yukon	Leave decisions are not currently listed online.	

NB: the information given on court websites is also usually available via CanLII or other online databases.

3.12 UNREPORTED DECISIONS WITHOUT A NEUTRAL CITATION

Style of cause | (date), | judicial district | docket number | (jurisdiction and court).

Indicate the style of cause, the full date of the decision in parentheses followed by a comma, the judicial district, and the docket number. Place the jurisdiction and court in parentheses at the end of the citation.

R v Crête (18 April 1991), Ottawa 97/03674 (Ont Prov Ct).

3.13 JURISPRUDENCE EXPRESS

Jurisprudence Express is an unofficial reporter providing summaries for cases from Quebec. Even though reference to Jurisprudence Express should be of last resort, some cases are only reported in Jurisprudence Express. The abbreviation **JE** is at the beginning. Then, include the year of the reporter followed by the number of the reported decision (do not provide the page number). Starting with the year 2000, include the four digits of the year. For years up until 1999, use only the last two digits.

Lalancette c Gagnon, [1995] JQ no 3573 (QL), **JE 95-1255** (CQ).

Commission des normes du travail c Mercier, [2000] JQ no 7821 (QL), **JE 2000-2257** (CQ (Civ Div)).

3.14 INTERLOCUTORY JUDGMENTS AND MOTIONS

Style of cause or names of parties | (date), | judicial district, | court identifier | docket number | type of document (e.g. motion to dismiss).

Marris Handold v Tyson Blair (23 April 2011), Montreal, Que CA 500-02-019902-944 (interlocutory judgment).

3.15 ADMINISTRATIVE BODIES AND TRIBUNALS

3.15.1 Decisions in Printed Reporters

Include the style of cause and indicate whether the case is adversarial (separate the parties with ***v***) or non-adversarial (prefix the style of cause with ***Re***). Where there is no style of cause, use the decision number instead.

Clarke Institute of Psychiatry ***v*** *Ontario Nurses' Assn (Adusei Grievance)* (2001), 95 LAC (4th) 154 (OLRB).

Re *Writers' Union of Canada Certification Application (Certification)* (1998), 84 CPR (3d) 329 (Canadian Artists and Professional Relations Tribunal).

Include the abbreviation as provided by the administrative body or tribunal in parentheses at the end of the citation if it is not evident from the title of the cited reporter (if an abbreviation cannot be found, use the full name). Abbreviate provinces and territories to the shortest provincial abbreviations (the Ontario Securities Commission is abbreviated **OSC**, and the Newfoundland and Labrador Human Rights Commission is abbreviated **NLHRC**). Note that abbreviations of a printed reporter (e.g., **OSC Bull**) may be different from the abbreviation of the agency (e.g., **OSC**).

3.15.2 Online Decisions

Style of cause | (date), | decision number, | online: | administrative body or tribunal | <URL>.

The Commissioner of Competition v Elkhorn Ranch & Resort Ltd (23 November 2009), CT-2009-018, online: Competition Tribunal <www.ct-tc.gc.ca/CMFiles/CT-2009-018_Registered%20Consent%20Agreement_1_45_11-23-2009_6123.pdf>.

Enclose the date of the decision in parentheses after the style of cause. Place a comma after the date. If applicable, include the decision number followed by **online**: and the abbreviation used by the administrative body or tribunal. These abbreviations usually do not contain periods. Note that most abbreviations consist of single letters for each important word in the name. Abbreviate provinces and territories to the shortest provincial abbreviations (e.g., the Ontario Securities Commission is abbreviated **OSC** and the Newfoundland and Labrador Human Rights Commission is abbreviated **NLHRC**).

> *Acuity Funds Ltd* (13 March 2009), online: **OSC** <www.osc.gov.on.ca/en/SecuritiesLaw_ord_20110218_217_acuity.htm>.

For further guidance regarding citation to online ressources, see section 1.6.

3.16 ARGUMENTS AND EVIDENTIARY DOCUMENTS

When referring to a **factum**, provide the full citation of the case. Then, indicate in parentheses **Factum of**, the party (**Appellant** or **Respondent**), and the page number or paragraph number. A short form can be established following the first reference to the document (e.g., **Factum of the Appellant at para 16 [FOA]**).

> *Reference re Secession of Quebec*, [1998] 2 SCR 217 **(Factum of the Appellant at para 16)**.

When referring to an **oral argument**, provide the full citation of the case, then place **Oral argument** and the party in parentheses.

> *Vriend v Alberta*, [1998] 1 SCR 493 **(Oral argument, Appellant)**.

When referring to a **public settlement agreement**, provide the style of cause, followed by **Settlement Agreement** in brackets before the other elements of the citation. If the agreement was announced through a news release, see section 6.14.

> *Mulroney v Canada (AG)* **[Settlement Agreement]**, [1997] QJ No 45 (QL) (Sup Ct).

When referring to **evidence**, provide the full citation of the case, followed by **Evidence** in parentheses with a brief statement identifying the item.

> *R v Swain*, [1991] 1 SCR 933 **(Evidence, Dr Fleming's recommendation that the appellant be released in the community)**.

For other types of documents (e.g., **testimonies, depositions, affidavits, subpoenas, memoranda, transcripts,** etc.), provide the full citation of the case and in parentheses indicate the type of documents referred to followed by the author of the content of the document.

3.17 ARBITRATION CASES

Reference to arbitration cases is covered by the same rules as for jurisprudence (see sections 3.3, 3.4, 3.6 and 3.7) even if they have little authority. For **international arbitration** cases, see section 5.2.11. For **WIPO** cases, see section 5.2.12.

Style of cause or case number | (year of decision), | reporter or identifier | pinpoint | (Arbitrator: | name of arbitrator).

Indicate the style of cause or the case number, followed by the year of the decision in parentheses. If the case is published in a print reporter, cite the arbitration reporter. If the case is published on an online database, write the identifier given by the service. Add the abbreviation of the service in parentheses if not already included in the identifier. If available, add the **name of the arbitrator** in parentheses, preceded by **Arbitrator:**. This is strongly recommended as it may be the only efficient way to distinguish an arbitration case from a regular case.

California State University v State Employers Trade Council - United (2009), 126 Lab Arb (BNA) 613 (Arbitrator: Bonnie Bogue).

Winona School District ISD 861 Winona v Winona Education Association (2006), 2006 WL 3876585 (Arbitrator: Daniel J Jacobowski).

4 Government Documents E-59

4 GOVERNMENT DOCUMENTS

4.1 PARLIAMENTARY PAPERS

This section applies to documents directly published by a parliamentary body (debates, journals, order papers, sessional papers, votes and proceedings, and reports). Apply the general rules of section 4.1.1, unless the document falls into one of the specific categories covered by sections 4.1.2-4.1.5.

4.1.1 General Form

Jurisdiction, | legislature, | *title*, | legislative session, | volume | number | (date) | pinpoint | (speaker).

Indicate the jurisdiction (if a province) and the legislature, unless this information is mentioned in the title of the document. For every federal government document, indicate the jurisdiction (**Canada**) only when other citations to international materials may confuse the reader.

House of Commons Debates, 37-1, No 64 (17 May 2001) at 4175 (Hon Elinor Caplan).
Quebec, National Assembly, *Votes and Proceedings*, 39-1, No 48 (18 June 2009) at 517.
Saskatchewan, *Journals of the Legislative Assembly*, 23-3, vol 105 (9 March 1998) at 7.
Quebec, National Assembly, *Feuilleton et préavis*, 38-1, No 79 (6 May 2008).

Write the title, in italics, as it appears on the title page of the document. Indicate the legislative session. The first number is the number of the parliament or legislature and the second is the number of the session. Use cardinal numbers. For example, **37th Parliament, 1st Session** becomes **37-1**.

Place the volume and/or document number, if any, after the title, preceded by a comma. Include the full date in parentheses followed by the pinpoint. Include the name of the speaker, if any, in parentheses at the end of the citation.

4.1.2 Debates

Where relevant, indicate the title of the bill being debated in quotation marks and the reading before the jurisdiction, legislature and title.

"Bill C-8, An Act to amend the Copyright Act and the Trade-marks Act and to make consequential amendments to other Acts", 2nd reading, *House of Commons Debates*, 41-2, No 9 (28 October 2013) at 1504 (Hon Steven Blaney).

When referring to a debate with a committee, use the same form, but add the name of the committee after the legislature. The title is the title of the work produced by the committee.

House of Commons, **Standing Committee on Justice and Human Rights**, *Evidence*, 39-2, No 12 (7 February 2008) at 15:30 (Tony Cannavino).

4.1.3 Order Papers

At the federal level, the ***Order Paper*** and the ***Notice Paper*** are two parts of a single publication. Only cite the relevant part in the title.

> House of Commons, ***Order Paper***, 39-1, No 175 (20 June 2007).

4.1.4 Sessional Papers

From Confederation in 1867 to 1925, the Library of Parliament bound all the Sessional Papers into volumes. Older sessional papers are published in the ***Sessional Papers***. Indicate the title of the report in quotation marks after the legislature. If an author is given, place by and the name after the title of report. Indicate the year only, not the full date, in parentheses.

> Ontario, Legislative Assembly, **"Report on Workmen's Compensation for Injuries" by James Mavor**, *Sessional Papers*, No 40 (1900) at 6-7.

Modern sessional papers are kept loose. Instead of the title, place **Sessional Paper** in roman font. House of Commons sessional papers are provided numbers that are indicated in the Journal when the document is tabled.

> House of Commons, "Report of the Canadian International Trade Tribunal for the fiscal year ended March 31, 2015" by Oliver (Minister of Finance), **Sessional Paper**, 41-2, **No 8560-412-553-02** (2 August 2015).

4.1.5 Reports

After the name of the legislature, add the name of issuing body and the title of the report.

Reports published in debates:

Place the title of the report in quotation marks.

> Ontario, Legislative Assembly, Standing Committee on Regulations and Private Bills, **"Election of Chair"**, *Official Report of Debates (Hansard)*, No T-6 (26 September 2001) at 41.

Reports published separately:

Place the title of the report in italics. If the Chair is indicated on the cover page, add the information in parentheses. This section applies to reports directly published by a parliamentary body. If the report is published by any other body, see section 4.2 on non-parliamentary documents.

> House of Commons, ***Labelling of Genetically Modified Food and its Impact on Farmers: Report of the Standing Committee on Agriculture and Agri-Food*** (June 2002) **(Chair: Charles Hubbard)**.

4.2 NON-PARLIAMENTARY DOCUMENTS

This section applies to all government-published documents that do not emanate directly from a legislative body. Apply the general rules of section 4.2.1, unless the document falls into one of the specific categories covered by sections 4.2.2–4.2.4.

4.2.1 General Form

Jurisdiction, | issuing body, | *title,* | (type of document), | other information | (publication information) | pinpoint.

Canada, Royal Commission on Electoral Reform and Party Financing, *Reforming Electoral Democracy*, vol 4 (Ottawa: Communication Group, 1991) at 99.

Include the jurisdiction unless it is mentioned in another element of the citation. Include the issuing body unless it is mentioned in the title. If there is an individual author, or an institutional author that differs from the issuing body, provide the author's name after the title preceded by the word **by**. In all other respects, follow the rules of section 6.2.2.

Statistics Canada, *Police-Reported Crime Statistics in Canada, 2011*, **by Shannon Brennan**, Catalogue No 82-002-X (Ottawa: Statistics Canada, 11 October 2012).

After the document title, and following the name of an individual or institutional author if included, provide all other information that would help readers to locate a source (e.g. catalogue information), or to assess a source's authority (e.g. the date on which a source was updated, or whether the source is currently under review or cancelled). Separate each element by a comma. If the document is divided into multiple volumes, follow the rules at section 6.2.4. The name of the president or commissioner associated with the issuing body may also be placed in parentheses after the title.

Statistics Canada, *Mixed Unions*, by Anne Milan & Brian Hamm, in *Canadian Social Trends*, **Catalogue No 11-008-X** (Ottawa: Statistics Canada, 2004).

Canadian Intellectual Property Office, *Manual of Patent Office Practice*, **December 2010 update** (Ottawa: Industry Canada, 1998) at 12.

Quebec, Ministère de la justice, *Commentaires du ministre de la justice: Le Code civil du Québec*, **vol 1** (Quebec: Publications du Québec, 1993) at 705.

Where the issuing body is also the publisher of the document, its name may be shortened or replaced by an acronym in the publication information section. In all other respects, provide publication information according to the rules of sections 6.2.5-6.2.9.

Quebec, **Office de révision du Code civil**, *Rapport sur les obligations*, by the Comité du droit des obligations (Montreal: **ORCC**, 1975).

If the type of document is indicated on the title page, provide this information between parentheses after the title of the document.

Commission de la santé et de la sécurité du travail du Québec, *Planification des mesures d'urgence pour assurer la sécurité des travailleurs* **(Guide)** (Quebec: CSST, 1999) at 53.

Canada, Department of National Defence, *Defence Terminology Programme* **(Defence Administrative Orders and Directives)**, No 6110-1, under review (Ottawa: DND, 29 January 2010).

Do not provide the type of document if obvious from the title of the document or if it would not help readers to locate or understand the source.

Canadian Agency for Drugs and Technology in Health, ***CEDAC Final Recommendation*****: Abacavir/ Lamivudine**, by Canadian Expert Drug Advisory Committee (Ottawa: CADTH, 16 November 2005) at paras 2-4.

Nova Scotia, Workers' Compensation Board, *Chronic Pain* (Halifax: WCB, April 2008).

Unless another location appears in the document itself, presume that federal documents are published in Ottawa, and that provincial/territorial documents are published in the provincial/territorial capital. Provide the most complete publication date available based on information contained in the source document.

Use the same format for law reform publications. If available, provide the report number, followed by the year in parentheses.

Law Reform Commission of British Columbia, *Report on Non-Charitable Purpose Trusts*, Report 128 (1992).

Alberta Law Reform Institute, *Estate Administration*, Final Report 102 (2013) at para 91.

4.2.2 Tax Interpretation Bulletins (ITs) and Information Circulars (ICs)

ITs are income tax interpretation bulletins published by the Canada Revenue Agency. **ICs** are information circulars, also published by the Canada Revenue Agency. Analogous documents exist at the provincial level.

Canada Revenue Agency, Interpretation Bulletin IT-459, "Income Tax Act Adventure or Concern in the Nature of Trade" (8 September 1980).

Canada Revenue Agency, Information Circular IC-70-6R5, "Advance Income Tax Rulings" (17 May 2002).

If the bulletin has been revised insert **R** after the document number. The number of revisions is indicated by the number following the R.

Revenu Québec, Interpretation Bulletin IMP 1131-1/R3, "Capital Tax Liability" (30 June 2011) at para 4.

When tax documents are divided into paragraphs, pinpoint to a paragraph.

4.2.3 Reports of Inquiries and Commissions

Jurisdiction, | issuing body, | *title*, | volume | (publication information) | (Chair) | pinpoint.

Include the jurisdiction unless it is mentioned in another element of the citation. Include the issuing body unless it is mentioned in the title of the report. To distinguish the volumes, indicate **vol** or any other appellation used in the report (such as "book"). Do not repeat the volume number in subsequent references unless there is a citation to a different volume anywhere else in the citing document.

> *Commission of Inquiry on the Blood System in Canada: Final Report*, vol 1 (Ottawa: Public Works and Government Services Canada, 1997) at 100.
>
> Canada, Commission of Inquiry into the Sponsorship Program and Advertising Activities, *Who is Responsible? Fact Finding Report* (Ottawa: Public Works and Government Services Canada, 2005) at 33.

To cite a report published in multiple volumes with different titles, include a full citation for each volume separated by a semicolon. Treat the title of the volume as a subtitle of the entire work. Subsequent references must include the volume number following the short title.

> *Report of the Royal Commission on Aboriginal Peoples: Looking Forward, Looking Back*, **vol 1** (Ottawa: Supply and Services Canada, 1996); *Report of the Royal Commission on Aboriginal Peoples: Restructuring the Relationship*, **vol 2** (Ottawa: Supply and Services Canada, 1996) at 14.

4.2.4 Public Papers of Intergovernmental Conferences

Name of conference or committee, | *title*, | document number | (location of conference: | date of conference).

Indicate the name of the conference or committee in full, followed by the title of the paper and the document number. Provide the location and full date of the conference in parentheses.

> Meeting of the Continuing Committee of Ministers on the Constitution, *The Canadian Charter of Rights and Freedoms*: *Discussion Draft, July 4, 1980*, Doc 830-81/027 (Ottawa: 8–12 September 1980).
>
> Federal-Provincial-Territorial Meeting of Ministers Responsible for Justice, *Dealing with Impaired Driving in Prince Edward Island: A Summary 1986-1997*, Doc 830-600/021 (Montreal: 4–5 December 1997).

4.2.5 Intergovernmental Documents

4.2.5.1 General Form

Title, | date, | pinpoint, | online: | *title of the website* | <URL> | [archived URL].

Most intergovernmental documents are available online in PDF format. Provide the full path in accordance with the rules of section 1.6.

> *Accord de coopération et d'échanges entre le gouvernement du Québec et le gouvernement de l'Ontario en matiÒre d'affaires francophones*, 2 June 2006, art 2, online (pdf): *Secrétariat aux affaires intergouvernementales canadiennes* <www.saic.-gouv.qc.ca/francophonie-canadienne/politique/accords-cooperation/accord-ontario.pdf> [perma.cc/B8U4-N2TR].
>
> *Convention de la Baie-James et du Nord québécois et conventions complémentaires*, 11 November 1975, art 28.3.4, online (pdf): *Association of Employees of Northern Quebec* <www.aenq.org> [perma.cc/KA58-QSB9].

4.2.5.2 Indigenous Treaties and Land Claims Agreements

Online versions of Indigenous treaties are found on the website of the Government of Canada in the section on Indigenous and Northern Affairs: <www.aadnc-aandc.gc.ca/eng>. Provide the short form for numbered treaties even in absence of subsequent references.

> *Treaty 3 between Her Majesty the Queen and the Saulteaux Tribe of the Ojibbeway Indians at the Northwest Angle on the Lake of the Woods with Adhesions*, 3 October 1873, online: *Government of Canada* <www.aadnc-aandc.gc.ca> [perma.cc/NN5G-4J6T] **[*Treaty 3*]**.

Indicate the full title of the treaty or the agreement. Do not provide the date if it is already indicated in the title.

> *Treaty No 8 Made June 21, 1899*, online: *Government of Canada* <www.aadnc-aandc.gc.ca> [perma.cc/5JU9-2D2M] [*Treaty 8*].
>
> *Agreement Between the Inuit of the Nunavut Settlement Area and Her Majesty the Queen in Right of Canada*, **25 May 1993**, online (pdf): *Government of Nunavut* <www.gov.nu.ca> [perma.cc/J38P-FAMC].

5 International Materials E-67

5 INTERNATIONAL MATERIALS

5.1 INTERNATIONAL DOCUMENTS

5.1.1 Treaties, UN Documents, and Other International Agreements

Treaty Name, | parties, if applicable, | date of signature, | treaty series reference | pinpoint | (date of entry into force | optional additional information).

Write the complete title of the treaty. If the names of the parties to a bilateral treaty are not mentioned in the title, include the shortened (but not abbreviated) names of the parties after the title, between commas. The names of the parties to a multilateral treaty may be included in parentheses at the end of the citation.

Provide the date when the treaty was first signed or opened for signature. Provide the date of entry into force at the end of the citation, in parentheses. Provide the treaty series citation after the date. Following the treaty series citation, optionally provide a parallel citation to other treaty series, referring to treaty series in the following order of preference: (1) *United Nations Treaty Series* [UNTS] or *League of Nations Treaty Series* [LNTS]; (2) official treaty series of a state involved (e.g., *Canada Treaty Series* [Can TS], *United Kingdom Treaty Series* [UKTS]); (3) other series of international treaties. If available, provide a parallel citation to *International Legal Materials* [ILM]. See **Appendix A-5** for a list of treaty series and their abbreviations.

Provide any additional information at the end of the citation, following the date of entry into force (e.g., the names of the parties to a multilateral treaty, the number of ratifications, and the status of particular countries).

Treaty Relating to Boundary Waters and Questions Arising with Canada, United States and United Kingdom, 11 January 1909, 36 US Stat 2448 (entered into force 5 May 1910).

Convention for the Protection of Human Rights and Fundamental Freedoms, 4 November 1950, 213 UNTS 221 at 223 (entered into force 3 September 1953) [*ECHR*].

International Covenant on Civil and Political Rights, 19 December 1966, 999 UNTS 171 arts 9–14 (entered into force 23 March 1976, accession by Canada 19 May 1976) [*ICCPR*].

North American Free Trade Agreement Between the Government of Canada, the Government of Mexico and the Government of the United States, 17 December 1992, Can TS 1994 No 2 (entered into force 1 January 1994) [*NAFTA*].

General Agreement on Tariffs and Trade, 30 October 1947, 58 UNTS 187 (entered into force 1 January 1948) [*GATT 1947*].

5.1.1.1 Australian Treaty Neutral Citation

The Australian Commonwealth government has adopted a method of neutral citation for treaties that should precede citation to a printed source. The form consists of the publication year in brackets, the identifier (**ATS, ATNIA or ATNIF**), and the document number. This citation should follow the treaty name and the year of signing.

> *Agreement on the Conservation of Albatrosses and Petrels*, 19 June 2001, [2004] ATS 5.

5.1.2 United Nations Documents

Not all UN documents contain every element found in the examples below. Adapt the citation and provide the information necessary to identify the document clearly. See **Appendix A-5** for a list of commonly used works and phrases in UN documents.

5.1.2.1 Charter of the United Nations

The *Charter of the United Nations* does not require a full citation. Cite it as: ***Charter of the United Nations*, 26 June 1945, Can TS 1945 No 7**.

5.1.2.2 Official Records

Official records published by UN organizations contain three parts: **Meetings**, **Supplements**, and **Annexes**. The official records are identified by the particular body's acronym followed by **OR**. Provide the full names of UN bodies that have no official acronym.

5.1.2.2.1 Meetings

UN body's acronym and OR, | session number **or** number of years since the body's inception, | meeting, | UN doc number (and sales number) | (year of document) | pinpoint | [provisional].

Indicate UN (unless UN is part of the body's acronym) followed by the **UN body's acronym** and **OR** (**Official Records**). Do not add a space between UN and the acronym.

Provide the **session number** after the name of the body. If the session number is not available, give the year of the body since its inception. If neither the session number nor the year of the body are available, provide the calendar year.

Provide the **meeting number** after the sessional information. Provide the **UN document number** after the meeting number. If a document has more than one document number, indicate all the numbers, separated by a hyphen. Give the **sales document number** after the document number in parentheses (e.g., Sales No #) (if applicable).

Provide the **calendar year** in parentheses after the UN document number, unless previously indicated. Indicate **provisional documents** by placing **[provisional]** at the end of the citation.

> UNCTAD TDBOR, 23rd Sess, 565th Mtg, UN Doc TD/B/SR.565 (1981).
> UNSCOR, 53rd Year, 3849th Mtg, UN Doc S/PV.3849 (1998) [provisional].
> UNESCOR, 1984, 23rd Plen Mtg, UN Doc E/1984/SR.23.

5.1.2.2.2 Supplements

UN resolutions, decisions, and reports appear as supplements to documents published in the Official Records.

Author, | *title*, | UN body Res **or** Dec number, | UN body's acronym and OR, | session number **or** calendar year, | Supp No, | UN Doc number | (calendar year) | 1st page | pinpoint.

For reports, provide the name of the author if not mentioned in the title.

> **Commission on Crime Prevention and Criminal Justice**, *Report on the Ninth Session*, UNESCOR, 2000, Supp No 10, UN Doc E/2000/30.
>
> *Report of the UN Commissioner for Refugees*, UNGAOR, 15th Sess, Supp No 11, UN Doc A/4378/Rev.1 (1960).

For decisions and resolutions, provide the **decision or resolution number** after the title.

> *Universal Declaration of Human Rights*, **GA Res 217A (III)**, UNGAOR, 3rd Sess, Supp No 13, UN Doc A/810 (1948) 71.
>
> *Protection of the heritage of indigenous people*, **ESC Dec 1998/ 277**, UNESCOR, 1998, Supp No 1, UN Doc E/1998/98, 113 at 115.

Indicate **UN** (unless UN is part of the body's acronym) followed by the **UN body's acronym** and **OR** (**Official Records**). Do not add a space between **UN** and the acronym. For resolutions and decisions, provide this information after the resolution or decision number. For reports, provide this information immediately after the report's title.

Provide the **session number** after the UN body's official records acronym. If the session number is not available, give the **year of the body since its inception**. If neither the session number nor the year of the body is available, provide the **calendar year**. Provide the **supplement number** and the UN document number after the sessional information. Provide the **calendar year** in parentheses after the UN document number, unless it has been indicated previously. If possible, conclude the citation with the first page number and pinpoint. Add a comma when there is no information provided between the UN document number and the first page.

5.1.2.2.3 Annexes

Title, | UN body's acronym and OR, | session number **or** number of years since the body's inception, | annex, agenda item no, | UN Doc number | (year) | 1st page | pinpoint.

Provide the UN body's acronym and **OR** (**Official Records**) after the title. Do not add a space between **UN** and the acronym.

Provide the **session number** after the UN body's acronym. If the session number is not available, give the **year of the body since its inception**. If neither the session number nor the year of the body is available, provide the **calendar year**.

Indicate **Annex** and the agenda item number, followed by the UN document number. Provide the calendar year in parentheses after the UN document number, unless it has been indicated previously. Conclude the citation with the first page number if the document is part of a bound collection of documents. Add a comma when there is no information provided between the UN document number and the first page.

> *Protectionism and structural adjustment*, UNCTAD TDBOR, 32nd Sess, Annex, Agenda Item 6, UN Doc TD/B/1081 (1986) at 23.
>
> *USSR: Draft Resolution*, UNESCOR, 3rd year, 7th Sess, Annex, Agenda Item 7, UN Doc E/884/Rev.1 (1948) at para 3.

5.1.2.3 UN Masthead Documents (Mimeographs)

> Name of body, | name of sub-body or commission | author, | *title,* | session, | meeting, | Supplement, | UN Doc number, | date | pinpoint | [short form].

A mimeograph is an official document of the UN. Refer to one only when the document has not been reproduced in the Official Reports. Mimeographs are available at <documents.un.org>.

Not every document will indicate all of the elements listed above. The most important element is the **UN Doc number**, as that is the easiest way to find the document online, followed by the name of the body, the title, and the date. The other elements are less essential, but should be included if they are on the title page.

> UNSC, Disarmament Commission, *Questions about Arms Manufacturing in Eastern Iraq*, UN Doc S/CN.10/L.666, July 1993.

5.1.2.4 Periodicals

When referring to periodical articles published by the UN, follow the rules for citing articles (see section 6.1). If it is unclear from the title of the periodical that the UN is the publisher, include UN and the particular body responsible for the publication in parentheses at the end of the citation.

> CP Romulo, "External Debt in Central America" (1987) CEPAL Review No 32 (UN, Economic Commission for Latin America and the Caribbean).

5.1.2.5 Yearbooks

Cite UN yearbooks using the same rules as those provided for collections of essays, at section 6.3. Give the UN document number of the article cited and of the yearbook, if available.

> "Report of the Commission to the General Assembly on the work of its thirty-ninth Session" (UN Doc A/42/10) in *Yearbook of the International Law Commission 1987*, vol 2, part 2 (New York: UN, 1989) at 50 (UNDOC. A/CN 4/SER.A/1987/Add. 1).

5.1.2.6 Sales Publications

Cite sales publications using the rules for books, at section 6.2.

> UN, *Recommendations on the Transport of Dangerous Goods*, 9th ed (New York: UN, 1995) at 18.

5.1.3 Council of Europe Documents

Council of Europe, | body, | sessional information, | *title*, | official publication, | other information | (year) | pinpoint.

Write **Council of Europe**, followed by the particular body responsible for the instrument. Abbreviate **Parliamentary Assembly** to **PA**, and **Consultative Assembly** to **CA**. Provide the sessional information followed by the title of the document, if applicable. Indicate the official publication in abbreviated form.

Abbreviate *Official Report of Debates* to **Debates**.

> Council of Europe, PA, 2001 Ordinary Sess (First Part), **Debates**, vol 1 (2001) at 67.

Abbreviate *Texts Adopted by the Assembly* to **Texts Adopted**.

> Council of Europe, CA, 21st Sess, Part 3, **Texts Adopted**, Rec 585 (1970) at 1.

Abbreviate *Orders of the Day and Minutes of Proceedings* to **Orders**.

> Council of Europe, CA, 21st Sess, Part 2, **Orders**, 10th Sitting (1969) at 20.

Abbreviate *Documents: Working Papers* to **Documents**.

> Council of Europe, PA, 2000 Ordinary Sess (Third Part), *Situation of lesbians and gays in Council of Europe member states*, **Documents**, vol 5, Doc 8755 (2000) at 1.

Abbreviate *Information Bulletin on Legal Affairs* to **Inf Bull**. See section 6.1 for the format.

> Council of Europe, Committee of Ministers, *Recommendation R(82)1*, (1980) 12 **Inf Bull** 58.

5.1.4 Organization of American States Documents

OAS, | issuing body, | session number, | *title*, | OAS document number | (year) | pinpoint.

OAS documents do not have an author. Include the particular issuing body, if one exists, unless it is clear from the title of the report. Where applicable, put the session or meeting number after the name of the issuing body. Place **OR** before the OAS document number. The document number begins with the letters **OEA** (Organización de los Estados Americanos) and not OAS.

> OAS, General Assembly, 2d Sess, *Draft Standards Regarding the Formulation of Reservations to Multilateral Treaties*, OR OEA/Ser.P/AG/Doc.202 (1972).

OAS, Inter-American Commission on Human Rights, *Draft of the Inter-American Declaration on the Rights of Indigenous Peoples*, OR OEA/Ser.L/V/II. 90/Doc.14, rev. 1 (1995) at 1.

5.1.5 World Trade Organization (WTO) and the General Agreement on Tariffs and Trade (GATT) Documents

GATT **or** WTO, | *title,* | Decision, Recommendation, **or** Document number, | session number, | BISD | online information.

WTO, General Council, *Minutes of Meeting* (held on 22 November 2000), WTO Doc WT/GC/M/60, online: WTO <docsonline.wto.org>.

Decisions and recommendations do not have an author. GATT and WTO are the authors of all reports. Include the particular issuing body, if one exists, unless it is clear from the title of the report. Give the decision, recommendation, or document number. If none, give the full date of the decision or recommendation. Abbreviate **Contracting Parties** to **CP**, **Decision** to **Dec** and **Recommendation** to **Rec**.

Accession of Guatemala, GATT CP Decision L/6824, 47th Sess, 38th Supp BISD (1991) 16.

Freedom of Contract in Transport Insurance, GATT CP Recommendation of 27 May 1959, 15th Sess, 8th Supp BISD (1960) 26.

Where possible, cite GATT documents to the ***Basic Instruments and Selected Documents*** (**BISD**). If a report is printed independently with no document number, use the rules for books, at section 6.2 (e.g., **GATT, *The International Markets for Meat: 1990/91* (Geneva: GATT, 1991)**).

GATT, *Report of the Panel adopted by the Committee on Anti-Dumping Practices on 30 October 1995*, GATT Doc ADP/137, 42nd Supp BISD (1995) 17.

WTO, *Report of the Working Party on the Accession of Bulgaria*, WTO Doc WT/ACC/BGR/5 (1996), online: WTO <docsonline.wto.org>.

5.1.6 Organisation for Economic Co-operation and Development (OECD) Documents

OECD, | authoring body, | *title*, | series title, | working paper number **or** other publication information, | Doc No | (publication information **or** year).

Indicate **OECD** and the authoring body, followed by the title in italics. If the document is a work in a series, provide the series title.

OECD, Development Assistance Committee, *Japan (No 34)*, Development Cooperation Review Series, (Paris: OECD, 1999).

If the document is a working paper, provide the working paper number, if applicable, and the OECD document number. Note that some document numbers begin with **OCDE**, in French or English.

OECD, Economics Department, *Encouraging Environmentally Sustainable Growth in Australia*, Working Paper No 309, Doc No ECO/WKP (2001) 35 (2001).

Include other information such as the volume number for a periodical or series. Provide the publication information in parentheses at the end of the citation. For periodicals, provide the month of publication, if applicable.

OECD, *OECD Economic Surveys: China*, Economic Surveys, vol 2005, No 13, (2005).

5.2 CASES

See **Appendix A-5** for a list of abbreviations of international organizations and their reporters.

5.2.1 Permanent Court of International Justice (1922–1946)

To cite acts and rules of the PCIJ, write the title, volume number, and name of publication, followed by the first page or document number (e.g., ***Revised Rules of the Court*** **(1926), PCIJ 33 (Ser D) No 1**).

5.2.1.1 Judgments, Orders, and Advisory Opinions

Style of cause (names of parties) | (year), | type of decision, | reporter | case No | pinpoint.

Judgments of the PCIJ are published in *Series A: Collection of Judgments* (**PCIJ (Ser A)**) and in *Series A/B: Judgments, Orders and Advisory Opinions* (**PCIJ (Ser A/B)**). Do not specify the type of decision.

Panevezys-Saldutiskis Railway Case (Estonia v Lithuania) (1939), PCIJ (Ser A/B) No 76 at 16.

Orders of the PCIJ are published in *Series A/B: Judgments, Orders and Advisory Opinions* (**PCIJ (Ser A/B)**). Do not provide the year after the style of cause, but provide the full date after the type of decision (**Order of** day | month | year).

Panevezys-Saldutiskis Railway Case (Estonia v Lithuania), **Order of 30 June 1938**, PCIJ (Ser A/B) No 75 at 8.

Advisory opinions of the PCIJ are published in *Series B: Collection of Advisory Opinions* (**PCIJ (Ser B)**) and in *Series A/B: Judgments, Orders and Advisory Opinions* (**PCIJ (Ser A/B)**). Do not provide the name of the parties after the style of cause.

Case of the Customs Régime Between Germany and Austria (1931), Advisory Opinion, PCIJ (Ser A/B) No 41 at 3.

5.2.1.2 Pleadings, Oral Arguments, and Documents

Style of cause (names of parties), | "title of document" | (date), | reporter | case number, | first page | pinpoint.

Indicate the PCIJ Series and the case number. Pleadings, oral arguments, and other documents from **before 1931** are published in *Series C: Acts and Documents Relating to Judgments and Advisory Opinions Given by the Court* (**PCIJ (Series C)**), and **after 1931** in *Series C: Pleadings, Oral Statements and Documents* (**PCIJ (Series C)**). **Basic Documents**, **Annual Reports** and **Indices** are published in series D through series F.

> *Lighthouses Case Between France and Greece (France v Greece)*, "Oral argument of Professor Basdevant" (5 February 1934), PCIJ (Series C) No 74, 222 at 227.
> *Pajzs, Csáky, Esterházy Case (Hungary v Yugoslavia)*, "Application Instituting Proceedings" (1 December 1935), PCIJ (Series C) No 79, 10 at 12.

5.2.2 International Court of Justice (1946–present)

To cite acts and rules of the ICJ, write the title, volume number, and name of publication, followed by the first page or document number (e.g., ***Travel and Subsistence Regulations of the International Court of Justice*, [1947] ICJ Acts & Doc 94**).

5.2.2.1 Judgments, Orders, and Advisory Opinions

Judgments, orders, and advisory opinions of the International Court of Justice are published in the court's official reporter: ***Reports of Judgments, Advisory Opinions and Orders*** (**ICJ Rep**). Refer to the ICJ website <www.icj-cij.org> for ICJ judgments, opinions, or orders not yet printed. Follow the online citation rules of section 1.6.

Style of cause (names of parties), | type of decision | [year of reporter] | reporter | first page | pinpoint.

Although the ICJ Reports sometimes separates the parties' names with a slash (El Salvador/ Honduras), always separate them with a **v** (**El Salvador v Honduras**).

Judgments: Do not specify the type of decision.

> *Case concerning East Timor (Portugal v Australia)*, [1995] ICJ Rep 90 at 103.

Orders: Provide the full date after the type of decision (**Order of** day | month | year).

> *Certain Activities Carried Out by Nicaragua in the Border Area (Costa Rica v Nicaragua)*, **Order of 8 March 2011**, [2011] ICJ Rep 6.

Advisory Opinions: Do not provide the name of the parties after the style of cause.

> *Legality of the Threat or Use of Nuclear Weapons Case*, Advisory Opinion, [1996] ICJ Rep 66 at 70.

5.2.2.2 Pleadings, Oral Arguments, and Documents

Style of cause (names of parties), | "title of document" | (date), | [year of reporter] | reporter | (vol) | first page | pinpoint.

The ICJ publishes pleadings and other documents in Pleadings, Oral Arguments and Documents (ICJ Pleadings). Pleadings are available on the ICJ website: <www.icj-cij.org>.

If there is a volume number, cite it in Arabic numerals (e.g., **1, 2, 3**) and in parentheses before the number of the first page. After 1981, ICJ Pleadings do not indicate the date of publication of the reporter.

> *Case concerning Right of Passage over Indian Territory (Portugal v India)*, "Oral argument of Shri MC Setalvad" (23 September 1957), [1960] ICJ Pleadings (vol 4) 14 at 23.
>
> *Fisheries Jurisdiction Case (Spain v Canada)*, "Application Instituting Proceedings Submitted by Spain" (28 March 1995), ICJ Pleadings 3.

5.2.3 European Court of Human Rights and European Commission of Human Rights

5.2.3.1 Before 1999

Style of cause | (year of judgment), | volume number | reporter | first page, | parallel citation.

Cite the official reporters of the Court and Commission: ***European Court of Human Rights, Series A: Judgments and Decisions*** (**ECHR (Ser A)**); ***Collection of Decisions of the European Commission of Human Rights*** (**Eur Comm'n HR CD** (1960-1974)); ***Decisions and Reports of the European Commission of Human Rights*** (**Eur Comm'n HR DR** (1975-1999)).

Provide a parallel citation to the ***Yearbook of the European Convention on Human Rights*** (**YB Eur Conv HR**) or to the ***European Human Rights Reports*** (**EHRR**).

> *Kurt v Turkey* (1998), 74 ECHR (Ser A) 1152, 27 EHRR 373.
>
> *Spencer v United Kingdom* (1998), 92A Eur Comm'n HR DR 56, 41 YB Eur Conv HR 72.

5.2.3.2 1999 and Later

Protocol No 11 to the Convention for the Protection of Human Rights and Fundamental Freedoms came into force on 1 November 1998, replacing the old court and commission with a new full-time court.

Style of cause, | application number, | [year] | volume number | reporter | first page, | parallel citation.

Add **[GC]** at the end of the style of cause, before the comma, if the judgment was given by the Grand Chamber of the Court.

Other information may also be added in parentheses after the style of cause, before the comma: **(dec)** for a **decision on admissibility**, **(preliminary objections)** for a judgment concerning only **preliminary objections**, **(just satisfaction)** for a judgment concerning only **just satisfaction**, **(revision)** for a judgment concerning **revision**, **(interpretation)** for a judgment concerning **interpretation**, **(striking out)** for a judgment **striking the case out**, or **(friendly settlement)** for a judgment concerning a **friendly settlement**.

If there is more than one application number, include only the first number.

For unreported decisions, give the application number followed by the date the judgment was rendered (e.g., ***Roche v United Kingdom*, No 32555/96 (19 October 2005)**).

> *Allard v Sweden*, No 35179/97, [2003] VII ECHR 207, 39 EHRR 321.
> *Cyprus v Turkey*, No 25781/94, [2001] IV ECHR 1, 35 EHRR 731.

5.2.4 Inter-American Court of Human Rights

5.2.4.1 Judgments, Orders, and Advisory Opinions

> *Style of cause (name of state concerned)* | (year of judgment), | type of decision and number, | reporter | case or report No, | pinpoint, | parallel citation.

Indicate the style of cause. If the case involves an individual state, include the name of that state in parentheses. Provide the year of the decision in parentheses. Indicate the reporter and case number. Provide a parallel citation to the **annual report of the court**, to ***International Legal Materials*** **(ILM)** or to the ***Inter-American Yearbook on Human Rights***.

The Inter-American Court of Human Rights publishes **judgments** in *Inter-American Court of Human Rights, Series C: Decisions and Judgments* **(Inter-Am Ct HR (Ser C))**. Do not indicate the type of decision.

> *Neira Alegría Case (Peru)* (1996), Inter-Am Ct HR (Ser C) No 29 at para 55, *Annual Report of the Inter-American Court of Human Rights: 1996*, OEA/Ser.L/V/III.19/doc.4 (1997) 179.

The Inter-American Court of Human Rights publishes **advisory opinions** in Inter-American Court of Human Rights, Series A: Judgments and Opinions **(Inter-Am Ct HR (Ser A))**. Specify if the document is an **advisory opinion** and provide the advisory opinion number.

> *Reports of the Inter-American Commission on Human Rights (Art 51 of the American Convention on Human Rights) (Chile)* (1997), **Advisory Opinion OC-15/97**, Inter-Am Ct HR (Ser A) No 15 at para 53, *Annual Report of the Inter-American Commission on Human Rights: 1997*, OEA/ Ser.L/V/III.39/doc.5 (1998) 307.

5.2.4.2 Pleadings, Oral Arguments, and Documents

> *Style of cause (name of the state concerned),* | type of decision and number, | "title of document" | (date of document), | reporter and (series) | first page | pinpoint.

Indicate the style of cause. If the name of the state concerned is not already included in the style of cause, write the name in parentheses. Specify if it is an **advisory opinion** and give the advisory opinion number. Provide the reporter and first page. The Inter-American Court of Human Rights publishes pleadings, oral arguments, and other documents in *Inter-American Court of Human Rights, Series B: Pleadings, Oral Arguments and Documents* **(Inter-Am Ct HR (Ser B))**.

Proposed Amendments to the Naturalization Provisions of the Constitution of Costa Rica, Advisory Opinion OC-4/84, "Verbatim Record of Public Hearing" (7 September 1983), Inter-Am Ct HR (Ser B) 23.

5.2.5 Inter-American Commission on Human Rights

Style of cause | (year of judgment), | Inter-Am Comm HR, | case or report number | pinpoint, | *annual report,* | document number.

Decisions of the Inter-American Commission on Human Rights are published in the commission's annual reports. Cite the commission's annual report and the document number. The document number starts with the letters **OEA** (Organización de les Estados Americanos) and not OAS, no matter the language of the document.

Sánchez v Mexico (1992), Inter-Am Comm HR, No 27/92 *Annual Report of the Inter-American Commission on Human Rights: 1992-93*, OEA/Ser.L/V/II.83/doc.14 104.

5.2.6 International Criminal Tribunals

This section provides guidelines for citing documents created by the International Criminal Court; the International Criminal Tribunal for the former Yugoslavia; the International Criminal Tribunal for Rwanda; the Special Court for Sierra Leone; and the Special Panels for Serious Crimes (East Timor).

Style of cause, | case number, | title of document (version) | (date of document) | pinpoint | (tribunal), | source.

Deputy General Prosecutor for Serious Crimes v Sito Barros, 01/2004, Final Judgment (12 May 2005) at para 12 (Special Panels for Serious Crimes (East Timor)), online: *Judicial System Monitoring Program* <www.jsmp.tl/en>.

Include the **given name** of the accused where available in the style of cause. If there are **multiple accused** in the style of cause, use only the name of the first accused. Include **informal designation** in parentheses, after the title, if necessary.

*Prosecutor v Zdravko Mucic (**Celebici Camp Case**)*, IT- 96-21-*Abis*, Judgment on Sentence Appeal (8 April 2003) at para 8 (International Criminal Tribunal for the former Yugoslavia, Appeals Chamber), (WL).

The title reflects the nature of the document, which can vary considerably. Indicate whether the document cited is the **public version** (designated **Public** or **Public redacted**) or the **confidential version** to which public access is limited. For Internet citations, see section 1.6. The official Internet sites of the adjudicative bodies report only a limited portion of available documents. Some commercial online databases provide wider coverage. If the name of the website is the same as that of the tribunal, use only the initials when identifying the website.

Prosecutor v Théoneste Bagosora, ICTR-98-41-T, Minutes of Proceedings (2 April 2002) (International Criminal Tribunal for Rwanda, Trial Chamber), online: ***ICTR*** <www.unictr.org>.

5.2.7 General Agreement on Tariffs and Trade (GATT) 1947 Panel Reports

Style of cause (complainant) | (year of decision), | GATT document number, | BISD volume | (year) | first page | pinpoint, | parallel citation.

Cite the GATT's **BISD** (***Basic Instruments and Selected Documents***) by providing the supplement number, followed by **BISD**, the year in parentheses, and the initial page of the document.

Republic of Korea—Restrictions on Imports of Beef (Complaint by New Zealand) (1989), GATT Doc L/6505, 36th Supp BISD (1988-89) 234 at 237.

United States—Countervailing Duties on Fresh, Chilled and Frozen Pork from Canada (Complaint by Canada) (1991), GATT Doc DS7/R, 38th Supp BISD (1990-91) 30.

5.2.8 World Trade Organization (WTO) Panel and Appellate Body Reports

Style of cause (complainant) | (year of decision), | WTO Doc number | pinpoint | (type of report), | parallel citation.

Provide the style of cause, followed by the names of the complainants. If the **complaints are treated as one** in the report, provide the names of all complainants after the style of cause. If there are **many complainants** and each complaint is treated separately, provide only the name of the complainant to which the report is destined. If there are more than three complainants, provide the name of one complainant followed by **et al**.

Provide the WTO document number. A report can have more than one document number (e.g., **WT/DS 8, 10, 11/AB/R**). In the document number, **WT/DS** indicates **World Trade Dispute Settlement**, **AB** indicates an **Appellate Body**, and **R** indicates **report**. If the case involves more than one complainant, different reports may be addressed to particular complainants. In such cases, the last element of the document number will indicate the name of the particular complainant to which the report is destined (e.g., **WT/DS27/R/USA**).

United States—Sections 301-310 of The Trade Act of 1974 (Complaint by the European Communities) (1999), *WTO* Doc WT/DS152/R at para 3.1 (Panel Report), online: *WTO* <docs.wto.org> [perma.cc/U4TY-NESC].

India—Patent Protection for Pharmaceutical and Agricultural Chemical Products (Complaint by the United States) (1997), *WTO* Doc WT/DS50/AB/R (Appellate Body Report), online: *WTO* <docsonline.wto.org> [perma.cc/QJY2-HVDW].

5.2.9 Canada-United States Free Trade Agreement Panels

Style of cause ∣ (year of decision), ∣ file number, ∣ reporter ∣ (type of panel), ∣ parallel citation.

Indicate a reporter reference, if the panel is published. Provide the chapter under which the complaint was brought. Abbreviate the various panels as follows: **Ch 18 Panel** (**Canada-United States Trade Commission Panel under Chapter 18**), **Ch 19 Panel** (**Canada-United States Binational Panel under Chapter 19**), and ECC (**Extraordinary Challenge Committee**).

> *Re Red Raspberries from Canada* (1990), USA-89-1904-01, 3 TCT 8175 (Ch 19 Panel), online: *NAFTA Secretariat* <www.nafta-sec-alena.org>.
>
> *Re Fresh, Chilled or Frozen Pork from Canada* (1991), ECC-91-1904-01USA (ECC), online: *NAFTA Secretariat* <www.nafta-sec-alena.org>.

5.2.10 North American Free Trade Agreement (NAFTA) Binational Panels

Style of cause (names of parties) ∣ (year of decision), ∣ file number ∣ (type of panel), ∣ parallel citation.

Provide the chapter under which the complaint was brought. Abbreviate the various panels as follows: **Chapter 19 Binational Panel** to **Ch 19 Panel**, **Chapter 20: Arbitral Panel** to **Ch 20 Panel**, and **Chapter 19 Extraordinary Challenge Committee** to ECC.

> *Re Certain Softwood Lumber from Canada (United States v Canada)* (2005), ECC-2004-1904-01USA (ECC), online: *NAFTA Secretariat* <www.nafta-sec-alena.org>.
>
> *Re Polystyrene and Impact Crystal from the United States of America (United States v Mexico)* (1995), MEX-94-1904-03 (Ch 19 Panel), online: *NAFTA* Secretariat <www.nafta-sec-alena.org>.
>
> *Re Tariffs Applied by Canada to Certain US-Origin Agricultural Products (United States v Canada)* (1996), CDA-95-2008-01 (Ch 20 Panel), online: *NAFTA Secretariat* <www.nafta-sec-alena.org>.

5.2.11 International Arbitration Cases

Style of cause **or** Case number ∣ (year of decision), ∣ reporter ∣ pinpoint ∣ (framework) ∣ (names of arbitrators).

Indicate the style of cause including the parties' names, if available.

> *Southern Pacific Properties v Egypt* (1992), 32 ILM 933 at 1008 (International Centre for Settlement of Investment Disputes) (Arbitrators: Dr Eduardo Jiménez de Aréchaga, Mohamed Amin El Mahdi, Robert F Pietrowski Jr).

If parties are reported anonymously, indicate the case number.

Case No 6248 (1990), 19 YB Comm Arb 124 at 129 (International Chamber of Commerce).

Specify the organization responsible for providing the arbitration framework or mechanism in parentheses at the end of the citation. Provide names of arbitrators in parentheses at the end of the citation (optional).

5.2.12 World Intellectual Property Organization (WIPO) Arbitration Cases

5.2.12.1 Uniform Domain Name Dispute Resolution Policy (UDRP)

Style of cause, | case number | <domain name> | (WIPO Arbitration and Mediation Center (UDRP)).

After the style of cause, include the case number and the domain name that is the subject of the arbitration.

CareerBuilder, LLC v Names for sale, D2005-0186 <careersbuilder.com> (WIPO Arbitration and Mediation Center (UDRP)).

5.2.13 International Law Cases Decided Before National Courts

Style of cause, | domestic reporter, | international | reporter | (country, | court).

Cite a national reporter if a national court decides an international case. Provide a second citation to an internationally available reporter, e.g., the ***Annual Digest and Reports of Public International Law Cases*** **(Ann Dig ILC)**, the ***International Law Reports*** **(ILR)**, the ***Common Market Law Reports*** **(CMLR)**, or the ***Common Market Reporter*** **(CMR)**. After 1950, the Ann Dig ILC became the ILR.

Re Noble and Wolf, [1949] 4 DLR 375, [1948] Ann Dig ILC 302 (Can, Ont CA).
Lindon v Commonwealth of Australia (No 2) (1996), 136 ALR 251, 118 ILR 338 (Austl, HC).
Institute of Chartered Accountants in England and Wales v Customs and Excise Commissioners, [1999] 2 All ER 449, [1999] 2 CMLR 1333 (UK, HL).

6 Secondary Sources and Other Materials E-83

6 SECONDARY SOURCES AND OTHER MATERIALS

6.1 LEGAL JOURNALS

6.1.1 General Form

Author, | "title of article" | (year) | volume: | issue | abbreviation of journal | page | pinpoint | (electronic service).

John Borrows, "Creating an Indigenous Legal Community" (2005) 50 McGill LJ 153 at 155 (QL).

6.1.2 Author

6.1.2.1 Single Author

Indicate the author's name **as it is presented on the title page of the article**. Include all names and initials used, but do not add a space between two initials. Do not substitute names when initials are used, and do not substitute initials when names are used. Include **titles** such as **The Honourable**, **Madam Justice**, **Rabbi**, **Professor**, or **Lord** if they appear on the title page. Include **name suffixes** such as **Jr** or **IV**. Do not include authors' degrees or other credentials.

Lynn A Iding, "In a Poor State: The Long Road to Human Rights Protection on the Basis of Social Condition" (2003) 41:2 Alta LR 513.

HW Arthurs, "The Political Economy of Canadian Legal Education" (1998) 25:1 JL & Soc'y 14.

6.1.2.2 Joint Authors

Include up to three authors. If there are **two authors**, separate the authors' names with an ampersand (&). If there are **three authors**, separate the first two authors with a comma and place an ampersand (&) before the last one. If there are **more than three authors**, include only the first author's name and **et al**. For **collaborations** other than full joint authorship, follow the usage on the title page.

David Weissbrodt & Muria Kruger, "Norms on the Responsibilities of Transnational Corporations and Other Business Enterprises with Regard to Human Rights" (2003) 97:4 AJIL 901.

Rafael La Porta et al, "Law and Finance" (1998) 106:6 Journal of Political Economy 1113 at 1152.

6.1.3 Title of Article

Place the title of the article **in quotation marks**. Do not put a comma after the title. Separate a title from a subtitle with a colon. Do not use an em-dash (—) or an en-dash (–). Capitalize the title according to the conventions of the language of the title and follow the punctuation rules of the language of the title. Always use double quotation marks (e.g., **"Title"**) around the title if you are writing in English.

> Suzanne A Kim, **"'Yellow' Skin, 'White' Masks: Asian American 'Impersonations' of Whiteness and the Feminist Critique of Liberal Equality"** (2001) 8:1 Asian LJ 89.

For further rules on language and punctuation of titles, see section 6.2.3.

6.1.4 Year of Publication

If a journal is **organized by volume number**, indicate the year of publication **in parentheses**.

> David M Brown, "Freedom From or Freedom For?: Religion As a Case Study in Defining the Content of Charter Rights" **(2000)** 33:3 UBC L Rev 551.

If a journal is **not organized by volume number, but by year**, provide the year **in brackets**.

> Frédéric Pollaud-Dulian, "À propos de la sécurité juridique" **[2001]** RTD civ 487.

6.1.5 Volume, Issue, and Series

Place the **volume number** after the year of publication, followed by a colon and the **issue number**. Do not put spaces before and after the colon. Since many online databases do not provide the issue number, this element is optional. The only case where the issue number is a mandatory element is when the issues of a volume are not consecutively paginated. Where two issues are published at once, separate the numbers with a slash (e.g., **6/7**).

Provide the volume and issue number in Arabic numerals (e.g., **1, 2, 3**), even if the journal itself uses Roman numerals. Indicate the **series number** (if applicable) in parentheses after the title of the journal. The abbreviations used for ordinal numbers should be written in English irrespective of the language of the journal.

> RRA Walker, "The English Property Legislation of 1922-6" (1928) **10:1** J Comp Legis & Intl L **(3rd)** 1.

6.1.6 Title of Journal

Abbreviate the title of the periodical according to the list of abbreviations in **Appendix D**.

If the journal does not appear in **Appendix D**, apply the following abbreviation rules. Write out in full any word that does not appear on the following list. The titles of French-language journals that do not appear in **Appendix D** should be abbreviated following the rules in the French section of this Guide.

Secondary Sources and Other Materials

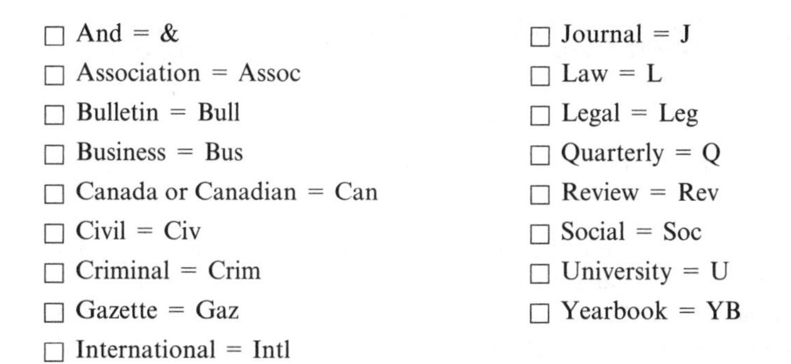

- ☐ And = &
- ☐ Association = Assoc
- ☐ Bulletin = Bull
- ☐ Business = Bus
- ☐ Canada or Canadian = Can
- ☐ Civil = Civ
- ☐ Criminal = Crim
- ☐ Gazette = Gaz
- ☐ International = Intl
- ☐ Journal = J
- ☐ Law = L
- ☐ Legal = Leg
- ☐ Quarterly = Q
- ☐ Review = Rev
- ☐ Social = Soc
- ☐ University = U
- ☐ Yearbook = YB

Omit the words "of" and "the" from the abbreviated title. Place a space between any two words that have lower-case letters, and between an ampersand and the words or letters on each side of it (e.g., **Crim Rev** or **Can J Tax & Bankruptcy**. Do not place a space between adjacent capital letters (e.g., **JL Policy & Freedom**). Apply the jurisdiction abbreviations of the journals column of **Appendix A-1** to place names. If there is no such abbreviation, write the place name out in full. Where a journal has a subtitle, omit the subtitle and abbreviate only the main title. Do not italicize the title or the abbreviation.

> Janet Conway, "Civil Resistance and the 'Diversity of Tactics' in the Anti-Globalization Movement: Problems of Violence, Silence, and Solidarity in Activist Politics" (2003) 41:2/3 **Osgoode Hall LJ** 505.

6.1.7 First Page of Article

Indicate the first page of the article after the title of the journal. **Do not include** "at".

> Darren O'Toole, "La revendication du titre 'indien' par les Métis du Manitoba" (2006) 39:3 Revue canadienne de science politique/Canadian Journal of Political Science **529**.

6.1.7.1 Article Published in Parts

If parts of the article are published in **different volumes**, provide the author and the title as usual. Include both full citations, separated by an ampersand (**&**).

> RA Macdonald, "Enforcing Rights in Corporeal Moveables: Revendication and Its Surrogates" (1986) 31:4 McGill LJ 573 **&** (1986) 32:1 McGill LJ 1.

If the article is published in parts of **one volume**, include both first page numbers, separated by an ampersand (**&**).

> Edward W Keyserlingk, "The Unborn Child's Right to Prenatal Care" (1982) 3:1 Health L Can **10 & 31**.

6.2 BOOKS

6.2.1 General Form

Author, | *title*, | edition | other elements | (place of publication: | publisher, | year of publication) | pinpoint | (electronic service).

As a general rule, provide any additional element between the edition and the place of publication. Their order of presentation is the following: **name of translator** (section 6.2.2.4), **total number of volumes or number of cited volume** (section 6.2.4), **volume title, series title and volume number within series, loose-leaf** (section 6.2.6). Separate these elements with commas, but never place a comma before the parenthesis introducing the publication information. Since some of these elements are exceptionally included at a different place in the citation, always refer to the specific rules for every additional element. If the book is a collection of essays, see section 6.3.

> Philip Girard, *Bora Laskin: Bringing Law to Life* (Toronto: University of Toronto Press for the Osgoode Society for Canadian Legal History, 2005) at 20.
>
> Martha Derthick, *Up in Smoke: From Legislation to Litigation in Tobacco Politics*, 2nd ed (Washington, DC: CQ Press, 2005).
>
> Jean-Louis Baudouin & Yvon Renaud, *Code civil du Québec annoté*, 20th ed (Montreal: Wilson & Lafleur, 2017) at note 7/3.

Secondary Sources and Other Materials

6.2.2 Author

6.2.2.1 Single Author

Indicate the author's name **as it is presented on the title page of the book** (not the cover page). Include all names and initials used, but note that there is no space between two initials. Do not substitute names when initials are used, and do not substitute initials when names are used. Include **titles** such as **The Honourable**, **Madam Justice**, **Rabbi**, **Professor**, or **Lord** if they appear on the title page. Include **name suffixes** such as **Jr** or **IV**. Do not include authors' degrees or other credentials.

> **Ellen Anderson**, *Judging Bertha Wilson: Law as Large as Life* (Toronto: University of Toronto Press for The Osgoode Society for Canadian Legal History, 2001).
>
> **Rt Hon Lord Denning**, *What Next in the Law* (London, UK: Butterworths, 1982).
>
> **H Patrick Glenn**, *Legal Traditions of the World* (Oxford: Oxford University Press, 2000).
>
> **David Fraser**, *Cricket and the Law: the Man in White is Always Right* (London, UK: Routledge, 2005).

6.2.2.2 Joint Authors

Include **up to three authors**, separating the first two authors' names with a comma, and the last two with an ampersand (&).

Monique Mattei Ferraro & Eoghan Casey, *Investigating Child Exploitation and Pornography: The Internet, the Law and Forensic Science* (Boston: Elsevier/Academic Press, 2005).

If there are **more than three authors**, include only the first author's name followed by **et al**.

Joel Bakan et al, *Canadian Constitutional Law*, 3rd ed (Toronto: Emond Montgomery, 2003).

For **collaborations** other than full joint authorship, follow the usage on the title page of the book.

Pierre-Gabriel Jobin with the collaboration of Nathalie Vézina, *Baudouin et Jobin : Les obligations*, 6th ed (Cowansville, QC: Yvon Blais, 2005).

6.2.2.3 Editor or Reviser of the Text of Another

Editor, | ed, | *title*, | edition | (publication information).

If the author's name is part of the title, treat the editor as the author, followed by **ed**.

HG Beale, ed, *Chitty on Contracts*, 29th ed (London, UK: Sweet & Maxwell, 2004).

Author, | *title*, | edition | ed by | editor | (publication information).

If the author's name is not part of the title, indicate the editor after the edition.

Precede the name(s) of editor(s) with **ed by**. If there is a numbered edition, mention it (e.g., **5th ed by**).

Provide the names of both the author(s) and the editor(s) as they appear in the publication.

SA De Smith, *Judicial Review of Administrative Action*, 5th ed by Lord Woolf & Jeffrey Jowell (London, UK: Sweet & Maxwell, 1995).

6.2.2.4 Translator

Translate languages likely to be unfamiliar to readers. The original language of a quotation may be provided in the footnote.

6.2.2.4.1 Published Translation

For published translations, include the translator's name, preceded by **translated by**, before the publication information. If it is necessary to modify the translation, indicate this with **[modified by author]** after the publication information, but before the final period. If providing both the editor or reviser's information (section 6.2.2.3) and the translator's information (section 6.2.2.3), always provide the editor's information first.

Averroës, *The Book of the Decisive Treatise Determining the Connection Between the Law and Wisdom*, **translated by** Charles E Butterworth (Provo: Brigham Young University Press, 2001).

Secondary Sources and Other Materials

6.2.2.4.2 Providing a Translation

When writing and providing a translation for ease of understanding, cite to the work and insert **[translated by author] in the footnote** (and not after the translated text, as required in the French rule). The expression refers to you, the author, and not to the author of the work being cited.

> María José Falcón y Tella, *La desobediencia civil* (Madrid: Marcial Pons, 2000) at 28 **[translated by author]**.

6.2.3 Title

Indicate the title of the book in full, in italics. Use the spelling and punctuation of the published title.

> Janet Dine, ***Companies, International Trade and Human Rights*** (New York: Cambridge University Press, 2005).

Precede subtitles by a colon in italic font. If referring to a book in French, include a space before the colon.

> Petri Mäntysaari, ***Comparative Corporate Governance: Shareholders as a Rule-maker*** (New York: Springer, 2005).
>
> Frédéric Garron, ***La caducité du contrat : étude de droit privé*** (Aix-en-Provence: Presse universitaires d'Aix-Marseille, 2000).

Place a comma before dates included at the end of the title.

> WR Cornish & G de M Clark, ***Law and Society in England, 1750-1950*** (London, UK: Sweet & Maxwell, 1989).

If the title of a book is in a language other than English, French, or any language that will be familiar to readers, provide the title in the original language, followed by a translation of the title into English. Place the translation in non-italic font, in brackets with no punctuation between the original title and translation.

> Cesare Beccaria, ***Dei delliti e delle pene*** **[On Crimes and Punishment]**, 5th ed (London, UK: Transaction Publishers, 2009).

Transliterate titles in languages that are not written in Latin characters, such as Chinese and Hebrew (e.g., **Menachem Elon**, ***Ha-Mishpat Ha-Ivri*** **[Jewish Law]**).

6.2.3.1 Published Proceedings of Conferences or Symposia

Treat information about the conference or symposium as part of the title. Place this information in italics after a comma.

> Paul Brand, Kevin Costello & WN Osborough, eds, *Adventures of the Law: Proceedings of the Sixteenth British Legal History Conference, Dublin, 2003* (Dublin: Four Courts Press in association with The Irish Legal History Society, 2005).

6.2.4 Volume Number

6.2.4.1 Books in English

Provide the volume number in Arabic numerals (e.g., **1, 2, 3**), even if the book itself uses Roman numerals. Do not repeat the volume number in subsequent references unless there is a citation to a different volume elsewhere in the citing document.

If the volumes are published under separate titles, place the volume before the publication information.

> David Gillies, *Telecommunications Law*, **vol 1** (London, UK: Butterworths, 2003).

If the volumes are subdivisions of a single title, insert the volume after the publication information.

> Karl Marx, Capital: *A Critical Analysis of Capitalist Production*, ed by Friedrich Engels, translated by Samuel Moore & Edward B Aveling (London, UK: Swan Sonnenschein, 1908) **vol 1** at 15.

6.2.4.2 Books in French

Author, | *title*, | tome, | volume, | edition | editor | (publication information).

> Jean Carbonnier, *Droit civil : les obligations*, t 4, 22nd ed (Paris: Presses universitaires de France, 2000).

French legal writing may be divided into **tomes** (**t**), with each tome further subdivided into **volumes** (**v**). Tome and volume information appears after the title. Use only Arabic numerals (e.g., **1, 2, 3**) for tome and volume numbers. If applicable, place the title of the volume after a colon following the volume number.

> Henri Mazeaud et al, *Leçons de droit civil*, t 3, vol 1, 7th ed by Yves Picod (Paris: Montchrestien, 1999).

Do not repeat the tome or volume number in subsequent references unless there is a citation to a different tome or volume elsewhere in the citing document.

6.2.5 Edition

If the work has appeared in several editions, place the number of the edition (e.g., **8th ed**) after the title. Do not superscript the **st**, **nd**, **rd** or **th** following the number. Abbreviate **edition** to **ed**. If the work has been revised but no edition number is given, insert **revised ed** after the title.

> Richard Clayton & Hugh Tomlinson, eds, *Civil Actions Against the Police*, **3rd ed** (London, UK: Sweet & Maxwell, 2004).
>
> Carlos L Israels & Egon Guttman, *Modern Securities Transfer*, **revised ed** (Boston: Warren, Gorham & Lamont, 1971).

6.2.6 Books in Loose-leaf Form

Author, | *title* | (publication information) | (loose-leaf revision | supplement number or date), | pinpoint.

This section applies to **books that are continually updated**. For legislation in loose-leaf format, see section 2.1.6. After the publication information, place in parentheses the phrase **loose-leaf** followed by the revision or supplement number.

Optionally include the year of the revision if it is not already indicated as part of the revision or supplement number.

> JD Green, *The Law of Tort* (Toronto: Thomson Reuters, 2011) (loose-leaf **updated 2013**, release 20), ch 5 at 71.

Use the publication date that appears on the copyright page, even if it differs from a date that appears elsewhere in the loose-leaf manual. Use the chapter and the page number to pinpoint if available.

> Georges Audet et al, *Le congédiement en droit québécois en matière de contrat individuel de travail* (Cowansville, QC: Yvon Blais, 1991) (loose-leaf revision 18:1), ch 5 at 71.
>
> Madeleine Lemieux, *Tribunaux administratifs du Québec : Règles et législation annotées* (Cowansville, QC: Yvon Blais, 2002) (loose-leaf revision 15), ch R9 at 85
>
> Robert W Hillman, *Hillman on Lawyer Mobility: The Law and Ethics of Partner Withdrawals and Law Firm Breakups*, 2nd ed (New York: Wolters Kluwer, 1998) (loose-leaf 2009 supplement), ch 2 at 85.

6.2.7 Place of Publication

Include place of publication where it is available. Place of publication may signal to the reader the jurisdiction relevant to the cited material. Indicate the place of publication as it appears on the title page or on the verso of the title page. Use an **English form** of a name if it exists (e.g., **Munich** and not München; **Prague** and not Praha). If **more than one place of publication** is listed, include the place that appears on the title page (not those indicated on the verso of the title page) or, if many places are listed on the recto of the title page, include only the first place.

If additional information is required to identify the place of publication (e.g., the province, state, or country) include that information, in abbreviated form, after the place of publication. If a location could be confused with another, provide additional information (e.g., **London, Ont** and **London, UK**). See the commonly used Canadian province abbreviations of **Appendix A-1** and the American state abbreviations of **Appendix A-2**.

> Bruce MacDougall, *Queer Judgments: Homosexuality, Expression, and the Courts in Canada* (**Toronto**: University of Toronto Press, 2000).
>
> Lee Edwards, ed, *Bringing Justice to the People: the Story of the Freedom-Based Public Interest Law Movement* (**Washington, DC**: Heritage Books, 2004).

6.2.8 Publisher

Write the publisher's name **as it appears on the title page**. Do not abbreviate it (e.g., **University Press** and not **UP**). Omit the definite article (**the**) if it is the first word of the publisher's name and omit terms that identify corporate status (e.g., **Ltd**, **Inc**).

> Martha M Ertman & Joan C Williams, *Rethinking Commodification: Cases and Readings in Law and Culture* (New York: **New York University Press**, 2005).

Omit the words "Publishing" or "Publishers" and "éditions" unless it is part of an indivisible whole (e.g., **Éditions de l'Homme**). Follow the same rule for other languages (e.g., **Verlag**). Write **Press** in English and **Presses** in French if included in the publisher's name on the title page.

> Gaëlle Breton-LeGoff, *L'influence des organisations non gouvernementales (ONG) sur la négociation de quelques instruments internationaux* (Cowansville, QC: **Yvon Blais**, 2001).

For references to **copublishers**, provide the places of publication first, followed by the names of the publishers and the year. Separate the places of publication from each other by an ampersand (&). Similarly, separate the names of the publishers from each other by an ampersand. Separate the places and names by a colon.

> (Latzville, BC & Montreal: Oolichan Books & Institute for Research on Public Policy, 1992).

If a publisher is **working for an organization** write **for** immediately before the organization's name (e.g., **Janet E Gans Epner for The Commission on Women in the Profession**).

If **no publisher** is listed, write **publisher unknown**.

6.2.9 Year of Publication

Indicate the year of the **current edition**, not of the first edition. Generally, use the most recent copyright date, unless a year of publication is given explicitly. Do not cite the year of printing.

> Michael Hames-García, *Fugitive Thought: Prison Movements, Race and the Meaning of Justice* (Minneapolis: University of Minnesota Press, **2004**).

6.3 ESSAYS OR ENTRIES FROM COLLECTIONS OF ESSAYS, DICTIONARIES AND ENCYCLOPEDIAS

6.3.1 General Form

For the purposes of the present Guide, **collections of essays, dictionaries** and **encyclopedias** will be subject to the same rules.

Author of essay or entry, | "title of essay or entry" | in | editor, | ed, | *title of book*, | edition | (place of publication: | publisher, | year of publication) | first page | pinpoint.

Provide as many elements as possible among those suggested in the general form. Note however that several elements may not be found.

Place the name of the author and the title of the essay or entry. Provide the elements relating to the book using the same rules and in the same order as prescribed in section 6.2. Do not confuse the name of the editor with the name of the author of the essay or entry. Follow the name(s) of the editor(s) by **ed** or **eds**, placed between commas.

If referring to the foreword, preface, introduction, or conclusion of a book, indicate it as if it were an entry in a collection of essays. Use **Foreword**, **Preface**, etc. or the title of that section in lieu of the title of the essay.

Where there are other elements to be added (see section 6.2.1), insert them between the title of the collection and the publication information.

6.3.2 Collections of Essays

A collection of essays is a book containing various essays or chapters written by different authors.

> Gabriel J Chin, "Race, the War on Drugs and Collateral Consequences of Criminal Conviction" in Christopher Mele & Teresa A Miller, eds, *Civil Penalties, Social Consequences* (New York: Routledge, 2005) 43 at 45.

6.3.3 Encyclopedias

An encyclopedia is a work providing information on a branch of knowledge (to distinguish from the dictionary at section 6.3.4). Cite the contributing author's name where available. Note that many encyclopedias do not explicitly credit contributors.

> Rev Edward Mewburn Walker, "Constitution of Athens" in Hugh Chisholm, ed, *Encyclopaedia Britannica*, 11th ed (New York: Encyclopaedia Britannica, 1911).

Include additional elements where relevant (e.g., the volume number). See section 6.2.1.

6.3.4 Dictionaries

A dictionary is a work listing the words of a language or specific field. It provides information as to the meaning and grammatical use of the entries. Refer only to the name of the author or editor of the work since the author of the entry is generally unknown. Indicate the keyword in quotation marks as a pinpoint, preceded by the Latin phrase **sub verbo** for "under the word".

> F Allard et al, eds, *Private Law Dictionary of Obligations and Bilingual Lexicons*, (Cowansville, QC: Yvon Blais, 2003) **sub verbo** "code".
>
> Desmond Brice-Bennett, *Legal Glossary: English/Inuktitut/French* (Iqaluit: Nunavut Arctic College, 1997) **sub verbo** "piqujaq".

6.4 ENCYCLOPEDIC DIGESTS

6.4.1 Canadian Encyclopedic Digest

The *Canadian Encyclopedic Digest* (CED) is published in loose-leaf format and provides a broad narrative of the law. Each volume is organized by subject matter (e.g., criminal law, family law).

6.4.1.1 CED Print Edition

CED | (series | edition), | volume, | title | section.

Write **CED**, not the name of the digest in full. Indicate the series: **Ontario CED (Ont)** or **Western CED (West)**.

> CED (Ont 4th), vol 1, title 2 at § 10.

6.4.1.2 CED Online Edition

CED | edition | (online), | *subject matter* | (series), | "detailed subject heading & sub-headings" | (CED subheading code) | section.

CED editions are cited by number only (**4th,** not **4th ed**). Separate the detailed subject headings and subheadings by colons. Indicate the numerical subheading code as it appears in the CED online.

Prefer citing to the online version. If you wish to cite to a print version, cite according to the rule in section 6.4.1.1 above, including the series. Westlaw provides a link to print citation information for all subjects through the online version of the CED.

> CED 4th (online), *Actions* (Ont), "Forms and Classes of Action: Penal Actions: General" (II.5.(a)) at § 3.
>
> CED 4th (online), *Securities and Stock Exchanges*, "Securitues Offences Under the Criminal Code: Fraudulent Manipulation of Stock Exchange Transactions" (II.1) at § 191-195.

6.4.2 Halsbury's Laws of Canada

Halsbury's Laws of Canada provides summary statements of a broad range of legal subjects. Each volume is organized by subject matter (e.g., criminal procedure, insurance). Updates are made through cumulative supplements, issued annually. If the cited section has been updated in a cumulative supplement, cite the supplement and its release number in parentheses following the section, using an abbreviated form (**Cum Supp Release** x).

6.4.2.1 Halsbury's Laws of Canada Print Edition

Halsbury's Laws of Canada, | volume, | *subject matter* | section | (update).

Halsbury's Laws of Canada, vol 2, *Business Corporations* at HBC-298 "Focus on Interests" (Cum Supp Release 4).

6.4.2.2 *Halsbury's Laws of Canada Online Edition*

Halsbury's Laws of Canada (online), | *subject matter*, | "detailed subject heading & subheadings" | (subheading code) | section | update.

Halsbury's Laws of Canada (online), *Business Corporations*, "Shareholder Remedies: The Oppression Remedy: Meaning of Oppression" (XIII.2.(2)) at HBC-298 "Focus on Interests" (Cum Supp Release 4).

6.4.3 JurisClasseur Québec

JurisClasseur Québec is published in loose-leaf format and is also available online on Quicklaw. Note however that the bibliographical information provided is different depending on the version used. Pinpoint should be made to numbers (**no**, **nos**) that are indicated at the beginning of every titled paragraph. Do not refer to paragraphs (**para**, **paras**) since many paragraphs are not numbered.

Author, | "fascicule number: | fascicule heading" | pinpoint, | in | editor, | ed, | JCQ | *title of the collection.*

6.4.3.1 *JurisClasseur Québec Print Edition*

Write the name of the author of the fascicule. In absence of numbers, pinpoint should be made to page numbers, which comprise the fascicule number and the page number within that fascicle separated with a slash (**10/30**, **5/26**).

Louise Tremblay, "Fascicule 4: Testament - règles de forme" at no 62, in Pierre-Claude Lafond, ed, JCQ *Successions et libéralités.*

6.4.3.2 *JurisClasseur Québec on Quicklaw*

Omit the name of the author since it is not provided on the online version. Place **(QL)** at the end of the citation.

"Fascicule 4: Testament - règles de forme" at no 62, in Pierre-Claude Lafond, ed, JCQ *Successions et libéralités* (QL).

6.5 CODES OF PROFESSIONAL CONDUCT

Issuing body, | *title of the code,* | publication information, | pinpoint.

If the issuing body and the editor is the same entity, use the official abbreviation in the publication information.

The Canadian Bar Association, *CBA Code of Professional Conduct,* Ottawa: CBA, 2006, ch III, commentary 1.

The Law Society of Manitoba, *Code of Professional Coduct,* Winnipeg: Law Society of Manitoba, 2007, ch 6.1(1)(f).

Some codes of professional conduct are enacted by legislation. Cite them like regular laws (see section 2.1).

6.6 BOOK REVIEWS

Author of book review, | "title of book review", | Book Review of | *title of book being reviewed* | by | author or editor of book reviewed, | citation information.

If the review has a title, include it after the author of the review, followed by a comma. Insert **Book Review of** before the title of the book reviewed. Change the expression to Book Note of if that terminology is used in the publication.

After the title of the book being reviewed, indicate the name of the author of the book introduced with **by**. If the title of the review includes **both the title of the book reviewed and its author**, do not repeat this information. Instead, just write **Book Review**, leaving out "of". If the title of the review includes ***either*** **the author or the title**, but not both, then all the information should be indicated after **Book Review of**, even if some of it will be repeated. If the book being reviewed has an editor instead of an author, write **ed** after the name of the editor of the book reviewed and a comma (e.g., **Ronald E Dimock, ed**).

Heather Jensen, Book Review of *Girl Trouble: Female Delinquency in English Canada* by Joan Sangster, (2004) 67:2 Sask L Rev 658.

Christopher Heer, Michael Hong & Jason J Kee, Book Review of *Intellectual Property Disputes: Resolution and Remedies* by Ronald E Dimock, ed, (2004) 62:1 UT Fac L Rev 93.

Larry Lee, "Reading the Seattle Manifesto: In Search of a Theory", Book Review of *Whose Trade Organization? Corporate Globalization and the Erosion of Democracy: An Assessment of the World Trade Organization* by Lori Wallach & Michelle Sforza, (2003) 78:6 NYUL Rev 2305.

6.7 CASE COMMENTS AND COMMENTS ON LEGISLATION

Author, | "title", | type of comment | on | style of cause **or** title of law or bill, | (citation).

Indicate the title of the comment (if available) in quotation marks. Also include the style of cause preceded by **on**, unless it is in the title.

For **case comments**, indicate **Case Comment**.

Jessie L Givener, "*Lavoie v Canada*: Reconciling Equality Rights and Citizenship-based Law", Case Comment, (2003-2004) 35:2 Ottawa L Rev 277.

For **legislative comments**, indicate **Legislative Comment**.

Secondary Sources and Other Materials

John Boston, "The *Prison Litigation Reform Act*: The New Face of Court Stripping", Legislative Comment on Pub L No 104-134, 110 Stat 1321-66 (1996), (2001) 67:2 Brook L Rev 429.

6.8 COMMENTS, REMARKS, AND NOTES

Author, | "title", | type of document, | citation.

Include the type of document (**Note**, **Comment** or **Remark**) before the citation information. Do not enclose it in quotation marks. If the document has a title, place the title in quotation marks.

Thomas M Franck, "Criminals, Combatants, or What — An Examination of the Role of Law in Responding to the Threat of Terrorism", **Editorial Comment**, (2004) 98:4 AJIL 686.

Eric J Feigin, "Architecture of Consent: Internet Protocols and Their Legal Implications", **Note,** (2004) 56:4 Stan L Rev 901.

6.9 UNPUBLISHED MANUSCRIPTS

6.9.1 General Form

Author, | *title* **or** "title" | (date of creation) | [unpublished, | archived at | location].

Include the title according to the genre. If it is an article, place the title in quotation marks. If it is a book, place the title in italics. Include the date of creation in parentheses after the title. Indicate that the manuscript is unpublished by enclosing **unpublished, archived at** and the location of the manuscript in brackets.

Irwin Cotler, *Canadian Charter of Rights and Freedoms* (1998) [unpublished, archived at McGill University Faculty of Law Library].

6.9.2 Forthcoming Manuscripts

Author, | *title*, **or** "title", | publication information | [forthcoming in | projected date of publication].

Indicate the title according to the type of manuscript. If the manuscript is an article, place the title in quotation marks. If the manuscript is a book, place the title in italics. Include the publication information according to the classification of the document, but do not indicate the year of publication. If the publication is a journal and the forthcoming issue number is known, include the issue number. Indicate that the manuscript has not yet been published by enclosing **forthcoming in** and with the projected date of publication in brackets, if available.

6.9.3 Theses and Dissertations

Author,	*title*	(degree, | institution, | year)	[unpublished].

After the author's name and the title of the thesis or dissertation, indicate the degree for which it was written, the institution, and the year in parentheses. If the degree or institution is unknown, include the **field of study** (e.g., law, political science, economics). At the end of the citation include **unpublished** in brackets. Cite theses issued by microform services (e.g., **University Microfilms International**) in the same manner as published books, with the service in lieu of publisher.

> Julie Desrosiers, *L'isolement, le retrait et l'arrêt d'agir dans les centres de réadaptation pour jeunes* (DCL Thesis, McGill University Institute of Comparative Law, 2005) [unpublished].
>
> Val Napoleon, *Ayook: Gitksan Legal Order, Law and Legal Theory* (PhD Dissertation, University of Victoria, 2009) [unpublished].

6.10 ADDRESSES AND PAPERS DELIVERED AT CONFERENCES

Speaker,	"title" or Address	(lecture series, paper, or other information | delivered at the | conference or venue, | date),	publication information **or** [unpublished].

If the address has a title, provide the title. If it has **no title**, indicate **Address**. Include the lecture series in which the address was delivered, if available. Indicate the **location** or institution where the address was delivered or the paper presented. Provide the publication information, preceded by a comma, if the address has been published. If the address is **unpublished**, insert **[unpublished]** at the end of the citation. Indicate, if available, where a transcript of the unpublished address is available (see section 6.19.1). If the unpublished address is available online, indicate its location in lieu of publication information (see section 6.19). If the address is **published as a collection**, cite it in the same manner as a collection of essays (see section 6.3).

> Chris Tollefson, "The Implications of *Okanagan Indian Band* for Public Interest Litigants: A Strategic Discussion Paper" (Paper delivered at the AGM of the Court Challenges Program of Canada, Winnipeg, 19 November 2005) [unpublished].
>
> John Borrows, "Creating an Indigenous Legal Community" (John C Tait Memorial Lecture in Law and Public Policy delivered at the Faculty of Law, McGill University, 14 October 2004), (2005) 50 McGill LJ 153.

6.11 COURSE MATERIALS

Professor, | *title* | type of document | (faculty, | date **or** year) | pinpoint.

Indicate the type of document if it is not already included in the title. Insert a comma between the title and the type of document. **Coursepacks** are booklets of material put together by professors for a particular class. Although it is always preferable to cite to the original material, if the citation or pinpoint is unavailable, one may cite to the coursepack. **Lecture notes** are notes written by the professor for use in a particular class.

> Shauna Van Praagh, *Coursepack: Extra-contractual Obligations/Torts* (Faculty of Law, McGill University, 2011) at 20.
>
> Jean-Sébastien Brière, *Droit des brevets,* Coursepack (Faculté de droit, Université de Sherbrooke, Fall 2008) at 331.

6.12 MAGAZINES

Author, | "title of article", | *title of magazine* | volume number: | issue number | (date) | first page of article, | pinpoint | electronic source.

Include the name of the author of the article, if available, followed by the title of the article in quotation marks. Provide the name of the magazine in italics. Enclose any other optional identifying information, such as the place of publication, in brackets and italics immediately following the name of the magazine. Include the **volume number** and **issue number**, separated by a colon. Insert the **full date** in parentheses. If the date is a timespan rather than a precise date, indicate the **first day of coverage**.

> "The Case Against Clones", *The Economist* (2 February 2013), online: <www.economist.com> [perma.cc/S339-KH9D].
>
> Benjamin Phelan, "Buried Truths", *Harper's Magazine* 309:1855 (December 2004) 70.

6.13 NEWSPAPERS, NEWSWIRES, AND OTHER NEWS SOURCES

Author | "title of article", | *newspaper* | (date) | page | electronic source.

Provide the name of the author, if available, followed by the title of the article in quotation marks. Provide the name of the newspaper, newswire, or other source in italics. If geographic information is required to identify the source, indicate it within brackets in the title.

Newspapers:

If pages are numbered by section, provide the section identifier. If the article is contained on a single page, do not repeat that page for a pinpoint.

Newswires:

A newswire is a service transmitting the latest news via satellite and various other electronic media. Replace the newspaper name in italics with the newswire name in italics. For further information on citing to online sources, see section 6.19.

Naomi Wolf, "Take the Shame Out of Rape", *The Guardian* (25 November 2005), online: <www.guardian.co.uk> [perma.cc/5BE2-55CQ].

"Ottawa Eyes Six Candidates in Search of New Supreme Court Judge", *Canadian Press* (17 October 2005) (QL).

"Ruling on Baby with Three Mothers", *BBC News* (10 November 2005), online: <news.bbc. co.uk> [perma.cc/EZ75-LSGB].

Bill Curry, "PM, Premiers Work Out Deal on Aboriginal Health Care", *The Globe and Mail* (26 November 2005) A4.

6.13.1 Editorials and Letters to the Editor

Author, | "title of the editorial", | style of document, | *newspaper* | (date) | page | electronic source.

Indicate **Letter to the Editor** after the author of a letter to the editor and **Editorial** after the title of an editorial. Italicize the name of the newspaper, magazine, or other source. Enclose any other optional identifying information, such as the place of publication, in brackets and italics.

Harold von Cramon, Letter to the Editor, *The [Montreal] Gazette* (26 September 2005) A26.

Ken Lum, Letter to the Editor, *The Vancouver Sun* (6 December 2004) A10.

6.14 NEWS RELEASES

Issuing body, | type of document, | document number, | "title" | (date) | electronic source.

Indicate the type of document as it appears at the top of the page. If the document is **numbered**, provide the number immediately after the type of document. Include the **date** at the end of the citation, before the electronic source.

Indian and Northern Affairs, News Release, 2-02688, "Inuit Firms Secure Three Contaminated Sites Contracts" (6 July 2005).

United Nations, Press Release, SG/SM/12548-OBV/820-WOM/1764 "Secretary-General, Marking International Day of Rural Women, Calls for Scaling Up Investments in Resources, Infrastructure, Services to Improve Rural Women's Lives" (15 October 2009), online: *UN Meetings Coverage & Press Releases* <www.un.org/en/unpress>. [perma.cc/G9BD-U3FG]

6.15 LETTERS, MEMORANDA, AND INTERVIEWS

Type of document | persons involved | (date) | further information.

Indicate a **letter** by writing **Letter from**, an interview by writing **Interview of**, or a memorandum by writing **Memorandum from**, followed by the parties' names at the beginning of the citation. Include the parties' names, followed by the date the letter was written.

If the position of a person involved is not obvious or is not mentioned in the text, include as much detail on the position as necessary, preceded by a comma. If the author is not the interviewer, include the name of the interviewer. If the author (you) is the interviewer, it is not necessary to do so. If the letter, memorandum, or interview is published, appears online, or is held in an archive, include the appropriate citation for such sources.

> Letter from Sir Robert Wilmot to Lord George Sackville (16 November 1753) in James Walton, ed, "*The King's Business*"*: Letters on the Administration of Ireland 1740-1761, from the Papers of Sir Robert Wilmot* (New York: AMS Press, 1996).
>
> Interview of Edward Beauvais by Douglas Sanderson (29 May 1948) on *This Week*, CBC Radio, Toronto, CBC Radio Archives.

6.16 ARCHIVAL MATERIALS

Title of document | (other information), | location of archive, | name of archive | (classification number).

If a document is located in an archive, provide as much information on the document as possible using the traditional citation rules, followed by the archival information.

> *Daniel Tracey v Jean Baptiste Bourtron dit Larochelle* (23 December 1830), Montreal, Archives Nationales du Québec (files of the Court of Quarter Sessions).
>
> Chief Andrew Paull to TA Crerar (22 June 1944), Ottawa, National Archives of Canada (RG 10, vol 6826, file 496-3-2, pt 1).

6.17 INTELLECTUAL PROPERTY

6.17.1 Patents

"Title of Invention", | country | Patent No | PCT patent No | (filing date), | pinpoint.

Indicate the **title of the invention** in quotation marks followed by the abbreviation of the **country where the patent was granted** and the **patent number**. If a patent was granted through the **Patent Cooperation Treaty** (PCT), use the form **PCT Patent No** for citation. If necessary, include both the country and the PCT patent numbers, separated by a comma. Indicate the **filing date**. Pinpoint to the abstract (**abstract**), a claim number (**clm**) or a figure (**fig**). For **patent applications**, write **application filed on** before the **filing date** (e.g. **application filed on 30 August 2008**).

"Violin Shoulder Cradle", Can Patent No 2414383, PCT Patent No PCT/US2001/021243 (29 June 2001), clm 10.

"Parallel network processor array", US Patent No 6854117 (31 October 2000), fig 9.

6.17.2 Trade-marks

"Trade-mark", | registrant, | country | registration number | (registration date) | status.

Indicate the **trade-mark** in quotation marks. Indicate the abbreviation of the **country where the trade-mark was registered**. Write the **registration number**. The format of the number varies for every jurisdiction. Indicate the registration date in parentheses. Write the **status** of the trade-mark in the register. Add **dead** or **live** for United States trade-marks, and **registered** or **expunged** for Canada.

"Kellogg's Cinnamon Mini Buns à la Cannelle", Kellogg Company, Can No TMA424258 (4 March 1994) expunged.

"Lego", Lego Juris A/S, USA 78882203 (3 June 2008) live.

6.17.3 Copyright

"Title of the protected work" | (type of work) | owner of the copyright, | country | registration number | (registration date) | status.

Indicate the **title of the protected work** in quotation marks. In Canada, the type of work includes original **literary, artistic, dramatic** and **musical** works, **performer's performances, sound recordings** and **communication signals**, as well as **mechanical contrivance**. Indicate the **owner of the copyright** and the **abbreviation of the country** where the copyright was issued. Write the **registration number**. The format of the number varies for each jurisdiction. Indicate the **registration date** in parentheses. If provided, indicate the status (**registered** or **expunged**) of the copyright in the register.

"Twilight" (music) Mary Chapin Carpenter, USA Pau002997899 (20 December 2005).

"Feel Happy" (sound recording) Warner Music Canada, Can 1035760 (24 January 2006) registered.

"Agrippa : Le livre noir" (literary) Éditions Michel Quintin, Can 1056747 (11 March 2003) registered.

6.18 WORKING PAPERS

Author, | "title" | (year) | institution | Working Paper | series number.

If the working paper is available online, indicate the location after the series number (see section 1.6).

Suzanne Scotchmer, "Patents in the University: Priming the Pump and Crowding Out" (2013) National Bureau of Economic Research Working Paper No 19252.

Bram Akkermans & Eveline Ramaekers, "Lex rei sitae in Perspective: National Developments of a Common Rule?" (2012) Maastricht European Law Institute Working Paper No 2012/14.

6.19 ELECTRONIC SOURCES

This section provides guidance for sources found solely or primarily online. For general guidance in citing to online sources, see section 1.6. For specific guidance with respect to certain sources available both online and in print, see the relevant section (e.g., jurisprudence (section 3.8), encyclopedic digests (section 6.4), newspapers (section 6.13)).

6.19.1 Websites

Author, | "title of the page/article" | (date of the page/article), | online: | *title of the website* | <URL> | [archived URL].

Richard Gold, "The Midas Conundrum: Why less can be more when it comes to intellectual property protection" (25 April 2017), online: *Centre for International Governance Innovation* <www.cigionline.org/articles/midas-conundrum> [perma.cc/XAP7-VWDR].

"Tribunaux canadiens" (last modified 21 June 2017), online: *Cour fédérale* <cas-cdc-www02.cas-satj.gc.ca> [perma.cc/WB8C-E55X].

It is likely that some information will not be found. In such cases, exercise judgment and include basic, critical information so that readers can track the source.

The author is the person who wrote the cited material. Where no author is clearly indicated, provide the name of the institutional owner of the domain. Omit author information if obvious from the title of the website.

The title of the page/article indicates the location of the section referred to in relation to the rest of the site. In the absence of clear page numbering on the site, the title is the most specific marker with which to refer to a given part of the website.

In the following order, indicate the date of publication of the page/article in parentheses (day, month and year) where available, the date of the last modification of the website preceded by **last modified**, or the date of access preceded by **last visited**.

Indicate the title of the website, the main title page, or the domain in which the reference is found in italics.

Indicate the full URL enclosed in angle brackets (< ... >). Exclude the **http://** and **https://** protocol, but include any protocol of different form. Include **www** only where it is included by the source.

6.19.1.1 PDF Documents

Use the same form as for websites (section 6.19.1), but provide the pinpoint after the date and add **(pdf)** after **online**.

Bernard Dafflon, "L'économie politique et la gestion territoriale des services environnementaux" (2013) at 37, online **(pdf)**: *Université de Fribourg* <www.unifr.ch> [perma.cc/2V4H-CWAU].

6.19.1.2 Podcasts

Use the same form as for websites (section 6.19.1), but provide the pinpoint after the date and add **(podcast)** after **online**. If available, write the name of the speaker instead of the author.

"Clerks! Part I" (26 October 2017) at 00h:03m:19s, online **(podcast)**: *McGill Law Journal* <lawjournal.mcgill.ca/fr/text/96> [perma.cc/C5W6-ANC4].

6.19.1.3 Online Video & Video Aggregators

Online videos are frequently reposted without permission or attribution. Always cite the website of origin, or the original account that uploaded the video if available. Use the same form as for websites (section 6.19.1), but provide the pinpoint after the date and add **(video)** after **online**. Include the author and title of the video. Omit author information if obvious from the title of the website.

UCTelevision, "Russ Feingold - Legally Speaking" (27 June 2013) at 00h:12m:15s, online **(video)**: *YouTube* <www.youtube.com> [perma.cc/AW5F-7QNQ].

"Supreme Court Hearings: Supreme Court Reference Case on the Appointment of Justice Marc Nadon" (15 January 2014) at 02h:29m:30s, online **(video)**: *CPAC* <www.cpac.ca/en/programs/supreme-court-hearings/episodes/29928389> [perma.cc/J2EH-TFXL].

6.19.1.4 Blogs

6.19.1.4.1 Blog Posts

Use the same form as for websites (section 6.19.1), but add **(blog)** after **online**. Include the author and the title of the post.

Michael Geist, "Posner on Copyright: Restrictive Fair Use a Risk to Creativity" (2 October 2012), online **(blog)**: *Michael Geist* <www.michaelgeist.ca/content/view/6645/125> [perma.cc/9RQ9-BSEF].

6.19.1.4.2 Blog Comments

Name or handle | (date and time), | online: | <URL>, | comment on | full blog post reference.

Indicate the blog comment reference, followed by **comment on** and the full blog post reference (see section 6.19.1.4.1). For sites which allow linking directly to an individual comment, provide the URL to that comment rather than the URL to the main blog entry. Indicate the timestamp of publication of the post or comment. To avoid confusion, use the 24-hour clock system.

Gary P Rodriguez (16 February 2011 at 11:14), **comment on** Daniel Poulin & Frédéric Pelletier, "Are We to Live with Useless Periods Forever?" (15 February 2011), online (blog): *Slaw* <www.slaw.ca/2011/02/15/are-we-to-live-with-useless-periods-forever> [perma.cc/6TF9-58LZ].

petes_PoV (6 October 2012 at 12:09), online (blog): *Slashdot* <news.slashdot.org/comments.pl?sid=3167773&cid=41568655> [perma.cc/XR2Z-L2VQ], **comment on** Timothy, "Gas Prices Jump: California Hardest Hit" (6 October 2012).

6.19.1.5 Social Media

Author, | "first sentence of post" | (date posted), | other information, | online: | *social medium* | <URL>.

If the length of the first sentence is excessive, truncate appropriately and add an ellipsis before the closing quotation mark (e.g., "**Again our mighty Senators are blowing our tax money ...**").

6.19.1.5.1 Facebook Posts

As "other information", include **posted on**, followed with the name of the group or individual whose page contains the cited post. If citing a group page or an individual profile page rather than a specific post, replace the first sentence of the post with the name of the group or individual profile, followed by the date of creation of the group or profile, if available.

Barack Obama, "When I left office, I told you all that the single most important thing ..." (5 October 2017), **posted on** *Barack Obama*, online: *Facebook* <www.facebook.com/barackobama> [perma.cc/9LXB-7URP].

6.19.1.5.2 Twitter Posts

Instead of the first sentence, include the full content of tweet in quotation marks. Indicate the timestamp of publication of the post after the date. To avoid confusion, use the 24-hour clock system.

White House Archived, "Detailed, thorough timeline from Day 1: The Ongoing Administration-Wide Response to the BP Oil Spill http://bit.ly/aYOIA3" (5 May 2010 **at 9:00**), online: *Twitter* <twitter.com/whitehouse/status/13433979066> [perma.cc/E2TK-E98U].

6.19.1.5.3 Reddit Posts

As "other information", include **posted on**, followed by the title of the thread in which the cited post is published.

Lawrence Lessig, "I spend as little time with lawmakers as possible" (2 July 2013), **posted on** *I am Lawrence Lessig (academic, activist, now collaborator with DEMAND*

PROGRESS) AMA, online: *Reddit* <www.reddit.com/r/IAmA/comments/1hibzy/i_am_lawrence_lessig_academic_activist_now/caum9w2> [perma.cc/BXB6-7VNT].

6.19.2 Other Digital Media

Traditional citation, | type of digital media: | *title of the media* | (publication information).

Provide the traditional citation for the document being cited, including if available the name of the author, the title and the date. Indicate the type of digital media (e.g., **CD-ROM**, **DVD, BluRay, MiniDisc**). Indicate the title of the media in italics, if different from the title in the traditional citation. In parentheses, provide the publication information for the digital medium.

Peter W Hogg & Mary Ellen Turpel, "Implementing Aboriginal Self-Government: Constitutional and Jurisdictional Issues," CD-ROM: *For Seven Generations: An Information Legacy of the Royal Commission on Aboriginal Peoples* (Ottawa: Libraxus, 1997).

The Paper Chase, 1973, DVD (Beverly Hills, Cal: 20th Century Fox Home Entertainment, 2003).

7 Foreign Sources E-111

Foreign Sources

7 FOREIGN SOURCES

7.1 COMMON LAW JURISDICTIONS

7.1.1 General Form

To cite a source from a common law jurisdiction that is not listed in this chapter, use the following model as a guide.

Style of cause | (year of the decision), | main citation | pinpoint | parallel citation | (court, | jurisdiction) | [*short title*].

Singh v Punjab, [1980] 2 Supreme Court Journal 475 at 524 (India) [*Singh*].
Hong Kong v Chan Hing Hung, [1998] 4 Hong Kong Court 487 at 488C (CFI HK) [*Chan*].
Alla Rahka v Mohamed Ahmed (1956), 29 LRK 6 (Kenya) [*Alla Rahka*].
Campbell v MGN Ltd, [2004] UKHL 22, [2004] 2 AC 457 (UK) [*MGN*].

7.1.2 Style of Cause, Pinpoint, Short Form, and Case History

Use the rules for Canadian jurisprudence for the style of cause (section 3.3), pinpoints (section 3.6), printed reporters (section 3.7), and case history (section 3.11). For guidance on short forms, see section 1.4.1.

7.1.3 Year

Generally, provide the year of the decision or omit it following the rules in section 3.4. When necessary to avoid ambiguity (e.g., when citing an unreported decision) indicate the full date rather than the year alone.

7.1.4 Neutral Citation, Printed Reporter, Online Database, or Unreported Decision

year and/or volume | reporter or tribunal identifier | (series) | first page or decision number | (online database) | pinpoint.

Prefer neutral citation to a printed reporter. Follow the conventions for the neutral citation adopted by the country (e.g., the UK uses square brackets around the year), but otherwise follow the advice given in the section on Canada (year, volume, reporter, series, page). Prefer a printed reporter to an online database. Follow section 3.7 for printed reporters.

For online databases, use the citation provided. Unless the database is likely to be known to the reader, append its name in parentheses.

For unreported judgments for which none of the above exist, follow the convention adopted by the jurisdiction, if one exists, or provide clear identifying information such as the judicial district followed by docket number (as in section 3.12). Indicate the full date in parentheses following the style of cause, rather than simply the year of the decision.

Among printed reporters, the order of preference from highest to lowest is (1) official reporters; (2) semi-official reporters; and (3) reporters with the broadest possible geographic scope.

Neutral citation

[2004] UKHL 22.

Printed reporter

11 F Supp (2d) 858 at 860.

Online database

[1995] FCJ no 206 (QL).

7.1.5 Jurisdiction and Court

Write the name of the country and the court in full, with the following exceptions: (1) abbreviations that are very likely to be familiar to the reader (e.g., US or UK); (2) a distinctive name that is commonly used in place of a country's official name (e.g., Netherlands rather than "Kingdom of the Netherlands"); and (3) clear indication of the name of the court and/or its jurisdiction elsewhere in the citation.

7.1.6 Judge

Use abbreviations for their titles only if they are likely to be familiar to the reader (e.g. CJ can usually be assumed to mean Chief Justice).

7.2 CIVIL LAW JURISDICTIONS

7.2.1 Civil Codes

To cite the civil code of a jurisdiction that is not listed in this section, use the following form as a guide. Do not italicize **Civil Code**.

Pinpoint | Civil Code | (jursidiction).

Art 46 Civil Code (Germany).
Art 123 Civil Code (Louisana).

This section applies to foreign civil codes (apart from French codes). For Canadian codes, see section 2.3. For French codes, see section 7.5.1.2.

7.2.2 Jurisprudence

Court and chamber, | city, | date, | *style of cause* | (year of publication), | reporter or journal | section | page and/or decision number | (annotated by author) | (country).

Include all elements that are applicable. Include an English translation of the name of the court or chamber, in brackets, if it would help the reader.

> Tribunal de Commerce, Ostende, 12 October 1987 (1988), Revue de Droit Commercial Belge 268 (annotated by Verougstraete) (Belgium).
>
> Corte Suprema de Justicia [Supreme Court], 15 November 1954, *Suàrez, Alfredo c Perez Estella*, 190 Revista Gaceta Jurídica 145, No 124-2008 (Chile).
>
> Interm People's Court, Shanghai, 11 May 1988, *China National Technical Importer/ Exporter v Industry Res* (22 August 1988), China Law & Practice 26 (China).
>
> Mahkamat al-Tamiez [Court of Cassation Tamiez], 6 March 1974, year 5, 1 Al-Nashra al-Qadaiah 161, No 1428 (Iraq).

7.3 UNITED KINGDOM

For general rules, see ***Oxford Standard for Citation of Legal Authorities*** (**OSCOLA**).

7.3.1 Legislation

7.3.1.1 Statutes

7.3.1.1.1 United Kingdom

Include **(UK)** after the title of the statute to indicate its origin. Never place a comma before the year where the title includes a year. Where the title does not include a year, indicate the calendar year after the comma following **(UK)**, followed by a comma.

Before 1963:

Title | (UK), | year, | regnal year | monarch, | chapter, | pinpoint.

Cite the regnal year in Arabic numerals (e.g., **1, 2, 3**). Following that number, include the abbreviation for the monarch in Roman numerals (**Geo V**).

> *Statute of Westminster 1931* (UK), **22 & 23 Geo V**, c 4, s 2.

1 January 1963 and after:

Title | (UK), | year, | pinpoint.

> *Northern Ireland Act 1998* (UK), s 5.

Foreign Sources

7.3.1.1.2 Northern Ireland

When citing Acts of the former Parliament of Northern Ireland or the Northern Ireland Assembly, include **(NI)** instead of **(UK)**.

> *National Insurance Act* (NI), 1946, s 7.

7.3.1.1.3 Scotland

For Acts of Scottish Parliament, include **(Scot)** instead of **(UK)** and provide the ASP number preceded by **ASP**.

> *Crofting Reform etc Act 2007* (Scot), ASP 7.

7.3.1.1.4 Wales

For measures of the Welsh Assembly, include **(Wales)** instead of **(UK)** and refer to the National Assembly of Wales Measure (**NAWM** or **MCCC**).

> *Learner Travel (Wales) Measure 2008* (Wales), NAWM 2.

7.3.1.2 Bills

Title | (jurisdiction), | session, | bill number, | pinpoint | (additional information).

For bills that originate in the House of Lords, indicate **[HL]** (not italicized) in the title. See **Appendix A-4** for abbreviations of jurisdictions.

> *Harbours Bill* [HL] (UK), 2005-2006 sess, Bill 40, s 2.
>
> *A Bill to amend the Game Preservation (Northern Ireland) Act 1928* (NI), 2001-2002 sess, Bill 15/00, s 2 (Committee Stage Extension 29 October 2001).

When the year is not obvious from the session, include the year after the session in parentheses.

> *Human Tissue (Scotland) Bill* (Scot), sess **2 (2005)**, Bill 42, s 6 (1st reading 3 June 2005).

7.3.1.3 Statutory Instruments

Title | (jurisdiction), | SR & O or SI | year/number, | pinpoint.

For regulations before 1948, abbreviate **Statutory Rules & Orders** to **SR & O**. For regulations after 1948, abbreviate **Statutory Instruments** to **SI**.

> *Penalties for Disorderly Behaviour (Amendment of Minimum Age) Order 2004* (UK), SI 2004/3166.
>
> *Cheese Regulations 1970* (NI), SR & O 1970/14.

7.3.2 Jurisprudence

7.3.2.1 General Form

Follow the same format as used for Canadian jurisprudence (see section 3).

Neutral citation available:

> *Campbell v MGN Ltd*, [2004] UKHL 22, [2004] 2 AC 457.

Neutral citation not available:

> *R v Woollin* (1998), [1999] 1 AC 82 (HL (Eng)).

See **Appendix B-2** for a list of courts and their abbreviations, and **Appendix C-2** for a list of United Kingdom reporters and their abbreviations.

7.3.2.2 Neutral Citation

Many courts in the United Kingdom have officially adopted a system of neutral citation. The form is the same as that of Canadian neutral citation (section 3.5), with the exception that the year is placed in brackets. Many older cases, especially those of the House of Lords and the Privy Council, have been assigned retroactive neutral citations. Treat these retroactive neutral citations as court-assigned neutral citation. Retroactive neutral citations are available on **BAILII**.

7.3.2.3 Appeal Courts

Supreme Court of The United Kingdom	[year] UKSC number
House of Lords	[year] UKHL number
Privy Council	[year] UKPC number
England and Wales Court of Appeal (Civil Division)	[year] EWCA Civ number
England and Wales Court of Appeal (Criminal Division)	[year] EWCA Crim number

The neutral citations for the Appeal Courts and the Administrative Court of the High Court became **official on 11 January 2001**. The Supreme Court of the United Kingdom assumed the judicial functions of the House of Lords on 1 October 2009. Place the year of the decision in brackets followed by the court identifier and the case number.

> *Campbell v MGN Limited*, [2004] UKHL 22.
> *Fraser v HM Advocate*, [2011] UKSC 24.
> *Copping v Surrey County Council*, [2005] EWCA Civ 1604 at para 15.

7.3.2.4 High Court

[Year] | court | number | (division) | pinpoint.

Neutral citations to the High Court were **officially adopted on 14 January 2002**. For cases heard in the High Court, the division of the Court is placed in parentheses *after* the case number. The High Court has three principal divisions and several specialist courts.

High Court Divisions and Abbreviations:

Queen's Bench Division	**QB**
Administrative Court	Admin
Commercial Court	Comm
Admiralty Court	Admlty
Technology & Construction Court	TCC

Chancery Division	**Ch**
Patents Court	Pat
Companies Court	Comp

Family Division	**Fam**

[2005] EWHC 1974 (Admlty) at para 10.
[2005] EWHC 2995 (Comm).

7.3.2.5 Reporter

Law Reports are **divided into series**. Do not refer to the *Law Reports*, but rather to the series. Since there is no separate reporter for the Court of Appeal, include **(CA)** at the end of each citation to a case heard in that court. For the abbreviations of the *Law Reports*, see **Appendix C-2**.

Beattie v E & F Beattie Ltd, [1938] Ch 708 **(CA)** 720 at 723.

Note the distinction between this later series of *Law Reports* and the 1865-1875 series of reporters with the same name (abbreviated **LR**).

Rylands v Fletcher (1868), **LR** 3 HL 330.

For cases prior to 1865, cite to *English Reports* (**ER**) in preference to a nominate reporter, or provide a parallel citation. The complete *English Reports* are publicly accessible on the CommonLII website.

Lord Byron v Johnston (1816), 2 Mer 28, **35 ER 851** (Ch).

7.3.2.6 Yearbooks

Style of cause | (year), | yearbook | term | regnal year | monarch, | folio number, | plea number.

Abbreviate Michaelmas to **Mich**, Hilary to **Hil**, Easter to **Pach**, and Trinity to **Trin**. Indicate the regnal year in Arabic numerals (e.g., **1, 2, 3**). Cite the monarch using Roman numerals. Abbreviate plea to **pl** and folio to **fol**.

Waldon v Marshall (1370), YB Mich 43 Edw III, fol 33, pl 38.

7.3.2.7 Reprints

Yearbook citation, | reprinted in, | translated by | translator / editor, | citation.

When citing to a reprint, provide as much information about the original yearbook entry as possible. Cite to the location where the reprint is found.

Randolph v Abbot of Hailes (1313-14), YB 6&7 Edw II (Eyre of Kent), reprinted in *Yearbooks of 6 Edward II* (1926), translated by William Craddock, ed, 27 Selden Soc 32 at 33.

7.3.2.8 Scotland and Northern Ireland

Where the jurisdiction is not obvious from the title of the reporter, and there is no neutral citation, abbreviate Scotland to **Scot** and Northern Ireland to **NI.** Enclose the abbreviation in parentheses at the end of the citation. As each volume is divided according to the court reported and each section is paginated separately, include the name of the court. See **Appendix B** for court abbreviations and **Appendix C** for reporter abbreviations.

M'Courtney v HM Advocate, [1977] JC 68 (HCJ **Scot**).
R v Crooks, [1999] **NI** 226 (CA).

7.3.2.8.1 Neutral Citation

The rules for neutral citation are the same for Scotland and Northern Ireland. The rules are similar to those of Canadian neutral citation (section 3.5), with the exception that the year is placed in square brackets.

7.3.2.8.1.1 Scotland

High Court of Justiciary	HCJT
Court of Criminal Appeal	HCJAC
Court of Session, Outer House	CSOH
Court of Session, Inner House	CSIH

Smith v Brown, [2005] HCJT 2 (Scot).
Kinross v Dunsmuir, [2005] HCJAC 3 at para 12 (Scot).
McBride v MacDuff, [2005] CSOH 4 (Scot).

7.3.2.8.1.2 Northern Ireland

Court of Appeal	NICA
Crown Court	NICC
County Court	NICty
Magistrates Court	NIMag
Queen's Bench Division	NIQB
Family Division	NIFam
Chancery Division	NICh

McDonnell v Henry, [2005] NICA 17.
Barkley v Whiteside, [2004] NIQB 12 at para 12.

7.3.2.9 Judge

Lord Justice	LJ
Lord Justices	LJJ
Master of the Rolls	MR
Lord Chancellor	LC
Vice Chancellor	VC
Baron	B
Chief Baron	CB

7.3.2.10 Online Databases

7.3.2.10.1 BAILII

Style of cause, | identifier given by service | (BAILII) | pinpoint | (jurisdiction | court).

Do not confuse BAILII's identifier with a neutral citation. Add **(BAILII)** after the identifier to avoid confusion.

London Borough of Harrow v Johnstone, [1997] UKHL 9 **(BAILII)** at para 6.

7.3.2.10.2 Service with No Identifier (Justis)

Style of cause | (year), | pinpoint | (jurisdiction | court) | (available on | name of the online database).

R v Woollin (1998), at para 23 (HL) (available on Justis).

7.3.3 Government Documents

Indicate **UK** at the beginning of the citation.

7.3.3.1 Debates

UK, | HL/HC | Deb | (date), | volume, | column | pinpoint | (speaker).

After UK, indicate the house. Abbreviate House of Commons to **HC** and House of Lords to **HL**. Indicate the speaker (if provided) in parentheses at the end of the citation.

UK, HL Deb (3 May 1983), vol 442, col 6 (Baroness Masham of Ilton).
UK, HC Deb (27 May 1774), vol 17, col 1357.

7.3.3.2 Command Papers

UK, | issuing body, | *title* | (Command paper number, | year) | pinpoint | (president).

Indicate the title as it appears on the title page of the report. Place the Command paper number after the title of the paper. Include the name of the president (if provided) in parentheses at the end of the citation. The proper abbreviation of Command is essential for identifying the document. It is indicated on the title page of each Command Paper:

1833–1869	c (1st series)
1870–1899	C (2nd series)
1900–1918	Cd
1919–1956	Cmd
1957–1986	Cmnd
1986–	Cm

UK, HC, *Report of the Committee on the Law Relating to Rights of Light* (Cmnd 473, 1957-58) at 955 (CE Harman).
UK, Department for Children, Schools and Families, *2008 Autumn Performance Report* (Cm 7507, 2008) at 54.

7.3.3.3 *Non-parliamentary Papers*

UK, | issuing body, | *title* | (nature of paper) | authors | (publication information).

Cite non-parliamentary papers in the same manner as Canadian non-parliamentary papers, according to the rules at section 4.2.

Do not write the issuing body if it is already in the title.

> UK, Royal Commission on the Press, *Studies on the Press* (Working Paper No 3) by Oliver Boyd-Barrett, Dr Colin Seymour-Ure & Professor Jeremy Turnstall (London: Her Majesty's Stationery Office, 1978).
>
> UK, Law Commission, *Contempt of Court* (Consultation Paper No 209) (London: The Stationery Office, 2012).

7.4 UNITED STATES

See the latest edition of ***The Bluebook: A Uniform System of Citation***.

7.4.1 Legislation

7.4.1.1 *Federal and State Constitutions*

Abbreviate **article** to **art**, **section** to **§**, and **sections** to **§§**. A paragraph within a section is labeled a **clause**, and is abbreviated to **cl** or **cls** in the plural.

> US Const art III, § 2, cl 3.

Abbreviate **amendment** to **amend**. Abbreviate **preamble** to **pmbl**. Indicate article and amendment numbers in capital Roman numerals. Indicate section and clause numbers in Arabic numerals (e.g., **1**, **2**, **3**).

> US Const amend XIV, § 1.

See **Appendix A-2** for a list of state abbreviations.

> NM Const art IV, § 7.

7.4.1.2 *Federal and State Statutes*

Order of preference of sources:

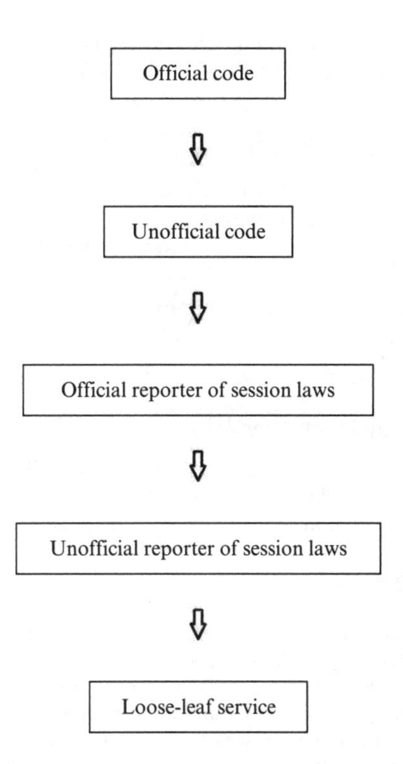

7.4.1.2.1 Codes

A code in the United States is a consolidation and codification by subject matter of the general and permanent federal or state laws. An **official code** is a code of the laws of the United States organized under fifty subject titles, prepared under the supervision of an appropriate government authority (e.g., federal Department of Justice). The official federal code is the ***United States Code*** (USC).

To determine whether a state code is official or unofficial consult the list of state codes available at Findlaw (<statelaws.findlaw.com/state-codes.html>).

An **unofficial code** is a code of the laws of the United States prepared by a private publisher. Unofficial federal codes include the ***United States Code Service*** (USCS) and the ***United States Code Annotated*** (USCA).

Title, | division of code | abbreviated code name | title number | section | (publisher | supplement | year).

Once a statute has been codified, its original title is usually not cited. **Include the title only for a special reason** (e.g., because it is commonly known by that name). Italicize the title.

> *Patient Protection and Affordable Care Act*, 42 USC § 18001 (2010).

If the code is **divided** into separate numbered titles, chapters, or volumes, include the number of that division. When citing federal codes, indicate the division before the code abbreviation.

> Pa Stat Ann **tit 63** § 425.3 (West Supp 1986).

Do not italicize the abbreviated name of the code. For citations to the Internal Revenue Code, it is possible to replace **26 USC** with **IRC**.

> **IRC** § 61 (2000).

When citing to an unofficial code, include the name of the publisher before the year, or before **Supp** where applicable.

When citing a supplement found in a pocket insert, place **Supp** before the year.

> Wis Stat Ann § 939.645 (**West Supp** 1992).

Include the year of publication of the code in parentheses at the end of the citation. When citing a **bound volume**, provide the year that appears on the spine of the volume. When citing a **supplement**, provide the year that appears on the title page of the supplement.

7.4.1.2.2 Session Laws

Session laws are the statutes passed by a session of Congress, bound and indexed chronologically. Session laws track the historical development of a law.

Title **or** date of enactment, | public law number **or** chapter number, | section, | session laws reporter | first page of act | pinpoint to reporter | (year) | (codification information).

Provide the name of the statute in italics. If it has no name, identify it by the date of its enactment in Roman type, not italics (**Act of 25 April 1978**). If no date of enactment is available, identify it by the date on which the act came into effect (**Act effective [date]**). Provide the public law number, introduced by the abbreviation **Pub L No**, or the chapter number of the statute, introduced by **c**. The number before the hyphen in the public law number is the session. The number following the hyphen is the identifier. To cite a **particular section**, indicate the section number directly after the public law number or the chapter number. Include a pinpoint to the reporter.

For federal statutes, the **official reporter** is the *Statutes at Large*, abbreviated to **Stat**. The abbreviation of the reporter is preceded by the volume number, followed by the first page of the act. Indicate a **pinpoint** following the citation to the first page of the act. Include a pinpoint to the particular section after the public law number or the chapter number.

Indicate the **year the statute was enacted** in parentheses at the end of the citation, unless the year is part of the name of the statute. The year in the title might not coincide with the year in which the statute was published, in which case you must provide both. See the *Antiterrorism and Effective Death Penalty Act of 1996* example.

Codification information for the law should be provided if it is available. If a single statute is divided and codified under many subject-headings of the code, indicate this with parenthetical information at the end of the citation (**(codified as amended in scattered sections of 26 USC)**).

> *The Indian Child Welfare Act of 1978*, Pub L No 95-608, 92 Stat 3069 (codified as amended at 25 USC § 1901–1963 (1988)).
>
> *Antiterrorism and Effective Death Penalty Act of 1996*, Pub L No 104–132, § 327, 110 Stat 1214 at 1257 (1997).
>
> Act of 25 April 1978, c 515, § 3, 1978 Ala Acts 569 at 570 (codified as amended at Ala Code § 9-3-12 (1987)).

7.4.1.2.3 Unofficial Reporters of Session Laws

Title, | public law number, | [volume] | unofficial reporter | pinpoint, | session law citation.

The most important unofficial reporter of session laws is the ***United States Code Congressional and Administrative News***, abbreviated to **USCCAN**. When citing to the USCCAN, indicate the volume and page number of the ***Statutes at Large*** (**Stat**) in which the law will subsequently appear.

> *Veteran's Benefits Improvements Act of 1996*, Pub L No 104-275, [1996] **USCCAN** 3762, 110 **Stat** 3322.

7.4.1.3 Uniform Codes, Uniform Acts, and Restatements

Title | section | (year of adoption).

Uniform Codes and **Uniform Acts** are proposed legislation, published by the National Conference of Commissioners of Uniform State Laws, to be adopted in all state legislatures, districts, and protectorates. **Restatements** are reports of the state of US common law on given topics and interpretation of statutes, published by the American Law Institute.

Italicize the title, unless it is a code. Do not place a comma after the title of a code or a restatement. When more than one restatement has been produced, indicate the number in parentheses. At the end of the citation, in parentheses, indicate the year of adoption, promulgation, or latest amendment, which often appears on the title page.

> UCC § 2-012 (1995).
>
> *Uniform Partnership Act* § 23 (1969).
>
> *Restatements of Security* § 51 (1941).
>
> *Restatement (Second) of the Law of Property* § 15 (1977).

7.4.1.4 Bills and Resolutions

7.4.1.4.1 Federal Bills

US, | Bill | house | number, | *title*, | Congress number, | year, | pinpoint | (status, if enacted).

Abbreviate **House of Representatives** as **HR** and **Senate** as **S**.

> US, Bill HR 1, *No Child Left Behind Act of 2001*, 107th Cong, 2001 (enacted).
>
> US, Bill S 7, *Prescription Drug Benefit and Cost Containment Act of 2003*, 108th Cong, 2003, s 107.

7.4.1.4.2 Federal Resolutions

US, | type of resolution | number, | *title*, | Congress number, | year | (status, if enacted).

> US, HR Con Res 6, *Expressing the Sense of the Congress Regarding the Need to Pass Legislation to Increase Penalties on Perpetrators of Hate Crimes*, 107th Cong, 2001.
>
> US, HR Res 387, *Providing for consideration of the bill (HR 3283) to enhance resources to enforce United States trade rights*, 109th Cong, 2005 (enacted).

Abbreviations of the type of resolution:

House Concurrent Resolutions	HR Con Res
House Resolutions	HR Res
House Joint Resolutions	HRJ Res
Senate Concurrent Resolutions	S Con Res
Senate Resolutions	S Res
Senate Joint Resolutions	SJ Res

7.4.1.4.3 State Bills and Resolutions

US, | type of bill or resolution | number, | *title*, | year or legislature number, | number **or** designation of legislative session, | state, | year, | pinpoint | (status, if enacted).

In addition to Regular Sessions, state legislatures may hold **First, Second, and Third Extraordinary Sessions**. Abbreviate these as **1st Extra Sess, 2d Extra Sess**, and **3d Extra Sess**, respectively. **Special Sessions** may be abbreviated **Spec Sess**. Abbreviate the state according to the list in **Appendix A-2**.

> US, AB 31, *An Act to Add Section 51885 to the Education Code, Relating to Educational Technology*, 1997-98, Reg Sess, Cal, 1996, s 1.
>
> US, SR 10, *Calling for the Establishment of a Delaware State Police Community Relations Task Force*, 141st Gen Assem, Reg Sess, Del, 2001 (enacted).

7.4.1.5 Regulations

7.4.1.5.1 The Code of Federal Regulations

The ***Code of Federal Regulations*** is the codification of the regulations of the United States, organized under the same 50 subject titles as the United States Code.

Title, | volume | reporter | section | (year).

Indicate the title of the rule or regulation when it is commonly known under that name. When possible, cite federal rules and regulations to the *Code of Federal Regulations*. The *Code of Federal Regulations* (**CFR**) is the official compilation of the federal government.

> *EPA Effluent Limitations Guidelines*, 40 CFR § 405.53 (1980).
> 47 CFR § 73.609 (1994).

7.4.1.5.2 Administrative Registers

Administrative registers report, among other things, administrative regulations enacted by government authorities.

Title | volume | Fed Reg | first page | (year) | (codification information | pinpoint).

When rules and regulations have not been codified, cite them to an administrative register. For federal rules and regulations, cite the ***Federal Register*** (**Fed Reg**). Include the number of the volume, the abbreviation of the register, the page number, and the year. When possible, at the end of the citation indicate where the rule or regulation will appear in the official compilation.

> 44 Fed Reg 12437221 (1979) (to be codified at 29 CFR § 552).
> *Outer Continental Shelf Air Regulations Consistency Update for California*, 70 Fed Reg 19472 (2009) (to be codified at 40 CFR § 55).

7.4.2 Jurisprudence

7.4.2.1 General Form

Style of cause, | vol | reporter | (series) | first page | pinpoint | (jurisdiction | court | year of decision) | (other information).

Administrative adjudications and arbitrations are cited in the same manner as other cases For arbitrations, place the name of the arbitrator followed by a comma and **Arb** in parentheses at the end of the citation.

> *Texas Beef Group v Winfrey*, 11 F Supp (2d) 858 (ND Tex 1998).
> *Dell Computer Corp*, 121 FTC 616 at 619 (1996).
> *Distribution Center of Columbus*, 83 Lab Arb Rep (BNA) 163 (1984) (Seidman, Arb).

Foreign Sources

7.4.2.2 Style of Cause

Indicate the style of cause according to the rules in section 3.3. For a state or country, use the common name, not the full formal name or abbreviation.

California v United States

If the case involves a city whose name could be mistaken for a state, enclose the relevant identifying information in parentheses: **New York (City of)** or **Washington (DC)**.

7.4.2.3 Neutral Citation

There is currently **no one uniform standard for neutral citation** in the United States, although some jurisdictions have adopted such citations.

7.4.2.4 Reporter and Series

After the style of cause, provide the volume number, the reporter abbreviation, the series number, and the first page of the case. **There is always a space between the reporter abbreviation and the series number.**

Murray v Earle, 405 F (3d) 278 (5th Cir 2005).

***US Reports* prior to 1875** are also numbered consecutively for each editor. Place this number and the editor's name in parentheses after **US**.

Scott v Sanford, 60 US (19 How) 393 (1857).

Abbreviations of editors:

Wallace	Wall
Black	Black
Howard	How
Peters	Pet
Wheaton	Wheat
Cranch	Cranch
Dallas	Dall

For the United States Supreme Court, cite reporters in the following order of preference: **US → S Ct → L Ed (2d) → USLW**. For federal courts, cite to **F** or **F Supp**. For state courts, cite to a regional reporter in preference to a state reporter. See **Appendix C-2** for a list of common reporters and their abbreviations.

7.4.2.5 *Pinpoint*

Place **at** before a pinpoint reference.

> *United States v McVeigh*, 153 F (3d) 1166 **at 1170** (10th Cir 1998).

7.4.2.6 *Court*

7.4.2.6.1 Federal Courts

The **United States Supreme Court** does not require an abbreviation unless the citation is to the ***United States Law Week*** (USLW). When citing to the USLW, place US and the full date in parentheses at the end of the citation.

> *Bush v Gore*, 531 US 98 (2000).
> *Boy Scouts of America v Dale*, 68 USLW 4625 (US 28 June 2000).

For Courts of Appeal cite the numbered circuit.

> *United States v Kaczynski*, 154 F (3d) 930 (**9th Cir** 1998).

Abbreviate the **District of Columbia Circuit Court** to DC Cir and the **Federal Circuit Court** to **Fed Cir**.

For district courts provide the abbreviated name of the district.

> *A&M Records v Napster*, 114 F Supp (2d) 896 (**ND Cal** 2000).

7.4.2.6.2 State Courts

Provide the court and the jurisdiction in parentheses, using the abbreviations from **Appendices A-2 and B.**

> *Peevyhouse v Garland Coal & Mining*, 382 P (2d) 109 (**Okla Sup Ct** 1963).

Omit the jurisdiction if it is obvious from the name of the reporter.

> *Truman v Thomas*, 165 **Cal** Rptr 308 (1980).

Omit the court if it is the highest court in its jurisdiction.

> *Hinterlong v Baldwin*, 308 **Ill App** (3d) 441 (App Ct 1999).

7.4.2.7 *Year of Decision*

Place the year of decision in parentheses at the end of the citation. If there is also a court abbreviation, combine the two within the same parentheses: (**App Ct 1999**).

7.4.2.8 *Online Databases*

7.4.2.8.1 Westlaw

Style of cause, | identifier given by service | pinpoint | (jurisdiction | court).

If the only identifier is the one provided by Westlaw, the judgment is otherwise unreported.

> *Fincher v Baker*, 1997 WL 675447 at 2 (Ala Civ App).

7.4.2.8.2 LexisNexis

Style of cause, | identifier given by service | pinpoint | (jurisdiction | court).

If the only identifier is the one reported by LexisNexis, the judgment is otherwise unreported.

> *Association for Molecular Pathology v Myriad Genetics*, 2013 US Lexis 4540 at 5 (USSC).

7.4.3 Government Documents

Indicate **US** at the beginning of the citation.

7.4.3.1 *Debates*

US | *Cong Rec*, | edition, | volume, | part, | pinpoint | (date) | (speaker).

Cite congressional debates after 1873 to the ***Congressional Record*** (**Cong Rec**).

Use the **daily edition** only if the debate is not yet in the bound edition.

> US, *Cong Rec*, vol 125, 15, at 18691 (1979).
> US, *Cong Rec*, daily ed, vol 143, 69, at H3176 (22 May 1977) (Rep Portman).

7.4.3.2 *Committee Hearings*

7.4.3.2.1 Federal

US, | *title*, | Congress number | (publication information) | pinpoint | (speaker).

Always cite the year of publication, and provide further publication information if available.

> US, *Federal Property Campaign Fundraising Reform Act of 2000: Hearing on HR 4845 Before the House Committee of the Judiciary*, 106th Cong (2000) at 2–3.
>
> US, *Assisted Suicide: Legal, Medical, Ethical and Social Issues: Hearing Before the Subcommittee on Health and Environment of the House Committee on Commerce*, 105th Cong (Washington, DC: United States Government Printing Office, 1997) at 2 (Dr C Everett Koop).

7.4.3.2.2 State

US,	*title*,	number of the legislative body **or** the year,	legislature number or designation,	state	(publication information)	pinpoint	(speaker).

Abbreviate the state according to the list in **Appendix A-2**. Always cite the year of publication, and provide further publication information if available.

> US, *Rico Litigation: Hearing on S 1197 Before the Senate Comm On Commerce and Econ Dev*, 41st Legis, 1st Reg Sess 5, Ariz (1993) (Barry Wong, policy analyst).

7.4.3.3 Reports and Documents

7.4.3.3.1 Federal

7.4.3.3.1.1 Numbered Documents and Reports

US,	issuing body,	*title*	(number)	(publication information)	pinpoint.

Indicate the issuing body unless it is named in the title of the report. Always cite the year of publication, and provide further publication information if available.

> US, *Secrecy: Report of the Commission on Protecting and Reducing Government Secrecy: Pursuant to Public Law 236, 103rd Congress* (S Doc No 105-2) (Washington, DC: US Government Printing Office, 1997) at 3.
>
> US, Senate Committee on the Budget, 111th Cong, *Concurrent Resolution on the Budget FY 2010* (Washington, DC: US Government Printing Office, 2009) at 213.

Abbreviations of numbers:

Documents	Reports
HR Doc No	HR Rep No
HR Misc Doc No	HR Conf Rep No
S Doc No	S Rep No
S Exec Doc No	

7.4.3.3.1.2 Unnumbered Documents and Committee Prints

US,	issuing body,	*title*	Committee Print	(publication information)	pinpoint.

Include the Congress number with the issuing body, if relevant. Always cite the year of publication, and provide further publication information if available.

US, Staff of House Committee on Veterans' Affairs, 105th Cong, *Persian Gulf Illnesses: An Overview*, Committee Print (1998) at 15.

US, National Commission on Children, *Beyond Rhetoric: A New American Agenda for Children and Families* (Washington, DC: The Commission, 1991) at 41.

7.4.3.3.2 State

US, | issuing body, | *title* | (number) | (publication information) | pinpoint.

Provide the document number, if available.

US, California Energy Commission, *Existing Renewable Resources Account, vol 1* (500-01-014V1) (2001).

Always cite the year of publication, and provide further publication information if available.

US, Washington State Transport Commission, *Washington's Transportation Plan 2003-2022* (Washington State Department of Transportation, 2002).

7.5 FRANCE

7.5.1 Legislation

7.5.1.1 Statutes and Other Legislative Instruments

Title, | JO, | publication date | (NC), | page or document number, | parallel citation.

Cite the title of the statute in French, but provide the date of publication and all related information in English. If the legislation has a number, then the descriptive title is optional. If the legislation does not have a number, include its descriptive title in full.

Always cite first the **Journal officiel de la République française**, abbreviated to **JO**. The Journal officiel is available free of charge on Légifrance (www.legifrance.gouv.fr). Include the publication date and the page or document number. When referring to the print version of the Journal official, provide the page number. When referring to the online version, provide the document number introduced by **no**. For JO supplements, place **(NC)** for **numéro complémentaire** after the publication date. For a list of earlier versions of the Journal officiel, consult section 7.5.3.2.

Ordonnance n° 2001-766 du 29 août 2001, JO, 31 August 2001, 13946, [2001] D 2564.

Décret du 5 décembre 1978 portant classement d'un site pittoresque, JO, 6 December 1978 (NC), 9250.

Arrêté du 24 mai 2017 relatif à l'insaisissabilité de biens culturels, JO, 17 June 2017, no 16.

Foreign Sources

7.5.1.2 Codes

***Code civil des Français* (1804–1807)**	art 85 **CcF**
***Code Napoléon* (1807–1814)**	art 85 **CN**
***Code civil* (1815–)**	art 1536 **C civ**
Code pénal	art 113-10 **C pén**
Code de procédure civile	art 1439 **C proc civ**
Code de propriété intellectuelle	art 123(8) **CPI**
Code de procédure pénale	art 144(2) **C proc pén**

Full citations are never used when referring to codes. To cite to one of the codes illustrated here, use the abbreviated name. To cite to another code, write the full title of the code at the first reference, and create a short form if needed (e.g., **art 1 *Code de la consommation* [C cons]**).

7.5.2 Jurisprudence

Use the **document numbers at the top** of the pages of *La semaine juridique*. Use the numbers at the bottom only to pinpoint to a specific page.

7.5.2.1 General Form

Court or chamber | city, | date, | *style of cause*, | [year of publication | session] | reporter | section | page or document number | pinpoint, | decision number | (annotation).

See **Appendix B-2** for the abbreviations of the names of the French courts and chambers.

7.5.2.2 Courts

7.5.2.2.1 Courts of First Instance

Trib admin Rouen, 27 December 2007, [2008] JCP G II 10041 (note Colette Saujot).
Trib gr inst Paris, 10 September 1998, [1999 1er sem] Gaz Pal Jur 37.

7.5.2.2.2 Courts of Appeal

CA Paris, 21 May 2008, *K c E et Sté nationale de télévision France 2* [2008] JCP Jur 390, No 06/07678.
CA Paris, 24 February 1998, [1998] D Jur 225 at 225.

7.5.2.2.3 Cour de cassation

Cass civ 1re, 14 December 1999, [1999] Bull civ I 222, No 97-15.756.
Cass crim, 24 February 2009, [2009] D 951 at 951, No 08-87.409.

7.5.2.2.4 Conseil d'État

Abbreviate **Conseil d'état** to CE.

CE, 27 January 1984, *Ordre des avocats de la Polynésie française*, [1984] Rec 20.

7.5.2.2.5 Conseil constitutionnel

Abbreviate **Conseil constitutionnel** to Cons const.

Cons const, 25 June 1986, *Privatisations*, [1986] Rec 61, 86-207 DC.

7.5.2.3 Style of Cause

Omit the style of cause except: (1) when citing a decision from an administrative tribunal or the Conseil d'État (but not in every case); (2) when citing an unpublished decision or one that is summarized in the *Sommaire* section of a reporter; (3) to avoid confusion (e.g. where two decisions were rendered on the same day by the same court); (4) when the case is better known by the names of the parties than by the usual information.

When the style of cause is included, italicize it and place it after the date, set off by commas.

Cass civ 1re, 5 February 1968, *Ligny-Luxembourg*, [1968 1er sem] Gaz Pal Jur 264.

7.5.2.4 Year and Session

Include the year of publication in square brackets before the abbreviation of the reporter. If citing the online version of the **Gazette du Palais** (**Gaz Pal**), the year of publication should be in parentheses before the issue number.

Cons const, 19 June 2008, **[2008]** JCP G Jur 449, 2008-564 DC.
Cass civ 1re, 15 February 2005, **(2006)** 337 Gaz Pal 46 (note S Lafargeas).

When citing an issue of the **Gazette du Palais** published in or before 2000, include the session after the year of publication, before the closing bracket. Keep the abbreviations for the ordinal number in French and write sem for **semestre**.

CA Orléans, 23 October 1997, [1999 1er sem] Gaz Pal Jur 217, (note Benoît de Roquefeuil).

7.5.2.5 Reporter

Place a single space between each informational element: **(1998 1re sem) Gaz Pal Jur 176**.

Cass civ 3e, 23 June 1999, [2000] JCP II 10333.

See **Appendix C-2** for the abbreviations of French reporters.

7.5.2.6 Section

When the sections in the volume are numbered, indicate the section number in Roman numerals after the year of publication. When the sections are not numbered, provide the abbreviation of the section title. Do not include the section when citing the ***Recueil Lebon*** **(Rec)**, the ***Actualité juridique de droit administratif*** **(AJDA)**, the ***Semaine juridique*** **(JCP)** after the 24th issue of 2009, or ***Dalloz*** **(D)** as of 2001.

Abbreviation of section titles:

Chroniques	Chron
Doctrine	Doctr
Informations rapides	Inf
Jurisprudence	Jur
Législation, Lois et décrets, Textes de lois, etc.	Lég
Panorama de jurisprudence	Pan
Sommaire	Somm

7.5.2.7 Page and Decision Number

Indicate the page number after the section or the year of publication. For the ***Semaine Juridique***, provide the decision number (e.g., **10000 bis**).

Ass plén, 6 November 1998, [1999] JCP G II **10000 bis.**

For the ***Bulletin de la Cour de cassation*** cite both the page and decision number separated by a comma and a space.

Cass civ 2e, 7 June 2001, [2001] Bull civ II **75, No 110.**

7.5.2.8 Pinpoint

Pinpoint citations are rarely used, given the brevity of most decisions. If required, it is always placed after the page number and introduced by **at**.

Trib gr inst Narbonne, 12 March 1999, [1999 1er sem] Gaz Pal Jur 405 **at 406.**

7.5.2.9 Notes

Any annotation or other writing appended to or included with a case must be indicated at the end of the citation, in parentheses. Irrespective of the type of writing referred to, write **note** followed by the author's name.

Cass civ 1re, 6 July 1999, [1999] JCP G II 10217 **(note Thierry Garé).**

7.5.3 Government Documents

Indicate **France** at the beginning of the citation of every government document.

7.5.3.1 Debates

7.5.3.1.1 From 1787 to 1860

France, | *Archives parlementaires,* | series, | tome, | date, | pinpoint | (speaker).

Cite to *Archives parlementaires: Recueil complet des débats législatifs et politiques des chambres françaises*, using the short title ***Archives parlementaires***. Indicate the series after the title. The first series covers 1787–1799, the second 1800–1860. Pinpoint to **sections**, not to articles. Add the name of the speaker (if provided) in parentheses at the end of the citation.

> France, *Archives parlementaires*, 1st series, t 83, 5 January 1794, s 3.

7.5.3.1.2 1871 to the Present

France, | *journal*, | house, | Débats parlementaires, | division, | number and date, | pinpoint, | (speaker).

From 1871 to the present, parliamentary debates are published in the ***Journal officiel de la République française***, abbreviated ***JO***. Indicate the house, followed by **Débats parlementaires**. For parliamentary debates published between 1871 and 1880 inclusive, omit both the house and **Débats parlementaires**. For parliamentary debates published between 1943 and 1958 inclusive, indicate only **Débats de [name of house]**.

> France, *JO*, Assemblée nationale, Débats parlementaires, Compte rendu intégral, 2nd session of 10 February 2004, at 1570, (Pascal Clément).
>
> France, *JO*, Sénat, Débats parlementaires, Compte rendu intégral, Session of 20 November 2003.

Indicate the division only from 1980 to the present for the Assemblée nationale, and from 1983 to the present for the Sénat. The divisions are **Compte rendu intégral** and **Questions écrites remises à la Présidence de l'Assemblée nationale et réponses des ministres** for the Assemblée nationale, and **Compte rendu intégral** and **Questions remises à la Présidence du Sénat et réponses des ministres aux questions écrites** for the Sénat.

Indicate the number (if provided) and the date of the session followed by the pinpoint. The name of the speaker may be added in parentheses at the end of the citation.

7.5.3.2 Earlier Versions of the Journal officiel

France, | *title*, | year **or** date of publication, | tome **or** volume | pinpoint.

Foreign Sources

Before 1871, parliamentary debates, parliamentary documents, and non-parliamentary documents were generally published in the various precursors to the *Journal officiel de la République française*:

1789–1810	*Gazette nationale, ou le Moniteur universel*
1811–1848	*Moniteur universel*
1848–1852	*Moniteur universel, Journal officiel de la République*
1852–1870	*Journal officiel de l'Empire français*

France, *Journal officiel de l'Empire français*, 1868, t 1 at 14.
France, *Gazette nationale, ou le Moniteur universel,* 1 July 1791, t 9 at 3.

The citation form varies according to the organization of the journal. In general, the citation should include at least the title, the year in question or the date of publication, the tome or volume (if any), and the pinpoint.

7.5.3.3 Parliamentary Documents

7.5.3.3.1 Travaux et réunions parlementaires

France, | house, | issuing body, | "title", | Compte rendu **or** *Bulletin* | (date) | (President).

Indicate the title of the *travaux*, then the number of the corresponding ***Compte rendu*** (for *travaux* of the Assemblée nationale) or the date of the ***Bulletin*** (for *travaux* of the Sénat). Unlike **Compte rendu**, ***Bulletin*** should be in italics. Add the name of the president (if provided) in parentheses at the end of the citation.

France, Assemblée nationale, Délégation aux droits des femmes, "Auditions sur le suivi de l'application des lois relatives à l'IVG et à la contraception", Compte rendu No 4 (6 November 2001) (President: Martine Lignières-Cassou).

France, Sénat, Commission des affaires étrangères, "Auditions de M. Dominique de Villepin, Ministre des affaires étrangères", *Bulletin* de la semaine du 27 janvier 2003 (28 January 2003) (President: André Dulait).

7.5.3.3.2 Rapports d'information (Reports)

France, | house, | issuing body, | *title*, | by author(s), | report number | (date) | pinpoint.

France, Sénat, Délégation pour l'Union européenne, *Le projet de traité établissant une Constitution pour l'Europe*, by Hubert Haenel, Report No 3 (1 October 2003) at 4.

France, Assemblée nationale, *Rapport d'information déposé en application de l'article 145 du Règlement par la mission d'information commune sur le prix des carburants dans les départements d'outre-mer,* by Jacques Le Guen & Jérôme Cahuzac, Report No 1885 (23 July 2009) at 63.

7.5.3.4 Non-parliamentary Documents

France, | issuing body, | *title*, | report number or volume, | publication information | pinpoint | (additional information).

Follow the rules for Canadian non-parliamentary documents in section 4.2.

France, *Commission d'enquête sur la sécurité du transport maritime des produits dangereux ou polluants*, Report No 2535, vol 1, (5 July 2000; President: Daniel Paul).

France, Conseil économique et social, *La conjoncture économique et sociale en 2005*, Avis et rapports du Conseil économique et social, *JO*, No 2005-09 at I-8 (1 June 2005; report by Luc Guyau).

France, Ministère de la justice, *Bulletin officiel*, No 82 at 3 (1 April–30 June 2001).

7.5.4 Doctrine

7.5.4.1 General Form

Author, | "title of article" | [year of publication] | reporter | section | first page or document number, | pinpoint.

Refer to sections 6.1.2, 6.1.3, 7.5.2.4, 7.5.2.5, and 7.5.2.6 to cite the author and title of articles published in French general reporters. See **Appendix C-2** for the abbreviations of French reporters.

Jean-Christophe Galloux, "La loi du 6 mars 1998 relative à la sécurité et à la promotion d'activités sportives" [1998] JCP G I 1085.

Nicolas Molfessis, "La controverse doctrinale et l'exigence de transparence de la doctrine" [2003] RTD civ 161 at 161.

Hélène Popu & Jean-Philippe Tricoit, "Le partage des cendres" [2004] 19 Defrénois 1285.

If the article is not paginated, include the document number (and the type of document if applicable).

Alain Gauvin, "La question récurrente de la qualification juridique des dérivés de crédit" [2004] 3 R Dr bancaire & financier, étude 1000032, see the text accompanying note 9.

Use the same form for comments published in general French reporters.

Xavier Labbée, "Esquisse d'une définition civiliste de l'espèce humaine" [1999] D Chron 437 at 440.

7.5.4.2 Notes

Author, | note of | court, | date of decision, | [year of publication] | reporter | section | first page or document number.

Foreign Sources

French reporters often publish notes below the summary of a case. To cite to a note, include the name of the author followed by the words **note of**. Provide the case citation according to the rules on citing French jurisprudence at section 7.5.2.

> Danielle Corrignan-Carsin, **note of** Cass soc, 10 May 1999, [1999] JCP G II 1425.

7.5.4.3 Encyclopedic Digests

7.5.4.3.1 General Form

Title of collection, | edition, | subject heading | by | author of the section, | pinpoint.

Provide the full title of the collection in italics. If **more than one edition** of the encyclopedia has been published, include the number of the edition.

> *Encyclopédie juridique Dalloz: répertoire de droit commercial*, 2nd ed, "Publicité foncière" by Luc Bihl, No 256.
> *Juris-classeur civil*, art 1354, fasc A by Roger Perrot.

7.5.4.3.2 Subject Headings

Regardless of the system of classification of the subject headings, indicate the number of the fascicle after the volume number, separated by a comma. Do not cite the date of the revision of the fascicle.

Organized alphabetically:

Include the keyword indicating the section in quotation marks.

> *Encyclopédie juridique Dalloz: répertoire de droit civil*, "Personnalité (droits de la)" by D Tallon, No 153.

If there is a fascicle number corresponding to the section, insert **fasc** followed by the alphanumeric indication.

> *Juris-classeur civil annexes*, **"Associations", fasc 1-A** by Robert Brichet.

Organized by articles of a code:

Provide the article number under which the section is classified. Use the same form as is used in the collection. If applicable, indicate the fascicle.

> *Juris-classeur civil*, **arts 1315-1326, fasc 20** by Daniel Veaux.

Organized by volume:

Provide the number of the volume in which the section is found. If applicable, indicate the fascicle.

> *Juris-classeur commercial: banque et crédit*, **vol 2, fasc 32** by Jean Stoufflet.

7.6 AUSTRALIA

7.6.1 Legislation

Title | (jurisdiction), | year/number, | pinpoint.

This section applies to statutes and delegated legislation (regulations). Cite the act's official short title in italics. Include the year of act as part of the title. Place the abbreviation of the jurisdiction after the title. See **Appendix A-3** for the abbreviations of jurisdictions for Australia.

Statute:

Marine Pollution Act 1987 (NSW), 1987/299, s 53(1)(d).

Delegated legislation:

Admiralty Amendment Rules 2002 (No 1) (Cth), 2002/109, r 5(b).

7.6.2 Jurisprudence

Recent Australian caselaw is accessible on the free online database AustLII.

7.6.2.1 General Form

Follow the same format as used for Canadian jurisprudence, except for the year, which is placed in square brackets (see section 3).

Neilson v Overseas Projects Corporation of Victoria Ltd, [2005] HCA 54.

In absence of neutral citation, **always provide the year of judgment** in parentheses after the style of cause.

Standard Portland Cement Company Pty Ltd v Good (1983), 57 ALJR 151 (PC).

Provide the year of the reporter **only if it differs from the year of judgment**.

Thwaites v Ryan (1983), [1984] VR 65 (SC).

7.6.2.2 Neutral Citation

Many Australian courts have adopted neutral citation. All cases on AustLII have a neutral citation. The format is the same as Canadian neutral citation (see section 3.5) except that the year is placed in square brackets.

7.6.2.3 Reporter

See **Appendix C-2** for the abbreviations of the series for the *Law Reports*. For **Privy Council** (PC) and **High Court of Australia** (HCA) decisions, cite to the official **CLR** before **ALR**. For other federal court decisions, cite to the official **FCR** before **FLR**. For Australian States and Territories, cite to the official state or territorial court reporter when possible.

7.6.2.4 Jurisdiction and Court

See **Appendix B-2** for the abbreviations of Australian courts. For state and territorial courts, if the jurisdiction is obvious from the reporter cited, only indicate the level of court.

7.6.3 Government Documents

Place **Austl** at the beginning of the citation.

7.6.3.1 Debates

Austl, | jurisdiction, | house, | *Parliamentary Debates* | (date) | pinpoint | (speaker).

After **Austl**, indicate the jurisdiction. See **Appendix A-3** for Australian abbreviations.

Always indicate the reporter as **Parliamentary Debates**.

> Austl, Commonwealth, House of Representatives, *Parliamentary Debates* (17 September 2001) at 30739 (Mr Howard, Prime Minister).
>
> Austl, Victoria, Legislative Assembly, *Parliamentary Debates* (23 October 1968) at 1197.

7.6.3.2 Parliamentary Papers

Austl, | jurisdiction | *title*, | number | (year) | pinpoint.

The number is preceded by **Parl Paper No**.

> Austl, Commonwealth, *Department of Foreign Affairs Annual Report 1975*, Parl Paper No 142 (1976) at 5.

7.6.3.3 Non-Parliamentary Papers

Austl, | jurisdiction, | issuing body, | *title* | (nature of paper) | by author(s) | (publication information) | pinpoint.

> Austl, Commonwealth, Royal Commission into Aboriginal Deaths in Custody, *Report of the Inquiry into the Death of Stanley John Gollan* by Commissioner Elliott Johnston (Canberra: Australian Government Publishing Service, 1990) at 31.
>
> Austl, Commonwealth, Law Reform Commission, *Annual Report 1998* (Report No 49) (Canberra: Australian Government Publishing Service, 1988).

7.6.3.4 Ministerial Documents

Author, | jurisdiction, | *title*, | document service, | number | (date) | pinpoint.

If additional information is required to identify the jurisdiction as within Australia, include **Austl** in parentheses following the jurisdiction named and before the comma preceding the title.

Paul Keating, Commonwealth (Austl), *Opening of the Global Cultural Diversity Conference*, Ministerial Document Service, No 172/94-95 (27 April 1995) at 5977.

7.7 NEW ZEALAND

7.7.1 Legislation

Title	(NZ),	year/number,	volume RS	first page.

This section applies to statutes and delegated legislation (regulations). Cite the act's official short title in italics. Include the year of act as part of the title. Place the abbreviation of the jurisdiction after the title. Provide the volume number followed by **RS** (for Reprint Series) if available.

Statute:

Abolition of the Death Penalty Act 1989 (NZ), 1989/119, 41 RS 1.

Delegated legislation:

High Court Amendment Rules (No 2) 1987 (NZ), 1987/169, 40 RS 904.

For delegated legislation, include the Gazette year and the Gazette page where available.

Ticketing of Meat Notice 1979 (NZ), Gazette 1979, 2030.

7.7.2 Jurisprudence

7.7.2.1 General Form

Follow the same format as for Canadian jurisprudence, except for the year, which is placed in square brackets (see section 3).

R v Clarke, [2005] NZSC 60.
Pfizer v Commissioner of Patents, [2005] 1 NZLR 362 (HC).

7.7.2.2 Neutral Citation

The Supreme Court of New Zealand officially adopted the use of neutral citation for judgments rendered in 2005 and after. Neutral citation in New Zealand follows the same format as Canadian neutral citation (see section 3.5) except that the year is placed in square brackets.

7.7.2.3 Reporter

7.7.2.3.1 Law Reports

Law Reports are divided into series. **Reference is not made to the *Law Reports* but rather to the series**.

There is no separate reporter for the **Judicial Committee of the Privy Council** (post-1932), the **Court of Appeal**, or the **High Court**. Include abbreviations **PC**, **CA**, or **HC** at the end of each citation to a case heard in that court. See **Appendix C-2** for the abbrevations of the series for the *Law Reports*.

7.7.2.4 Court

See **Appendix B-2** for the abbreviations of courts in New Zealand. Note that the ***Supreme Court Act 2003*** established the Supreme Court of New Zealand and abolished appeals from New Zealand to the Privy Council.

7.7.3 Government Documents

Indicate NZ at the beginning of the citation.

7.7.3.1 Debates

NZ, | *Hansard,* | stage: | subject | (question number) | date | (speaker)

Hansard provides the type of stage: **Questions to Ministers, Debate-General, Report of [a named] Committee** or **Miscellaneous.** Indicate the title of the debate as the subject (e.g., **Labour, Associate Minister-Accountability**). If the stage and the subject are the same, do not repeat the information.

> NZ, *Hansard,* Questions To Ministers: Biosecurity Risk-Motor Vehicle and Equipment Imports (No 3) 1 March 2000 (Ian Ewen-Street).

7.7.3.2 Parliamentary Papers

NZ, | "title", | date, | session | (chair) | shoulder number.

Do not add a space between the prefix of the shoulder and the actual number.

> NZ, "Report of the Government Administration Committee, Inquiry into New Zealand's Adoption Laws", August 2001, 46th Parliament (Dianne Yates, Chair).
>
> NZ, "Report of the Game Bird Habitat Trust Board for the year ended 31 August 1999", February 2000, C22.

7.8 SOUTH AFRICA

7.8.1 Legislation

If the jurisdiction is not obvious from the title, include (**S Afr**) after the title.

7.8.1.1 Statutes

Title | (S Afr), | number | of year, | pinpoint.

Constitution of the Republic of South Africa, 1996, No 108 of 1996.
Consumer Protection Act (S Afr), No 68 of 2008, s 33.

7.8.1.2 Amendments and Repeals

For further information, see section 2.1.11.

Constitution of the Republic of South Africa, 1996, No. 108 of 1996 **as amended by** *Constitution of the Republic of South Africa Amendment Act*, No. 3 of 1999.

7.8.1.2 Bills

Number, | *title* | (S Afr), | session, | parliament, | year, | pinpoint.

B30-2005, *Precious Metals Bill* (S Afr), 3d sess, 3d Parl, 2005.
B26-2005, *Nursing Bill* (S Afr), 3d sess, 3d Parl 2005, s 17.

7.8.2 Jurisprudence

Style of cause, | main citation | pinpoint | parallel citation | (jurisdiction | court).

Recent South African case law is accessible on the free online database **SAFLII**. Since no specific identifier is provided for SAFLII, include the neutral citation as main citation if possible. Follow the same format as for Canadian jurisprudence, except for the year, which is placed in square brackets (see section 3).

To refer to print versions, cite to the ***South African Law Reports*** or to the ***Butterworths Constitutional Law Reports*** if possible. For abbreviations of reporters, see **Appendix C-2**. If it is not obvious from the rest of the citation, provide the jurisdiction and the court in parentheses. For South African court abbreviations, see **Appendix B-2**.

Messina Associated Carriers v Kleinhaus, [2001] ZASCA 46 at para 10, [2001] 3 S Afr LR 868.

7.8.3 Government Documents

7.8.3.1 Debates

S Afr, | *Hansard*, | House, | date | pinpoint | (speaker).

S Afr, *Hansard*, National Assembly, 9 February 2009 at 1 (MJ Ellis).

7.8.3.2 Reports, Discussion Papers, and Issue Papers

Title, | Commission, | Project number | (date) | pinpoint.

Write the name of the commission if it is not included in the title of the report.

Truth and Reconciliation Commission of South Africa Report (29 October 1998) at ch 1, para 91.

Report on Trafficking in Persons, South African Law Reform Commission, Project No 131 (August 2008) at 23.

7.9 EUROPEAN UNION

7.9.1 Regulations, Directives, Decisions, Information, and Notices

European Union regulations, directives, decisions, information, notices, and other documents are published in the ***Official Journal of the European Union*** (OJ). The title replaced the *Official Journal of the European Communities* as of 1 February 2003.

The OJ is published every working day in every official language. It consists of two related series (the L series for **legislation** and the C series for **information and notices**) and a supplement (the S series for **public tenders**, which is available only in electronic format as of 1 July 1998).

Legislation from the European Communities includes instruments referred to as regulations, directives, and decisions. They are published in the L series (legislation) of the *Official Journal of the European Union.*

EC, | *title*, | [year of journal] | OJ, | series | issue number/first page | pinpoint.

Write EC for European Community and provide the full title of the instrument in italics. The instrument number is included in the title. The **number in directives and decisions** consists of the year and a sequential number (e.g., **98/85** or **2004/29**). To cite regulations, write the sequential number first, followed by the year (e.g., **2514/98**).

To refer to the *Official Journal of the European Union*, include **OJ**, followed by the series, the issue number, and the first page of the instrument, separated by a slash (e.g., **L 15/45**).

Regulations:

EC, *Commission Regulation (EC) 218/2005 of 10 February 2005 opening and providing for the administration of an autonomous tariff quota for garlic from 1 January 2005*, [2005] OJ, L 39/5 at 6.

Directives:

EC, *Commission Directive 2004/29/EC of 4 March 2004 on determining the characteristics and minimum conditions for inspecting vine varieties*, [2004] OJ, L 71/22.

Decisions:

EC, *Commission Decision 98/85/EC of 16 January 1998 concerning certain protective measures with regard to live birds coming from, or originating in Hong Kong and China*, [1998] OJ, L 15/45 at 45.

Information and notices:

EC, *Explanatory note concerning Annex III of the EU-Mexico Agreement (Decision 2/2000 of the EU-Mexico Joint Council)*, [2004] OJ, C 40/2.

7.9.2 Jurisprudence

Style of cause, | case number, | [year of reporter] | reporter | first page | pinpoint.

Write the style of cause. Abbreviate the names of institutions (e.g., **Council** rather than **Council of the European Communities**). Write the case number. **C-** indicates a decision of the **Court of Justice of the European Communities**, also known as the European Court of Justice (ECJ). **T-** indicates a decision of the **European Court of First Instance** (CFI).

Cite the reporter and indicate the first page of the case. Decisions of the ECJ and the CFI are published in the Courts' official reporter *Reports of Cases before the Court of Justice and the Court of First Instance*. Cite it as the ***European Court Reports*** (**ECR**). Precede page numbers by **I-** for **ECJ decisions** and by **II-** for **CFI decisions**.

Court of Justice of the European Communities:

Commission v Luxembourg, C-26/99, [1999] ECR I-8987 at I-8995.

European Court of First Instance:

Kesko v Commission, T-22/97, [1999] ECR II-3775 at II-3822.

7.9.3 Debates of the European Parliament

EC, | *date of sitting or title*, | [year] | OJ, | Annex and issue number/first page | pinpoint.

The debates of the European Parliament can be found in the Annex to the *Official Journal of the European Union* (OJ). Write **EC** and provide the title of the document or the date of the sitting. Provide the year the sitting was reported in brackets, followed by **OJ**, then **Annex**, the issue number, and the first page. A slash separates the issue number from the first page (e.g., **4-539/144**).

EC, *Sitting of Wednesday, 5 May 1999*, [1999] OJ, Annex 4-539/144 at 152.

7.10 OTHER LEGAL TRADITIONS

7.10.1 Roman Law

Refer to the **traditional divisions** of the work (generally book, title, section), not to the page number of the particular edition or translation. There are no spaces between the numbers of the different divisions. Use Arabic numerals (e.g., **1, 2, 3**) separated by periods to indicate the divisions, regardless of the usage of the edition or translation used.

The abbreviation **pr** means "*principium*" or "beginning" and refers to the unnumbered material before the first section of a title. Indicate the particular edition or translation used in parentheses at the end of the citation.

For **Justinian's *Digest***, indicate the author of the passage in question parenthetically after the citation.

Collection	Abbreviation	Example
Laws of the Twelve Tables	XII Tab	XII Tab 8.2
Institutes of Gaius	G	G 3.220
Code of Theodosius	Cod Th	Cod Th 8.14.1
Institutes of Justinian	Inst	Inst 4.4 pr (translated by Birks & McLeod)
Digest of Justinian	Dig	Dig 47.10.1 (Ulpian)
Codex of Justinian	Cod	Cod 6.42.16
Novels	Nov	Nov 22.3

7.10.2 Canon Law

Refer to the **traditional divisions** of the work, not the page number of the particular edition or translation. Use Arabic numerals (e.g., **1, 2, 3**) to indicate the divisions, regardless of the usage of the edition or translation. Indicate the particular edition or translation used in parentheses at the end of the citation.

Collection	Abbreviation	Example
Decretum of Gratian	–	**Part 1**: D 50 c 11 **Part 2**: C 30 q 4 c 5 **Part 2, *De poenitentia***: De poen D 1 c 75 **Part 3**: De cons D 1 c 5
Decretals of Gregory IX (*Liber extra*)	X	X 5.38.12
Decretals of Boniface VIII (*Liber sextus*)	VI	VI 5.2.16
Constitutions of Clement V (*Clementinae*)	Clem	Clem 3.7.2

Extravagants of John XXII (*Extravagantes Johannis XXII*)	Extrav Jo XII	Extrav Jo XII 14.2
Common Extravagants (Extravagantes communes)	Extrav Com	Extrav Com 3.2.9
Codex Iuris Canonici (1917)	1917 Code	1917 Code c 88, § 2
Codex Iuris Canonici (1983)	1983 Code	1983 Code c 221, § 1

7.10.3 Talmudic Law

Talmud, | *tractate*, | pinpoint.

Indicate Babylonian or Jerusalem Talmud. Italicize the tractate. When using the Babylonian Talmud, refer to the **traditional pagination** (Vilna edition) and not to the page number given by the publisher or translator. When using a different edition (e.g. Warsaw), indicate the edition in parentheses following the pinpoint.

When referring to a **particular edition or translation**, indicate the publication information in parentheses following the pinpoint (see sections 6.2.2.4.1 and 6.2.7 to 6.2.9). When providing a translation, insert **[translated by author]** after the initial citation and pinpoint (see section 6.2.2.4.2).

Use Arabic numerals (e.g., **1, 2, 3**) to indicate the leaf number and **a** or **b** to indicate the page. Pinpoint the **Jerusalem Talmud** to the Mishna (**Mish**) and the Halacha (**Hal**) and not to the page, as there are various editions with different pagination. Pinpoint to a page if the full publication information in parentheses can be provided, as set out in sections 6.2.7 to 6.2.9.

Babylonian Talmud, *Bava Metzia*, 11b.
Jerusalem Talmud, *Sanhedrin*, Mish 1 Hal 5.

INDEX

Index

MOT DU RÉDACTEUR

Depuis plus de trente ans, la Revue de droit de McGill contribue au développement de la référence juridique grâce à son *Manuel*. Nous avons toujours présenté notre ouvrage comme un repère pancanadien en la matière. Le terme « uniform » dans la version anglaise du titre suscite bien des débats et ne constitue pas de l'indifférence de notre part. Nous avons établi un ouvrage qui tient compte de la réalité canadienne comme aucun autre manuel de référence juridique ne l'a fait. Nous nous battons constamment pour préserver son bilinguisme et, à chaque édition, nous nous appliquons à établir des normes qui tiennent en compte les particularités des différentes cultures et des différents types de sources juridiques du Canada.

Les deux principaux objectifs qui nous ont guidés dans la préparation de cette neuvième édition sont la concision et l'accessibilité. Si ces deux caractéristiques vont généralement de pair, nous avons parfois dû prendre des décisions déchirantes afin de les concilier. Nous avons conservé au nom de l'accessibilité de nombreuses précisions que la concision nous commandait de retrancher. Ce fut un travail de moine que de déterminer les éléments à conserver et à retirer, mais chacune des décisions que nous avons prises ont été longuement étudiées et débattues avec des experts. Nous avons notamment convenu d'éliminer plusieurs tableaux d'exemples et de supprimer les listes à puces. Un manuel de référence juridique ne doit pas ressembler à un protocole scientifique, mais doit plutôt contenir des règles et des principes généraux et cohérents afin que toutes les sources, aussi singulières soient-elles, puissent être citées.

Si les sources de droit civil et de *common law* ont toujours été représentées de manière équilibrée dans notre *Manuel*, les sources de droit autochtone ont généralement été négligées. Dans la présente édition, nous avons inclus des règles pour faire référence à des documents constitutionnels autochtones et à des documents intergouvernementaux (traités et accords de revendications territoriales), sans compter des nouveaux exemples tirés du droit autochtone disséminés dans les sections existantes. Cependant, afin d'augmenter la quantité de sources autochtones traitées dans la prochaine édition du *Manuel*, nous prévoyons mener des consultations avec plusieurs experts dans le domaine.

Dans la rédaction de cet ouvrage, nous avons consacré énormément d'efforts à l'accessibilité des normes de référence pour les sources électroniques. Le Manuel étant publié suivant une base quadriennale, il est essentiel que chaque édition soit constamment à jour en matière de références en ligne. Si les documents électroniques sont souvent éphémères et peu formels, ils sont néanmoins très accessibles et de plus en plus utilisés par les juristes canadiens. Il existe maintenant de nombreux systèmes d'archivage de liens internet, qui résolvent à la fois le problème de la rupture des liens et celui des adresses interminables. À l'instar du

Bluebook, le *Manuel* encourage désormais la référence à des liens permanents chaque fois qu'un site internet doit être identifié.

Notre reconfiguration de la hiérarchie des sources jurisprudentielles confère également aux bases de données en ligne un statut plus important. Il ne sert à rien de nier qu'un grand nombre d'utilisateurs du *Manuel* n'ont pas recours aux versions imprimées des sources jurisprudentielles; ils consultent les décisions sur CanLII, LexisNexis ou Westlaw, puis choisissent les recueils imprimés parmi ceux énumérés sur ces services électroniques pour les inclure dans leur référence. Selon cette neuvième édition, les versions trouvées sur les bases de données en ligne ont le même statut que tout recueil non officiel. En effet, c'eût été aberrant de décourager l'utilisation d'un service comme CanLII, qui est à la fois gratuit, fiable et accessible.

Grèce aux nombreux changements orchestrés dans cette édition, nous avons bon espoir que le Manuel continuera de figurer à l'avant-plan en matière de référence juridique. En décembre 2017, la Société québécoise d'information juridique (SOQUIJ) a mis sur pied un outil électronique d'aide à la citation qui permet d'inscrire automatiquement les références juridiques conformément aux normes du *Manuel.* En avril 2018, Hein Online a également instauré un système qui fournit les références juridiques suivant les normes du *Manuel* pour tous les documents dans sa base de données. Ce sont là deux exemples qui démontrent la portée du *Manuel* et sa présence dans l'univers de la recherche juridique en ligne.

Lorsque nous avons entamé cette neuvième édition, nous avions une pléthore de projets ambitieux à l'esprit et avons établi de longues listes d'améliorations à apporter. L'appui de nombreux experts a été déterminant dans l'avancement de ces nombreux projets. Nous avons donc inclus pour la première fois une liste de remerciements afin de rendre compte de l'apport inestimable de chacun des experts qui ont rendu la présente édition possible. Il convient aussi de souligner la contribution de la rédactrice du *Manuel* de référence, (pour l'année 2018-2019), Barhilla Jesse-Buadoo, qui a finalisé le présent ouvrage.

Il est impensable d'atteindre la perfection dans une entreprise qui évolue constamment et c'est pourquoi d'autres éditions suivront. L'essentiel est de pouvoir se maintenir à jour sur une base régulière et d'améliorer certaines sections à chaque édition. Nous avons grandement besoin des opinions des membres de la communauté juridique et de leur appui pour parfaire notre *Manuel.* Par conséquent, nous vous prions de nous faire parvenir vos commentaires et suggestions à l'adresse suivante :

Revue de droit de McGill
3644 Rue Peel
Montréal, Québec H3A 1W9
Canada

Tel : 514-398-7397
Fax : 514-398-7360
http://lawjournal.mcgill.ca
journal.law@mcgill.ca

Nicolas Labbé-Corbin
Rédacteur du Manuel de référence, 2017-2018

Préface par l'honorable Ian Binnie

Cette neuviéme édition du *Manuel canadien de la référence juridique* constitue la mise à jour tant attendue d'un ouvrage à la fois pratique et indispensable. Les avocats et les juges ont régulièrement recours à des sources antérieures afin d'asseoir la légitimité de leurs points de vue. Cette observation va certes de soi en *common law*, mais la jurisprudence québécoise regorge également de références à des décisions antérieures, rendues au regard du *Code civil* ou de tout autre document législatif. L'invocation de précédents et d'autres sources notables rend compte de la nécessité de références exactes. On ne peut attendre du lecteur qu'il consulte des sources qu'il ne peut identifier efficacement.

Effectuer une recherche à la fois englobante et minutieuse, qui tienne compte du caractére plurijuridique et bilingue du droit canadien, constitue une tâche laborieuse. Si l'opération semble simple à première vue, la référence juridique se caractérise par ses fréquents revirements. Il existe de nombreux exemples de conventions qui ont changé au fil du temps. Si le présent *Manuel* explique en détail l'utilisation de formules telles que supra, la Cour suprême elle-même a décidé d'exclure ce mot de ses recueils. L'usage d'une langue morte n'est apparemment plus approprié de nos jours. De la même maniére, alors que la Cour suprême s'abstenait fermement d'utiliser des notes de bas de page même lorsqu'un supplément d'information était à-propos, des notes de bas de page apparaissent désormais de maniére relativement fréquente dans ses décisions, bien que leur utilisation varie énormément en fonction des juges. La personnalisation d'un jugement est admissible. Ainsi, plusieurs juges d'appel évitent d'utiliser l'expression « tribunal inférieur », car un tel langage élitiste présuppose une supériorité individuelle, qui est complétement inappropriée. Mais ce sont peut-être là des préoccupations qui n'ont pas leur place dans le *Manuel.*

Les rédacteurs ont parfaitement raison d'encourager la référence aux recueils officiels (par ex. les *Recueils de la Cour suprême*) lorsqu'ils sont disponibles plutôt qu'aux recueils privés (par ex. les *Dominion Law Reports*), car cela facilite l'accés à l'information juridique. En outre, la référence à des sources électroniques pose parfois probléme, et ce, pour diverses raisons. Par exemple, on ne peut pas indiquer le numéro de paragraphe lorsqu'on se réfère à la version électronique des RCS pour les décisions rendues dans les années 1990 ou antérieurement parce qu'à cette époque les paragraphes des décisions de la Cour suprême n'étaient pas numérotés. Par conséquent, la référence précise se faisait à la page et non au paragraphe. Toutefois, le *Manuel*, dans son souci du détail et de la précision, prescrit que la référence précise doit être faite au paragraphe lorsque cela est possible. De surcroît, dans le cas des recueils fédéraux officiels, deux versions, dans l'une et l'autre des langues officielles, se tiennent côte à côte. Chacune des versions a la même autorité et plusieurs juges se réfèrent à la deuxiéme version lorsque la première est ambiguë. C'est pour cette raison qu'une citation qui fait uniquement référence aux DLR, aux WWR ou à une version électronique d'une décision est fortement déconseillée selon le *Manuel* quand une version bilingue est autrement disponible.

Le présent ouvrage est grandement utile, car, au-delà des notions de base comme l'utilisation des parenthèses ou des crochets, les règles alambiquées qui régissent la référence juridique ne nous sont pas toutes familières. Nous ne pouvons mettre en pratique ce que nous ignorons. Plusieurs ignorent la marche à suivre pour faire référence à un « tweet », mais, dans cet ouvrage, le juriste averti peut trouver la réponse à cette question à la section 6.19.5.1.2. Un autre exemple est la gradation entre les différentes formules introductives, telles que « voir », « voir notamment », « voir par ex » ou « voir aussi », qui sont obscures pour la majorité des juristes qui n'ont pas pris part à la rédaction de ce *Manuel*, mais qui deviennent claires à la simple lecture de la section 1.3.6. À présent, grâce aux règles prévues dans les pages qui suivent, la communauté juridique est plus à même de contribuer à l'établissement de standards uniformes.

La Faculté de droit de l'Université McGill est un environnement propice au développement d'un ouvrage bilingue et plurijuridique, car elle s'intéresse aux systèmes canadiens de droit civil, de *common law* et de droit autochtone. De plus, cette neuvième édition du *Manuel* montre que la Faculté est nantie de rédacteurs industrieux et innovateurs. Nous leur sommes donc grandement redevables.

L'honorable Ian Binnie CC QC
Ancien juge à la Cour suprême du Canada
Mai 2018

Préface par l'honorable Patrick Healy

C'est en 1981 que le Comité de rédaction de la Revue de droit de McGill a envisagé pour la première fois de produire un manuel de référence juridique. En 1986, la première édition a été publiée, puis d'autres éditions se sont succédées tous les quatre ans. Chaque édition, y compris cette neuvième édition, a comporté une multitude de changements et d'améliorations. La quantité impressionnante de publications et d'institutions qui se servent du *Manuel* rend compte de sa qualité. Je réfère ici à la majorité des revues de droit canadiennes, à certains tribunaux et à bien d'autres institutions.

La publication du *Manuel* a indiscutablement comblé un besoin au Canada. Autrefois, les références juridiques souffraient de nombreuses incohérences, tant dans leur forme que dans leur contenu. Il était possible d'en relever entre différentes publications, mais aussi entre plusieurs textes d'un même ouvrage, voire au sein d'un même texte. Plusieurs ouvrages traitaient spécifiquement des méthodes de recherche juridique et certains d'entre eux proposaient des normes de référence juridique. Cependant, aucun consensus n'existait quant à la forme ou aux principes à adopter. Aujourd'hui, les chercheurs, les professionnels et les tribunaux ont à leur portée différents styles et modèles de référence juridique. Les normes demeurent donc hétérogènes et c'est pour cette raison qu'il est complètement insensé de prétendre qu'un ensemble de règles de référence fait autorité, encore moins qu'il est unanime. Toutefois, les règles énoncées par la Revue de droit de McGill dans son *Manuel* ont véritablement une portée inégalée. L'adoption étendue du Manuel assure une approche plus cohérente et disciplinée en matière de référence juridique au Canada.

Un manuel de référence est une forme particulière de manuel de rédaction, mais il ne s'intéresse pas à la qualité esthétique du texte. Ses objectifs sont plutôt de promouvoir la communication efficace de renseignements, généralement sous forme de références techniques, qui étayent ou expliquent le texte correspondant. Les références sont pratiquement au texte ce qu'est la preuve à la thèse. La référence juridique est utile, voire indispensable, à la communication efficace, autant que la preuve est essentielle à la thèse qu'elle étaye. Toute référence doit être perçue comme une partie intégrante du texte. Elle est incluse uniquement si elle y mérite une place et si elle assure que le message du texte pris dans son ensemble est véhiculé.

Si la concision est une vertu, les références doivent néanmoins être complètes, exactes et cohérentes. Ces caractéristiques générales ne suggèrent toutefois pas qu'il existe un style ou une pratique uniforme en matière de référence. Cette réalité est démontrée non seulement par l'hétérogénéité des modèles au Canada, mais aussi par les débats tapageurs à propos de la légitimité des différents manuels aux

États-Unis.[1] Dans le plus optimiste des cas, les manuels de référence fournissent des recommandations et des conventions assurant une pratique constante, mais qui ne peut prétendre à l'autorité du dogme orthodoxe.

Cette neuvième édition témoigne d'un effort soutenu afin de maintenir la rigueur et la légitimité du *Manuel.* En plus de son caractère bilingue, une attention toute particulière a été accordée à la qualité du français et aux enjeux de référence juridique dans les différents ressorts nationaux, continentaux et internationaux. Les rédacteurs cherchent constamment à simplifier le format des références, par exemple en retranchant la majorité des points, virgules et autres complications esthétiques, mais il serait encore possible de simplifier davantage. La plus récente amélioration du *Manuel* reste probablement la prise en considération des sources disponibles en ligne ou via d'autres médias électroniques. Vraisemblablement, il est désormais possible d'accéder au répertoire de plusieurs bibliothèques nationales et à des sources juridiques datant parfois de plusieurs siècles tout en restant confortablement assis derrière son écran.

Le passage de la forme imprimée aux autres supports médiatiques est radical et surpasse en magnitude l'apparition non moins révolutionnaire de l'imprimerie elle-même. Il sied de se demander si ce virage mènera également à des changements pratiques radicaux en matière de référence. Par exemple, le *Manuel* encourage toujours l'utilisation de références parallèles pour la jurisprudence et même pour d'autres sources d'information. Si le recours aux versions imprimées n'est visiblement pas un vestige du passé, la décision de privilégier les références neutres au détriment des références parallèles mérite notre attention. Nombreux sont ceux qui regrettent les heures écoulées dans les bâtiments souvent anciens que sont les bibliothèques en présence des artéfacts poussiéreux que sont les livres. En dépit de cette nostalgie, l'avancée irrésistible des technologies de l'information éclipse le plaisir saugrenu que certains éprouvent à manipuler des liasses de feuilles reliées. Les pratiques courantes de recherche et de rédaction tendent à atténuer la portée des sources en format papier et il est même probable que, dans un proche avenir, seules les références électroniques soient requises et que les références parallèles disparaissent complètement. Un tel changement assurerait davantage de simplicité, de concision et d'accessibilité.

D'une édition à l'autre, les rédacteurs de la Revue de droit de McGill s'assurent que le *Manuel canadien de la référence juridique* garde le rythme malgré les changements étourdissants qui bouleversent le monde de l'information. Ils veillent également à ce que le *Manuel* réponde à la demande en matière de règles de

1 Voir Susie Salmon, « Shedding the Uniform: Beyond a 'Uniform System of Citation' to a More Efficient Fit » (2016) 99:3 Marq L Rev 763; Fred R Shapiro et Julie Graves Krishnaswami, « The Secret History of the Bluebook » (2016) 100:4 Minn L Rev 1563; Richard A Posner, « The *Bluebook* Blues » (2011) 120:4 Yale LJ 850; Richard A Posner, « Goodbye to the Bluebook » (1986) 53:4 U Chicago L Rev 1343.

référence. La communauté juridique leur doit de sincères félicitations pour cette neuvième édition, qui établit des normes à la fois utiles et fort à-propos.

L'honorable Patrick Healy
Cour d'appel du Québec
Mai 2018

Préface par Me Daniel Boyer

La référence fait partie intégrante de tout écrit juridique. Elle guide le lecteur, tout comme l'auteur a lui-même été guidé, vers la bonne source, qu'elle soit loi, jurisprudence ou doctrine. Tout bon juriste se doit donc d'acquérir une maîtrise sans faille de l'emploi de la référence. Cette neuvième édition du *Manuel canadien de la référence juridique* lui en donne la clef, en proposant une marche à suivre conviviale et des standards flexibles afin de décrypter aisément l'univers de la référence juridique.

Une référence n'est ni vraie ni fausse au sens juridique, mais elle peut certes être exacte ou inexacte, selon qu'elle remplit ou non sa fonction d'indiquer précisément au lecteur la source juridique pertinente. Une référence inexacte ou incomplète risque de susciter exaspération et contrariété chez le lecteur, surtout lorsqu'elle l'entraîne sur une mauvaise piste.

La référence juridique ne relève pas de l'*elegantia juris* et demeure essentiellement un exercice de forme. Si sa cohérence est garante de références claires, son homogénéité ne l'est pas; ainsi le recours aux citations commande l'exercice constant de jugement critique. Dans son ouvrage à la fois remarquable et spirituel portant sur les éléments primordiaux de la rédaction scientifique, l'écrivain et sémioticien italien Umberto Eco synthétise ainsi l'objectif et la fonction de la référence juridique :

> Ce sont des normes très importantes et vous devez avoir la patience de vous familiariser avec elles. Vous verrez que ce sont surtout des normes *fonctionnelles* qui doivent vous permettre, ainsi qu'à vos lecteurs, d'identifier le livre dont il est question. Mais ce sont aussi des normes que l'on pourrait appeler d'*étiquette universitaire* : l'auteur qui les respecte montre qu'il est familier de sa discipline, les transgresser trahit le *parvenu* scientifique et cela peut parfois jeter une ombre de discrédit sur un travail par ailleurs bien fait. Ce qui ne signifie pas que ces normes d'étiquettes soient dépourvues d'importance réelle ou qu'elles ne soient que des tracasseries formalistes. [. . .] Mais avant de dire qu'il n'est pas nécessaire de mettre le titre d'un livre en italique, il faut *savoir* qu'on le met italique et pourquoi[1].

Les normes de référence juridique emportent leur lot de critiques, qu'elles soient de nature pragmatique, académique, ou même, conceptuelle. Les débats quant à la forme, au contenu et à l'accessibilité des manuels de référence juridique ne sont pas près d'être clos. Malgré tout, des développements, voire des progrès, surgissent régulièrement, et ce, grâce à un consensus sur le « pourquoi » des règles de référence, pour reprendre le terme d'Eco. Les perpétuelles transformations de forme et de contenu que subissent les sources juridiques et, bien entendu, la place de plus en plus importante de l'intertextualité au sein de l'écriture juridique moderne constituent les raisons d'être de ce manuel.

---

[1] Umberto Eco, *Comment écrire sa thèse*, traduit par Laurent Cantagrel, Paris, Flammarion, 2016 aux pp 114-115.

La majorité, si ce n'est la totalité, des règles de référence juridique nécessitent l'utilisation d'abréviations et quiconque aspire à devenir un juriste à part entière se doit de les apprivoiser. Tout comme un fan de baseball sait que la lettre « K » désigne un retrait au bâton et un fan de Mozart sait que « K » représente le catalogue *Köchel*, tout juriste qui se respecte sait que « KB » signifie *King's Bench*. Les abréviations juridiques nous accompagnent depuis l'époque de l'empereur Justinien, qui malgré son rôle remarquable dans le processus de codification du droit romain, a pitoyablement failli à sa parole en n'éliminant pas les abréviations juridiques, tel qu'il l'avait ordonné dans le *Corpus Juris Civilis* : « nous vous défendons d'écrire les mots en abrégé (*siglorum captiones & compendiosa aenigmata*) [...] vous ne vous servirez pas de chiffres ou notes abrégées » [2]. L'empereur est allé jusqu'à prévoir des mesures de répression contre ceux qui « entreprendront par la suite d'écrire nos lois par notes (*siglorum obscuritates*). »[3] Cependant, quiconque prend le temps de feuilleter un ouvrage ou une revue de droit constate que Justinien n'a manifestement pas su juguler l'emploi d'abréviations dans les documents juridiques. Grâce aux règles et aux exemples du *Manuel*, tant les auteurs que les lecteurs pourront déchiffrer et employer ces abréviations de manière efficace.

Les normes de référence juridique reflètent les particularités des différents ressorts. En l'absence d'une théorie unificatrice, ces normes demeurent essentiellement hétéroclites. Comme on peut le constater à la section 7.5.2 du *Manuel*, pour citer une décision française, il faut tout d'abord inclure le nom du tribunal et le nom de la ville, suivis de la date précise. Généralement, on omet les noms des parties, ce qui est bien s«r contraire à la pratique établie en *common law*. Que dirait un sémioticien du droit de cette insistance européenne sur le tribunal qui rend la décision alors que la *common law* met plutôt l'accent sur les noms des parties, et ce, quand le principe même du *stare decisis* repose sûr les notions de tribunal et de date?

Bien qu'impliqué dans l'élaboration du *Manuel* depuis sa première parution dans les années 1980, je n'ai jamais succombé au fétichisme de la référence juridique. Je suis heureux de constater le périple décidé du *Manuel* depuis un formalisme intempérant, luttant sans relâche contre la référence floue, jusqu'è son ouverture à l'innovation et à l'accessibilité du savoir juridique.

Me Daniel Boyer
Conseiller académique pour le
Manuel canadien de la référence juridique
Mai 2018

---

[2] Cod 1.17.1 s 13 (P-A Tissot, dir, *Les douze livres du Code de l'empereur Justinien: Code et novelles de Justinien; novelles de l'empereur Léon, fragmens de Gaÿus, d'Ulpien et de Paul traduction faite sur l'édition d'Elzévirs*, Metz, Behmer, 1806-1810).

[3] *Ibid*, 1.17.3 s 22.

TABLE DES MATIÈRES

1 Règles fondamentales F-3

1 RÈGLES FONDAMENTALES

Les règles établies dans ce *Manuel* s'appliquent seulement aux **notes de bas de page**, aux **références dans le texte** et aux **bibliographies**. Elles ne s'appliquent pas au corps du texte ou aux notes textuelles (par ex. aux phrases et aux clauses qui existent en dehors des limites de la citation); un guide de style devrait alors être utilisé. Utiliser les règles de la partie française pour écrire en français, et ce, même lorsque la source originale est dans une autre langue. N'utiliser les règles de la partie anglaise que pour écrire en anglais. Si la règle impose des parenthèses ( ), ne pas les remplacer par des crochets **[ ]** et vice-versa. Les caractères gras en couleur de ce *Manuel* mettent les exemples en évidence.

1.1 BIBLIOGRAPHIES

Diviser les bibliographies et les listes d'autorités de textes juridiques en sections (par ex. **législation**, **jurisprudence** et **doctrine**). Si certaines sources ne correspondent pas à l'une de ces catégories, ajouter une section résiduelle (**autres sources**). Il peut être utile de diviser la section contenant la doctrine en sous-sections (par ex. **monographies**, **périodiques** et **ouvrages collectifs**). Il est également possible de diviser les sources entre **sources internes** et **sources étrangères**.

Dans chaque section, classer les sources par **ordre alphabétique**. Classer la législation selon le titre de la loi, la jurisprudence selon l'intitulé et la doctrine selon le nom de famille de l'auteur. Pour la doctrine contenue dans une bibliographie, présenter le **nom de famille de l'auteur en premier** pour faciliter le classement par ordre alphabétique. Attention : l'ordre du prénom et du nom de famille change selon les traditions culturelles (avant, après ou entre les prénoms). Si le nom de famille apparaît en premier sur l'édition, omettre la virgule après ce nom (par ex. **Wang Sheng Chang**). Si le prénom apparaît en premier, mettre une virgule après le nom (par ex. **Smith, Graham JH**). Afin d'assurer l'exactitude de la forme et de respecter la source originale, présenter le nom de l'auteur tel qu'il apparaît sur la page titre de la publication, en incluant les initiales, et ce, même si le nom d'un même auteur est différent dans une référence ultérieure.

S'il y a une référence avec plus d'un auteur, écrire le prénom avant le nom de famille pour tous les auteurs excepté le premier (par ex. **Baudouin, Jean-Louis et Pierre-Gabriel Jobin**). S'il y a une référence à une œuvre par un seul auteur, ainsi qu'une œuvre par cet auteur et d'autres auteurs (par ex. **Baudouin** et **Baudouin et Jobin**), écrire celle avec un seul auteur d'abord. Chaque référence devrait avoir un **retrait** de 1/4 de pouce ou 0,63 cm (mettre en retrait toutes les lignes sauf la première ligne).

Suivre les règles des notes de bas de page du *Manuel* pour tout élément d'une référence à la doctrine (excepté pour l'ordre des noms de l'auteur ou du directeur d'un ouvrage collectif).

LÉGISLATION

Barristers and Solicitors Act, RSBC 1979, c 26.
Loi antiterroriste, LC 2001, c 41.
Loi de 1991 sur les sages-femmes, LO 1991, c 31.
Loi sur les sociétés de fiducie et les sociétés d'épargne, RLRQ c S-29.01.

JURISPRUDENCE

Delgamuukw c Colombie-Britannique, [1997] 3 RCS 1010, 153 DLR (4e) 193.
Kendle v Melsom, [1998] HCA 13.
Cass civ 1re, 26 juin 2001, (2001) D Jur 2593 (note V Avena-Robardet).
Létourneau c Laflèche Auto Ltée, [1986] RJQ 1956 (CS).
Nouvelle-Écosse (Workers' Compensation Board) c Martin, 2003 CSC 54.

DOCTRINE : MONOGRAPHIES

Lafond, Pierre-Claude, *Précis de droit des biens*, Montréal, Thémis, 1999.
Médina, Annie, *Abus de biens sociaux : prévention, détection, poursuite*, Paris, Dalloz, 2001.
Nadeau, Alain-Robert, *Vie privée et droits fondamentaux*, Cowansville (QC), Yvon Blais, 2000.
Tan, Cheng Han, *Matrimonial Law in Singapore and Malaysia*, Singapour, Butterworths Asia, 1994.

DOCTRINE : ARTICLES

Lamontagne, Denys-Claude, « L'imbrication du possessoire et du pétitoire », (1995) 55 R du B 661.
Lamontagne, Denys-Claude, « L'influence du droit public sur le droit immobilier », [1986] RDI 401.
Turp, Daniel, « Le droit au Québec à l'autodétermination et à l'indépendance : la loi sur la *clarté* du Canada et la loi sur les *droits fondamentaux* du Québec en collision » dans Marie-Françoise Labouz, dir, *Intégrations et identités nord-américaines : vues de Montréal*, Bruxelles, Bruylant, 2001, 137
Wang Sheng Chang, « Combination of Arbitration with Conciliation and Remittance of Awards — with Special Reference to the Asia-Oceana Region » (2002) 19 J Intl Arb 51.

1.2 RÉFÉRENCES DANS LE TEXTE : NOTE DE SERVICE ET FACTUM

La règle habituelle exige l'utilisation de notes en bas de page pour la rédaction de textes juridiques. Toutefois, dans certains types de documents, les références doivent être incluses **dans le corps même du texte**.

1.2.1 Note de service

Inclure la référence entre parenthèses immédiatement après le texte pertinent. La première fois qu'une référence apparaît, suivre les règles habituelles pour les notes de bas de page. Si la référence est répétée par la suite, créer un titre abrégé après la première référence (voir *Hill*). Si la référence n'est pas répétée, ne pas créer de titre abrégé (voir *Robitaille*).

À partir de la deuxième apparition d'une référence, utiliser uniquement le titre abrégé. Ajouter la référence précise (par ex. ***Hill* au para 195**).

> En plus des conditions pour « méfait donnant ouverture à un droit d'action » indépendamment de la violation pour laquelle on poursuit, les dommages-intérêts punitifs seront accordés lorsque la conduite du défendeur est si « malveillante, opprimante et abusive qu'elle choque le sens de dignité de la cour » (***Hill c Église de scientologie de Toronto***, [1995] 2 RCS 1130 au para 196, 184 NR 1, juge Cory [***Hill***]). Une telle conduite comprend la diffamation (***ibid***), l'omission de fournir des soins médicaux (***Robitaille v Vancouver Hockey Club Ltd*, 124 DLR (3e) 228, [1981] 3 WWR 481 (BCCA))**, et exceptionnellement les comportements abusifs des compagnies d'assurance (***Whiten c Pilot Insurance Co*, 2002 CSC 18 [*Whiten*]**).
>
> Puisque le premier mécanisme punitif est le droit criminel, la modération doit primer dans les recours aux dommages punitifs (***ibid* au para 69**). Il faut aussi noter qu'il ne peut y avoir responsabilité solidaire à l'égard de dommages-intérêts punitifs, car seul le responsable de la mauvaise conduite doit être condamné à les verser (***Hill* au para 195**).

1.2.2 Factum

Les paragraphes doivent être numérotés. Ces numéros commencent habituellement à la section « Faits ». Fournir un titre abrégé pour chaque source citée. Écrire le titre abrégé entre parenthèses immédiatement après le texte auquel la référence s'applique.

Indiquer la référence complète **à la fin du paragraphe**. Mettre en retrait les marges de gauche et de droite et utiliser une plus petite police de caractères.

Mettre les références **dans l'ordre de leur apparition dans le corps du texte**. Changer de ligne après chaque référence (ne pas mettre de point-virgule).

Écrire le titre abrégé, utilisé dans le corps du texte, en italiques et entre crochets, après la première référence complète de chaque source. Suivre les règles habituelles pour l'utilisation du ***supra*** (section 1.4.3). Toutefois, au lieu de se référer au numéro d'une note de bas de page, l'indicatif suivant le *supra* se réfère au numéro du paragraphe dans lequel est apparue la source pour la première fois (par ex. ***Whiten*, *supra* para 5 au para 69**). **Ne pas utiliser *ibid*** (section 1.4.2) dans un factum.

À la fin du paragraphe, inclure les références précises s'appliquant à tout le paragraphe (par ex. ***Whiten c Pilot Insurance*, 2002 CSC 18 aux para 69, 101, 110**).

> 5. En plus des conditions pour « méfait donnant ouverture à un droit d'action » indépendamment de la violation pour laquelle on poursuit, les dommages-intérêts punitifs seront accordés lorsque la conduite du défendeur est si « malveillante, opprimante et abusive qu'elle choque le sens de dignité de la cour » (*Hill*). Une telle conduite comprend la diffamation (*Hill*), l'omission de fournir des soins médicaux

(*Robitaille*), et exceptionnellement, les comportements abusifs des compagnies d'assurance (*Whiten*).

***Hill c Église de scientologie de Toronto* [1995] 2 RCS 1130 au para 196, 186 NR 1, juge Cory [*Hill* avec renvois aux RCS].**

***Robitaille v Vancouver Hockey Club Ltd*, 124 DLR (3e) 228, [1981] 3 WWR 481 (BCCA) [*Robitaille*].**

***Whiten c Pilot Insurance Co*, 2002 CSC 18 [*Whiten*].**

6. Puisque le premier mécanisme punitif est le droit criminel, la modération doit primer dans les recours aux dommages punitifs (*Whiten*). Il faut aussi noter qu'il ne peut y avoir responsabilité solidaire à l'égard de dommages-intérêts punitifs, car seul le responsable de la mauvaise conduite doit être condamné à les verser (*Hill*).

***Whiten, supra* para 5 au para 69.**

***Hill, supra* para 5 au para 195.**

1.3 RÈGLES CONCERNANT LES NOTES DE BAS DE PAGE

Les notes en bas de page des textes juridiques sont habituellement des notes discursives ou des notes de référence. Les **notes discursives** regroupent les commentaires pertinents mais périphériques qui risquent de dévier le lecteur du sujet principal. Les **notes de référence** indiquent les sources desquelles proviennent les arguments ou les citations. Des renseignements discursifs et des renseignements de référence peuvent être combinés dans une même note.

1.3.1 La création des notes de bas de page

Créer des notes de bas de page dans les cas suivants : (1) à la première référence à la source en question, (2) à chaque référence ou allusion à un passage particulier de la source et (3) à chaque citation ultérieure tirée de la source. Fournir la référence complète dans la première référence à la source uniquement.

1.3.2 L'indication des notes de bas de page dans le texte

Indiquer les notes de bas de page par des numéros en chiffres arabes (par ex. **1, 2, 3**) placés en exposant. Ne pas utiliser de chiffres romains ou de caractères tels que *, † et ‡.

De préférence, mettre le numéro de la note de bas de page à la fin d'une phrase, mais avant la ponctuation[1]. Cet ordre diffère de celui exigé pour les textes anglais, dans lesquels le numéro suit la ponctuation. Pour faire référence à un seul mot, placer le numéro de la note[2] immédiatement après le mot en question. Si le mot est suivi d'un signe de ponctuation[3], le numéro précède la ponctuation. S'il s'agit d'une citation placée « entre guillemets »[4], le numéro suit les guillemets et précède la ponctuation.

1.3.3 L'emplacement des notes de bas de page

Les notes de bas de page figurent au bas de la page, sous le texte, et se trouvent autant que possible sur la même page que le texte auquel elles correspondent. Distinguer les notes de bas de page du texte par une **plus petite police de caractères** et par une séparation du texte à l'aide d'une **ligne horizontale**.

1.3.4 La combinaison des notes de bas de page

Ne jamais mettre plus d'un numéro de note à un même endroit dans le texte. Combiner plutôt les références en une seule note de bas de page. Lorsque plusieurs références figurent dans une même note, elles sont séparées par un point-virgule et la note se termine par un point.

Si cela n'entraîne aucune confusion, il est possible de combiner les références à plusieurs documents en une note dont le numéro est placé à la fin du paragraphe. Éviter la combinaison s'il s'agit de citations provenant de sources différentes.

> [7] *Godbout c Longueuil (Ville de)*, [1997] 3 RCS 844; *Aubry c Vice-Versa*, [1998] 1 RCS 591.

1.3.5 Les références aux sources non françaises

L'écriture en français exige le respect des règles de référence françaises, quelle que soit la langue dans laquelle la source est rédigée. Conserver le titre (incluant l'usage des majuscules et de la ponctuation) dans la langue d'origine, mais pour tout autre élément de la référence, respecter les règles françaises, particulièrement en ce qui a trait à l'usage de la ponctuation.

> [1] David Kairys, dir, *The Politics of Law: A Progressive Critique*, 3e éd, New York, Basic Books, 1998 à la p 76.
> [2] *Credit Union Act*, SNS 1994, c 4.

1.3.6 Formules introductives

Les formules introductives permettent d'expliquer le lien logique entre la source à laquelle se réfère la note et l'idée énoncée dans le texte. En règle générale, il faut **mettre une formule introductive** :

> . . . le nom d'une société doit être indiqué dans les statuts constitutifs[1].
>
> [1] **Voir** *Loi canadienne sur les sociétés par actions*, LRC 1985, c C-44, art 6(1).

Il existe toutefois **deux exceptions** :

1) Lorsque la note de bas de page fait référence à une source directement citée dans le texte.

> . . . « les fruits de l'enquête qui se trouvent en la possession du substitut du procureur général n'appartiennent pas au ministère public pour qu'il s'en serve afin d'obtenir une déclaration de culpabilité, mais sont plutôt la propriété du public qui doit être utilisée de manière à s'assurer qui justice soit rendue. »[1] . . .
>
> [1] *R c Stinchcombe*, [1991] 3 RCS 326 à la p 333, 1991 CanLII 45 (CSC).

2) Lorsque le titre de la source apparaît pour la première fois dans le texte et que la note de bas de page ne sert qu'à fournir les autres éléments de la référence.

> Dans *R c Stinchcombe*[1], la Cour a déterminé que . . .
>
> 1 [1991] 3 RCS 326 à la p 333, 1991 CanLII 45 (CSC).

Chaque formule introductive se rapporte à **toutes les références de la même phrase**. Dans l'exemple ci-dessous, la formule **voir** se rapporte aux deux monographies citées dans la première phrase et **voir aussi** se rapporte à la dernière monographie citée.

> **Voir** Madeleine Cantin Cumyn, *L'administration du bien d'autrui*, Cowansville (QC), Yvon Blais, 2000 aux n° 24-51; Emmanuel Gaillard, *Le pouvoir en droit privé*, Paris, Economica, 1985 aux pp 150-55. **Voir aussi** Paul Roubier, *Droits subjectifs et situations juridiques*, Paris, Dalloz, 1963 aux pp 186-87.

Mettre seulement ***contra*** en italique. Ne pas mettre de signe de ponctuation entre la formule introductive et la source citée. Sans être exhaustif, le tableau ci-dessous présente les formules introductives courantes.

Voir	La source citée **appuie directement** l'idée exprimée dans le texte.
Voir aussi	La source citée **s'ajoute à d'autres qui appuient** l'idée exprimée dans le texte, mais elle n'est pas la plus concluante et n'est pas entièrement à propos.
Voir toutefois	La source citée **est en désaccord partiel** avec l'idée exprimée dans le texte, mais elle ne la contredit pas directement.
Voir par ex	La source citée **en est une parmi plusieurs qui appuient** l'idée exprimée dans le texte, mais ces autres sources ne sont pas citées.
Voir généralement	La source citée **appuie l'idée exprimée dans le texte et fournit des renseignements généraux** sur le sujet. Il est alors recommandé d'ajouter des informations supplémentaires entre parenthèses (voir la section 1.3.7).
Voir notamment	La source citée **est la plus concluante parmi plusieurs références qui appuient** l'idée exprimée dans le texte. Utiliser cette formule lorsque seules les meilleures sources sont présentées.
Comparer	La source citée fournit une idée différente de celle exprimée dans le texte, mais elle **permet tout de même d'établir une comparaison intéressante**. Il est alors recommandé d'ajouter des informations supplémentaires entre parenthèses (voir la section 1.3.7).
Contra	La source citée **contredit directement** l'idée exprimée dans le texte.

1.3.7 Information entre parenthèses dans les notes de bas de page

Lorsque l'idée affirmée ou infirmée par une cause manque de clarté, il peut être utile de fournir **entre parenthèses** une **brève description d'une phrase ou moins**. Une citation courte de la cause peut également être incluse entre parenthèses, suivie de la référence précise.

L'information entre parenthèses poursuit l'idée de la phrase précédente et débute par une minuscule. Si la citation débute par une majuscule, changer la première lettre par une minuscule entre crochets.

> [1] *Roncarelli c Duplessis*, [1959] RSC 121,16 DLR (2e) 689, juge Rand **(une décision discrétionnaire « [must] be based on considerations pertinent to the object of the administration » à la p 140)**; *Oakwood Development Ltd c St François Xavier (Municipalité)*, [1985] 2 RCS 164, 20 DLR (4e) 641, juge Wilson [*Oakwood* avec renvois aux RCS] **(« [l]'omission d'un organe de décision administrative de tenir compte d'un élément très important constitue une erreur au même titre que la prise en considération inappropriée d'un facteur étranger à l'affaire » à la p 174)**.

L'information entre parenthèses concerne la référence précèdente. Ainsi, dans l'exemple suivant, l'information entre parenthèses doit être placée après la décision à laquelle l'information se réfère.

> [3] *R c Robillard* (2000), [2001] RJQ 1, 151 CCC (3e) 296 (CA) **(le juge de la Cour supérieure a commis une erreur en déclarant que la réception en preuve des communications non confidentielles était susceptible de déconsidérer l'administration de la justice)**, infirmant [1999] JQ n° 5583 (CS) (QL).

1.4 RÉFÉRENCES ULTÉRIEURES ET ANTÉRIEURES

Lorsqu'une source apparaît plus d'une fois, **ne mentionner la référence complète que la première fois**. Les références ultérieures renvoient à cette première référence.

1.4.1 Titre abrégé

1.4.1.1 Modèle de base

Ne pas créer de titre abrégé si la référence n'est mentionnée qu'une fois dans le texte. Si le titre d'une source est court (environ trois mots ou moins), le titre complet peut être utilisé dans toutes les références ultérieures (voir note 10). Si le titre d'une source est plus long, créer un titre abrégé et l'utiliser dans toutes les références ultérieures.

Mettre le titre abrégé entre crochets à la fin de la référence, avant l'information entre parenthèses (section 1.3.7) et les étapes successives de la cause (section 3.11). Ne pas mettre les crochets en italique.

Placer les titres abrégés de législation et de jurisprudence en italique (par ex. ***Charte***). Toutefois, les abréviations comme **CcQ** ne sont pas considérées comme des titres abrégés et ne doivent pas être placées en italique. Il est tout de même possible d'utiliser ***Code*** en tant que titre abrégé. Si un seul code est mentionné dans le texte, il n'est pas nécessaire d'inclure cette forme abrégée entre crochets après la première référence.

Toutes les références ultérieures (***supra***, ***ibid***) doivent être précédées du titre abrégé de la source pour guider le lecteur à la note de la référence complète (voir note 80).

> [4] *Lamborghini (Canada) inc c Automobili Lamborghini SPA* (1996), [1997] RJQ 58 (CA) [***Lamborghini***].
> [7] *R c W (R)*, [1992] 2 RCS 122 au para 1, 74 CCC (3e) 134.
> [10] ***R c W (R)***, *supra* note 7 au para 3.
> [21] *Lamborghini*, *supra* note 4 à la p 66.
> [41] Christine Gagnon, « Les effets de la publication de la déclaration de copropriété » dans *La copropriété divise*, 2e éd, Cowansville (QC), Yvon Blais, 2007.
> [80] **Gagnon**, *supra* note 41 à la p 1.

1.4.1.2 Législation

Si une loi a un **titre abrégé officiel**, lui seul devrait être fourni dans la première référence. Si ce titre abrégé officiel est suffisamment court, il peut être utilisé pour les références ultérieures.

> [1] ***Code criminel***, LRC 1985, c C-46.

Si une loi n'a **pas de titre abrégé officiel ou que celui-ci est trop long** pour les références ultérieures, il peut être abrégé par un titre distinctif indiqué entre crochets à la fin de la référence.

> [2] *Charte des droits et libertés de la personne*, RLRQ c C-12 [***Charte québécoise***].
> [4] *Charte canadienne des droits et libertés*, partie I de la *Loi constitutionnelle de 1982*, constituant l'annexe B de la *Loi de 1982 sur le Canada* (R-U), 1982, c 11 [***Charte canadienne***].

Les abréviations bien connues peuvent également être utilisées.

> [3] *Loi sur la Gendarmerie royale du Canada*, LRC 1985 (2e supp), c 8 [***Loi sur la GRC***].

1.4.1.3 Jurisprudence

Choisir **une partie distinctive de l'intitulé ou le nom de l'une des parties** pour créer un titre abrégé.

> *PPL Corp v Commissioner of Internal Revenue*, 569 US ___, 133 S Ct 1897 (2013) [***PPL***].

Il est possible d'utiliser d'autres éléments afin d'identifier une cause :

1) Un intitulé plus connu provenant d'une cour inférieure.

> *Québec (PG) c A*, 2013 CSC 5 [***Éric c Lola***].

2) Le nom d'un navire pour la jurisprudence maritime.

Overseas Tankship (UK) Ltd v Miller Steamship Co (1966), [1967] 1 AC 617 à la p 625, [1966] 2 All ER 709 [***Wagon Mound No 2***].

3) Le nom d'un médicament pour les litiges en matière de brevets pharmaceutiques.

Apotex c Pfizer, 2009 CAF 8 [***Viagra***].

Afin d'éviter toute confusion lorsqu'il y a plusieurs causes portant le même nom, utiliser l'année de la décision. Noter que la date doit être en caractères romains.

R c Morgentaler, [1993] 3 RCS 462, 1993 CanLII 158 (CSC) [***Morgentaler* 1993**].

Afin de différencier les décisions d'une même cause émanant de différentes cours, utiliser les abréviations de l'**annexe B-2**. Noter que l'abréviation de la cour doit être en caractères romains.

[13] *Pappajohn c R*, [1980] 2 RCS 120, 1980 CanLII 13 (CSC) [***Pappajohn* CSC**].

[14] *R c Pappajohn* (1978), 45 CCC (2e) 67, [1979] 1 WWR 562 (BCCA) [***Pappajohn* CA**].

Si la référence originale comporte une référence parallèle, mais pas de référence précise, indiquer le recueil utilisé pour les références précises subséquentes à l'aide de la mention **avec renvois aux**, suivie de l'abréviation du recueil. Si une référence précise est indiquée dans la référence originale, cela sous-entend que toutes les références subséquentes seront effectuées à la même source. Ne pas inclure **avec renvois aux** dans ce cas. Les références précises subséquentes doivent être effectuées à la même source. Pour les causes ayant une **référence neutre**, il n'est pas nécessaire d'indiquer à quel recueil les références ultérieures appartiennent puisque la référence précise se fait aux paragraphes. La numérotation des paragraphes est déterminée par les cours et est uniforme pour tous les recueils.

[2] *R c Van der Peet*, [1996] 2 RCS 507, 1996 CanLII 216 (CSC) [***Van der Peet* avec renvois aux RCS**].

[3] *R c Ruzic*, 2001 CSC 24 au para 2 [***Ruzic***].

1.4.1.4 Doctrine

Ne pas inclure de forme abrégée à la fin de la référence originale. **Indiquer seulement le nom de famille de l'auteur** dans les références ultérieures.

[2] Marie-Thérèse Chicha, *L'équité salariale : mise en œuvre et enjeux*, 2e éd, Cowansville (QC), Yvon Blais, 2000.

[12] **Chicha**, *supra* note 2 à la p 183.

Si plusieurs auteurs cités ont le même nom de famille, inclure les initiales du prénom pour ces auteurs.

[7] Stephen A Smith, « Duties, Liabilities, and Damages » (2012) 125:7 Harv L Rev 1727.

[9] Lionel Smith, « The Province of the Law of Restitution » (1992) 71:4 R du B can 672.

[20] **S Smith**, *supra* note 7 à la p 1731.

[27] **L Smith**, *supra* note 9 à la p 675.

Si **plusieurs ouvrages d'un même auteur sont mentionnés**, utiliser le nom de famille de l'auteur et un titre abrégé. Respecter la forme typographique du titre du document dans le titre abrégé, soit l'utilisation de l'italique pour les livres ou l'utilisation des guillemets pour les articles.

[3] Aline Grenon, « La protection du consommateur et les sûretés mobilières au Québec et en Ontario : solutions distinctes? » (2001) R du B can 917 **[Grenon, « Protection »]**.

[14] **Grenon, « Protection »**, *supra* note 3 à la p 923.

Pour faire référence à **deux articles différents ou plus publiés dans un même ouvrage collectif**, inclure une forme abrégée de l'ouvrage collectif en appliquant les règles ci-dessus. À chaque première référence à un article de cet ouvrage, inclure la forme abrégée à la suite du nom de l'auteur et du titre de l'article. Pour les références subséquentes à un article, appliquer les règles ci-dessus.

[13] Louise Rolland, « La simulation dans le droit civil des obligations : le mensonge révélateur » dans Nicholas Kasirer, *Le faux en droit privé*, Montréal, Thémis, 2000 à la p 93

[86] Philippe Jestaz, « Faux et détournement d'institution en droit français de la famille » dans **Kasirer**, *supra* note 13 à la p 13.

[91] **Jestaz**, *supra* note 86 à la p 15.

1.4.2 *Ibid*

Ibid est l'abréviation du mot latin *ibidem*, qui signifie « au même endroit ». Utiliser *ibid* pour indiquer la **référence immédiatement précédente**. Ne pas indiquer le numéro de la note référée.

Utiliser *ibid* **après une référence complète** (voir note 2), **après un *supra*** (voir note 6) ou même **après un autre *ibid*** (voir note 7). S'il y a plus d'une référence dans la note de bas de page précédente, utiliser *supra* au lieu de *ibid*. Quand *ibid* est utilisé sans référence précise, *ibid* indique la même référence précise que la note précédente (voir note 6). Utiliser *supra* pour indiquer la référence originale complète lorsque la source précédente contenait une référence précise (voir note 8).

Pour faire référence à la source précédente dans une même note, utiliser *ibid* entre parenthèses (voir note 98).

[1] Voir *Lapointe c Hôpital Le Gardeur*, [1992] 1 RCS 382, 90 DLR (4e) 27 [*Lapointe*].

[2] ***Ibid*** à la p 383. Voir aussi *Laferrière c Lawson*, [1991] 1 RCS 541 à la p 592, 78 DLR (4e) 609 [*Laferrière*]; *Wilson c Rowswell*, [1970] RCS 865, 11 DLR (3e) 737 [*Wilson*].

[5] *Laferrière*, ***supra*** *note 2* à la p 595.

[6] ***Ibid.***

[7] ***Ibid*** à la p 599.

[8] *Laferrière, supra* note 2.

[98] Voir aussi *Pelletier c Roberge*, [1991] RRA 726, 41 QAC 161 [*Pelletier*]. *Pelletier* emploie la théorie de la perte de chance en droit québécois (voir ***ibid*** à la p 737).

1.4.3 *Supra*

Supra est le mot latin pour « ci-dessus ». Utiliser *supra* et le titre abrégé pour indiquer la **référence précédente contenant la référence complète**. *Supra* indique toujours la référence originale complète et non un autre *supra* ou *ibid*. Si la source est identifiée clairement dans le corps du texte, il n'est pas nécessaire de la répéter dans la note (voir note 58).

Pour faire référence **à la fois à la note et au corps du texte accompagné par la note**, utiliser la formule suivante : ***supra* note # et texte correspondant** (voir note 59). Pour faire référence **uniquement au texte** et non aux notes de bas de page, utiliser **ci-dessus** (section 1.4.4) et non *supra*.

[1] *Canada (PG) c Biorex inc*, [1996] RDJ 548 (disponible sur QL) (CA) [*Biorex*]; voir aussi *Loi sur les jeunes contrevenants*, LRC 1985, c Y-1.
[56] *Biorex*, ***supra*** note 1 à la p 551.
[57] *Loi sur les jeunes contrevenants*, ***supra*** note 1, art 5.
[58] ***Supra*** note 1 à la p 550.

1.4.4 Ci-dessus et ci-dessous

Utiliser les expressions ***ci-dessus*** et ***ci-dessous*** pour référer le lecteur à une **partie du texte** plutôt qu'aux notes de bas de page.

[1] Voir la partie III-A, **ci-dessus**, pour l'analyse de cette question.
[2] Voir la discussion plus approfondie de cette cause aux pp 164-70, **ci-dessous**.

Si le texte n'est pas divisé en parties ou en paragraphes facilement identifiables (par ex. en sous-titres ou en numéros de paragraphes) ou si la pagination finale du texte n'est pas définitive au moment de la rédaction, utiliser la formule ***texte correspondant à la note*** #.

[3] Voir l'analyse de la décision dans l'arrêt *Oakes* au **texte correspondant à la note** 41.

1.5 RÉFÉRENCES PRÉCISES

	page	**paragraphe**	**article**	**note de bas de page**	**numéro**
singulier	*Ibid* **à la p** 512.	*Ibid* **au para** 6.	*Ibid*, **art** 1457.	*Ibid* à la p 512, **n** 139.	*Ibid*, **n°** 45.
pluriel	*Ibid* **aux pp** 512—14.	*Ibid* **aux para** 6, 12.	*Ibid*, **arts** 1457–69.	*Ibid* à la p 512, **nn** 139, 142–46.	*Ibid*, **n°** 45-47.

Utiliser une référence précise pour faire référence à une portion spécifique du texte. Si possible, faire référence aux paragraphes, aux articles, aux notes de bas de page, aux numéros ou à toute autre division qui est plus précise que le numéro de page. Faire référence au numéro de page s'il n'existe pas de plus petite division. Pour les divisions qui ne sont pas incluses dans le tableau ci-dessus, indiquer **à**, le déterminant approprié, le nom de la division et le numéro (par ex. **à la note 7/3**).

Séparer les **références précises non-consécutives** par une **virgule**, et les **références précises consécutives** par un **tiret court** (–) et non un **trait d'union** (-). Retenir au moins les deux derniers chiffres après le tiret court (par ex. **159-60**). Si le modèle d'indexation des pages contient des traits d'union (par ex. 70.1-3, 70.1-4 etc.) ou tout autre modèle pouvant rendre ambiguë la séquence numérique lorsque unie avec un tiret court, privilégier la formule **à** pour unir la séquence de pages (par ex. 70.1-3 à 70.1-5).

Bien qu'il soit généralement préférable de faire référence à un numéro ou à une étendue spécifique, pour faire référence à une **zone générale**, placer **et s** (l'abréviation de « et suivantes ») immédiatement après le numéro de la première page de cette zone.

Ne pas abréger les éléments non numérotés (par ex. Préambule, Annexe, Disposition Préliminaire, etc.) dans une référence précise.

1.6 RESSOURCES ÉLÉCTRONIQUES

Un site internet constitue un ensemble de pages hébergées sur un serveur et accessible via internet. Aux fins du présent ouvrage, cette section ne s'applique pas aux bases de données en ligne, qui sont plutôt traitées dans les sections pertinentes relatives aux différents types de sources. Les sites internet ont l'avantage d'être accessibles à tous, mais présentent malheureusement un contenu souvent éphémère et n'ont pas toujours un statut officiel. Il est possible de se référer seulement à une version électronique d'une source lorsqu'il s'agit d'une version officielle, lorsqu'elle est la seule version existante ou lorsqu'elle est la seule version raisonnablement accessible. Pour chaque type de sources, consulter les règles spécifiques relatives aux ressources électroniques. Voir notamment la section 6.19 lorsque le site internet est la référence principale.

1.6.1 Archivage des sources internet

Afin de pallier au caractère éphémère du contenu disponible en ligne et d'empêcher la rupture des liens, il est préférable de se référer à une URL archivée à la suite de l'URL originale. Placer l'URL archivée entre crochets à la fin de la référence. L'utilisation du système d'archivage Perma est hautement recommandée (voir les exemples de la section 1.6.2).

Lorsqu'une URL archivée est indiquée dans la référence, n'inclure que l'URL de la racine du site internet si l'URL originale est trop longue ou peu conviviale.

1.6.2 Référence parallèle à des sources électroniques

Lorsque le contenu d'un site internet est disponible dans un autre format, privilégier une référence principale à cet autre format. Il est toutefois conseillé d'inclure une référence parallèle au format internet de la source puisque les lecteurs y ont généralement plus facilement accès. Inclure l'URL à la suite de la référence traditionnelle. La référence traditionnelle suit les règles prévues pour chaque type de sources.

Référence traditionnelle, | en ligne : | <URL> | [URL archivée].

Henry Samuel, « March for Girl Set Alight After Marriage Refusal », *The Daily Telegraph* (28 novembre 2005), en ligne : <www.telegraph.co.uk> [perma.cc/HC6D-K9M9].

Kahikino Noa Dettweiler, « Racial Classification or Cultural Identification?: The Gathering Rights Jurisprudence of Two Twentieth Century Hawaiian Supreme Court Justices » (2005) 6:1 Asian Pac L & Pol'y J 5, en ligne : <www.hawaii.edu/aplpj> [perma.cc/8EYU-FMGV].

Jean Teillet, *Metis Law in Canada*, Vancouver, Pape Salter Teillet, 2013, en ligne : <www.pstlaw.ca/resources/Metis-Law-in-Canada-2013.pdf> [perma.cc/TT3D-R42Z].

1.6.3 Identifiants numériques d'objet

Un identifiant numérique d'objet (DOI) est un repère de ressource permanent et unique qui identifie un document en ligne sans égard à son emplacement. Pour trouver un document qui a un DOI, entrer l'identifiant dans un outil de recherche qui reconnaît les DOI. Lorsqu'un DOI est disponible, ajouter le DOI à la fin de la référence traditionnelle.

Référence traditionnelle, | DOI : | <identifiant numérique d'objet>.

Anne Pineau, « Conjuguer relations tripartites et sous-traitance avec travail décent » (2013) 54:2 C de D 461, DOI : <10.7202/1017621ar>.

1.7 RÉFÉRENCES AUX SOURCES CITANT OU REPRODUISANT LA SOURCE ORIGINALE

Il est toujours préférable de faire référence à la source originale. Si une source originale se trouve en partie dans une autre source (la source citante), consulter la source originale afin de vérifier le contexte et l'exactitude de la citation.

1.7.1 Source orginale difficile à trouver

Lorsque la source originale est difficile à trouver ou a été détruite, il est possible de se référer à la source originale telle qu'elle se trouve dans la source citante, en fournissant le plus de renseignements possible sur la source primaire, suivis de **tel que cité dans** et de la référence à la source citante.

George R au Gouverneur Arthur Phillip, Instruction royale, 25 avril 1787 (27 Geo III), **reproduite dans** *Historical Documents of New South Wales*, t 1, 2e partie, Sydney, Government Printer, 1892-1901 à la p 67.

Dans certains cas, la version originale d'un document entièrement réimprimé dans un ouvrage collectif (par ex. les collections reproduisant les débats, les lettres, les traités ou les manuscrits) est uniquement disponible dans les archives. Dans ce cas, fournir le plus de renseignements possible sur le document original, suivis de **reproduit(e) dans** et de la référence à la source citante. Ne pas faire référence aux éditions reproduisant des extraits de sources originales facilement disponibles (par ex. des manuels).

> *Papers Relating to the Commission appointed to enquire into the state and condition of the Indians of the North-West Coast of British Columbia*, British Columbia Sessional Papers, 1888 aux pp 432-33, **tel que cité dans** Hamar Foster, « Honouring the Queen's Flag: A Legal and Historical Perspective on the Nisga'a Treaty » (1998) 120 BC Studies 11 à la p 13.

1.7.2 Accent sur la source citante

Pour souligner le fait qu'une source citante utilise la source originale (par ex. lorsque la source citante est plus éminente ou a plus de crédibilité), inclure la référence de la source citante, suivi de **citant** et de la source originale.

> *Canada (Citoyenneté et Immigration) c Khosa*, 2009 CSC 12 au para 38, **citant** Pierre-André Côté, *Interprétation des lois*, 3e éd, Cowansville (QC), Yvon Blais, 1999 à la p 91, n 123.

1.8 RÈGLES GÉNÉRALES CONCERNANT LES CITATIONS

Ces règles s'appliquent tant au corps du texte qu'aux notes de bas de page.

1.8.1 Emplacement des citations

Insérer les citations courtes (de **moins de quatre lignes**) dans le texte entre guillemets. Mettre les citations plus longues (de **quatre lignes ou plus**) en retrait des marges, à simple interligne et sans guillemets. Les dispositions législatives peuvent également être citées en retrait des marges même si elles ont moins de quatre lignes.

> Il rejette cet argument au motif que, selon lui, il n'existe « **aucune contradiction entre le refus de permettre le paiement d'honoraires extrajudiciaires et le droit d'accorder des honoraires spéciaux** »[4].
>
> La juge Dutil est également amenée à traiter de l'importance du fait que l'usine s'est établie à cet endroit avant les réclamants. À ce sujet, elle affirme que
>
> > **[l]a preuve ne démontre pas que les résidents du quartier Villeneuve savaient, à leur arrivée, qu'ils s'exposaient à des inconvénients aussi importants que ceux qu'ils ont vécus. Ils pouvaient s'attendre à certains inconvénients du fait qu'ils étaient voisins d'une cimenterie, cependant, ils s'installaient dans un quartier résidentiel [. . .]**[5].
>
> L'art. 32 C.c.Q. accorde à l'enfant un statut qui lui a longtemps été dénigré à travers l'histoire. Il se lit comme suit :
>
> > **Tout enfant a droit à la protection, à la sécurité et à l'attention que ses parents ou les personnes qui en tiennent lieu peuvent lui donner.**

1.8.2 Forme des citations

L'orthographe, les majuscules et la ponctuation d'une citation **reproduisent la source originale**; toute modification doit être clairement indiquée entre crochets. Si la phrase devient grammaticalement incorrecte, faire un ajustement entre crochets au début de la citation (par ex. changer une majuscule pour une minuscule ou vice-versa). Utiliser **l'ellipse entre crochets [. . .]** lorsque la citation est incomplète ou que la phrase citée se poursuit. Omettre les ellipses au début ou à la fin d'une citation, sauf dans les cas où la phrase est délibérément laissée grammaticalement incomplète.

Lorsque la source originale contient une faute, **inclure la correction entre crochets**. Ne pas utiliser [*sic*], à moins d'avoir une raison particulière de vouloir signaler l'erreur ou de vouloir la conserver.

Pour mettre l'accent sur une partie d'une citation, la mettre en italique et ajouter **[nos italiques]** immédiatement après la citation. Si les italiques étaient déjà indiquées dans la version originale, ajouter **[italiques dans l'original]**. Lorsque le texte original contient des notes de bas de page et qu'elles ne sont pas reproduites dans la citation, ajouter **[notes omises]** après la citation. Cette règle est contraire aux règles de la partie anglaise, selon lesquelles ces expressions sont placées à la fin de la référence et non à la fin de la citation.

> « [L]'objection identitaire s'avère [. . .] bien fondée »[32], et représente ainsi un élément important du débat.
>
> Donc, « [c]ette dichotomie découle tout naturellement de *l'impossibilité des juges de se dégager de leurs principes nationaux* » **[nos italiques]**[53].
>
> « L'intérêt d'autrui, auquel l'exercice d'un pouvoir est subordonné, le distingue essentiellement du droit subjectif que son titulaire exerce librement. La poursuite de l'intérêt d'autrui intègre nécessairement au pouvoir un but, dont l'attributaire doit tenir compte dans son exercice » **[notes omises]**.

1.8.3 Citation d'une source dans une autre langue

Utiliser autant que possible la version française de la source lorsque le texte rédigé est en français et une version anglaise lorsqu'il est rédigé en anglais. Le Canada, le Québec, le Manitoba, le Nouveau-Brunswick, l'Ontario, les Territoires du Nord-Ouest et le Yukon adoptent leurs lois en français et en anglais. Cependant, avant une certaine date, il est possible que celles-ci n'existent qu'en version anglaise.

Dans un texte juridique, il n'est pas nécessaire de traduire un passage tiré d'une source dans une autre langue. Toutefois, si cela facilite la compréhension, la référence doit clairement indiquer qui a traduit la citation. Pour une traduction professionnelle, voir la section 6.2.2.4.1. Pour une traduction de l'auteur (vous), indiquer **[notre traduction]** après la citation.

> Comme l'indique Robin, « les faits de l'espèce ne permettent pas de conclure à la mauvaise foi » **[notre traduction]**[79].

1.9 RÉDACTION D'UN TEXTE EN LANGUE ÉTRANGÈRE

Les règles de ce *Manuel* s'appliquent particulièrement à la rédaction de textes dans les deux langues officielles du Canada. Toutefois, il est possible d'adapter ces règles pour toute autre langue en s'inspirant de la section anglaise **ou** française, selon le degré de maîtrise de l'auteur. Les règles d'or sont l'**uniformité**, la **clarté** et la **facilité** pour le lecteur **de retracer les sources**. Les indications suivantes ne sont que des exemples d'adaptation des règles.

Traduire les formules comme « voir », « en accord avec », « tel que cité dans », « nos italiques » ou « avec renvois aux », mais conserver les expressions latines dans la langue d'origine. Conserver les règles de **forme** telles quelles, comme l'ordre des éléments et la structure du document. Suivre les **règles de ponctuation** de la langue de rédaction. Consulter un ouvrage grammatical si nécessaire. S'assurer que la forme employée est toujours constante, tant dans les notes de bas de page que dans le corps du texte.

Pour la **législation et la jurisprudence**, suivre le modèle de base canadien, ou adapter les règles des « Sources étrangères » (section 7). Utiliser l'acronyme du recueil et de la législature tel que présenté dans un document officiel de la loi. Inclure une indication géographique. Pour les sources jurisprudentielles, suivre la hiérarchie des sources. Toujours garder en tête le public cible et s'assurer que l'information est accessible aux lecteurs. Utiliser l'acronyme du recueil tel que présenté dans la source et toujours inclure l'indication géographique et la cour.

2 Législation F-21

2 LÉGISLATION

2.1 LOIS

2.1.1 Modèle de base

Titre, | recueil | indication géographique | année, | chapitre, | autres éléments d'indexation | (session ou supplément), | référence précise.

> *Code criminel*, LRC 1985, c C-46, art 745.

Ne pas mettre d'espace entre le recueil et l'indication géographique.

Si la référence à une loi contient une session ou un supplément, omettre la virgule qui suivrait normalement l'élément qui précède.

> *Loi de l'impôt sur le revenu*, LRC 1985, c 1 (5e supp), art 18(1)(m)(iv)(c).

La *Charte québécoise* et la *Déclaration canadienne des droits* doivent être citées en conformité avec les règles de la présente section malgré leur statut quasi constitutionnel.

> *Charte des droits et libertés de la personne*, RLRQ c C-12, art 10.
> *Déclaration canadienne des droits*, LC 1960, c 44, art 2.

Pour faire référence à des documents législatifs autochtones, inclure les renseignements essentiels et nécessaires afin que le lecteur puisse retracer la source. Si le titre du document n'est ni en français ni en anglais, fournir une description entre parenthéses ou une traduction entre crochets. Ne pas mettre ces renseignements supplémentaires en italique. Ce n'est pas nécessaire de traduire les noms des nations autochtones.

> *Akwesasne Tekaia'torehthà:ke Kaianerénhsera* [Loi relative aux tribunaux d'Akwesasne], Kaiahnehronshera Iehiontakwa [Registre de lois] No 2016-01, (2016), adoptée en vertu de la Mohawk Council Resolution 2015/2016-332, en ligne (pdf): *Mohawk Council of Akwesasne* <webdev.akwesasne.ca> [perma.cc/9MW6-VXTZ].
> *Tk'emlúps te Secwépemc Property Transfer Tax Law*, 2017, art 4, en ligne (pdf): *Tk'emlúps* <tkemlups.ca> [perma.cc/BV5R-5LW3].

2.1.2 Référence à un moment précis

Pour faire référence à une loi telle qu'elle parut à un moment précis lorsque la forme de référence standard est inadéquate, utiliser **telle que parue le [jour mois année]** ou **telle que parue en [mois année]** pour clarifier le moment auquel on se réfère.

> *Loi de l'impôt sur le revenu*, LRC 1985, c 1 (5e supp), art 20(1)(c) **telle que parue le 12 octobre 2012**.

2.1.3 Sources

Dans cet ordre, chercher la législation dans (1) les versions électroniques officielles de chaque juridiction. Si la version officielle n'est pas disponible en ligne, faire référence aux

(2) volumes imprimés de lois révisées, refondues ou réadoptées. En dernier recours, faire référence aux (3) recueils annuels. Ne faire référence aux recueils annuels que lorsqu'une loi est adoptée après la publication de la plus récente révision ou lorsque les articles pertinents ont été ajoutés ou modifiés depuis la publication de la plus récente révision.

Consulter le tableau ci-dessous pour trouver les versions électroniques officielles. Ce tableau fournit les sites internet les plus pertinents pour chercher la législation dans chaque juridiction. Pour plusieurs juridictions, les versions officielles ne sont pas disponibles en ligne. Les sites internet suivis d'un astérisque (*) renvoient à des versions non officielles de la législation. Les versions électroniques officielles sont citées de la même manière que les versions imprimées; indiquer l'URL seulement lorsqu'une version non officielle est citée.

Juridiction	Site internet
Canada	lois-laws.justice.gc.ca/fra
Alberta	www.qp.alberta.ca/Laws_Online.cfm
Colombie-Britannique	www.bclaws.ca*
Île-du-Prince-Édouard	www.princeedwardisland.ca/fr/legislation/all*
Manitoba	web2.gov.mb.ca/laws/index.fr.php*
Nouveau-Brunswick	www2.gnb.ca/content/gnb/fr/ministeres/procureur_general/lois_et_reglements.html
Nouvelle-Écosse	nslegislature.ca/fr/legislative-business/bills-statutes
Nunavut	www.nunavutlegislation.ca/fr
Ontario	www.ontario.ca/fr/lois
Québec	legisquebec.gouv.qc.ca/fr/home
Saskatchewan	www.publications.gov.sk.ca/freelaw*
Terre-Neuve-et-Labrador	www.assembly.nl.ca/legislation
Territoires du Nord-Ouest	www.justice.gov.nt.ca/fr/legislation-des-tno*
Yukon	www.gov.yk.ca/legislation/fr/index.html*

Nunavut : Pour les lois adoptées par les Territoires du Nord-Ouest spécifiquement à l'égard du Nunavut et avant le 1er avril 1999, ajouter **telle qu'adoptée pour le Nunavut, conformément à la *Loi sur le Nunavut*, LC 1993, c 28** à la suite de la référence standard.

> *Loi sur l'organisation judiciaire*, LTN-O 1998, c 34, telle qu'adoptée pour le Nunavut, conformément à la *Loi sur le Nunavut*, LC 1993, c 28.

Beaucoup de lois des Territoires du Nord-Ouest sont appliquées *mutatis mutandis* au Nunavut en vertu de l'article 29 de la loi fédérale *Loi sur le Nunavut*, LC 1993, c 28. Le cas échéant, ajouter la formule **telle que dupliquée pour le Nunavut par l'article 29 de la*Loi sur le Nunavut*, LC 1993 c 28** à la suite de la référence standard.

Loi sur les langues officielles, LRTN-O 1998, c O-1, telle que dupliquée pour le Nunavut par l'article 29 de la *Loi sur le Nunavut*, LC 1993, c 28.

Québec : Le Québec entretient le Recueil des lois et des règlements du Québec (**RLRQ**), un **recueil officiel des lois en vigueur constamment mis à jour** disponible en ligne. Les références faites à cette base de données utilisent la désignation RLRQ au lieu de LQ ou LRQ. Cette base de données est constamment mise à jour et n'est pas datée; ainsi, il ne faut pas écrire de date pour faire référence au RLRQ.

Loi sur les valeurs mobilières, **RLRQ** c V-1.1, art 9.

Les **versions historiques officielles** depuis 1969 sont disponibles en ligne au <www3.publicationsduquebec.gouv.qc.ca/loisreglements/loisannuelles.fr.html>. Utiliser la désignation **LQ** ou **LRQ** pour faire référence aux versions historiques. Actuellement, les années 1977-1995 ne sont disponibles qu'en français.

Loi sur les caisses d'entraide économique, **LRQ** c C-3, art 1.

2.1.4 Titre

Utiliser le **titre abrégé officiel**, qui se trouve généralement dans le premier article de la loi. S'il n'y a aucun titre abrégé, indiquer le titre qui se trouve au début de la loi. N'ajouter l'article défini (**le**, **la**) que s'il fait partie du titre (tel qu'indiqué dans le titre abrégé officiel ou au début de la loi). Si le titre de la loi est indiqué dans le corps du texte, ne pas le répéter dans la référence.

Indiquer le titre de la loi en italique et mettre une virgule non italique après le titre. Si l'année fait partie du titre de la loi, elle doit être indiquée comme telle en italique (par ex. *Loi de 2000 sur la cour d'appel*). Inclure l'année après la législature même si l'année fait partie du titre. Respecter l'usage des majuscules dans le titre de la loi.

N.B. Les lois sont adoptées en français et en anglais dans les juridictions suivantes : Canada, Manitoba, Nouveau-Brunswick, Ontario, Québec, Nunavut, les Territoires du Nord-Ouest et Yukon. Toutefois, il est possible que des lois adoptées avant une certaine date n'existent qu'en anglais.

Loi de 2000 sur la cour d'appel, LS 2000, c C-42.1, art 11.
Health Care Protection Act, SA 2000, c H-3.3.

2.1.5 Lois révisées et recueils annuels

Abréger **Lois révisées**, **Lois refondues** et **Lois réadoptées** par **LR**. Abréger **Lois** et **Statuts** par **L** pour les références aux volumes annuels. Abréger **Statutes** par S. Utiliser **L** pour **Lois** (et non **O** pour **Ordonnances**) pour une référence à un recueil de lois des Territoires du Nord-Ouest ou du Yukon.

Code des droits de la personne, **LRO** 1990, c H.19.
Loi sur les compagnies, **RLRQ** c C-38, art 29.
Protected Areas of British Columbia Act, **SBC** 2000, c 17.

Lorsqu'une loi ne se trouve pas dans les recueils actuels de lois révisées, ne pas présumer que la loi n'existe pas ou qu'elle n'est plus pertinente. Par exemple, la *York University Act, 1965*, SO 1965, c 143 reste en vigueur même si elle n'est pas incluse dans une révision. Certaines provinces, comme l'Ontario, listent ces lois dans une table des lois non consolidées.

2.1.6 Recueils à feuilles mobiles

Les recueils à feuilles mobiles sont des consolidations de législation continuellement mises à jour. Ainsi, une référence à un recueil à feuilles mobiles ne contient pas de date et le recueil est présumé être la version la plus récente (si plus de précision est nécessaire, faire référence à un moment précis, section 2.1.2). Avec l'arrivée des consolidations en ligne, les recueils à feuilles mobiles sont de moins en moins utilisés.

Les provinces du Manitoba et de la Nouvelle-Écosse publient une version officielle des recueils à feuilles mobiles. (Certaines juridictions, telles que l'Alberta, publient un recueil à feuilles mobiles non officiel).

Le Manitoba, qui n'a pas de base de données officielle en ligne, maintient un service de recueil à feuilles mobiles intitulé *la Codification permanente des lois du Manitoba* (CPLM); cependant, cette publication ne doit être utilisée qu'en tant que source parallèle optionnelle, accompagnant une référence principale faite soit aux lois révisées, soit aux recueils annuels. Ne pas mettre de virgule entre le recueil et le numéro de chapitre.

> *Code des droits de la personne*, LM 1987-88, c 45, **CPLM c H175**, art 8.

Le Québec a cessé de produire les mises à jour des recueils à feuilles mobiles du RSQ en 2010 quand ce service a été remplacé par le Recueil des lois et règlements du Québec.

2.1.7 Indication géographique

Inscrire l'indication géographique immédiatement après le recueil. Voir la colonne des lois et des gazettes de **l'annexe A-1** pour les abréviations d'autres juridictions.

Voir **l'annexe A-1** pour les abréviations d'autres juridictions.

> *Loi sur les agences de voyages*, **LRO** 1990, c T.19.
> *Workers Compensation Act*, **SPEI** 1994, c 67.

2.1.8 Année, session et supplément

Écrire l'année après l'indication géographique, suivie d'une virgule. Si un numéro de session ou de supplément suit l'année, placer la virgule après l'indication de ce numéro ou de ce supplément. Ne pas indiquer l'année pour le Recueil de lois et règlements du Québec (RLRQ) ou pour les recueils à feuilles mobiles du Manitoba (**CPLM**), puisque ces sources sont continuellement mises à jour et ne contiennent pas de date de publication. S'il est nécessaire d'ajouter plus de précision, utiliser la référence à un moment précis dans le temps (section 2.1.2).

> *Loi de 1998 sur l'adoption internationale*, LO **1998**, c 29.

Lorsqu'une **session s'étend sur plus d'une année**, se référer à toutes les années sur lesquelles s'étend le recueil (par ex. **1980–81**).

> *Hospital Act*, LY **1989-90**, c 13.

Si un **recueil contient les lois de plusieurs sessions**, les chapitres sont numérotés indépendamment pour chaque session. Indiquer entre parenthèses le numéro de la session (**1re**, **2e**, **3e** ou **4e**), suivi de **sess** après l'année.

> *An Act to Amend the Labour Act*, SPEI **2000 (1re sess)**, c 7.

Faire référence au **supplément** pour les lois et modifications qui ont été adoptées pendant l'année d'une révision ou d'une refonte des lois, mais qui n'ont pas été comprises dans la refonte. Par exemple, le LRC 1985 n'a été mis en vigueur qu'à la fin de l'année 1988. Ainsi, les lois de 1985–1988 ont été réimprimées pour les mettre à niveau avec les lois nouvellement révisées (Premier supplément = lois de 1985; Deuxième supplément = lois de 1986; Troisième supplément = lois de 1987; Quatrième supplément = lois de 1988; Cinquième supplément = *Loi de l'impôt sur le revenu*). Indiquer entre parenthèses le numéro de supplément, suivi de **supp** après le chapitre.

> *Loi sur les douanes*, LRC 1985, c 1 **(2e supp)**.

Pour les lois fédérales adoptées avant 1867, ainsi que pour les lois provinciales adoptées avant que la province ne se joigne à la confédération, indiquer **l'année du règne** entre parenthèses, à la suite de l'année du calendrier.

Anne	Ann
Edward	Edw
Elizabeth	Eliz

George	Geo
Victoria	Vict
William	Will

> *An Act respecting the Civilization and Enfranchisement of certain Indians*, S Prov C 1859 **(22 Vict)**, c 9.

2.1.9 Chapitre

Abréger chapitre par **c** et écrire la référence du chapitre telle qu'indiquée dans le recueil, **incluant les traits d'union et les points**.

> *Chester Trails Act*, RSNS 2001, **c 21**.
> *Loi sur les tribunaux judiciaires*, RLRQ **c T-16**.
> *Loi sur le cadastre*, RLRQ **c C-1**.

Entre 1934 et 1975–76, les lois des recueils annuels de Terre-Neuve sont désignées par un numéro. Abréger **numéro** par **n°**.

> *Landlord and Tenant (Residential Tenancies) Act, 1973*, SN 1973, **n° 18**.

2.1.10 Référence précise

Pour indiquer un article particulier d'une loi, insérer une virgule à la suite du chapitre, puis écrire la référence précise. Abréger **article** et **articles** par **art** et **arts** (et non **à l'art**) dans les notes de bas de page, mais jamais dans le corps du texte.

> *Environmental Protection and Enhancement Act*, RSA 2000, c E-12, **arts** 2, 38-42, 84.

Indiquer les subdivisions plus précises (paragraphes, alinéas, sous-alinéas) comme elles apparaissent dans la loi citée. Mettre entre parenthèses chaque subdivision même s'il n'y a pas de parenthèses dans la version officielle de la loi. Noter que l'abréviation demeure **art** même si la référence est faite à une plus petite subdivision.

> *Legal Profession Act*, 1990, SS 1990, c L-10.1, **arts 4(1), 6(2)(b)(i)—(ii), 9**.

Faire référence à une subdivision non numérotée ou sans désignation alphabétique comme à un alinéa. Utiliser l'abréviation **al**.

> *Charte de la langue française*, RLRQ c C-11, préambule, **al** 3.

Consulter la section 1.5 pour obtenir des renseignements généraux sur les références précises.

2.1.11 Modifications, abrogations et remises en vigueur

Il est sous-entendu que les références se rapportent à la **loi telle que modifiée à la date de publication** du texte de l'auteur.

> *Loi sur les représentations théâtrales*, LRQ 1977, c R-25.

Indiquer que la loi a été modifiée uniquement si cette mention est pertinente à la question traitée dans le texte. Lorsqu'il y a une modification, faire référence d'abord à la loi originale, suivie de **modifiée par** et de la référence à la nouvelle loi. Indiquer le titre de la deuxième loi (qu'il s'agisse d'une loi modifiée ou abrogée, ou d'une loi modifiant ou abrogeant) uniquement s'il est différent du titre de la première loi ou s'il n'est pas compris dans le titre de celle-ci.

> *Loi sur les mesures d'urgence*, LM 1987-88, c 11, **modifiée par LM 1997, c 28**.
>
> *Municipal Government Act*, RSA 2000, c M-26, art 694(4), **modifiée par** *Municipal Government Amendment Act*, SA 2003, c 43, art 4.

Dans le cas d'une loi qui a été **abrogée**, se référer à la loi abrogative en l'introduisant par la formule **abrogée par**.

> *Loi sur les prestations familiales*, LRO 1990, c F.22, **abrogée par *Loi de 1997 sur la réforme de l'aide sociale*, LO 1997, c 25, art 4(1)**.

Indiquer **modifiant** lorsqu'une référence est faite à une **loi qui modifie une loi antérieure** et indiquer **abrogeant** lorsqu'il s'agit d'une loi qui abroge une loi antérieure.

> *Loi modifiant la Loi sur les normes du travail*, LTN-O 1999, c 18, **modifiant LRTN-O 1988, c L-1**.

Loi sur la Société de développement autochtone de la Baie James, RLRQ c S-9.1, **abrogeant** ***Loi constituant la Société de développement autochtone de la Baie James*****, LQ 1978, c 96**.

Si une loi ou une partie d'une loi a été **abrogée et remplacée par une autre**, se référer à la loi originale en premier, suivie de **remise en vigueur par** et de la référence complète de la nouvelle partie. N'utiliser cette terminologie que lorsque les dispositions abrogées et remplacées se trouvent dans le même article.

2.1.12 Annexes

Pour les lois paraissant dans une annexe, indiquer la révision ou le volume dont fait partie l'annexe, suivi d'une virgule et du numéro de l'annexe. Toujours indiquer la référence officielle, suivie de **reproduite dans** pour introduire la référence à l'annexe. Écrire le numéro de l'annexe en chiffres romains.

Déclaration canadienne des droits, LC 1960, c 44, **reproduite dans LRC 1985, annexe III**.

2.1.13 Loi contenue dans une autre loi

Faire référence au titre de la loi contenue dans la loi principale en premier lieu, suivi d'une virgule. Écrire ensuite la référence complète de la partie pertinente de la loi principale, introduite par **constituant**. Les références précises à la loi contenue sont indiquées avant la référence à la loi principale.

Loi sur la Société d'expansion du Cap-Breton, art 27, **constituant** la partie II de la *Loi organique de 1987 sur le Canada atlantique*, LC 1988, c 50.

2.2 LOIS CONSTITUTIONNELLES

Beaucoup de lois constitutionnelles ont été adoptées sous des noms différents de ceux couramment utilisés; il faut utiliser le **nouveau titre**. Consulter l'annexe de la *Loi constitutionnelle de 1982* pour trouver le nouveau titre de la loi. Si l'ancien titre est pertinent, l'indiquer entre parenthèses à la fin de la référence. Au besoin, inclure une référence à l'**annexe II des LRC 1985** après la référence officielle puisque la plupart des lois constitutionnelles canadiennes s'y trouvent.

Indiquer les références précises aux articles de la *Charte canadienne* et de la *Loi constitutionnelle de 1982* immédiatement après le titre. Indiquer les références précises aux autres lois constitutionnelles après le numéro du chapitre.

Pour faire référence à des documents constitutionnels autochtones, inclure les renseignements essentiels et nécessaires afin que le lecteur puisse retracer la source. Si le titre du document n'est ni en français ni en anglais, fournir une description entre parenthèses ou une traduction entre crochets. Ne pas mettre ces renseignements supplémentaires en italique.

Lois constitutionnelles :

> *Loi constitutionnelle de 1867* (R-U), 30 & 31 Vict, c 3, art 91, reproduit dans LRC 1985, annexe II, n° 5.
>
> *Loi constitutionnelle de 1982*, art 35, constituant l'annexe B de la *Loi de 1982 sur le Canada* (R-U), 1982, c 11.

Charte canadienne :

> *Charte canadienne des droits et libertés*, art 7, partie I de la *Loi constitutionnelle de 1982*, constituant l'annexe B de la *Loi de 1982 sur le Canada* (R-U), 1982, c 11.

Constitutions autochtones :

> *Nipissing Gichi-Naaknigewin* (constitution de Nipissing First Nation), (2014).
>
> *Nunatsiavut Constitution Act*, CIL 31-12-2012 N-3, en ligne (pdf) : <www.nunatsiavut.com/wp-content/uploads/2015/07/CIL-31-12-2012-N-3 Nunatsiavut-Constitiution-Act.pdf> [perma.cc/ZC35-89XB].

2.3 CODES

Ne pas fournir la référence complète pour désigner un code canadien. Pour un code mentionné ci-dessous, utiliser le nom abrégé dès la première référence. Noter que les titres complets sont en italique alors que les titres abrégés sont en caractères romains.

Titre complet	**Titre abrégé**
Code civil du Québec	CcQ
Code civil du Québec (1980)	CcQ (1980)
Code civil du Bas Canada	CcBC
Code de procédure civile	Cpc
Code de procédure pénale	Cpp

Pour un code canadien qui n'est pas dans cette liste, suivre le modèle de base de la section 2.1.1 pour la première référence et créer une version abrégée pour les références ultérieures si nécessaire. Pour faire référence à l'ancien *Code de procédure civile*, ajouter l'année d'adoption **(1965)** entre parenthèses à la suite de l'abréviation.

> Art 477 Cpc **(1965)**.

Pour faire référence aux Commentaires du ministre à propos du Code civil du Québec, voir la section 4.2.1. Pour faire référence à un code annoté, voir le dernier exemple de la section 6.2.1.

2.4 PROJETS DE LOI

Numéro, | *titre*, | session, | législature, | indication géographique, | année, | référence précise | (renseignements supplémentaires).

Le numéro des projets de loi de la Chambre des communes est précédé par **C-**, et le numéro des projets de loi du Sénat par **S-**.

Indiquer le **titre non abrégé** du projet de loi. Mettre le titre en italique et respecter l'usage des majuscules.

Pour une référence à un projet de loi provincial, mentionner l'indication géographique.

Ne pas indiquer l'année du règne.

Diviser les projets de loi en **articles** (**art** ou **arts**). Indiquer les renseignements supplémentaires (par ex. la date d'une des lectures ou l'étape franchie dans l'adoption du projet de loi) entre parenthèses à la fin de la référence, s'il y a lieu. Si possible, indiquer le numéro de chapitre de la future loi en tant que renseignement supplémentaire (par ex. **(sanctionnée le 21 juin 2001), LQ 2001, c 32**).

Canada

PL C-7, *Loi concernant l'Agence des services frontaliers du Canada*, 1re sess, 37e parl, 2005, art 5(1)(e) (adopté par la Chambre des communes le 13 juin 2005).

PL S-1, *Loi concernant les chemins de fer*, 2e sess, 40e lég, 2009, art 1 (première lecture le 26 janvier 2009).

Provinces et territoires

PL 161, *Loi concernant le cadre juridique des technologies de l'information*, 2e sess, 36e lég, Québec, 2001 (sanctionné le 21 juin 2001), LQ 2001, c 32.

2.5 RÈGLEMENTS

Le tableau ci-dessous fournit des renseignements quant à la forme à privilégier pour faire référence aux règlements selon l'indication géographique. Noter qu'il n'existe pas toujours une version refondue des règlements (le mot « refondu » signifie aux fins de la présente section « refondu », « révisé » ou « réadopté »). Dans la colonne du modèle de base des règlements, le mot « année » est suivi d'un astérisque (*) lorsque seulement les deux derniers numéros doivent être indiqués. Noter également que l'année dans le cas des règlements refondus est l'année de la refonte.

Indication géographique		**Modèle de base**	**Exemple**
Canada	Refondu	*Titre*, **CRC**, chapitre, référence précise (année).	*Règlement sur les oiseaux migrateurs*, CRC, c 1035, art 4 (1978).
	Non refondu	**DORS**/année-numéro, référence précise.	DORS/2000-111, art 4.

Législation

Indication géographique		Modèle de base	Exemple
Alberta		**Alta Reg** numéro/année, référence précise.	Alta Reg 184/2001, art 2.
Colombie-Britannique		**BC Reg** numéro/année, référence précise.	BC Reg 362/2000, art 6.
Île-du-Prince-Édouard		**PEI Reg EC** année-numéro, référence précise.	PEI Reg EC1999-598, art 3.
Manitoba	Refondu	**Règl du Man** numéro/année*R, référence précise.	Règl du Man 468/88R, art 2.
	Non refondu	**Règl du Man** numéro/année, référence précise.	Règl du Man 155/2001, art 3.
Nouveau-Brunswick		**Règl du N-B** année-numéro, référence précise.	Règl du N-B 2000-8, art 11.
Nouvelle-Écosse		**NS Reg** numéro/année, référence précise.	NS Reg 24/2000, art 8.
Nunavut		**Règl du Nu** numéro-année*, référence précise.	Règl du Nu 045-99, art 2.
Ontario	Refondu	**RRO** année, **Reg** numéro, référence précise.	RRO 1990, Reg 1015, art 3.
	Non refondu	**Règl de l'Ont** numéro/année*, référence précise.	Règl de l'Ont 426/00, art 2.
Québec	Refondu	**RLRQ** chapitre, numéro du règlement, référence précise.	RLRQ c C-11, r 9, art 10.
	Non refondu	**D** numéro-année*, date, référence à la *Gazette*, référence précise.	D 868-97, 2 juillet 1997, (1997) GOQ II 3692, art 2.
Saskatchewan	Refondu	**RRS** chapitre, **Reg** numéro, référence précise.	RRS c C-50.2, Reg 21, art 6.
	Non refondu	**Sask Reg** numéro/année, référence précise.	Sask Reg 67/2001, art 3.
Terre-Neuve-et-Labrador	Refondu	**CNLR** numéro/année*, référence précise.	CNLR 1151/96, art 6.
	Non refondu	**NLR** numéro/année*, référence précise.	NLR 08/02, art 2.

Indication géographique		Modèle de base	Exemple
Territoires du Nord-Ouest	Refondu	**RRTN-O** année, chapitre, référence précise.	RRTN-O 1990, c E-27, art 16.
	Non refondu	**Règl des TN-O** numéro-année*, référence précise.	Règl des TN-O 253-77, art 3.
Yukon		**YD** année/numéro, référence précise.	YD 2000/130, art 9.

Toujours inclure le titre du règlement pour faire référence à la Codification des règlements du Canada. Dans tous les autres cas, l'indication du titre du règlement au début de la référence est facultative, mais fortement conseillée. Le titre doit être italique et suivi d'une virgule.

Canada : Les règlements fédéraux promulgués après la codification se trouvent dans la **partie II de la Gazette du Canada**. Ne pas faire directement référence à la *Gazette*. Pour faire référence aux règlements promulgués à partir de l'année 2000, inclure les quatre numéros de l'année. Pour les règlements promulgués avant l'année 2000, utiliser exceptionnellement les deux derniers chiffres de l'année même s'il n'y a pas d'astérisque dans le tableau.

Règlement sur la compensation de la taxe (TPS/TVH), DORS/**91**-49, art 4.

Terre-Neuve : Toutes les références à Terre-Neuve ont été changées pour Terre-Neuve-et-Labrador. N'utiliser la section « Terre-Neuve » du tableau ci-dessus que pour les règlements qui ont été abrogés avant le 6 décembre 2001. Utiliser la section « Terre-Neuve-et-Labrador » pour tous les autres règlements.

Québec : Voir la section 2.6.1 pour faire référence à la *Gazette officielle du Québec*.

Le tableau ci-dessous donne la signification des différentes abréviations employées dans cette section. Pour les abréviations d'indications géographiques, consulter la colonne sur les règlements du tableau de l'**annexe A-1**.

Abréviation	Signification	Abréviation	Signification
CRC	Codification des règlements du Canada	RR	Revised Regulations
DORS	Décrets, ordonnances et règlements	EC	Executive Council
Reg/R	Regulation(s)	D	Décret
CNR	Consolidated Newfoundland Regulation	OC/OIC	Orders in Council
CNLR	Consolidated Newfoundland and Labrador Regulation	GOQ	*Gazette officielle du Québec*

Législation

Abréviation	Signification	Abréviation	Signification
Règl	Règlement(s)	RLRQ	Recueil des lois et des règlements du Québec

2.6 AUTRES INFORMATIONS PUBLIÉES DANS LES *GAZETTES*

2.6.1 Modèle de base

Titre (information supplémentaire), | (année) | abréviation de la *Gazette* | partie de la *Gazette*, | page | (renseignements supplémentaires).

Indiquer le titre du document s'il y a lieu. Si le document est numéroté, inclure le numéro avec le titre, tel qu'indiqué dans la *Gazette*. Inclure le numéro du texte réglementaire (**TR**) après l'abréviation s'il y en a un. Le nom de la personne ou de la partie concernée par un avis peut être inclus entre parenthèses après le titre.

Indiquer la partie de la *Gazette* après l'abréviation. Si la *Gazette* n'est pas publiée en plusieurs parties, indiquer la page immédiatement après le point suivant l'année (**GOQ, 74**). Inclure des renseignements supplémentaires nécessaires, comme le nom de la loi en vertu de laquelle un décret est promulgué (voir *Provincial Parks Act*).

Ministerial Order 36/91, (1991) A Gaz I, 1609.
Avis (Banque du Canada), (1995) Gaz C I, 4412.
D309/2001, (2001) A Gaz I, 1752 (*Provincial Parks Act*).

N.B. La version PDF de la *Gazette du Canada* est officielle depuis le 1er avril 2003 sur le site <www.gazette.gc.ca>.

2.6.2 Décrets

Un décret est un instrument du pouvoir exécutif mettant en œuvre une décision du gouvernement (par ex. la création d'un règlement).

2.6.2.1 Fédéral

Titre, | CP année-numéro **ou** numéro du texte réglementaire, | référence à la *Gazette*, | (renseignements supplémentaires).

Inclure le titre en italique s'il y en a un. Abréger **Conseil Privé** par **CP**. Inscrire le numéro du texte réglementaire (**TR**), s'il y a lieu. Inclure des renseignements supplémentaires entre parenthèses à la fin de la référence (par ex. le titre de la loi en vertu de laquelle le décret a été promulgué) s'il y a lieu.

CP 1997-627, (1997) Gaz C II, 1381.
Décret refusant d'annuler ou de référer au CRTC une décision concernant CFJO-FM, TR/97-51, (1997) Gaz C II, 1523.

Législation

2.6.2.2 *Provincial et territorial*

Titre, | numéro du décret, | référence à la *Gazette* | (renseignements supplémentaires).

Inclure le titre en italique s'il y a lieu. Pour les ***Orders in Council***, utiliser l'abréviation et le numéro qui apparaissent dans la Gazette. Utiliser D pour **Décret**. Le numéro comprend parfois l'année ou les deux derniers chiffres de l'année. Inclure des renseignements supplémentaires entre parenthèses à la fin de la référence si nécessaire (par ex. le titre de la loi en vertu de laquelle le décret est promulgué).

> D 1989/19, (1989) Gaz Y II, 57.
>
> *Town of Paradise Order*, OC 99-529, (1999) N Gaz II, 451 (*Municipalities Act*).
>
> *Règlement sur la levée de la suspension et sur l'application de l'article 411 de la* Loi sur les normes du travail à l'égard de certains salariés, D 570-93, (1993) GOQ II, 3309.

2.6.3 Proclamations et instructions royales

Référence à la loi entrée en vigueur ou émetteur de la Proclamation ou de l'Instruction, | type de document, | date, | numéro du texte réglementaire, | référence.

Inclure le type de document, soit **Proclamation** ou **Instruction royale** si le contexte l'exige.

Indiquer la date, suivie de la *Gazette* ou d'une autre référence. Pour les proclamations fédérales de 1972 à aujourd'hui, indiquer le numéro du texte réglementaire (TR).

> *Loi sur l'Agence spatiale canadienne*, LC 1990, c 13, entrée en vigueur le 14 décembre 1990, TR/91-5, (1991) Gaz C I, 74.
>
> Proclamation, 1er avril 1991, (1991) S Gaz I, 1174.
>
> George R, Proclamation, 7 octobre 1763 (3 Geo III), reproduite dans LRC 1985, ann II, nº 1.
>
> George R au Gouverneur Arthur Phillip, Instruction royale, 25 avril 1787 (27 Geo III), reproduite dans *Historical Documents of New South Wales*, t 1, 2e partie, Sydney, Government Printer, 1892-1901 à la p 67.

2.7 RÈGLEMENTS MUNICIPAUX

Ville, | Règlement ou Règlement refondu | numéro, | *titre* | (date), | référence précise.

Indiquer le titre complet s'il n'existe pas de titre abrégé.

Non refondus

> Ville de Blainville, Règlement nº 955-43, *Règlement de zonage* (10 janvier 1994), art 2366.

Refondus

> Ville de Montréal, Règlement refondu c S-011, *Règlement sur les Services de collecte*, art 5.

2.8 RÈGLES DE PRATIQUE

Indication géographique, | organisme, | *titre*, | numéro d'indexation, | information d'indexation additionnelle, | référence précise.

Les règles de pratique (ou règles de procédure) balisent et régissent le fonctionnement des organes ou organismes judiciaires et administratifs. Écrire l'indication géographique et l'organisme à moins que l'information ne fasse partie du titre des règles. Voir la colonne des abréviations postales de **l'annexe A-1**. Ne pas écrire **Canada** pour les règles de la Cour suprême du Canada, ni pour les règles de la Cour fédérale. Abréger **règle** par **r**. Pour faire référence au ***Code de procédure civile*** et au ***Code de procédure pénale*** du Québec, voir la section 2.3.

> *Règles de la Cour suprême du Canada*, r 16.
> Commission québécoise des liberations conditionnelles, *Règles de pratique*, r 10(4).
> Alberta, *Rules of Court*, AR 124/2010, vol 1, r 10.50.

2.9 COMMISSIONS DE VALEURS MOBILIÈRES

Titre, | commission | document | bulletin | (date), | référence précise.

Pour les **instructions canadiennes**, les **normes canadiennes**, et autres documents de valeurs mobilières, faire référence aux **commissions de valeurs mobilières provinciales**. Abréger **Instruction canadienne** par **IC** et **Norme canadienne** par **NC**. Pour les **modifications**, les **règlements en consultation**, les **avis du personnel** et d'autres textes de commission, faire référence au **Bulletin de commission** ou à une autre publication similaire. Si des règlements ou des textes sont uniquement publiés en anglais, indiquer le nom de la commission et du document en anglais.

> *Mutual Reliance Review System for Exemptive Relief Applications*, OSC NP 12-201, (2005) 28 Bull de CVMO 7166.
> *Proposed Amendments to Multilateral Instrument 52-109 Certification of Disclosure in Issuers' Annual and Interim Filings and Companion Policy 52-109CP*, MSC Notice 2005-19 (1 avril 2005).
> *Règlement 62-104 sur les offres publiques d'achat et de rachat*, AMF Consultation, (2006) 3:20 BAMF : Valeurs mobilières 1 à la p 2.

3 Jurisprudence F-37

3 JURISPRUDENCE

3.1 SOURCES

Ordre hiérarchique des sources :

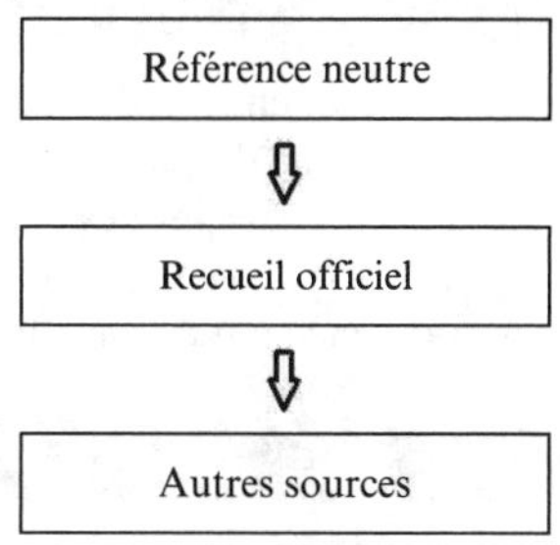

Il est fortement recommandé de citer au moins deux sources (référence principale et référence parallèle) en l'absence de référence neutre. Lorsque plusieurs sources sont identifiées, les lecteurs peuvent accéder plus facilement aux décisions citées. En conformité avec la hiérarchie des sources, la référence parallèle permet d'accentuer la pertinence d'une décision si elle se trouve dans un recueil prestigieux ou spécifique à un domaine du droit (par ex. DLR, CCC, Admin LR, etc.).

La référence principale doit être faite à la source disponible la plus élevée suivant la hiérarchie des sources. La référence parallèle doit être faite à la deuxième source disponible la plus élevée. **Avant de se référer aux sources qui font moins autorité, s'assurer que les sources faisant le plus autorité ne sont pas disponibles.**

Lorsqu'une référence neutre est disponible, elle doit toujours constituer la référence principale. En règle générale, une référence parallèle n'est pas requise lorsque la référence neutre est indiquée. N'inclure une référence parallèle que si la cour en question n'a pas assigné elle-même de numéros de paragraphe.

En l'absence de référence neutre ou lorsqu'une référence parallèle est tout de même requise, faire référence aux recueils officiels pour les juridictions nationales.

En dernier lieu, faire référence à d'autres sources, soit des recueils non officiels ou des services de bases de données en ligne. Le présent *Manuel* établit une hiérarchie entre les différentes sources comprises dans la catégorie des « autres sources ». Privilégier les services de bases de données en ligne qui sont aisément accessibles, et les recueils non officiels qui sont détenus par la majorité des bibliothèques de droit et qui contiennent des versions intégrales des décisions. Dans l'**annexe C-2**, les sources à privilégier sont suivies d'un astérisque (*).

3.2 MODÈLE DE BASE

Intitulé, ∣ référence principale ∣ référence précise, ∣ référence parallèle ∣ [*titre abrégé*].

Fisher v Fisher, 2008 ONCA 11 aux para 52-59 [*Fisher*].
Gordon c Goertz, [1996] 2 RCS 27 au para 13, 134 DLR (4e) 321 [*Gordon*].

Les sections subséquentes décrivent en détail chacun des éléments requis suivant ce modèle de base. À noter que plusieurs éléments exclus du modèle ci-dessus doivent être néanmoins incorporés à la référence dans certains cas spécifiques (année de la décision, indication géographique, cour, juge, étapes successives de la cause, etc.). Consulter les sections ci-après pour plus de renseignements quant à ces éléments supplémentaires.

3.3 INTITULÉ

L'intitulé est une version abrégée du titre d'une décision qui permet de s'y référer de manière informelle. **Lorsque l'intitulé est indiqué dans le recueil principal, utiliser cet intitulé tel quel.** Si la décision ne fournit pas d'intitulé, voir les sections 3.3.1 à 3.3.18. Ne pas répéter l'intitulé dans la note de bas de page s'il est déjà mentionné dans le texte. Mettre en italique les noms des parties et le *c* ou le *v* qui sépare les noms des parties. L'utilisation du *c* ou du *v* dans l'intitulé indique la langue dans laquelle la décision est rendue. Si la décision est rendue en anglais, utiliser le *v*.

Pacific Developments Ltd v Calgary (Ville de)

Si la décision est rendue en français, utiliser le *c*.

Traverse Trois-Pistoles Escoumins Ltée c Québec (Commission des transports)

Pour les décisions bilingues, utilisez le *c* pour la rédaction d'un texte en français.

Comité pour le traitement égal des actionnaires minoritaires de la Société Asbestos Ltée c Ontario (Commission des valeurs mobilières)

Quand l'intitulé comprend des termes qui apparaissent normalement en italique, il faut mettre ceux-ci en caractères romains (italique inversé). Ceci s'applique, par exemple, à un navire qui est poursuivi in rem (par ex. *Porter v The* **Pinafore**). Comme indiqué ci-haut, cette règle ne s'applique pas aux *v* et *c*.

3.3.1 Noms des parties

N'utiliser que les noms de famille. Omettre les prénoms et les initiales.

Blackburn-Moreault** c **Moreault
Marcil** c **Hétu

Lorsqu'il y a jonction de plusieurs instances, ne mentionner que la première instance. Éviter l'expression **et al** pour indiquer qu'il y a plusieurs parties.

Mettre en majuscule la première lettre du nom de chaque partie, ainsi que la première lettre des noms propres. Ne pas mettre en majuscule les prépositions, les conjonctions et les autres mots faisant partie des expressions procédurales (par ex. *in re*, *ex rel*). Traduire en français les descriptions telles que **Ville de**, mais ne traduire ni les mots qui appartiennent au nom d'une partie (par ex. **Université**) ni les abréviations (par ex. **Ltée** ou **srl**). Ne pas inclure **Le**, **La**, **L'**, **Les** ou **The** s'il s'agit du premier mot du nom d'une partie, même s'il s'agit d'une raison sociale. Toutefois, indiquer l'article défini s'il fait partie du nom d'une chose poursuivie *in rem* (tel qu'un navire ou un avion, par ex. ***Le Mihalis Angelos***).

3.3.2 Personne représentée par un tuteur

Les expressions telles que (***Tuteur à l'instance***) doivent être entre parenthèses après le nom de la personne représentée.

Dobson ***(Tuteur à l'instance)*** *c Dobson*

3.3.3 Noms corporatifs et noms de sociétés

Il est important d'identifier les entités commerciales comme telles. Ainsi, toujours inclure **Ltd**, **Ltée**, **srl** ou **LLP**. Ne pas traduire ces expressions ou abréviations. Indiquer les prénoms et les initiales qui font partie de la raison sociale. Indiquer les noms de tous les partenaires d'une société. Lorsqu'une compagnie a un nom bilingue, utiliser le nom de la compagnie dans la langue de la décision de référence. Si la décision est bilingue, utiliser le nom dans la langue du texte rédigé.

Pelletier c ***Madawaska Co Ltée***
JJ Joubert Ltée *c Lapierre*
KPMG ***srl*** *c Lachance*
Lemieux c ***Société*** *Radio-Canada*

3.3.4 Pays, unités fédérales, provinces et municipalités

Indiquer **le nom français du pays habituellement utilisé** et non son nom officiel ou son abréviation.

États-Unis *c Shulman*

Omettre **Province de**, **État de**, **Peuple de** ou tout autre identificateur du genre.

Québec (PG) c *Auger*

Placer les identificateurs, comme **Ville de**, **Communauté urbaine de**, **Comté de**, **District de** ou **Municipalité de** entre parenthèses après le nom du lieu.

Laurentide Motels Ltd c ***Beauport (Ville de)***
Charlesbourg-Est (Municipalité de) *c Asselin*
Vigi Santé Ltée c Montréal ***(Communauté urbaine de)***

3.3.5 Testaments et successions

Ne pas indiquer le nom des exécuteurs testamentaires, seulement le nom de la succession.

*Tremblay c **Trudel, succession***

Le terme **Re** doit précéder le nom de la succession lorsque le demandeur et le défendeur ne sont pas inclus dans l'intitulé.

Re Succession Eurig

Cependant, toujours suivre l'intitulé indiqué par le recueil, même si le **Re** est placé différemment.

Succession Lipton (Re)

3.3.6 Faillites et mises sous séquestre

Indiquer le nom du failli ou de la compagnie mise sous séquestre suivi de **syndic de**, **séquestre de** ou **liquidateur de** entre parenthèses.

*Chablis Textiles **(Syndic de)** c London Life Insurance*
*Lasalle Land Co **(Liquidateur de)** c Alepin*

3.3.7 Titres de lois

Si l'indication géographique ne peut être déduite du nom de la loi, elle doit être indiquée entre parenthèses à la suite du nom de la loi.

Re Code canadien du travail
Renvoi relatif à la Loi sur l'instruction publique (Québec)

3.3.8 La Couronne

Utiliser **R** pour identifier la Couronne pour remplacer les expressions telles que **La Reine**, **Regina**, **La Couronne**, **La Reine du chef de** ou tout terme semblable qui sert à identifier la Couronne.

***R** c Blondin*

3.3.9 Entités gouvernementales

Identifier l'indication géographique que l'entité gouvernementale représente. Utiliser le nom de l'indication géographique, suivi du nom de l'organisme gouvernemental (tel qu'une commission, un ministère ou un département) entre parenthèses. Ne pas répéter l'indication géographique dans la parenthèse.

*Chagnon c Québec **(Commission d'accès à l'information)***

Abréger **Ministre du Revenu national** par **MRN** et **Sous-ministre du Revenu national** par **Sous-MRN**.

*Savard c **MRN***

Écrire l'abréviation **PG** pour désigner **Procureur général**.

Jurisprudence

Schreiber c Canada (PG)

Ne pas inclure le nom d'un individu représentant un organisme gouvernemental.

Canada (Ministre de l'Emploi et de l'Immigration) c Jiminez-Perez

3.3.10 Sociétés d'État

Ne pas indiquer le nom de l'indication géographique avant le nom de la société d'État.

Westaim Corp c ***Monnaie royale canadienne***

3.3.11 Conseils et organismes municipaux

Indiquer le nom du conseil ou de l'organisme municipal après la juridiction.

Québec (PG) c Montréal (Communauté urbaine) ***Service de police***

3.3.12 Conseils scolaires

Omettre les termes tels que **Conseil scolaire** et **Conseil d'administration**; n'indiquer que le nom de l'institution.

Ross c ***District nº 15 du Nouveau-Brunswick***

3.3.13 Syndicats

Ne pas abréger le nom des syndicats, car de telles abréviations varient d'un cas à l'autre.

Lavigne c ***Syndicat des employés de la Fonction publique de l'Ontario***

3.3.14 Agences d'aide sociale

Inclure le nom de la communauté d'où provient l'agence, sauf si le nom de la communauté fait partie du nom de l'agence.

Doe c ***Metropolitan Toronto Child and Family Services***
Manitoba (Directeur de la protection de l'enfance) *c Y*

3.3.15 Noms de parties protégées

Si les noms des parties ne sont pas divulgués, utiliser les initiales disponibles ou le titre et la description numérique fournis dans le recueil.

DP** c **S
Droit de la famille - 1763

3.3.16 Intitulés différents pour une même cause : l'emploi de *sub nom*

Sub nom est l'abréviation de *sub nomine*, soit « sous le nom » en latin. Débuter toute référence par les noms des parties tels qu'ils paraissent dans le recueil le plus officiel (voir la hiérarchie des sources à la section 3.1). Si un autre recueil fait référence aux mêmes parties sous des noms différents, indiquer ***sub nom***, suivi de l'intitulé entre parenthèses immédiatement avant la référence en question.

> *Compagnie des chemins de fer nationaux du Canada c Canada (Commission des droits de la personne)*, [1987] 1 RCS 1114, (***sub nom*** *Action Travail des Femmes* c *Canadian National Railways Co*) 40 DLR (4e) 193.

3.3.17 Tierce partie agissant pour l'une des parties : *ex rel*

Ex rel est l'abréviation d'*ex relatione*, qui signifie « à cause de la relation ou de l'information » en latin.

Utiliser l'expression ***ex rel*** pour indiquer qu'une tierce partie agit au nom d'une autre partie.

> *Ryel c Québec (PG)* ***ex rel*** *Société immobilière du Québec*

3.3.18 Expressions procédurales et renvois constitutionnels

L'expression **Renvoi relatif à** n'est utilisée que pour les renvois constitutionnels. Dans tous les autres cas, écrire ***Re***.

> ***Renvoi relatif à la Loi sur les armes à feu***

Remplacer ***In re***, ***Dans l'affaire de*** et ***In the matter of*** par ***Re***.

> ***Re*** *Denis*

Dans l'intitulé d'une décision, l'expression ***ex parte*** signifie que la partie nommée après la mention a demandé l'action.

> ***Ex parte*** *Royal Dress Co*

Jurisprudence

3.4 ANNÉE DE LA DÉCISION

Lorsqu'une décision comporte une **référence neutre** ou que **l'année de la décision est la même que l'année indiquée dans la référence principale**, ne pas indiquer l'année après l'intitulé.

> *Cadbury Schweppes Inc c Aliments FBI Ltée* **(1999)**, [1999] 1 RCS 142, 59 BCLR (3e) 1.

Lorsque **l'année n'est pas mentionnée dans la référence principale**, fournir l'année de la décision entre parenthèses après l'intitulé. Cette règle vaut quand bien même l'année de la décision est la même que l'année mentionnée dans la référence parallèle. Ne pas mettre l'année en italique.

R v Borden (1993), 24 CR (4e) 184, 1993 CarswellNS 18 (WL Can) (NSCA).

Lorsque **l'année mentionnée dans la référence principale est différente de l'année de la décision**, fournir l'année de la décision entre parenthèses après l'intitulé en plus de l'année indiquée dans la référence principale.

Joyal c Hôpital du Christ-Roi (1996), [1997] RJQ 38, 1996 CarswellQue 1062 (WL Can) (CA).

3.5 RÉFÉRENCE NEUTRE

Les références neutres émanent directement de la cour qui a rendu la décision, et seule la désignation officielle doit être utilisée. Toutes les cours canadiennes et un nombre croissant de tribunaux administratifs ont adopté la référence neutre. Pour connaître leur date d'adoption, voir l'**annexe B-3**.

La référence neutre permet l'identification d'une cause indépendamment des recueils imprimés ou des services éléctroniques dans lesquels elle est publiée. Pour plus de renseignements, consulter la section 3.2.2 (« Référence neutre ») du document du Comité canadien de la référence intitulé *La préparation, la référence et la distribution des décisions canadiennes*, disponible sur <lexum.com/ccc-ccr/preparation/fr>.

R v Senko, 2004 ABQB 60 au para 12.

Ordre des arpenteurs-géomètres du Québec c Tremblay, 2001 QCTP 24 à la n 14.

L'indication géographique et le niveau de la cour sont identifiés dans la référence neutre elle-même. Ne pas ajouter d'abréviation ou d'indication géographique additionnelle. Certains services bases de données en ligne utilisent des codes de désignation qui ressemblent à la référence neutre (par ex. SCJ ou OJ de Quicklaw). N'utiliser ces désignations que pour citer une source provenant de ces bases de données, et non pas en lieu d'une référence neutre officielle.

Dans un texte destiné à un lectorat étranger, ou lorsque référence est faite à de la jurisprudence étrangère, il pourrait être utile d'ajouter avant la référence neutre le code de pays de trois lettres établi par la norme internationale **ISO 3166-1 alpha-3** (par ex. ***R c Law*, CAN 2002 SCC 10**). D'autres exemples de code sont **GBR** pour le Royaume-Uni, **FRA** pour la France, **AUS** pour l'Australie, **NZL** pour la Nouvelle-Zélande et **ZAF** pour l'Afrique du Sud.

3.5.1 Année

La référence neutre commence avec l'année au cours de laquelle la décision a été rendue par la cour.

3.5.2 Identifiant du tribunal

Le code de désignation du tribunal est assigné par la cour et peut contenir jusqu'à huit caractères. Le code de désignation des provinces et territoires débute par un préfixe de deux caractères qui, à l'exception des Territoires du Nord-Ouest, correspond au code de l'indication géographique traditionnelle de deux lettres (celles-ci sont les mêmes en anglais et en français). Voir la colonne des références neutres de **l'annexe A-1**.

Suivre le préfixe de **l'acronyme habituel du tribunal ou de la cour**, mais omettre la réintroduction de toute lettre représentant l'indication géographique (par ex. le Tribunal des professions du Québec est **QCTP** et non **QCTPQ**).

Les cours et les tribunaux fédéraux ne suivent pas la règle du préfixe décrite ci-haut (par ex. Cour suprême du Canada = **CSC**). Noter que la Cour fédérale portait l'abréviation CFPI de 2001 à 2003. Voir **l'annexe B-3** pour une liste complète d'abréviations pour les références neutres.

3.5.3 Numéro de la décision

Le numéro de séquence est assigné par la cour. Ce numéro revient à « 1 » le 1er janvier de chaque année.

3.6 RÉFÉRENCE PRÉCISE

3.6.1 Modèle de base

Indiquer la référence précise **après la référence principale.**

Toujours indiquer le paragraphe lorsqu'il y a une référence neutre ou s'il y a une numérotation officielle des paragraphes (c'est-à-dire une numérotation établie par la cour et suivie uniformément par tous les recueils). S'il n'y a pas de référence neutre ou de numérotation officielle des paragraphes, indiquer le numéro de page ou de paragraphe et identifier le recueil auquel les références sont faites (section 3.6.2). Lorsque les paragraphes sont numérotés, faire référence à un paragraphe unique en écrivant **au para** et à plusieurs paragraphes en écrivant **aux para**. Pour se référer à une page, utiliser **à la p** et, pour plusieurs pages, utiliser **aux pp**.

Ne pas mettre de virgule avant la référence précise.

Faire référence à une note de bas de page avec **n**. Pour faciliter la référence, inclure le numéro du paragraphe correspondant, et séparer la référence au paragraphe de celle à la note de bas de page par une virgule. Voir la section 1.5 pour les règles générales traitant des références précises.

R c Latimer, 2001 CSC 1 **au para 27**.
Madden c Demers (1920), 29 BR 505 **aux pp 510–12**, 1920 CarswellQue 62 (WL Can).
Ordre des arpenteurs-géomètres du Québec c Tremblay, 2001 QCTP 24 **au para 18, n 14**.

3.6.2 Recueil auquel les références sont faites

Lorsqu'il n'y a pas de référence neutre, la numérotation des paragraphes peut varier d'un recueil à l'autre. Le lecteur doit être en mesure d'identifier le recueil qui est la source de la référence précise.

La référence précise se fait autant que possible **au recueil imprimé le plus officiel, mentionné en premier lieu** (voir la section 3.1 pour la hiérarchie des sources). Pour des références subséquentes, utiliser le même recueil.

Ne pas spécifier la source de la référence précise lorsqu'il y a une référence neutre. Dans ce cas, les numéros des paragraphes sont établis par la cour et non par l'éditeur individuel.

> *R v Sharpe*, **2007 BCCA 191** [*Sharpe*].

Ne pas spécifier la source de la référence précise lorsqu'il y a une référence précise lors de la première mention d'un cas. Cela sous-entend que les références subséquentes suivront le même modèle et feront référence au même recueil.

> *Université du Québec à Trois-Rivières c Larocque*, [1993] 1 RCS 471 **à la p 473**, 101 DLR (4e) 494 [*Larocque*].

Pour faire des références précises subséquentes, ajouter **avec renvois au(x)** après le titre abrégé, suivi du nom du recueil.

> *Delgamuukw v British Columbia* (1991), 79 DLR (4e) 185, 1991 CanLII 2372 (BCSC) [*Delgamuukw* **avec renvois aux DLR**].

3.7 RECUEIL IMPRIMÉ

3.7.1 Année du recueil

Les recueils sont publiés en volumes classés par année de parution (par ex. RCS; RJQ) ou en volumes classés par série (par ex. DLR; CCC).

Si les volumes sont classés par **année de parution**, l'année est nécessaire à l'identification du volume. Fournir l'année du recueil entre crochets.

> **[2003]** RJQ 89 (CS)

Certains recueils classés par année de parution publient **plusieurs volumes à chaque année** (par ex. RCS). Indiquer l'année entre crochets, suivie du numéro du volume.

> **[1998]** 2 RCS 217

Si les volumes sont classés par **série**, ne pas indiquer l'année pour identifier le volume (mais se rappeler d'inclure l'année dans l'intitulé si elle n'est pas par ailleurs indiquée dans la référence : voir la section 3.4).

> **24** CR (4e) 184 (NSCA)

Noter aussi que **certains recueils ont changé leur mode de classification des volumes**.

Entre les années 1877 et 1923, les ***Supreme Court Reports*** ont été classés par volume (par ex. **27 CSC**). Entre 1923 et 1974, le recueil a été classé par année (par ex. **[1950]** CSC). Depuis 1975, plusieurs volumes sont publiés par année (par ex. **[1982] 2 CSC**).

Avant 1974, les ***Ontario Reports*** étaient classés par année de parution (par ex. **[1973] OR**). À partir de 1974, ils ont été organisés par série (par ex. **20 OR**). Si les volumes sont classés par **série**, ne pas indiquer l'année pour identifier le volume.

3.7.2 Recueil

Indiquer l'abréviation du nom du recueil selon la liste des abréviations des recueils de jurisprudence à l'**annexe C**.

3.7.2.1 Recueils officiels

Les recueils officiels s'appliquent aux juridictions fédérales et sont publiés par l'Imprimeur de la Reine.

S'il existe des différences entre deux versions du même jugement, la version publiée dans un recueil officiel a préséance.

3.7.2.2 Recueils non officiels

La catégorie des recueils non officiels comprend tous les recueils imprimés qui ne sont pas officiels; à noter que le présent *Manuel* ne fait plus de distinction entre les recueils semi-officiels et les recueils non officiels. Voir la liste non exhaustive des recueils non officiels à **l'annexe C-2**. Il est fortement conseillé de se référer aux recueils suivis d'un astérisque (*). Ces recueils ont été sélectionnés en conformité avec les principes suivants : (1) les recueils qui sont **facilement disponibles** sont à privilégier par rapport aux recueils moins accessibles, (2) les recueils **généraux** sont à privilégier par rapport aux recueils spécialisés et (3) les recueils couvrant un **grand territoire géographique** sont à privilégier par rapport aux recueils couvrant un territoire géographique plus limité.

Si un choix s'impose malgré tout (par ex. entre plusieurs recueils non officiels suivis d'un astérisque), les principes susmentionnés doivent être appliqués afin de sélectionner le recueil le plus approprié. Garder à l'esprit le lectorat visé. Si le texte est destiné à un lectorat spécialisé, il est possible de citer des recueils spécifiques au domaine du droit en question.

3.7.3 Série

Si le recueil a été publié en plusieurs séries, indiquer la série entre parenthèses, entre l'abréviation du recueil et la première page du jugement.

Remplacer **nouvelle série** ou *New Series* par **ns**.

> 1974), 18 CBR **(ns)** 99 (CS Qc

Indiquer le numéro de série en français (**(4e)** et non **(4th)**).

> 156 NSR **(2e)** 347 (CA)

N.B. Certaines bases de données en ligne ne reconnaissent pas les numéros de série français lorsque la décision est publiée en anglais uniquement. Adapter la recherche en conséquence.

3.7.4 Première page

Indiquer le numéro de la première page du jugement après le recueil.

[1988] 2 RCS 712

3.8 SERVICES DE BASE DE DONNÉES EN LIGNE

Les services de bases de données en ligne permettent notamment de trouver de la jurisprudence. Il est possible de citer leur contenu comme référence principale ou comme référence parallèle. Suivant la hiérarchie des sources, ils ont le même statut que les recueils non officiels (voir la section 3.1). Consulter l'**annexe E** pour trouver les abréviations des différents services (par ex. **CanLII**, **QL**, **WL Can**), mais consulter plutôt **l'annexe C-2** pour trouver les identifiants de chacune des bases de données des services (par ex. **CanLII**, **ACS**, **CarswellOnt**). Il est fortement conseillé de se référer aux identifiants suivis d'un astérisque (*). Puisque tous les services ne sont pas disponibles ou gratuits partout au Canada, il faut garder à l'esprit le lectorat visé lorsqu'une référence est faite à une base de données en ligne. Éviter de faire référence à un service de bases de données auquel la majorité des lecteurs ne pourront accéder.

Ne pas inclure l'URL lorsqu'une référence est faite à une base de données en ligne. N'utiliser que l'identifiant fourni par le service, généralement placé au-dessous de l'intitulé. Ne pas confondre l'identifiant et les recueils imprimés dans lesquels une décision est aussi disponible. Dans l'exemple suivant, la référence aux *Recueils de la Cour suprême* est la référence principale et **1993 CanLII 151** est la référence parallèle à la base de données de CanLII.

Caisse populaire de Maniwaki c Giroux, [1993] 1 RCS 282, **1993 CanLII 151**.

Lorsque l'identité d'un service de bases de données en ligne n'est pas évidente dans l'identifiant de la base de données ou que le service ne fournit aucun identifiant pour une décision donnée, indiquer le nom de la base de données entre parenthèses en utilisant les abréviations de l'**annexe E**.

Almad Investments Ltd v Mister Leonard Holding Ltd, 1996 CarswellOnt 4402 **(WL Can)** au para 3 (Div gén Ont).

Indiquer le numéro de paragraphe dans la référence précise. Ne pas se référer aux numéros de page de la source électronique, car ils sont spécifiques au service utilisé et sont susceptibles de varier selon le format du document (par ex. PDF, txt, html). Lorsque les paragraphes ne sont pas numérotés, éviter de se référer à la base de données comme référence principale.

Abitibi-Consolidated Inc v Doughan, EYB 2008-139174 (Référence) **au para 23** (Qc CS).

Utiliser les règles prévues à la section 3.4 lorsque l'année n'est pas fournie dans l'identifiant.

Desputeaux c Éditions Chouette **(2001)**, AZ-50085400 (SOQUIJ) au para 19 (Qc CA).

3.8.1 CanLII

L'**Institut canadien d'information juridique** (CanLII) est un service de bases de données en ligne accessible gratuitement à l'adresse <canlii.org>. Afin que tous les lecteurs puissent aisément accéder aux décisions citées, CanLII devrait être privilégié par rapport aux services payants. Les identifiants de CanLII sont généralement constitués de l'année, suivie de **CanLII** et du numéro de série du document. Lorsque la référence neutre est disponible, l'identifiant est constitué de la référence neutre elle-même, suivie de **(CanLII)**. Il faut alors inclure uniquement la référence neutre sans autre référence à la base de données.

1993 CanLII 2848	2016 CanLII 96404

3.8.2 LexisNexis Quicklaw

LexisNexis Quicklaw est un service payant de bases de données en ligne qui permet d'accéder à la jurisprudence canadienne, mais aussi à de nombreuses autres sources juridiques, telles que la législation et la doctrine. Les identifiants sont généralement constitués de l'année, de la cour ou de l'indication géographique suivie de **J** pour « Judgments » (par ex. **OJ** pour « Ontario Judgments ») et du numéro de série du document. La lettre **J** peut précéder la cour ou l'indication géographique lorsque la décision est rendue en français (par ex. **JQ** pour Jugements du Québec) et la lettre **J** est parfois remplacée par la lettre **A** pour Arrêts (par ex. **ACS** pour Arrêts de la Cour suprême). L'année doit être entre crochets et le numéro de série doit être précédé de **No** pour les décisions rendues en anglais ou de **no** pour les décisions rendues en français.

[2001] ACS no 1	[1995] OJ No 4335
[1995] ACF no 206	[2001] JQ no 1510

3.8.3 Westlaw Canada

WestlawNext Canada est un service payant de bases de données en ligne qui permet d'accéder à la jurisprudence canadienne, mais aussi à de nombreuses autres sources juridiques, telles que la législation et la doctrine. Les identifiants sont généralement constitués de l'année, du mot **Carswell**, suivi sans espace de l'indication géographique et du numéro de série du document.

2003 CarswellQue 343	1985 CarswellNat 145
2001 CarswellSask 4	1990 CarswellYukon 4

3.8.4 SOQUIJ

La **Société québécoise d'information juridique** (SOQUIJ) est un service de bases de données en ligne qui permet d'accéder à la jurisprudence du Québec et des cours fédérales, mais aussi à la législation, à la doctrine et aux plumitifs. Les identifiants sont généralement constitués de **AZ-**, suivi sans espace du numéro de série du document. L'année de la décision n'est jamais incluse dans l'identifiant.

AZ-50085400 AZ-5016965

3.8.5 La Référence

La Référence est un service de bases de données en ligne qui permet d'accéder à la jurisprudence du Québec et des cours fédérales, mais aussi à la législation et aux ouvrages de doctrine publiés par les Édition Yvon Blais. Les identifiants sont généralement constitués de **EYB**, de l'année et du numéro de série du document.

EYB 1993-84186 EYB 2011-191663

3.9 INDICATION GÉOGRAPHIQUE ET COUR

Fournir l'indication géographique et le niveau de la cour s'il n'y a **pas de référence neutre** (comportant l'indication géographique et la cour) **et** si ces **informations ne peuvent être déduites** du nom du recueil. Fournir l'indication géographique et la cour entre parenthèses après le numéro de page ou la référence précise, ainsi qu'après la référence parallèle. Ne pas ajouter d'espace entre les lettres majuscules des abréviations des cours. Toutefois, inclure un espace quand l'abréviation est formée de majuscules et de minuscules (par ex. **CQ; BCCA; Div gén Ont; CQ crim & pén**). Utiliser les abréviations françaises des indications géographiques et des cours lorsque le lieu en question est bilingue. Si la cour ne rend que des jugements en anglais, utiliser l'abréviation anglaise. Voir les abréviations des indications géographiques dans la colonne des cours de **l'annexe A-1** et les abréviations des cours à **l'annexe B**.

Beauchemin c Blainville (Ville de) (2001), 202 DLR (4e) 147 (CS Qc).
Re McEachern (1996), 147 Nfld & PEIR 146 (PEISC (TD)).
Rempel v Reynolds (1991), 94 Sask R 299 (QB).
Air Canada c Joyal, [1982] CA 39 (Qc).
Miller c Monit International, 2001 CSC 13, [2001] 1 RCS 432.

3.10 JUGE

Si cela est pertinent, indiquer le nom du juge à la fin de la référence. Ajouter **dissident(e)** précédé par une virgule s'il s'agit d'une dissidence. Lorsque le banc entier a entendu la cause, il est possible d'utiliser le terme **en banc**.

R c Sharpe, 2001 CSC 2 au para 14, **juge en chef McLachlin**.
Gosselin c Québec (PG), [1999] RJQ 1033 (CA), **juge Robert, dissident**.
R c Wholesale Travel Group Inc, [1991] 3 RCS 154, **en banc**.

3.11 ÉTAPES SUCCESSIVES D'UNE CAUSE

3.11.1 Étapes antérieures

Indiquer les étapes antérieures d'une cause à la fin de la référence si elles sont pertinentes. Séparer les décisions par une virgule.

> *Law c Canada (Ministre de l'Emploi et de l'Immigration)*, [1999] 1 RCS 497, **confirmant** (1996), 135 DLR (4e) 293 (CAF).
>
> *Wilson & Lafleur Ltée c Société québécoise d'information juridique*, [2000] RJQ 1086 (CA), **infirmant** [1998] RJQ 2489 (CS).
>
> *Tsiaprailis c Canada*, 2005 CSC 8, **confirmant** 2003 CAF 136, **infirmant** [2002] 1 CTC 2858, [2002] DTC 1563 (CCI [procédure générale]).

Les expressions **confirmant** et **infirmant** se rapportent à la première référence. Dans *Tsiaprailis*, la Cour suprême confirme la décision de la Cour d'appel qui avait infirmé la décision de la Cour canadienne de l'impôt.

Si la décision confirme ou infirme une décision antérieure pour des motifs autres que ceux discutés, utiliser **confirmant pour d'autres motifs** ou **infirmant pour d'autres motifs**. Si la décision confirme ou infirme une décision antérieure en partie seulement, **utiliser confirmant en partie** ou **infirmant en partie.**

3.11.2 Étapes postérieures

Indiquer les étapes postérieures d'une cause si celle-ci a été jugée postérieurement par d'autres cours. Les étapes postérieures d'une cause figurent à la fin de la référence. Les différentes décisions sont séparées par des virgules. Utiliser **conf par** pour abréger **confirmé par** et **inf par** pour abréger **infirmé par**.

> *Granovsky c Canada (Ministre de l'Emploi et de l'Immigration)*, [1998] 3 CF 175 (CA), **conf par** 2000 CSC 28.

Si la décision a été confirmée ou infirmée pour des motifs autres que ceux discutés, utiliser **conf pour d'autres motifs par** ou **inf pour d'autres motifs par**. Si la décision a été confirmée ou infirmée en partie seulement, utiliser **conf en partie par** ou **inf en partie par**.

> *Ontario English Catholic Teachers' Association c Ontario (PG)* (1998), 162 DLR (4e) 257 (Div gén Ont), **inf en partie par** (1999), 172 DLR (4e) 193 (CA Ont), **inf par** 2001 CSC 15.

Les expressions **conf par** et **inf par** se rapportent à la première référence. Ainsi, dans l'exemple *Ontario English Catholic Teachers' Association*, la Cour suprême a confirmé la décision de la Cour d'appel d'Ontario, selon laquelle la décision de la division générale de la Cour de justice de l'Ontario devait être infirmée. La Cour suprême n'a pas infirmé la décision de la Cour d'appel de l'Ontario.

3.11.3 Étapes antérieures et postérieures

Suivre les règles pour les étapes antérieures et postérieures des sections ci-dessus. Toute décision confirmative ou infirmative renvoie à la première référence.

> *Ardoch Algonquin First Nation v Ontario* (1997), 148 DLR (4e) 126 (CA Ont), **infirmant** [1997] 1 CNLR 66 (Div gén Ont), **conf par** 2000 CSC 37 [*Ardoch*].

Dans *Ardoch*, la Cour d'appel de l'Ontario a infirmé la décision de la Cour de justice de l'Ontario; cette infirmation a été confirmée par la Cour suprême du Canada.

> *Canada c Canderel Ltée*, [1995] 2 CF 232 (CA), **infirmant** [1994] 1 CTC 2336 (CCI), **inf par** [1998] 1 RCS 147 [*Canderel Ltée*].

Dans *Canderel Ltée*, la Cour fédérale d'appel a infirmé la décision de la Cour canadienne de l'impôt, mais sa propre décision a été infirmée par la Cour suprême du Canada (c'est-à-dire que la Cour suprême du Canada a confirmé la décision de la cour de l'impôt).

Indiquer les étapes antérieures avant les étapes postérieures.

3.11.4 Autorisation de pourvoi

Référence à la décision dont l'autorisation de pourvoi est demandée, | cour, | référence au recueil ou numéro de greffe (date).

Les décisions d'autorisation de pourvoi à la **Cour suprême du Canada** se trouvent sur CanLII, Lexum, Westlaw Canada et Quicklaw, ainsi qu'au début des RCS. Les décisions d'avant 2005 se trouvent uniquement au début des RCS. Les décisions de **cours d'appel** concernant l'autorisation de pourvoi se trouvent parfois dans les recueils de jurisprudence et dans les services de base de données en ligne. Inclure la référence à la décision pour laquelle l'autorisation de pourvoi est demandée.

> *White Resource Management Ltd v Durish* (1992), 131 AR 273 (CA), autorisation de pourvoi à la CSC **demandée**.

Indiquer la cour devant laquelle la demande de pourvoi a été faite. Si possible, indiquer si le pourvoi a été autorisé ou refusé et faire référence à cette décision.

> *Westec Aerospace v Raytheon Aircraft*, 1999 BCCA 243, autorisation de pourvoi à la CSC **accordée**, [2000] 1 RCS xxii.
>
> *Cie pharmaceutique Procter & Gamble Canada Inc c Canada (Ministre de la Santé)*, 2004 CAF 393, autorisation de pourvoi à la CSC **refusée**, 30714 (21 avril 2005).

Indiquer s'il s'agit d'un pourvoi de plein droit.

> *Whiten v Pilot Insurance* (1996), 132 DLR (4e) 568 (Div gén Ont), **pourvoi de plein droit** à la CA.

Fournir une référence soit à un recueil imprimé (voir *Westec* Aerospace), soit au numéro de greffe suivi par la date entre parenthèses (voir *Procter & Gamble*). Certaines requêtes sont publiées. Dans ces cas, utiliser les règles de référence pour une décision standard, et ajouter le résultat (**autorisation de pourvoi à [la cour] autorisée, ou autorisation de pourvoi à [la cour] refusée**).

R v Gallagher, 2013 ABCA 269, **autorisation de pourvoi à Alta CA refusée**.

Accès aux pourvois par juridiction		
Cour suprême	Les décisions d'autorisation de pourvoi sont disponibles sur CanLII, Lexum, Westlaw Canada, Quicklaw, ainsi qu'au début du RCS.	
Cour d'appel fédérale	Les décisions d'autorisation de pourvoi ne sont actuellement pas disponibles en ligne.	
Alberta	Certaines décisions d'autorisation de pourvoi ont une référence neutre et sont disponibles sur le site internet de la cour.	albertacourts.ca
Colombie-Britannique	Certaines décisions d'autorisation de pourvoi ont une référence neutre et sont disponibles sur le site internet de la cour.	www.courts.gov.bc.ca
Île-du-Prince-Édouard	Certaines décisions d'autorisation de pourvoi ont une référence neutre et sont disponibles sur le site internet de la cour.	www.gov.pe.ca/courts/supreme/reasons.php3
Manitoba	Certaines décisions d'autorisation de pourvoi ont une référence neutre et sont disponibles sur CanLII.	
Nouveau-Brunswick	Certaines décisions d'autorisation de pourvoi datant depuis 2012 sont listées dans les Décisions sur les motions.	www.gnb.ca/cour/03COA1/motions-f.asp
Nouvelle-Écosse	Certaines décisions d'autorisation de pourvoi ont une référence neutre et sont disponibles sur le site internet du Département de Justice.	decisions.courts.ns.ca/site/nsc/en/nav.do
Nunavut	Certaines décisions d'autorisation de pourvoi ont une référence neutre et sont disponibles sur le sites-web de la cour.	www.justice.gov.nt.ca/CourtLibrary/library_decisions.shtml
Ontario	Les pourvois datant depuis 2002 se trouvent listés avec leur numéro de greffe.	www.ontariocourts.ca/coa/en/leave/
Québec	Certaines décisions d'autorisation de pourvoi ont une référence neutre et sont disponibles sur une base de données en ligne de la province.	citoyens.soquij.qc.ca

Saskatchewan	Certaines décisions d'autorisation de pourvoi ont une référence neutre et sont disponibles sur CanLII ou sur une base de données en ligne de la province (qui mène à CanLII).	www.lawsociety.sk.ca/library/public-resources/court-of-appeal-judgments.aspx
Terre-Neuve-et-Labrador	Les décisions d'autorisation de pourvoi ne sont actuellement pas disponibles en ligne.	
Territoires du Nord-Ouest	Certaines décisions d'autorisation de pourvoi ont une référence neutre et sont disponibles sur le site internet du Département de Justice.	decisia.lexum.com/nwtcourts-courstno/fr/nav.do
Yukon	Les décisions d'autorisation de pourvoi ne sont actuellement pas disponibles en ligne.	

NB: les informations concernant les sites internet des tribunaux sont généralement aussi disponibles via CanLII ou d'autres bases de données en ligne.

3.12 JUGEMENTS NON PUBLIÉS ET SANS RÉFÉRENCE NEUTRE

Intitulé | (date), | district judiciaire | numéro de greffe | (indication géographique et cour).

Indiquer l'intitulé et la date de la décision entre parenthèses, suivis d'une virgule, du district judiciaire, du numéro de greffe, ainsi que de l'indication géographique et de la cour entre parenthèses.

R c Crète (18 avril 1991), Ottawa 97/03674 (CP Ont).

3.13 JURISPRUDENCE EXPRESS

Jurisprudence Express est un recueil non officiel, qui fournit des résumés jurisprudentiels de décisions rendues au Québec. Bien qu'il soit préférable de ne pas se référer à Jurisprudence Express, certaines décisions sont uniquement publiées dans ce recueil. L'abréviation **JE** doit être placée au début de la référence. Inclure ensuite l'année du recueil, suivie du numéro de la décision citée (ne pas indiquer le numéro de la page). Pour les recueils publiés avant l'année 2000, n'inclure que les deux derniers chiffres de l'année. À partir de 2000, inclure les quatre chiffres de l'année.

Lalancette c Gagnon, [1995] JQ no 3573 (QL), **JE 95-1255** (CQ).

Commission des normes du travail c Mercier, [2000] JQ no 7821 (QL), **JE 2000-2257** (CQ civ).

3.14 JUGEMENTS INTERLOCUTOIRES

Intitulé ou *nom des parties* | (date), | district judiciaire, | identifiant de la cour | numéro de dossier | type de document (par ex. requête en irrecevabilité).

Marris Handold v Tyson Blair (23 avril 2011), Montréal, CA QC 500-02-019902-944 (jugement interlocutoire).

3.15 ORGANES ET TRIBUNAUX ADMINISTRATIFS

3.15.1 Références aux recueils imprimés

Fournir l'intitulé de la décision tel qu'il apparaît dans le recueil et indiquer si le processus est contradictoire (séparer le nom des parties par ***c***) ou non (mettre ***Re*** avant l'intitulé). Lorsqu'il n'y a pas d'intitulé, indiquer le numéro de la décision.

Médecins (Ordre professionnel des) **c** *Latulippe (CD Méd)*, [1997] DDOP 89 (TP).

Re *Citric Acid and Sodium Citrate* (1985), 10 CER 88 (Tribunal canadien des importations).

Indiquer l'abréviation employée par l'organe ou le tribunal administratif entre parenthèses à la fin de la référence s'il est impossible de le déduire du titre du recueil (utiliser le nom si aucune abréviation n'est trouvée). Utiliser une abréviation courte pour les provinces et les territoires (par ex. la Commission des valeurs mobilières du Québec est abrégée **CVMQ**, la Commission des valeurs mobilières de l'Ontario est abrégée **CMVO** et la Newfoundland and Labrador Human Rights Commission est abrégée **NLHRC**). À noter que les abréviations d'un recueil imprimé peuvent être différentes de celles d'un organisme administratif (par ex. **OSC** ou **OSCB**).

3.15.2 Décisions en ligne

Intitulé | (date), | numéro de la décision, | en ligne : | organe ou tribunal administratif | <URL>.

Indiquer la date précise de la décision entre parenthèses après l'intitulé, et suivie d'une virgule.

Autorité des marchés financiers c Jean-Yves Mulet (9 septembre 2009), 2009-019, en ligne : *BDRVM* <www.bdrvm.com>.

Indiquer le numéro de la décision (s'il y a lieu), suivi de **en ligne :** et de l'abréviation utilisée par le tribunal ou l'organe administratif. Utiliser une abréviation courte pour les provinces et les territoires (par ex. la Commission des valeurs mobilières du Québec est abrégée **CVMQ**, la Commission des valeurs mobilières de l'Ontario est abrégée **CVMO** et la *Newfoundland and Labrador Human Rights Commission* est abrégée **NLHRC**).

Réexamen de la décision de radiodiffusion 2008-222 conformément aux décrets CP 2008-1769 et CP 2008-1770 (11 août 2009), CRTC 2009-481, en ligne : *CRTC* <www.crtc.gc.ca/fra/archive/2009/2009-481.htm>.

Voir la section 1.6 pour plus de renseignements sur la référence à des ressources électroniques.

3.16 PLAIDOIRIES ET DOCUMENTS DE PREUVE À L'AUDIENCE

Pour un **mémoire**, indiquer la référence complète de la cause. Ensuite, écrire entre parenthèses **mémoire de**, le nom de la partie (**appelant** ou **intimé**) et le numéro de la page ou du paragraphe. Utiliser les références complètes pour les parties. Créer un titre abrégé lors de la première référence au document (par ex. **mémoire de l'appelant au para 16 [MA]**).

Renvoi relatif à la sécession du Québec, [1998] 2 RCS 217 **(mémoire de l'appelant au para 16)**.

Pour une **plaidoirie orale**, indiquer la référence complète de la décision, suivie de **plaidoirie orale de** et du nom de la partie entre parenthèses.

Vriend c Alberta, [1998] 1 RCS 493 **(plaidoirie orale de l'appelant)**.

Pour un **règlement public hors cour**, fournir l'intitulé, suivi de **règlement hors cour** entre crochets, et des autres éléments de la référence. Si le règlement a été annoncé dans un communiqué de presse, voir la section 6.14.

Mulroney c Canada (PG) **[Règlement hors cour]**, [1997] AQ n° 45 (CS) (QL).

Pour un **élément de preuve**, indiquer la référence complète de la décision, suivie de **preuve** et d'une brève description de l'élément entre parenthèses.

R c Swain, [1991] 1 RCS 933 **(preuve, recommandation du Dr Fleming de remettre l'appelant en liberté)**.

Adapter la forme générale fournie ci-haut pour les autres types de documents, dont les témoignages, les dépositions, les affidavits, les assignations, les memoranda, les transcriptions, les plumitifs, etc.

Tremblay c Daigle, [1989] 2 RCS 530, 62 DLR (4e) 634 (affidavit de Daigle).

3.17 DÉCISIONS D'ARBITRAGE

Même si les décisions d'arbitrage font peu autorité, elles sont également régies par les règles de citation applicables à la jurisprudence (voir les sections 3.3, 3.4, 3.6 et 3.7). Pour les décisions d'**arbitrage international**, voir la section 5.2.11. Pour les décisions de l'**OMPI**, voir la section 5.2.12.

Intitulé ou numéro de la décision | (année de la décision), | recueil ou identifiant | référence précise | (arbitre : | nom de l'arbitre).

Indiquer l'intitulé ou le numéro de la décision, suivi de l'année de la décision entre parenthèses. Si la décision est publiée dans un recueil imprimé, faire référence au recueil d'arbitrage. Si la décision est publiée dans un service de bases de données en ligne, inclure l'identifiant fourni par le service. Ajouter l'abréviation du service entre parenthèses si elle n'est pas déjà mentionnée dans l'identifiant. Si possible, ajouter le **nom de l'arbitre ou des arbitres** entre parenthèses précédé par **arbitre :** ou **arbitres :**. Puisqu'il s'agit du moyen le plus efficace pour les lecteurs de comprendre qu'il s'agit d'une décision d'arbitrage et non d'une décision ordinaire, il est fortement conseillé d'inclure cet élément dans la citation.

California State University v State Employers Trade Council — United (2009), 126 Lab Arb (BNA) 613 (arbitre : Bonnie Bogue).

Winona School District ISD 861 Winona v Winona Education Association (2006), 2006 WL 3876585 (arbitre : Daniel J Jacobowski).

4 Documents gouvernementaux

4 DOCUMENTS GOUVERNEMENTAUX

4.1 DOCUMENTS PARLEMENTAIRES

Cette section s'applique aux documents publiés directement par un organe parlementaire (débats, journaux, feuilletons, documents parlementaires, procès-verbaux et rapports). Appliquer les règles générales prévues à la section 4.1.1 à moins que le document cité n'entre dans les catégories particulières prévues aux sections 4.1.2 à 4.1.5.

4.1.1 Modèle de base

Indication géographique, | législature, | *titre*, | numéro de la législature et session, | volume, | numéro | (date) | référence précise | (orateur).

Écrire l'indication géographique (s'il s'agit d'une province) et la législature à moins que ces informations ne fassent partie du titre du document. Pour tous les documents gouvernementaux fédéraux, n'ajouter l'indication géographique **(Canada)** que si des références à des documents internationaux dans le texte risquent de mélanger le lecteur.

> *Débats de la Chambre des communes*, 37-1, n° 64 (17 mai 2001) à la p 4175 (Hon Elinor Caplan).
>
> **Québec**, Assemblée nationale, *Procès-verbal*, 39-1, n° 48 (18 juin 2009) à la p 517.
>
> Saskatchewan, *Journals of the Legislative Assembly*, 23-3, vol 105 (9 mars 1998) à la p 7.
>
> Québec, **Assemblée nationale,** *Feuilleton et préavis*, 38-1, n° 79 (6 mai 2008).

Indiquer le titre en italique tel qu'il apparaît sur la page titre du document. Indiquer le numéro de la législature suivi du numéro de la session. Utiliser des nombres cardinaux. Par exemple, **37e parlement, 1re session** devient 37-1.

S'il y a lieu, inclure le volume et/ou le numéro du document après la virgule suivant le titre. Indiquer la date complète entre parenthèses, suivie de la référence précise. S'il y a lieu, indiquer le nom de l'orateur entre parenthèses à la fin de la référence.

4.1.2 Débats législatifs

Si pertinent, indiquer le titre du projet de loi en discussion entre guillemets et le numéro de la lecture devant l'indication géographique, la législature et le titre.

> **« Projet de loi C-8, Loi modifiant la loi sur le droit d'auteur, la loi sur les marques de commerce et d'autres lois en conséquence », 2e lecture**, *Débats de la Chambre des communes*, 41-2, n° 9 (28 octobre 2013) à la p 1504 (Hon Steven Blaney).

Utiliser le même modèle de base pour faire référence à un débat impliquant un comité, mais inclure le nom du comité après la législature. Le titre est le titre du document produit par le comité en question.

Chambre des communes, **Comité permanent de la justice et des droits de la personne**, *Témoignages*, 39-2, n° 12 (7 février 2008) à 15:30 (Tony Cannavino).

4.1.3 Feuilletons

Au fédéral, le ***Feuilleton*** et le ***Feuilleton des avis*** sont deux parties d'une seule publication. Indiquer uniquement le recueil pertinent comme titre.

Chambre des communes, ***Feuilleton***, 39-1, n° 175 (20 juin 2007).

4.1.4 Documents parlementaires

Les documents parlementaires étaient anciennement publiés dans les ***Sessional Papers***. Fournir le titre du rapport entre guillemets après la mention de la législature. S'il y a un auteur, indiquer son nom après le titre du rapport, suivi de **par**. Indiquer l'année et non la date complète entre parenthèses.

Ontario, Assemblée législative, « **Report on Workmen's Compensation for Injuries** » **par James Mavor**, *Sessional Papers*, n° 40 (1900) aux pp 6—7.

Les documents parlementaires modernes ne sont plus publiés dans des volumes. Au lieu du titre, inclure **document parlementaire** en caractères romains. Pour les documents parlementaires émanant de la Chambre des communes, inclure le numéro de série indiqué dans le journal.

Chambre des communes, « Rapport du Tribunal canadien du commerce extérieur pour l'exercice terminé le 31 mars 2015 » par Oliver (ministre des Finances), **document parlementaire**, 41-2, **n° 8560-412-553-02** (2 août 2015).

4.1.5 Rapports

Après la législature, inclure le nom de l'organisme et le titre du rapport.

Rapports publiés dans un journal des débats :

Placer le titre du rapport entre guillemets.

Québec, Assemblée nationale, Commission permanente de l'Éducation, « **Étude détaillée du projet de loi no 12 : Loi sur l'aide financière aux études** », *Journal des débats de la Commission permanente de l'Éducation*, vol 37, n° 11 (1er juin 2001) à la p 1.

Rapports publiés séparément :

Indiquer le titre du rapport en italique. Si le nom du président est indiqué sur la page couverture, ajouter cette information entre parenthèses. Cette section s'applique aux rapports publiés directement par un organe parlementaire. Si le rapport est publié par tout autre organe, voir la section 4.2 sur les rapports non parlementaires.

Chambre des communes, ***L'étiquetage des aliments génétiquement modifiés et son impact sur les agriculteurs : Rapport du Comité permanent de l'agriculture et de l'agroalimentaire*** (avril 2002) **(président : Charles Hubbard)**.

4.2 DOCUMENTS NON PARLEMENTAIRES

Cette section s'applique à tout document gouvernemental qui n'est pas publié par un organisme législatif. Suivre les règles générales de la section 4.2.1, sauf si le document fait partie d'une catégorie specifique comprise dans les sections 4.2.2–4.2.5.

4.2.1 Modèle de base

Indication géographique, | organisme, | *titre* | (type de document), | renseignements additionnels, | renseignements sur l'édition | référence précise.

Canada, Commission royale sur la réforme électorale et le financement des partis, *Pour une démocratie électorale renouvelée*, vol 4, Ottawa, Groupe Communication, 1991 à la p 99.

Inclure l'indication géographique à moins qu'elle ne fasse partie du nom de l'organisme ou du titre du document. Indiquer l'organisme responsable à moins qu'il ne fasse partie du titre. Si le document porte le nom d'un auteur spécifique au sein de l'organisme responsable, fournir le nom de l'auteur après le titre, précédé du mot **par**. Pour le reste de la référence, suivre les règles de la section 6.2.2.

Statistique Canada, *Statistiques sur les crimes déclarés par la police au Canada, 2011*, **par Shannon Brennan**, n° de catalogue 82-002-X, Ottawa, Statistique Canada, 11 octobre 2012.

Après le titre du document et le nom de l'auteur spécifique s'il y a lieu, fournir tout autre renseignement qui pourrait aider les lecteurs à trouver une source (par ex. données provenant d'un catalogue) ou à évaluer l'autorité d'une source (par ex. la date à laquelle la source a été mise à jour, ou une indication que la source est en examen ou a été annulée). Séparer chaque élément par une virgule. Si le document est divisé en plusieurs volumes, suivre les règles de la section 6.2.4. Le nom du commissaire ou du président peut être inclus entre parenthèses après le titre.

Statistique Canada, *Les unions interculturelles*, par Anne Milan et Brian Hamm, dans *Tendances sociales canadiennes*, **n° de catalogue 11-008-X**, Ottawa, Statistique Canada, 2004.

Office de la propriété intellectuelle, *Recueil des pratiques du Bureau des brevets*, **mise à jour décembre 2010**, Ottawa, Industrie Canada, 1998 à la p 12.

Québec, Ministère de la justice, *Commentaires du ministre de la Justice : le Code civil du Québec*, **t 1**, Québec, Publications du Québec, 1993 à la p 5.

Si l'organisme responsable est également l'éditeur du document, il est possible de l'abréger ou de le remplacer par un acronyme dans la section des renseignements sur l'édition. Pour tout autre renseignement sur l'édition, suivre les règles des sections 6.2.5 à 6.2.9.

Québec, **Office de révision du Code civil**, *Rapport sur les obligations*, par le Comité du droit des obligations, Montréal, **ORCC**, 1975.

Si le type de document est indiqué sur la page titre, fournir ce renseignement entre parenthèses après le titre du document.

Commission de la santé et de la sécurité du travail du Québec, *Planification des mesures d'urgence pour assurer la sécurité des travailleurs* **(Guide)**, Québec, CSST, 1999 à la p 53.

Canada, Ministère de la Défense Nationale, *Programme de terminologie de la Défense* **(Directives et ordonnances administratives de la Défense)**, n° 6110-1, en examen, Ottawa, MDN, 29 janvier 2010.

Ne pas indiquer le type de document s'il est évident dans le titre ou s'il n'aide pas les lecteurs à trouver ou à comprendre la source.

Agence canadienne des médicaments et des technologies de la santé, ***CEDAC Final Recommendation : Abacavir/Lamivudine***, par le Comité consultatif canadien d'expertise sur les médicaments, Ottawa, ACMTS, 16 novembre 2005 aux para 2—4.

Nouvelle-Écosse, Commission d'indemnisation des accidents du travail, *Chronic Pain* **(Fact sheet)**, Halifax, CIAT, avril 2008.

À moins que l'indication géographique ne soit précisée dans le titre lui-même, présumer que les documents fédéraux sont publiés à Ottawa et que les documents provinciaux ou territoriaux sont publiés dans la capitale de la province ou du territoire. Indiquer la date de publication la plus complète disponible sur la base des informations contenues dans le document de la source.

Utiliser le même modèle pour les documents des commissions de réforme du droit. Si possible, fournir le numéro du rapport, suivi de l'année entre parenthèses.

Law Reform Commission of British Columbia, *Report on Non-Charitable Purpose Trusts*, Report 128 (1992).

Alberta Law Reform Institute, *Estate Administration*, Final Report 102 (2013) au para 91.

4.2.2 Bulletins d'interprétation (IT) en matière d'impôts et circulaires d'information (IC)

Ministère, | Bulletin d'interprétation | numéro du bulletin, | « titre » | (date) | référence précise.

Les **IT** sont des bulletins d'interprétation courants en matière d'impôt sur le revenu et sont publiés par l'Agence du revenu du Canada. Les **IC** sont des circulaires d'information et sont également publiées par l'Agence du revenu du Canada. Des documents similaires sont publiés dans les provinces.

Agence du revenu du Canada, Bulletin d'interprétation **IT**-459, « Projet comportant un risque ou une affaire de caractère commercial » (8 septembre 1980).

Faire suivre le numéro de bulletin d'un **R** s'il a été révisé.

Agence du revenu du Canada, Bulletin d'interprétation IT-525**R**, « Artistes de la scène » (17 août 1995).

Le nombre de révisions est indiqué par le chiffre suivant le R.

Agence du revenu du Canada, Bulletin d'interprétation IT-244**R3**, « Dons de polices d'assurance-vie à des œuvres charitables » (6 septembre 1991) au para 4.

Lorsque les bulletins d'interprétation en matière d'impôt sont divisés en paragraphes, faire référence au numéro de paragraphe.

4.2.3 Rapports d'enquête et rapport de commissions

Indication géographique, | organisme, | *titre*, | volume | renseignements sur l'édition | (président) | référence précise.

Inclure l'indication géographique, à moins qu'elle ne paraisse ailleurs dans la référence.

Inclure le nom de l'organisme, à moins qu'il ne soit déjà mentionné dans le titre du rapport.

Si un mot comme **livre** ou **cahier** paraît sur la page titre du document, utiliser cette terminologie plutôt que **vol**.

Ne pas indiquer le numéro de volume dans les références ultérieures. Toutefois, pour faire référence à un autre volume du rapport dans une référence ultérieure, indiquer le numéro du volume pour éviter toute confusion.

Canada, Commission d'enquête sur le programme de commandites et les activités publicitaires, *Qui est responsable ? Rapport factuel*, Ottawa, Travaux publics et Services gouvernementaux Canada, 2005 à la p 14.

Pour faire référence à un rapport publié dans des volumes distincts portant des titres différents, indiquer la référence complète pour chaque division, séparées d'un point-virgule. Indiquer le titre du volume comme si c'était un sous-titre du document (précédé d'un deux-points).

Indiquer le volume (ou le livre ou le cahier) après le titre abrégé dans les références ultérieures.

Rapport de la Commission d'enquête sur la situation de la langue française et sur les droits linguistiques au Québec : la langue de travail, **livre 1**, Québec, Éditeur officiel, 1972 aux pp 150, 300; *Rapport de la Commission d'enquête sur la situation de la langue française et sur les droits linguistiques au Québec : les droits linguistiques*, **livre 2**, Québec, Éditeur officiel, 1972 à la p 38.

4.2.4 Documents de conférences intergouvernementales

Conférence **ou** comité, | *titre*, | numéro du document, | lieu de la conférence, | date de tenue de la conférence.

Indiquer le nom complet de la conférence ou du comité, suivi du titre du document et du numéro du document.

Indiquer le lieu et la date complète de la conférence.

Réunion fédérale-provinciale-territoriale des ministres responsables de la justice, *Groupe de travail fédéral-provincial-territorial sur la provocation, Rapport intérimaire*, Doc 830-600/020, Montréal, 4–5 décembre 1997.

Conférence fédérale-provinciale des Premiers ministres, *Compte rendu textuel de la Conférence fédérale-provinciale des Premiers ministres sur les questions constitutionnelles intéressant les autochtones*, Doc 800-18/004, Ottawa, 8–9 mars 1984.

4.2.5 Documents intergouvernementaux

4.2.5.1 Modèle de base

Titre, | date, | référence précise, | en ligne : | *titre du site internet* | <URL> | [URL archivée].

La majorité des documents intergouvernementaux sont disponibles en ligne en format PDF. Fournir l'URL conformément aux règles prévues à la section 6.19.

Accord de coopération et d'échanges entre le gouvernement du Québec et le gouvernement de l'Ontario en matière d'affaires francophones, 2 juin 2006, art 2, en ligne (pdf) : *Secrétariat aux affaires intergouvernementales canadiennes* <www.saic.-gouv.qc.ca/francophonie-canadienne/politique/accords-cooperation/accord-ontario.pdf> [perma.cc/B8U4-N2TR].

Convention de la Baie-James et du Nord québécois et conventions complémentaires, 11 novembre 1975, art 28.3.4, en ligne (pdf) : *Association des employés du nord québécois*, <www.aenq.org> [perma.cc/KA58-QSB9].

4.2.5.2 Traités autochtones et accords de revendications territoriales

Les versions électroniques des traités autochtones sont disponibles sur le site internet du gouvernement du Canada dans la section des Affaires autochtones et du Nord : <www.aadnc-aandc.gc.ca/fra>. Même en l'absence de références ultérieures, fournir la forme abrégée des traités numérotés.

Traité N° 3 conclu entre Sa Majesté la Reine et la tribu des Saulteux de la nation des Ojibeways et un point situé à l'angle Nord-Ouest du lac des Bois et adhésions à ce dernier, 3 octobre 1873, en ligne : *Gouvernement du Canada* <www.aadnc-aadnc.gc.ca> [perma.cc/K2PK-UA25] [*Traité 3*].

Indiquer le titre complet du traité ou de l'accord. Ne pas inclure la date du traité si elle fait déjà partie du titre.

Traité N° 8 conclu le 21 juin 1899 et adhésions, rapports et autres, **21 juin 1899**, en ligne : *Gouvernement du Canada* <www.aadnc-aandc.gc.ca> [perma.cc/YV7Y-GBHT] [*Traité 8*].

Accord entre les Inuit de la région du Nunavut et Sa Majesté la Reine du chef du Canada, **25 mai 1993**, en ligne (pdf) : *Gouvernement du Canada* <publications.gc.ca> [perma.cc/5UF7-DH5R].

5 Documentation internationale F-67

5 DOCUMENTATION INTERNATIONALE

5.1 TRAITÉS ET DOCUMENTS INTERNATIONAUX

5.1.1 Traités, documents des Nations Unies et autres accords internationaux

Titre, | parties (s'il y a lieu), | date de signature, | recueil de traités | référence précise, | (date d'entrée en vigueur | renseignements supplémentaires).

Indiquer le titre complet du traité. Si le nom des parties à un traité bilatéral n'est pas indiqué dans le titre, écrire la version courte (mais non abrégée) du nom des parties après le titre, entre virgules. Inclure le nom des parties à un traité multilatéral à la fin de la référence, si nécessaire.

Indiquer la date de la première signature du traité ou de son ouverture à la signature. Indiquer la date d'entrée en vigueur entre parenthèses à la fin de la référence.

Écrire la référence du recueil de traités après la date. À la suite de la citation de la série des traités, il est possible de fournir une référence parallèle à d'autres recueils de traités et de suivre l'ordre des recueils suivant : (1) *Recueil de traités des Nations Unies* [**RTNU**] ou *Recueil de traités de la Société des Nations* [**RTSN**], (2) recueils de traités officiels des États pertinents (par ex. *Recueil des traités du Canada* [**RT Can**], *United Kingdom Treaty Series* [**UKTS**]) et (3) autres recueils de traités et accords internationaux. Fournir une référence parallèle aux *International Legal Materials* [**ILM**] si possible. Consulter **l'annexe A-5** pour la liste des abréviations des organismes internationaux.

Fournir des renseignement supplémentaires à la fin de la référence, après la date d'entrée en vigueur, si nécessaire (par ex. le nom des parties au traité, le nombre de ratifications et le statut de certains États).

Traité sur l'extradition, Espagne et Costa Rica, 23 octobre 1997, 2025 RTNU 251 (entrée en vigueur : 30 juillet 1998).

Convention de sauvegarde des droits de l'homme et des libertés fondamentales, 4 novembre 1950, 213 RTNU 221 à la p 233 (entrée en vigueur : 3 septembre 1953) [*Convention européenne des droits de l'homme*].

Pacte international relatif aux droits civils et politiques, 19 décembre 1966, 999 RTNU 171 arts 9—14 (entrée en vigueur : 23 mars 1976, accession du Canada 19 mai 1976) [*PIDCP*].

Accord de libre-échange nord-américain entre le gouvernement du Canada, le gouvernement des États-Unis et le gouvernement du Mexique, 17 décembre 1992, RT Can 1994 nº 2 (entrée en vigueur : 1er janvier 1994) [*ALÉNA*].

Accord général sur les tarifs douaniers et le commerce, 30 octobre 1947, 58 RTNU 187 (entrée en vigueur : 1er janvier 1948) [*GATT de 1947*].

5.1.1.1 Référence neutre des traités australiens

Le gouvernement australien du Commonwealth a adopté sa propre méthode de référence neutre pour les traités, qui doit accompagner toute référence à un recueil imprimé. Introduire la référence neutre après le titre du traité et la date de signature. Indiquer l'année de publication entre crochets, suivie de l'identifiant du recueil et du numéro de document.

> *Agreement on the Conservation of Albatrosses and Petrels*, 19 juin 2001, **[2004] ATS 5**.

5.1.2 Documents des Nations Unies

Chaque document des Nations Unies ne contient pas toujours tous les éléments inclus dans les exemples ci-dessous. Adapter les références de manière à ce qu'elles fournissent les renseignements nécessaires à l'identification du document. Consulter **l'annexe A-5** pour la liste des abréviations des organismes internationaux.

5.1.2.1 Charte des Nations Unies

Une référence complète n'est pas nécessaire pour la *Charte des Nations Unies*. Il est possible de faire référence à la *Charte* de la façon suivante : ***Charte des Nations Unies*, 26 juin 1945, RT Can 1945 n° 7.**

5.1.2.2 Documents officiels

Les documents officiels publiés par les organes des Nations Unies se divisent en trois parties, soit les **séances**, les **suppléments** et les **annexes**. Faire référence aux documents officiels en inscrivant **Doc off** avant l'acronyme de l'organe qui en est responsable.

Fournir le nom complet des organes de l'ONU qui n'ont pas d'acronyme officiel.

5.1.2.2.1 Séances

> Doc off et acronyme de l'organe responsable, | numéro de sess ou nombre d'années écoulées depuis la création de l'organe ou année civile, | numéro de séance, | numéro de document de l'ONU et (numéro de vente) | (année du document) | référence précise | [provisoire].

Indiquer **Doc off** pour **Documents officiels**, suivi de **l'abréviation de l'organe des Nations Unies** et de la mention NU, si elle ne fait pas déjà partie de l'acronyme de l'organe.

Fournir le **numéro de session** après le nom de l'organe ou de la mention NU. Si le numéro n'est pas disponible, indiquer **le nombre d'années écoulées depuis la création de l'organe**. Si ni l'une ni l'autre des informations ne sont disponibles, indiquer **l'année civile**.

Indiquer le **numéro de séance** après le numéro de session. Indiquer le **numéro de document** après le numéro de séance. Si un document a plusieurs numéros, indiquer chacun d'entre eux, séparés par des virgules. Indiquer le numéro de vente (s'il y a lieu) entre parenthèses après le numéro de document.

Indiquer l'année civile du document entre parenthèses après le numéro de document si elle n'a pas été mentionnée précédemment dans la référence. Indiquer qu'un document est provisoire en ajoutant **[provisoire]** à la fin de la référence.

> Doc off CCED CNUCED, 23e sess, 565e séance, Doc NU TD/B/SR.565 (1981).
>
> Doc off CS NU, 53e année, 3849e séance, Doc NU S/PV.3849 (1998) [provisoire].
>
> Doc off CES NU, 1984, 23e séance plén, Doc NU E/1984/SR.23.

5.1.2.2.2 Suppléments

Les résolutions, les décisions et les rapports de l'ONU paraissent dans des suppléments aux documents officiels.

> Auteur, | *titre*, | Rés ou Déc et organe et no, | Doc off, | session ou année de l'organe ou année civile, | numéro de supp, | numéro de document de l'ONU | (année civile) | 1re page | référence précise.

Pour les rapports, indiquer l'auteur avant le titre, s'il n'est pas déjà mentionné dans celui-ci.

> ***Rapport du Secrétaire général Boutros-Ghali sur les travaux de l'Organisation***, Doc off AG NU, 46e sess, supp no 1, Doc NU A/46/1 (1991).
>
> **Commission on Crime Prevention and Criminal Justice**, *Report on the Ninth Session*, Doc off CES NU, 2000, supp n° 10, Doc NU E/2000/30.

Pour faire référence à une décision ou une résolution, indiquer le numéro de décision ou de résolution après le titre.

> *Déclaration universelle des droits de l'Homme*, **Rés AG 217A (III)**, Doc off AG NU, 3e sess, supp no 13, Doc NU A/810 (1948) 71.
>
> *Protection of the heritage of indigenous people*, **Déc CES 1998/277**, Doc off CES NU, 1998, supp no 1, Doc NU E/1998/98 113 à la p 115.

Indiquer **Doc off** pour **Documents officiels**, suivi de **l'abréviation de l'organe des Nations Unies** et de la mention **NU**, si celle-ci ne fait pas partie de l'acronyme de l'organe. Pour les résolutions et les décisions, indiquer cette information après le numéro de résolution ou de décision. Pour les rapports, indiquer cette information immédiatement après le titre du rapport.

Indiquer le **numéro de session**. S'il n'est pas disponible, indiquer **le nombre d'années écoulées depuis la création de l'organe**. Si ni l'une ni l'autre des informations ne sont disponibles, indiquer **l'année civile**. Après la session, faire référence au **numéro de supplément** et au **numéro de document**. Indiquer l'année civile du document entre parenthèses après le numéro de document, si elle n'est pas déjà mentionnée dans la référence. Placer ensuite le numéro de la première page du document et la référence précise, s'il y a lieu. Si aucune information n'est indiquée entre le numéro de document et le numéro de page, placer une virgule après le numéro de document afin d'éviter toute confusion.

5.1.2.2.3 Annexes

Titre, | Doc off et acronyme de l'organe responsable | numéro de sess ou année de l'organe ou année civile, | annexe, point numéro, | numéro de document de l'ONU | (année civile) | 1re page | référence précise.

Indiquer le titre en italique, suivi d'une référence aux documents officiels de l'organe responsable.

Si **le numéro de session** n'est pas disponible, indiquer **le nombre d'années écoulées depuis la création de l'organe**. Si ni l'une ni l'autre des informations ne sont disponibles, indiquer **l'année civile**.

Indiquer **l'annexe** et le point d'ordre du jour, suivis du numéro de document.

Si l'année civile n'a pas été précédemment indiquée, l'inscrire entre parenthèses après le numéro de document. Placer ensuite le numéro de la première page du document si celui-ci fait partie d'une collection reliée, suivi d'une référence précise s'il y a lieu. Si aucune information n'est indiquée entre le numéro de document et le numéro de page, placer une virgule après le numéro de document afin d'éviter toute confusion.

> *Protectionism and Structural Adjustment*, Doc off CNUCED CCED, 32e sess, annexe, point 6, Doc NU TD/B/1081 (1986) 23.
> *URSS : Projet de résolution*, Doc off CES NU, 3e année, 7e sess, annexe, point 7, Doc NU E/884/Rev.1 (1948) 29 au para 3.

5.1.2.3 Documents à en-tête de l'Organisation des Nations Unies (Documents miméographiés)

Nom du corps, | nom du sous-corps ou de la commission | auteur, | *titre*, | session, réunion, supplément, | Doc NU No, | date | référence précise | [*titre abrégé*].

La forme miméographique est officielle, mais ne devrait être citée que si le document n'est pas publié dans les documents officiels. Les documents miméographiés sont disponibles sur le site <documents.un.org>. Il est improbable qu'un document indique tous les éléments listés ci-haut. L'élément le plus important est le **Doc NU No**, puisque ceci est le moyen de recherche en ligne le plus facile, suivi du nom du corps, du titre et de la date. Les autres éléments sont moins essentiels, mais doivent être inclus s'ils se trouvent sur la page couverture.

> NUCS, Commission du désarmement, *Questions about Arms Manufacturing in Eastern Iraq,* Doc NU S/CN.10/L.666 Juillet 1993.

5.1.2.4 Périodiques

Pour faire référence à un **périodique publié par l'ONU**, suivre les règles de référence aux périodiques énoncées à la section 6.1. Si le titre n'indique pas que le périodique est publié par les Nations Unies, ajouter NU et l'organe responsable de la publication entre parenthèses à la fin de la référence.

« Emplois rémunérés dans les activités non agricoles » (1989) 63:9 Bulletin mensuel de statistiques 12 (NU, Département des affaires économiques et sociales internationales).

5.1.2.5 Annuaires

Pour les **articles d'annuaires des Nations Unies**, suivre les règles des ouvrages collectifs à la section 6.3. Si possible, inclure le numéro de document. Indiquer les noms de l'auteur et du directeur s'ils sont disponibles.

« Report of the Commission to the General Assembly on the work of its thirty-ninth Session » (Doc NU A/42/10) dans *Yearbook of the International Law Commission 1987*, vol 2, partie 2, New York, NU, 1989 à la p 50 (Doc NUA/CN.4/SER.A/1987/ Add.1).

5.1.2.6 Publications de vente

Faire référence aux **publications de vente** en utilisant les mêmes règles que pour les monographies (section 6.2).

NU, *Recommandations sur le transport des produits dangereux*, 9e éd, New York, NU, 1995 à la p 118.

5.1.3 Documents du Conseil de l'Europe

Conseil de l'Europe, | organe, | renseignements sur la session, | *titre*, | publication officielle, | autres renseignements | (année) | référence précise.

Indiquer **Conseil de l'Europe**, suivi de l'organe responsable. Abréger **Assemblée parlementaire** par **AP** et **Assemblée consultative** par **AC**. Fournir des renseignements sur la session, suivis du titre du document s'il y a lieu. Utiliser l'abréviation de la publication officielle.

Abréger *Comptes rendus des débats* par **Débats**.

Conseil de l'Europe, AP, 2001 sess ordinaire (1re partie), **Débats**, vol 1 (2001) à la p 67.

Abréger *Textes adoptés par l'Assemblée* par **Textes adoptés**.

Conseil de l'Europe, AC, 21e sess, partie 3, **Textes adoptés**, Rec 585 (1970) à la p 1.

Abréger *Ordres du jour et procès-verbaux* par **Ordres**.

Conseil de l'Europe, AC, 21e sess, partie 2, **Ordres**, 10e séance (1969) à la p 20.

Abréger *Documents de séance* par **Documents**.

Conseil de l'Europe, AP, 38e sess, *Déclaration écrite no 150 sur la protection du site archéologique de Pompei*, **Documents**, vol 7, Doc 5700 (1987) à la p 1.

Abréger *Bulletin d'information sur les activités juridiques* par **Bull inf**. Suivre le modèle prévu à la section 6.1.

Conseil de l'Europe, Comité des Ministres, *Recommandation R(82)1*, (1980) 12 **Bull inf** 58.

5.1.4 Documents de l'Organisation des États américains

OÉA, | organe, | numéro de session, | *titre*, | numéro de document | (année) | référence précise.

Les documents de l'OEA n'ont pas d'auteur. Indiquer l'organe responsable du document, à moins que le nom ne soit indiqué dans le titre du document.

s'il y a lieu, indiquer le numéro de session ou le numéro de séance après avoir indiqué l'organe responsable du document.

Écrire **Doc off** (Documents officiels) devant le numéro du document commençant par **OEA**. Le numéro du document débute avec les trois lettres **OEA** (Organización de los Estados Americanos) et non pas OÉA ou OAS.

OÉA, Assemblée générale, 2e sess, *Draft Standards Regarding the Formulation of Reservations to Multilateral Treaties*, Doc off OEA/Ser.P/AG/Doc.202 (1972).

OÉA, Commission interaméricaine des Droits de l'Homme, *Draft of the Inter-American Declaration on the Rights of Indigenous Peoples*, Doc off OEA/Ser.L/V/II.90/Doc.14, rev. 1 (1995) à la p 1.

5.1.5 Documents de l'Organisation mondiale du commerce (OMC) et de l'*Accord général sur les tarifs douaniers et le commerce* (GATT)

OMC ou GATT, | *titre*, | numéro de Déc, Rec ou Doc, | numéro de session, | IBDD | service électronique.

OMC, Conseil général, *Compte rendu de la réunion* (tenue le 22 novembre 2000), OMC Doc WT/GC/M/60, en ligne : *OMC* <docsonline.wto.org>.

Les décisions et les recommandations n'ont pas d'auteur. Indiquer le GATT, l'OMC et les organes plus précis comme responsables des rapports à moins que le nom ne soit indiqué dans le titre du rapport. Indiquer le numéro de décision ou de recommandation. S'il n'y a pas de numéro, indiquer la date complète de la décision ou de la recommandation. **PC** désigne **Parties contractantes**, **Déc** désigne **Décision** et **Rec** désigne **Recommandation**.

Accession of Guatemala, GATT PC Déc L/6824, 47e sess, supp n° 38 IBDD (1991) 16.

Liberté de contrat en matière d'assurance, GATT PC Rec du 27 mai 1959, 15e sess, supp n° 8 IBDD (1960) 26.

Si possible, se référer aux ***Instruments de base et documents divers*** (IBDD) du GATT. Si un rapport est publié indépendamment, sans numéro de document, suivre les règles pour les monographies (section 6.2) (par ex. **GATT, *Les marchés internationaux de la viande : 1990/91*, Genève, GATT, 1991**).

Report of the Panel adopted by the Committee on Anti-Dumping Practices on 30 October 1995, GATT Doc ADP/137, supp n° 42 IBDD (1995) 17.

OMC, *Rapport du groupe de travail sur l'accession de la Bulgarie*, OMC Doc WT/ ACC/BGR/5 (1996), en ligne : *OMC* <docsonline.wto.org>.

5.1.6 Documents de l'Organisation de coopération et de développement économiques (OCDE)

OCDE, organe, | *titre,* | titre de la série, | numéro du document de travail, | numéro du document | (renseignements sur l'édition).

Indiquer **OCDE** et l'organe particulier, suivi du titre en italique. Si le document fait partie d'une série, fournir le titre de la série.

OCDE, *Japon (n° 34)*, Examens en matière de coopération pour le développement, Paris, ODCE, 1999.

Si le document est un document de travail, fournir le numéro du document de travail (s'il y a lieu) ainsi que le numéro du document de l'OCDE. Noter que le numéro de document débute avec **OCDE** en français et en anglais.

OCDE, Département économique, *Pour une croissance écologiquement durable en Australie*, Document de travail n° 309, n° de doc ECO/ WKp(2001) 35 (2001).

Indiquer les renseignements sur l'édition. Si la seule information disponible est la date, mettre cette date entre parenthèses. Dans le cas d'un périodique, indiquer la date la plus précise possible.

OCDE, *Données OCDE sur l'environnement : Compendium 1995* (1995).

5.2 JURISPRUDENCE

Voir **l'annexe A-5** pour une liste des abréviations des organismes internationaux et de leurs recueils.

5.2.1 Cour permanente de Justice internationale (1922–1946)

Faire référence aux lois et aux règles de la CPJI par le titre, le numéro de recueil et le nom de l'édition, suivis de la première page ou du numéro de document (par ex. ***Revised Rules of the Court*** **(1926), CPJI 33 (sér D) n° 1**).

5.2.1.1 Arrêts, ordonnances et avis consultatifs

Intitulé (nom des parties) | (année), | type de décision, | recueil | numéro | référence précise.

Les **arrêts de la CPJI** sont publiés dans la *Série A : Recueil des arrêts* (**CPJI (sér A)**) et dans la *Série A/B : Arrêts, ordonnances et avis consultatifs* (**CPJI (sér A/B)**). Ne pas préciser le type de décision.

> *Affaire des zones franches de la Haute-Savoie et du pays de Gex (France c Suisse)* (1932), CPJI (sér A/B) n° 46 à la p 167.

Les **ordonnances de la CPJI** sont publiées dans la *Série A/B : Arrêts, ordonnances et avis consultatifs* **(CPJI (sér A/B))**. Ne pas indiquer l'année après l'intitulé, mais fournir la date complète après le type de décision (**Ordonnance du** jour | mois | année).

> *Chemin de fer Panevezys-Saldutiskis (Estonie c Lituanie)*, **Ordonnance du 30 juin 1938**, CPJI (sér A/B) n° 75 à la p 8.

Les **avis consultatifs de la CPJI** sont publiés dans la *Série B : Recueil des avis consultatifs* (**CPJI (sér B)**) et dans la *Série A/B : Arrêts, ordonnances et avis consultatifs* (**CPJI (sér A/B)**). Ne pas indiquer le nom des parties après l'intitulé.

> *Trafic ferroviaire entre la Lituanie et la Pologne* (1931), Avis consultatif, CPJI (sér A/B) n° 42 à la p 3.

5.2.1.2 *Plaidoiries, exposés oraux et autres documents*

Intitulé (nom des parties), | « titre du document précis » | (date du document), | recueil | numéro de décision, | 1re page | référence precise.

Faire référence à la série CPJI et indiquer le numéro de la décision. **Les plaidoiries, les exposés oraux** et **les autres documents avant 1931** sont publiés dans la *Série C : Actes et documents relatifs aux arrêts et aux avis consultatifs de la cour* (**CPJI (Sér C)**), et **les documents datant d'après 1931** dans la *Série C : Plaidoiries, exposés oraux et documents* (**CPJI (Sér. C)**). **Les documents de base**, **les annuaires** et **les indices** paraissent dans les séries D à F.

> *Affaire franco-hellenique des phares (France c Grèce)*, « Exposé oral de M le professeur Basdevant » (5 février 1934), CPJI (sér C) n° 74, 222 à la p 227.
>
> *Affaire Pajzs, Csáky, Esterházy (Hongrie c Yougoslavie)*, « Requête introductive d'instance » (1er décembre 1935), CPJI (sér C) n° 79, 10 à la p 12.

5.2.2 Cour internationale de Justice (1946 à aujourd'hui)

Faire référence aux lois et aux règles de la CIJ par le titre, le numéro de recueil et le nom de l'édition, suivis de la première page ou du numéro de document (par ex. ***Travel and Subsistence Regulations of the International Court of Justice***, **[1947] CIJ Acts & Doc 94**).

5.2.2.1 *Arrêts, ordonnances et avis consultatifs*

Les arrêts, les ordonnances et les avis consultatifs de la Cour internationale de Justice sont publiés dans le recueil officiel de la cour : **Recueil des arrêts, avis consultatifs et ordonnances** (**CIJ Rec**). Se référer au site internet de la CIJ <www.icj-cij.org> pour accéder aux arrêts, aux ordonnances et aux avis consultatifs qui ne sont pas encore publiés. Pour la référence aux sources électroniques, suivre les règles prévues à la section 1.6.

Intitulé (nom des parties), | type de décision, | [année du recueil] | recueil | première page | référence précise.

Bien que le recueil de la CIJ sépare parfois le nom des parties par une barre oblique (***El Salvador/Honduras***), remplacer la barre oblique par un *c* (***El Salvador c Honduras***).

Arrêts : Ne pas préciser le type de décision.

> *Affaire relative au Timor oriental (Portugal c Australie)*, [1995] CIJ Rec 90 à la p 103.

Ordonnances : Fournir la date complète après le type de décision (**Ordonnance du** jour | mois | année).

> *Certaines activités menées par le Nicaragua dans la région frontalière (Costa Rica c Nicaragua)*, **Ordonnance du 8 mars 2011**, [2011] CIJ Rec 6.

Avis consultatifs : Ne pas indiquer le nom des parties après l'intitulé.

> *Licéité de l'utilisation des armes nucléaires par un État dans un conflit armé*, Avis consultatif, [1996] CIJ Rec 66 à la p 70.

5.2.2.2 Mémoires, plaidoiries et documents

Intitulé officiel (nom des parties), | « titre du document précis » | (date du document), | [année du recueil] | recueil et numéro de volume | 1re page | référence précise.

Faire référence au recueil et à la première page du document. La CIJ publie les mémoires et autres documents dans ***Mémoires, plaidoiries et documents*** (**CIJ Mémoires**). Les mémoires sont disponibles sur le site internet de la CIJ : <www.icj-cij.org>.

S'il y a lieu, inclure un numéro de volume avant l'indication de la première page en chiffres arabes (par ex. **1, 2, 3**) et entre parenthèses. Après 1981, les mémoires n'indiquent pas la date de publication du recueil. Les volumes sont identifiés à partir du titre de la décision à laquelle le document se rapporte.

> *Affaire du droit de passage sur le territoire indien (Portugal c Inde)*, « Plaidoirie de Shri MC Setalvad » (23 septembre 1957), [1960] CIJ Mémoires (vol 4) 14 à la p 23.
>
> *Compétence en matière de pêcheries (Espagne c Canada)*, « Requête introductive d'instance par l'Espagne » (28 mars 1995), CIJ Mémoires 3.

5.2.3 Cour européenne des Droits de l'Homme et Commission européenne des Droits de l'Homme

5.2.3.1 Avant 1999

Intitulé | (année de la décision), | numéro de volume | recueil | 1re page | référence précise, | référence parallèle.

Renvoyer aux publications officielles de la Cour et de la Commission : ***Cour européenne des Droits de l'Homme, Série A : Arrêts et décisions*** (**Cour Eur DH (Sér A)**), ***Recueil de décisions de la Commission européenne des Droits de l'Homme*** (**Comm Eur DH Rec** (de 1960 à 1974)) et ***Décisions et rapports de la Commission européenne des Droits de l'Homme*** (**Comm Eur DH DR** (de 1975 à 1999)). Si possible, fournir une référence parallèle à **l'*Annuaire de la***

Convention européenne des Droits de l'Homme **(Ann Conv Eur DH)** ou aux ***European Human Rights Reports*** **(EHRR)**.

> *Kurt c Turquie* (1998), 74 CEDH (Sér A) 1152, 27 EHRR 373.
> *Spencer c Royaume-Uni* (1998), 92A Comm Eur DHDR 56, 41 YB Eur Conv HR 72.

5.2.3.2 À partir de 1999

Le Protocole n° 11 à la *Convention de sauvegarde des Droits de l'Homme et des Libertés fondamentales*, en vigueur depuis le 1er novembre 1998, a remplacé l'ancienne cour et l'ancienne commission par une nouvelle cour permanente.

Intitulé, | numéro de demande, | [année] | numéro de volume | recueil | 1re page, | référence parallèle.

Indiquer [GC] entres crochets après l'intitulé et avant la virgule, si l'arrêt ou la décision a été rendu par la Grande Chambre de la Cour.

Indiquer entre parenthèses après l'intitulé et avant la virgule s'il y a lieu : **(déc)** pour une **décision sur la recevabilité**, **(exceptions préliminaires)** pour un arrêt portant uniquement sur des **exceptions préliminaires**, **(satisfaction équitable)** pour un arrêt portant uniquement sur la **satisfaction équitable**, **(révision)** pour un arrêt de **révision**, **(interprétation)** pour un arrêt d'**interprétation**, **(radiation)** pour un arrêt **rayant l'affaire du rôle**, ou **(règlement amiable)** pour un arrêt sur un **règlement amiable**.

S'il existe **plus d'un numéro de demande**, inclure uniquement le premier numéro. Pour les **décisions non publiées**, indiquer le numéro de demande, suivi de la date du jugement (par ex. *Roche c Royaume-Uni* **[GC], n° 32555/96 (19 octobre 2005)**).

> *Allard c Suède*, n° 35179/97, [2003] VII CEDH 207, 39 EHRR 321.
> *Chypre c Turquie*, n° 25781/94, [2001] IV CEDH 1, 35 EHRR 731.

5.2.4 Cour interaméricaine des Droits de l'Homme

5.2.4.1 Jugements, ordonnances et avis consultatifs

Intitulé (nom de l'État impliqué) | (année de la décision), | type de décision et numéro, | recueil | numéro de la décision | référence précise, | référence parallèle.

Inscrire l'intitulé. Si la cause implique un État individuel, indiquer le nom de cet État entre parenthèses. Fournir l'année de la décision entre parenthèses. Indiquer le recueil et le numéro de la décision. Fournir une référence parallèle au **rapport annuel de la Cour**, aux ***International Legal Materials*** **(ILM)** ou à l'***Inter-American Yearbook on Human Rights***.

La Cour interaméricaine des Droits de l'Homme publie ses **jugements** dans *Inter-American Court of Human Rights, Series C: Decisions and Judgments* **(Inter-Am Ct HR (sér C))**. Ne pas indiquer le type de décision.

Affaire Neira Alegría (Pérou) (1996), Inter-Am Ct HR (sér C) n° 29 au para 55, *Annual Report of the Inter-American Court of Human Rights: 1996*, OEA/Ser.L/V/III.19/doc.4 (1997) 179.

La Cour interaméricaine des Droits de l'Homme publie ses **avis consultatifs** dans *Inter-American Court of Human Rights, Series A: Judgments and Opinions* (**Inter-Am Ct HR (sér A)**). Indiquer si le document est un **avis consultatif** et fournir le numéro de la décision.

Reports of the Inter-American Commission on Human Rights (Art 51 of the American Convention on Human Rights) (Chili) (1997), **Avis consultatif OC-15/97**, Inter-Am Ct HR (sér A) n° 15 au para 53, *Annual Report of the Inter-American Commission on Human Rights: 1997*, OEA/ Ser.L/V/III.39/doc.5 (1998) 307.

5.2.4.2 Mémoires, plaidoiries et documents

Intitulé (nom de l'État impliqué), | type de décision et numéro, | « titre du document » | (date du document), | recueil et (série) | 1re page, | référence précise.

Inscrire l'intitulé. Si l'information n'est pas déjà présente dans l'intitulé, indiquer le nom de l'État impliqué entre parenthèses. Indiquer si la décision est un **avis consultatif** et fournir le numéro de la décision. Indiquer le recueil et la première page de la décision. La Cour interaméricaine des Droits de l'Homme publie les mémoires, les plaidoiries et d'autres documents dans *Inter-American Court of Human Rights Series B: Pleadings, Oral Arguments and Documents* (**Inter-Am Ct HR (Sér B)**).

Proposed Amendments to the Naturalization Provisions of the Constitution of Costa Rica, Avis consultatif OC-4/84, « Verbatim Record of Public Hearing » (7 septembre 1983), Inter-Am Ct HR (Sér B) 203.

5.2.5 Commission interaméricaine des Droits de l'Homme

Intitulé | (année du jugement), | Inter-Am Comm HR, | numéro de la décision | référence précise, | *rapport annuel,* | numéro du document.

Les décisions de la Commission interaméricaine des Droits de l'Homme sont publiées dans ses rapports annuels. Faire référence au recueil annuel de la Commission et indiquer son numéro de document. Le numéro de document des publications de l'Organisation des États américains débute toujours avec **OEA** (Organización de los Estados Americanos) et non OÉA, quelle que soit la langue du document.

Sánchez c Mexico (1992), Inter-Am Comm HR, No 27/92, *Annual Report of the Inter-American Commission on Human Rights : 1992–93*, OEA/Ser.L/V/ II.83/doc.14 104.

5.2.6 Tribunaux de droit pénal international

Cette section s'applique aux documents provenant de la Cour pénale internationale, du Tribunal pénal international pour l'ex-Yougoslavie, du Tribunal pénal international pour le Rwanda, du Tribunal spécial pour la Sierra Leone et des Groupes d'enquête sur les crimes graves du Timor oriental.

Intitulé, | numéro de l'affaire, | titre du document (version) | numéro de la décision | référence précise | (tribunal), | référence parallèle.

> *Deputy General Prosecutor for Serious Crimes v Sito Barros*, 01/2004, Jugement final (12 mai 2005) au para 12 (Groupes d'enquête sur les crimes graves (Timor-Leste)), en ligne : *Judicial System Monitoring Program* <www.jsmp.tl/en>.

Indiquer le **prénom** de l'accusé dans l'intitulé, s'il y a lieu. S'il y a plus d'un accusé, indiquer uniquement le nom du premier accusé.

Inclure les **désignations informelles**, si désiré, entre parenthèses après le titre.

> *Le Procureur c Zdravko Mucic (**Jugement Celebici**)*, IT-96-21-*Abis*, Arrêt relatif à la sentence (8 avril 2003) au para 8 (Tribunal pénal international pour l'ex-Yougoslavie, Chambre d'appel) (WL).

Le titre du document indique sa fonction. Noter si le renvoi est la **version publique** du document ou la **version confidentielle** dont l'accès est limité au public. Suivre les directives fournies à la section 1.6 pour une référence à un site internet. Certains sites internet officiels des organismes judiciaires ne publient qu'une portion limitée des documents disponibles, alors que d'autres bases de données en ligne commerciales offrent une sélection de documents plus étendue. Si le nom du site internet est le même que celui du tribunal, indiquer uniquement les initiales pour identifier le site internet.

> *Le Procureur c Théoneste Bagosora*, ICTR-98-41-T, Procès-verbal d'audience (2 avril 2002) (Tribunal pénal international pour le Rwanda, Chambre de première instance), en ligne : ***TPIR*** <www.unictr.org>.

5.2.7 Groupes spéciaux de l'*Accord général sur les tarifs douaniers et le commerce* (GATT) 1947

Intitulé (plainte(s)) | (année du document), | numéro de document GATT, | numéro IBDD et (année) | 1re page | référence précise, | référence parallèle.

Se référer aux **IBDD** (***Instruments de base et documents divers***) du GATT en indiquant le numéro de volume suivi de **IBDD**, de l'année entre parenthèses et de la première page du document.

> *République de Corée – Restrictions à l'importation de la viande de bœuf (Plainte de la Nouvelle-Zélande)* (1989), GATT Doc L/6505, Supp n° 36 IBDD (1988-89) 234, en ligne : *OMC* <www.wto.org>.
>
> *États-Unis – Droits compensateurs sur la viande de porc fraîche, réfrigérée et congelée en provenance du Canada (Plainte du Canada)* (1991), GATT Doc DS7/R, Supp n° 38 IBDD (1990-91) 30, en ligne : *OMC* <www.wto.org>.

5.2.8 Rapports de Groupes spéciaux et de l'Organe d'appel de l'Organisation mondiale du commerce (OMC)

Intitulé (plainte(s)) | (année de la décision) | numéro du document de l'OMC | référence précise | (type de rapport), | référence parallèle.

Fournir l'intitulé du rapport, suivi du nom de l'auteur ou des auteurs de la plainte. Si les plaintes sont étudiées dans **un seul rapport**, indiquer les noms de tous les États ayant déposé une plainte après l'intitulé du rapport. Si plusieurs États ont déposé des plaintes **traitées séparément**, indiquer le nom de l'État visé par le rapport. Si plus de trois États ont déposé la plainte, indiquer le nom d'un seul État, suivi de **et al**.

Fournir le numéro du document. Un rapport peut avoir plusieurs numéros de document (par ex. **WT/DS 8, 10, 11/AB/R**). Dans le numéro du document, les lettres **WT-/DS** indiquent un **World Trade Dispute Settlement**, **AB** représente l'abréviation d'***Appellate Body*** et **R** indique un **rapport**. Si un rapport est destiné à un État particulier parmi plusieurs ayant déposé une plainte, l'abréviation du nom de cet État apparaît dans le numéro de document (par ex. **OMC doc WT/DS27/R/USA**).

États-Unis – Articles 301 à 310 de la Loi de 1974 sur le commerce extérieur (Plainte des communautés européennes) (1999), OMC Doc WT/DS152/R au n° 3.1 (Rapport du Groupe spécial), en ligne : *OMC* <docs.wto.org> [perma.cc/U4TY-NESC].

Inde – Protection conférée par un brevet pour les produits pharmaceutiques et les produits chimiques pour l'agriculture (Plaintes des États-Unis) (1997), OMC Doc WT/DS50/AB/R (Rapport de l'Organe d'appel), en ligne : *OMC* <docs.wto.org>. [perma.cc/QJY2-HVDW]

5.2.9 Rapports de Groupes spéciaux de l'Accord de libre-échange canado-américain

Intitulé | (année de la décision), | numéro de document, | recueil | (Groupe spécial), | référence parallèle.

Faire référence à un recueil imprimé si possible. Fournir des renseignements pour le chapitre sous lequel la plainte a été soumise. Abréger les divers groupes spéciaux de la façon suivante : **Groupe spéc ch 18** pour **Groupe spécial créé en vertu du chapitre 18**, **Groupe spéc ch 19** pour **Groupe spécial créé en vertu du chapitre 19** et **Comité pour cont extr** pour **Comité pour contestation extraordinaire**.

Re Framboises rouges du Canada (1990), USA-89-1904-01, 3 TCT 8175 (Groupe spéc c 19), en ligne : *Secrétariat de l'ALÉNA* <www.nafta-sec-alena.org>.

Re Porc frais, frigorifié et congélé du Canada (1991), ECC-91-1904-01 USA (Comité cont extr), en ligne : *Secrétariat de l'ALÉNA* <www.nafta-sec-alena.org>.

5.2.10 Rapports de Groupes spéciaux de l'Accord de libre-échange nord-américain (ALÉNA)

Intitulé (nom des parties) | (année de la décision), | numéro du document | (groupe spécial), | référence parallèle.

Re Certains produits de bois d'œuvre résineux du Canada (États-Unis c Canada) (2005), ECC-2004-1904-01USA (Comité cont extr), en ligne : *Secrétariat de l'ALÉNA* <www.nafta-sec-alena.org>.

Re Polystyrène et cristal impact en provenance des États-Unis d'Amérique (États-Unis c Mexique) (1995), MEX-94-1904-03 (Groupe spéc ch 19), en ligne : *Secrétariat de l'ALÉNA* <www.nafta-sec-alena.org>.

Re Tarifs douaniers appliqués par le Canada sur certains produits agricoles en provenance des États-Unis d'Amérique (États-Unis c Canada) (1996), CDA-95-2008-01 (Groupe arb ch 20), en ligne : *Secrétariat de l'ALÉNA* <www.nafta-sec-alena.org>.

Fournir des renseignements sur le chapitre dans lequel la plainte a été soumise. Abréger les noms des groupes spéciaux de la façon suivante : **Groupe spéc ch 19** pour **Groupe spécial binational créé en vertu du chapitre 19**, **Groupe arb ch 20** pour **Groupe arbitral créé en vertu du chapitre 20**, et **Comité cont extr** pour **Comité pour contestation extraordinaire**.

5.2.11 Décisions d'arbitrage international

Intitulé ou numéro de la décision | (année de la décision), | recueil, | référence précise | (cadre) | (arbitres).

Southern Pacific Properties c Egypt (1992), 32 ILM 933 à la p 1008 (International Center for Settlement of Investment Disputes) (Arbitres : Dr Eduardo Jiménez de Aréchaga, Mohamed Amin El Mahdi, Robert F. Pietrowski Jr).

Fournir l'intitulé avec les noms des parties si elles sont divulguées. Si les parties sont anonymes, indiquer le numéro de la décision.

Déc nº 6248 (1990), 19 YB Comm Arb 124 à la p 129 (International Chamber of Commerce).

Indiquer l'organisme qui a fourni le cadre ou le mécanisme d'arbitrage. Indiquer les noms des arbitres entre parenthèses à la fin de la référence (facultatif).

5.2.12 Décisions d'arbitrage de l'Organisation mondiale de la propriété intellectuelle (OMPI)

5.2.12.1 Principes directeurs régissant le règlement uniforme des litiges relatifs aux noms de domaine (UDRP)

Après l'intitulé, inclure le numéro du litige et le nom du domaine sur lequel porte la décision d'arbitrage.

Intitulé, | numéro du litige | <nom de domaine> | (Centre d'arbitrage et de médiation de l'OMPI (UDRP)).

CareerBuilder, LLC v Names for sale, D2005-0186 <careersbuilder.com> (Centre d'arbitrage et de médiation de l'OMPI (UDRP)).

5.2.13 Décisions de droit international prises devant des cours nationales

Intitulé, | recueil du pays d'origine, | recueil international | (pays et indication géographique).

Si une décision de portée internationale est rendue par une **cour nationale**, fournir une référence à un recueil du pays d'origine. Indiquer une référence à un recueil international tel que l'***Annual Digest and Reports of Public International Law Cases*** (**Ann Dig ILC**), l'***International Law Reports*** (**ILR**), les ***Common Market Law Reports*** (**CMLR**) ou le ***Common Market Reporter*** (**CMR**). En 1950, les Ann Dig ILC sont devenus les ILR.

Re Noble and Wolf, [1949] 4 DLR 375, [1948] Ann Dig ILC 302 (Can, CA Ont).

Lindon v Commonwealth of Australia (n° 2) (1996), 136 ALR 251, 118 ILR 338 (Austl, HC).

Institute of Chartered Accountants in England and Wales v Customs and Excise Commissioners, [1999] 2 All ER 449, [1999] 2 CMLR 1333 (R-U, HL).

6 Doctrine et autres documents F-85

6 DOCTRINE ET AUTRES DOCUMENTS

6.1 REVUES DE DROIT

6.1.1 Modèle de base

Auteur, | « titre de l'article » | (année) | volume | : | numéro | abréviation du périodique | première page | référence précise | (service électronique).

Marie-Claude Prémont, « La fiscalité locale au Québec : de la cohabitation au refuge fiscal » (2001) 46 RD McGill 713 à la p 720 (QL).

6.1.2 Auteur

6.1.2.1 Un seul auteur

Indiquer le nom de l'auteur **tel qu'il paraît à la première page de l'article**. Inclure tous les noms et initiales utilisés. Ne pas mettre d'espace entre les initiales. Ne pas inscrire un nom lorsque des initiales sont utilisées et ne pas inclure d'intiales lorsqu'un nom est utilisé. Si le nom de l'auteur sur la page de couverture est précédé d'un **titre honorifique** tel que **l'honorable**, **Rabbin**, **Professeur** ou **Lord**, inclure ce titre dans la référence. Inclure également les **suffixes** tels que **Jr** ou **IV**. Ne pas indiquer les diplômes ou autres références.

Frédéric Bachand, « L'efficacité en droit québécois d'une convention d'arbitrage ou d'élection de for invoquée à l'encontre d'un appel en garantie » (2004) 83:2 R du B 515.

L'honorable Louis LeBel, « La protection des droits fondamentaux et la responsabilité civile » (2004) 49:2 RD McGill 231.

6.1.2.2 Coauteurs

Ne pas indiquer plus de trois auteurs. S'il y a **deux auteurs**, séparer les noms des auteurs par **et**. S'il y a **trois auteurs**, séparer les deux premiers noms par une virgule et écrire **et** avant le dernier nom. S'il y a **plus de trois auteurs**, indiquer le nom du premier auteur, suivi de **et al**. Pour les autres types de **collaborations,** suivre la formule utilisée sur la page titre.

Murielle Paradelle, Hélène Dumont et Anne-Marie Boisvert, « Quelle justice pour quelle réconciliation ? : Le Tribunal pénal international pour le Rwanda et le jugement du génocide » (2005) 50:2 RD McGill 359.

Armel Huet et al, *Capitalisme et industries culturelles,* Grenoble, Presses Universitaires de Grenoble, 1978.

6.1.3 Titre de l'article

Indiquer le titre de l'article **entre guillemets**. Ne pas mettre de virgule après le titre.

Séparer un titre d'un sous-titre à l'aide d'un deux-points (:). Respecter les règles des **majuscules** et de la **ponctuation** de la langue du titre. Peu importe la langue du titre, utiliser des guillemets français avant et après le titre (par ex. « **Titre** »).

Ghislain Otis, « **Les sources des droits ancestraux des peuples autochtones** » (1999) 40:3 C de D 591.

Pour plus de détails concernant la langue et la ponctuation des titres, voir la section 6.2.3.

6.1.4 Année de publication

Si le périodique **est divisé en volumes numérotés**, indiquer la date de publication **entre parenthèses**.

Michel Poirier, « La convention d'emphytéose peut-elle être à titre gratuit ? » **(1998)** 58 R du B 401.

Si le périodique **n'est pas divisé en volumes numérotés, mais en années**, indiquer l'année **entre crochets**.

Frédéric Pollaud-Dulian, « À propos de la sécurité juridique » **[2001]** RTD civ 487.

6.1.5 Volume, numéro et série

Placer le **volume** après l'année de publication, suivi d'un deux-points et du **numéro** de la revue. Ne pas mettre d'espace ni avant ni après le deux-points. Puisque plusieurs bases de données en ligne ne fournissent pas le numéro, cet élément demeure facultatif. Le numéro est obligatoire uniquement lorsque les différents numéros d'un volume ne sont pas paginés consécutivement. Lorsque deux numéros sont publiés simultanément dans un même document, séparer ces numéros par une barre oblique (par ex. **6/7**).

Indiquer le volume et le numéro en chiffres arabes (par ex. **1, 2, 3**) même si la revue utilise des chiffres romains. Si une revue est aussi divisée en séries, indiquer entre parenthèses la **série** après le titre de la revue. Les abréviations des nombres ordinaux doivent apparaître en français dans la référence même si la revue est publiée dans une autre langue.

RRA Walker, « The English Property Legislation of 1922—6 » (1928) **10:1** J Comp Legis & Intl L **(3e)** 1.

6.1.6 Titre du périodique

Abréger le titre du périodique selon la liste des abréviations prévue à l'**annexe D**. Si le périodique n'apparaît pas dans l'**annexe D**, appliquer les règles suivantes. Écrire au complet les mots qui n'apparaissent pas dans la liste ci-dessous. Les titres de périodiques anglais qui n'apparaissent pas dans **l'annexe D** doivent être abrégés selon les règles de la section anglaise de ce Guide.

- ☐ Annuaire/annales = Ann
- ☐ Association = Assoc
- ☐ Barreau = B
- ☐ Gazette = Gaz
- ☐ International = Intl
- ☐ Journal = J

- ☐ Bulletin = Bull
- ☐ Canada ou canadien(ne) = Can
- ☐ Civil = Civ
- ☐ Criminel = Crim
- ☐ Droit = Dr
- ☐ Et = &
- ☐ Juridique = Jur
- ☐ Légal = Lég
- ☐ Revue = R
- ☐ Social/société = Soc
- ☐ Université = U

Omettre les mots « de/du », « un/une/des » et « le/la/les » dans les titres abrégés. Placer une espace entre deux mots ayant des caractères minuscules, et entre une esperluette et les mots ou lettres qui l'encadrent (par ex. Actu & dr int). Ne pas mettre d'espace entre des lettres majuscules adjacentes (par ex. RTD civ). Appliquer les abréviations de juridiction de la colonne des revues de **l'annexe A** pour les noms d'endroits. S'il n'y a pas de telle abréviation, écrire le nom du lieu au complet. Lorsqu'un journal a un sous-titre, omettre le sous-titre et n'abréger que le titre principal. Ne pas mettre l'abréviation ou le titre du périodique en italique.

> Will Kymlicka, « Federalism and Secession: At Home and Abroad » (2000) 13:2 **Can JL & Jur** 207.

6.1.7 Première page de l'article

Indiquer la première page de l'article après le titre de la revue. **Ne pas écrire** « p » ou « à la p ».

> Darren O'Toole, « La revendication du titre 'indien' par les Métis du Manitoba » (2006) 39:3 Revue canadienne de science politique/Canadian Journal of Political Science **529**.

6.1.7.1 Articles publiés en parties

Si les parties de l'article ont été publiées dans **plusieurs volumes**, indiquer l'auteur et le titre, suivis de la référence complète pour chaque partie, séparées par **et**.

> RA Macdonald, « Enforcing Rights in Corporeal Moveables: Revendication and Its Surrogates » (1986) 31:4 RD McGill 573 **et** (1986) 32:1 RD McGill 1.

Si les parties de l'article ont été publiées dans **un même volume**, indiquer les premières pages de chaque partie, séparées par **et**.

> Roderick A Macdonald, « L'image du Code civil et l'imagination du notaire » (1995) 74 R du B can **97 et 330**.

6.2 MONOGRAPHIES

6.2.1 Modèle de base

Auteur, | *titre*, | édition, | autres éléments | lieu d'édition, | maison d'édition, | année d'édition | référence précise | (service électronique).

En règle générale, inclure les autres éléments entre l'édition et le lieu d'édition. Leur ordre de présentation est le suivant : **nom du traducteur** (section 6.2.2.4), **numéro du volume** (section 6.2.4), **titre du volume**, **titre d'une collection et numéro du volume dans cette collection** et **feuilles mobiles** (section 6.2.6). Ces éléments doivent être séparés par des virgules. Puisque certains de ces éléments doivent exceptionnellement être inclus à un emplacement différent de la référence, toujours consulter les règles spécifiques pour chacun des éléments. Si le livre est un ouvrage collectif, voir la section 6.3.

> Éric Canal-Forgues, *Le règlement des différends à l'OMC*, 3e éd, Bruxelles, Bruylant, 2008 à la p 53.
>
> J Anthony VanDuzer, *The Law of Partnerships and Corporations*, Toronto, Irwin Law, 2009 ch 2 (B) (3) (QL).
>
> Jean-Louis Baudouin et Yvon Renaud, *Code civil du Québec annoté*, 20e éd, Montréal, Wilson & Lafleur, 2017 à la note 7/3.

6.2.2 Auteur

6.2.2.1 Un seul auteur

Indiquer le nom de l'auteur **tel qu'il paraît sur la page titre** (et non sur la page couverture). Inclure tous les noms et initiales utilisés. Ne pas mettre d'espace entre les initiales. Ne pas inscrire un nom lorsque des initiales sont utilisées et ne pas inclure d'intiales lorsqu'un nom est utilisé. Si le nom de l'auteur sur la page de couverture est précédé d'un **titre honorifique** tel que **l'honorable**, **Rabbin**, **Professeur** ou **Lord**, inclure ce titre dans la référence. Inclure également les suffixes tels que **Jr** ou **IV**. Ne pas indiquer les diplômes ou autres références.

> **Sylvio Normand**, *Introduction au droit des biens*, 2e éd, Montréal, Wilson & Lafleur, 2014.
>
> **Jean-Pierre Baud**, *L'affaire de la main volée : une histoire juridique du corps*, Paris, Seuil, 1993 à la p 4.
>
> **Lucie Laflamme**, *Le partage consécutif à l'indivision*, Montréal, Wilson & Lafleur, 1999.
>
> **Lord Denning**, *What Next in the Law*, Londres, Butterworths, 1982.

6.2.2.2 Coauteurs

Séparer les noms des deux derniers auteurs par **et**.

> **Jacques Bourdon, Jean-Marie Pontier et Jean-Claude Ricci**, *Droit des collectivités territoriales*, Paris, Presses universitaires de France, 1987.

Ne pas indiquer plus de trois auteurs. S'il y en a plus, indiquer le nom du premier auteur, suivi de **et al**.

> **Joel Bakan et al**, *Canadian Constitutional Law*, 3e éd, Toronto, Emond Montgomery, 2003.

Pour les **autres types de collaborations** (par ex. **avec la collaboration de**), suivre la formule utilisée sur la page titre de la monographie.

Pierre-Gabriel Jobin avec la collaboration de Nathalie Vézina, *Baudouin et Jobin : Les obligations*, 6e éd, Cowansville (QC), Yvon Blais, 2005.

6.2.2.3 Directeur ou correcteur de l'ouvrage d'un autre auteur

Directeur, | dir, | *titre*, | édition, | renseignements sur l'édition.

Si le nom de l'auteur fait partie du titre, faire référence au directeur, suivi de **dir** entre virgules.

M Dupin, dir, *Oeuvres de Pothier*, 2e éd, Paris, Pichon-Béchet, 1835.

Auteur, | *titre*, | édition | par | directeur, | renseignements sur l'édition.

Si le nom de l'auteur ne fait pas partie du titre, mettre le nom du directeur après la mention de l'édition, et l'introduire avec **par**. S'il y a plusieurs éditions, indiquer le numéro (par ex. **8e éd par**). Indiquer le(s) nom(s) du ou des auteur(s) et du ou des directeur(s) tels qu'ils apparaissent dans la publication.

Aubry et Rau, *Droit civil français*, 8e éd par André Ponsard et Ibrahim Fadlallah, Paris, Librairies techniques, 1989.

6.2.2.4 Traducteur

Traduire les textes en langues étrangères qui pourraient ne pas être connues des lecteurs. Le texte original d'une citation peut être inclus dans la note de bas de page.

6.2.2.4.1 Traduction professionnelle

Faire référence à une traduction professionnelle en indiquant le nom du traducteur avant les renseignements sur l'édition, introduit par **traduit par**. S'il est nécessaire de modifier la traduction, ajouter **[modifiée par l'auteur]** après les renseignements sur l'édition. Toujours inclure l'information sur le directeur ou le correcteur (section 6.2.2.3) avant l'information sur le traducteur (section 6.2.2.4).

Jürgen Habermas, *Droit et démocratie : entre faits et normes*, **traduit par** Rainer Rochlitz et Christian Bouchindhomme, Paris, Gallimard, 1997.

6.2.2.4.2 Traduction de l'auteur du texte (vous)

L'ajout **[notre traduction]** se réfère à l'auteur (vous) et non à l'auteur du texte cité. Traduire un passage tiré d'une source rédigée dans une autre langue que le français ou l'anglais. Insérer l'ajout **[notre traduction]** dans le corps même du texte, après les guillemets de la citation traduite et immédiatement avant l'appel de note.

Comme le dit Kronby, « la cour fut convaincue par la preuve de l'épouse » **[notre traduction]**[28].

Doctrine et autres documents

6.2.3 Titre

Indiquer le titre du livre en entier et en italique. Suivre l'orthographe et la ponctuation du titre tel que publié.

> Brigitte Lefebvre, *La bonne foi dans la formation du contrat*, Cowansville (QC), Yvon Blais, 1998.

Précéder le sous-titre d'un deux-points non italique. Lorsque le livre cité est en anglais, ne pas mettre d'espace avant le deux-points.

> Frédéric Garron, *La caducité du contrat* : *étude de droit privé*, Aix-en-Provence, Presses universitaires d'Aix-Marseille, 2000.
>
> Petri Mäntysaari, *Comparative Corporate Governance*: *Shareholders as a Rule-maker*, New York, Springer, 2005.

Insérer une virgule avant une date comprise à la fin du titre.

> Michel Verpeaux, *La naissance du pouvoir réglementaire, 1789-1799*, Paris, Presses universitaires de France, 1991.

Si le titre de l'ouvrage est dans une langue qui n'est pas le français, l'anglais ou une autre langue familière aux lecteurs, inscrire le titre original, suivi d'une traduction en français. Ne pas mettre la traduction en italique, mais entre crochets, sans ponctuation entre le titre original et la traduction.

> Jürgen Schwarze, *Europaïsches Varwaltungsrecht* [Droit administratif européen], 2e éd, Bruxelles, Bruylant, 2009.

Transcrire le titre en lettres latines lorsque le titre original est dans une autre écriture (par ex. **Menachem Elon, *Ha-Mishpat Ha-Ivri* [Droit juif]**).

6.2.3.1 *Procédures publiées d'une conférence ou d'un symposium*

> Marie-France Bich, « Petits éléments pour une réflexion polémique sur la solidarité en droit du travail » dans *Droits de la personne : solidarité et bonne foi. Actes des Journées strasbourgeoises de l'Institut canadien d'études juridiques supérieures 2000 tenues du 2 au 8 juillet 2000 à Strasbourg*, Cowansville (QC), Yvon Blais, 2000.

Traiter toute information concernant la conférence ou le symposium comme faisant partie du titre.

6.2.4 Numéro de volume

6.2.4.1 *Livres en français*

Auteur | *titre*, | tome, | volume : | édition, | directeur, | renseignements sur l'édition.

> Jean Carbonnier, *Droit civil : les obligations*, t 4, 22e éd, Paris, Presses universitaires de France, 2000.

Doctrine et autres documents

Les ouvrages en français peuvent être divisés en tomes et subdivisés en volumes. Utiliser **t** pour **tome** et **vol** pour **volume**. Les renseignements relatifs au tome et au volume doivent être fournis après le titre. Indiquer les numéros de tomes et de volumes en chiffres arabes (par ex. **1, 2, 3**). S'il y a lieu, inclure le titre du volume introduit par un deux-points à la suite du numéro de volume.

> Henri Mazeaud et al, *Leçons de droit civil*, t 3, vol 1 : Sûretés, publicité foncière, 7e éd, Yves Picod, dir, Paris, Montchrestien, 1999.

Ne pas répéter le numéro du tome et du volume dans les références suivantes, à moins qu'il n'y ait une référence à un tome ou un volume différent ailleurs dans le document citant.

6.2.4.2 Livres en anglais

Indiquer le numéro du volume en chiffres arabes (par ex. **1, 2, 3**) même si l'éditeur utilise des chiffres romains. Ne pas répéter le numéro du volume dans les références ultérieures à moins qu'il y ait une référence à un volume différent ailleurs dans le document citant.

Si les volumes sont publiés sous différents titres, indiquer le numéro du volume avant les renseignements sur l'édition.

> David Gillies, *Telecommunications Law*, **vol 1**, Londres (R-U), Butterworths, 2003.

Si les volumes sont publiés sous un même titre, indiquer le numéro du volume après les renseignements sur l'édition.

> Karl Marx, *Capital: A Critical Analysis of Capitalist Production*, Friedrich Engels, dir, traduit par Samuel Moore et Edward B Aveling, Londres (R-U), Swan Sonnenschein, 1908, **vol 1** à la p 15.

6.2.5 Édition

Indiquer le numéro de l'édition (par ex. **2e éd**) après le titre. Abréger **édition** par **éd**. Lorsque l'ouvrage a été révisé mais qu'aucun numéro d'édition n'est précisé, indiquer **éd révisée** après le titre.

> Germain Brière, *Le nouveau droit des successions*, **2e éd**, Montréal, Wilson & Lafleur, 1997.
>
> Maurice Tancelin, *Des obligations : contrat et responsabilité*, **éd révisée**, Montréal, Wilson & Lafleur, 1986.

6.2.6 Ouvrage à feuilles mobiles

Auteur, | *titre*, | renseignements sur l'édition, | (feuilles mobiles | date de la mise à jour | supplément), | référence précise.

Les règles de cette section s'appliquent aux **ouvrages de doctrine** dont le contenu est **continuellement renouvelé**. Pour faire référence à la législation sous forme de recueils à feuilles mobiles, voir la section 2.1.6. Après les renseignements sur l'édition, mettre entre parenthèses l'expression **feuilles mobiles** et le numéro de la mise à jour ou du supplément.

Si l'année de la révision n'est pas déjà indiquée dans le numéro de la mise à jour ou du supplément, il est possible de l'inclure dans la référence.

> *The Law of Tort*, Toronto, Thomson Reuters, 2011 (feuilles mobiles **mises à jour en 2013**, version 20), ch 5 à la p 71).

Utiliser la date d'édition qui paraît sur la page où sont indiquées les informations sur les droits d'auteur, même si cette date diffère de la date qui se trouve ailleurs dans le livre. Faire référence au chapitre en plus de la page si l'ouvrage est divisé en chapitres.

> Georges Audet et al, *Le congédiement en droit québécois en matière de contrat individuel de travail*, Cowansville (QC), Yvon Blais, 1991 (feuilles mobiles mises à jour 18:1), ch 5 à la p 71.
>
> Madeleine Lemieux, *Tribunaux administratifs du Québec : Règles et législation annotées*, Cowansville (QC), Yvon Blais, 2002 (feuilles mobiles mises à jour 15), ch R9 à la p 85.
>
> Robert W Hillman, *Hillman on Lawyer Mobility : The Law and Ethics of Partner Withdrawals and Law Firm Breakups*, 2e éd, New York, Wolters Kluwer, 1998 (feuilles mobiles supplément 2009), ch 2 à la p 85.

6.2.7 Lieu d'édition

Indiquer le lieu d'édition. Le lieu d'édition peut servir à signaler au lecteur la juridiction pertinente à l'œuvre citée. Indiquer le lieu d'édition tel qu'il figure au recto ou au verso de la page titre. Utiliser la **version française** du nom de la ville si elle existe (par ex. écrire **Londres (R-U)** et non **London (UK)**). S'il y a **plus d'un lieu d'édition**, inclure le lieu indiqué sur la page titre (et non ceux indiqués au verso de la page titre) ou, si plusieurs lieux sont indiqués sur le recto de la page titre, inclure seulement le premier lieu.

Si des renseignements supplémentaires sont requis pour identifier le lieu d'édition (par ex. la province, l'état ou le pays), abréger ces renseignements entre parenthèses après le lieu d'édition (par ex. **Cowansville (QC)**). Si deux villes peuvent être confondues, ajouter les renseignements supplémentaires nécessaires (par ex. **London (ON)** et **Londres (R-U)**). Voir les abréviations couramment utilisées des provinces canadiennes de l'**annexe A-1** et les abréviations des états américains de l'**annexe A-2**.

> Jean-Luc Aubert, *La responsabilité civile des notaires*, 3e éd, **Paris**, Defrénois, 1998.
>
> Andrée Lajoie, *Pouvoir disciplinaire et tests de dépistage de drogues en milieu de travail : illégalité ou pluralisme*, **Cowansville (QC)**, Yvon Blais, 1995.

6.2.8 Maison d'édition

Indiquer le nom de la maison d'édition **tel qu'il figure à la page titre**. Ne pas l'abréger (par ex. **Presses de l'Université Laval** et non **PUL**). Omettre l'article défini (**le**, **la**, **les**, **l'**, ***the***) si c'est le premier mot du nom de la maison d'édition et omettre les expressions indiquant le statut corporatif (par ex. **ltée**, **inc**).

> Mireille D-Castelli et Dominique Goubau, *Précis de droit de la famille*, Sainte-Foy (QC), **Presses de l'Université Laval**, 2000.

Écrire « édition(s) », « Publishing » ou « Publishers » uniquement s'il s'agit d'une partie inséparable du nom (par ex. **Éditions de l'Homme**). Si ces mots apparaissent dans une langue autre que le français ou l'anglais, ne pas les supprimer (par ex. **Verlag**). Indiquer **Presses** en français et **Press** en anglais si c'est inclus dans le nom de la maison d'édition sur la page titre.

> Pierre-Claude Lafond, *Précis de droit des biens*, 2e éd, Montréal, **Thémis**, 2007.

S'il y a **plus d'un éditeur**, fournir les lieux d'édition et les noms des coéditeurs, suivis de l'année. Séparer les lieux d'édition l'un de l'autre par **et**. De même, sépararer les noms des coéditeurs par **et**.

> Latzville (BC) et Montréal : Oolichan Books et Institute for Research on Public Policy, 1992.

Si un éditeur travaille pour une **organisation**, indiquer **pour** avant le nom de l'organisation (par ex. **Janet E Gans Epner pour la Commission on Women in the Profession**). Si **aucune maison d'édition** n'est indiquée, écrire **maison d'édition inconnue**.

6.2.9 Année d'édition

Indiquer l'année de **l'édition actuelle** et non celle de la première édition. En général, utiliser la date la plus récente indiquée sur l'édition, à moins que l'année de publication ne soit présentée de façon explicite. Ne pas indiquer l'année d'impression.

> Jean Pineau et Serge Gaudet, *Théorie des obligations*, 4e éd, Montréal, Thémis, **2001**.

6.3 ARTICLES OU ENTRÉES D'OUVRAGES COLLECTIFS, DE DICTIONNAIRES ET D'ENCYCLOPÉDIES

6.3.1 Modèle de base

Aux fins du présent *Manuel*, les **ouvrages collectifs**, les **encyclopédies** et les **dictionnaires** sont soumis aux mêmes règles.

Auteur de l'article ou de l'entrée, | « titre de l'article ou de l'entrée » | dans | directeur, | dir, | *titre de l'ouvrage*, | édition, | lieu d'édition, | maison d'édition, | année d'édition, | première page | référence précise.

Indiquer le plus de renseignements possible parmi ceux suggérés dans la forme générale. Noter toutefois que plusieurs renseignements ne seront pas disponibles.

Indiquer tout d'abord le nom de l'auteur et le titre de l'article ou de l'entrée, puis indiquer les renseignements relatifs à l'ouvrage dans le même ordre et en utilisant les règles prévues à la section 6.2. Ne pas confondre le nom du directeur et le nom de l'auteur de l'article ou de l'entrée. Suivre le nom du directeur de **dir** entre virgules.

Si le texte n'est pas un article ou une entrée, utiliser en guise de titre d'article ou d'entrée le nom donné à la section citée en suivant les règles qui s'appliquent aux articles (par. ex. **Avant-propos**, **Préface**, **Introduction**, **Conclusion**).

Lorsque des éléments autres que ceux suggérés dans le modèle de base peuvent être ajoutés (voir section 6.2.1), les placer entre le titre de l'ouvrage et les renseignements sur l'édition.

6.3.2 Ouvrages collectifs

Un ouvrage est collectif s'il est rédigé ou conçu par plusieurs auteurs. Les ouvrages collectifs comprennent notamment les livres regroupant des chapitres ou des essais rédigés par différents auteurs.

> Madeleine Cantin Cumyn, « Le Code civil et la gestion des biens d'autrui » dans Jean-Louis Baudouin et Patrice Deslauriers, dir, *La responsabilité civile des courtiers en valeurs mobilières et des gestionnaires de fortune : aspects nouveaux*, Cowansville (QC), Yvon Blais, 1999, 121 à la p 128.

6.3.3 Encyclopédies

Une encyclopédie est un ouvrage qui recense les connaissances liées à un domaine du savoir particulier (à distinguer du dictionnaire à 6.3.4). Indiquer le nom de l'auteur lorsqu'il est fourni. À noter que plusieurs encyclopédies ne reconnaissent pas explicitement les contributions d'auteurs.

> Rev Edward Mewburn Walker, « Constitution of Athens » dans Hugh Chisholm, dir, *Encyclopaedia Britannica*, 11e éd, New York, Encyclopaedia Britannica, 1911.

Inclure tous les éléments supplémentaires, par exemple le numéro de volume (voir section 6.2.1).

6.3.4 Dictionnaires

Un dictionnaire est un ouvrage qui recense l'ensemble des mots d'une langue ou d'un domaine d'activité et qui fournit des renseignements quant au sens et à l'emploi de chacune des entrées. L'auteur de l'entrée n'étant généralement pas connu, se référer uniquement au nom de l'auteur ou du directeur de l'ouvrage, mais indiquer entre guillemets le mot cherché comme référence précise à la suite de la locution ***sub verbo***, qui signifie « au mot » en latin.

> Gérard Cornu, dir, *Vocabulaire juridique*, 11e éd, Paris, Presses universitaires de France, 2016, ***sub verbo*** « minorité ».
> Desmond Brice-Bennett, *Legal Glossary: English/Inuktitut/French*, Iqaluit, Nunavut Arctic College, 1997, ***sub verbo*** « piqujaq ».

6.4 RECUEILS ENCYCLOPÉDIQUES

6.4.1 *Canadian Encyclopedic Digest*

Le *Canadian Encyclopedic Digest* (CED) est une encyclopédie publiée en feuilles mobiles donnant de l'information générale sur un sujet particulier du droit. Chacun des volumes est organisé par sujet (par ex. droit criminel, droit de la famille).

6.4.1.1 CED version imprimée

CED | (série | édition), | volume, | titre | section.

Écrire **CED** plutôt que le nom de l'encyclopédie au complet. Indiquer la série sous forme abrégée : **Ontario CED** (**Ont**) et **Western CED** (**West**).

CED (Ont 4e), vol 1, titre 2 à la s 10.

6.4.1.2 CED version électronique

CED | édition | (en ligne), | *sujet* | (série), | « | rubrique et sous-rubrique » | (code de la sous-rubrique CED) | section.

Séparer les rubriques et les sous-rubriques par un deux-points. Inscrire le code de la sous-rubrique tel qu'il apparaît dans le CED en ligne.

Favoriser une référence à la version électronique. Si vous souhaitez faire référence à la version imprimée, suivre les règles de la section 6.4.1.1. Westlaw fournit un lien vers les renseignements nécessaires pour une référence à la version imprimée à partir de la version électronique du CED.

CED 4e éd (en ligne), *Actions* (Ont), « Forms and Classes of Action : Penal Actions : General » (II.5.(a)) à la s 3.
CED 4e éd (en ligne), *Citizenship*, « Taking the Test and Oath of Citizenship : Oral Interview for Citizenship » (III.(6)) à la s 57.

6.4.2 Halsbury's Laws of Canada

Halsbury's Laws of Canada fournit des résumés d'un large éventail de sujets juridiques. Chaque volume est organisé par sujet (par ex. procédures criminelles, assurances). Les mises à jour sont faites par l'entremise de suppléments cumulatifs publiés annuellement. Lorsque la partie citée fut mise à jour par un supplément cumulatif, faire référence à ce supplément et à son numéro de version entre parenthèses et à la suite de la section, en utilisant la forme abrégée (**Supp Cum version** x).

6.4.2.1 Halsbury's Laws of Canada version imprimée

Halsbury's Laws of Canada, | volume, | *sujet*, | section | (mise à jour).

Halsbury's Laws of Canada, vol 2, *Business Corporations*, dans HBC-301 « Prescribed by statute » (Supp Cum version 4).

6.4.2.2 Halsbury's Laws of Canada version électronique

Halsbury's Laws of Canada | (en ligne), | *sujet*, | « rubrique et sous-rubrique » | (code de la sous-rubrique) | section | mise à jour.

Halsbury's Laws of Canada (en ligne), *Business Corporations*, « Shareholder Remedies : The Oppression Remedy : Standing » (XIII.2.(6)) dans HBC-301 « Prescribed by statute » (Supp Cum version 4).

6.4.3 JurisClasseur Québec

Le ***JurisClasseur Québec*** est un recueil encyclopédique disponible en version imprimée sous forme de feuilles mobiles et en version électronique sur Quicklaw. Les renseignements bibliographiques à inclure dans la référence sont différents selon la version utilisée. Les références précises doivent être faites aux numéros (n°) indiqués devant le titre de certains paragraphes. Ne pas faire référence aux paragraphes (**para**), car plusieurs paragraphes ne sont pas numérotés.

Auteur, | « numéro du fascicule : | titre du fascicule » | référence précise, | dans | directeur, | dir, | JCQ | *titre de la collection.*

6.4.3.1 *Version imprimée du JurisClasseur Québec*

Indiquer le nom de l'auteur du fascicule. Si la source n'est pas divisée en numéros, la référence précise doit être faite aux numéros de page. Les numéros de page sont constitués du numéro du fascicule et du numéro de la page à l'intérieur du fascicule en question. Les deux numéros sont séparés d'une barre oblique (**10/30, 5/26**).

Louise Tremblay, "Fascicule 4 : Testament – règles de forme" au n° 62, dans Pierre-Claude Lafond, dir, JCQ Successions et libéralités.

6.4.3.2 *Version Quicklaw du JurisClasseur Québec*

Omettre le nom de l'auteur puisque ce renseignement n'est pas fourni dans la version électronique. Inscrire **(QL)** à la fin de la référence.

« Fascicule 4 : Testament – règles de forme » au no 62, dans Pierre-Claude Lafond, dir, JCQ *Successions et libéralités* **(QL)**.

6.5 CODES DE DÉONTOLOGIE

Organisme, | *titre du code,* | renseignements sur l'édition, | référence précise.

Si l'organisme et l'éditeur sont les mêmes, indiquer l'abréviation officielle de l'organisme dans les renseignements sur l'édition.

L'Association du Barreau canadien, *Code de déontologie professionnelle*, Ottawa, ABC, 2006, ch VI, r 1(a).

Association des infirmières et infirmiers du Canada, *Code de déontologie des infirmières et infirmiers*, Ottawa, AIIC, 2008, préambule à la p 2.

Abréger **règle** par **r**. Certains codes de déontologie sont établis par la législation. Faire référence à ces codes comme à des lois ordinaires (section 2.1).

Doctrine et autres documents

6.6 RECENSIONS

Auteur, | « titre de la recension », | recension de | *titre de l'ouvrage recensé* | de | auteur ou éditeur de l'ouvrage recensé | renseignements sur l'édition.

Les recensions sont l'équivalent des *book reviews* en anglais.

Si la recension porte un titre, l'indiquer après le nom de l'auteur, suivi d'une virgule. Indiquer **recension de** avant le titre de l'ouvrage recensé. Introduire par **de** le nom de l'auteur après le titre de l'ouvrage recensé.

Si le titre de la recension indique **à la fois le titre de l'ouvrage recensé et son auteur**, omettre ces informations dans le reste de la référence. Si le titre de la recension indique ***soit*** **le titre de l'ouvrage recensé,** ***soit*** **son auteur**, indiquer cette information après **recension de** même si une partie de l'information sera répétée.

Si l'ouvrage recensé possède un éditeur plutôt qu'un auteur, écrire **éd** entre virgules après le nom de l'éditeur de l'ouvrage recensé.

> Bjarne Melkevik, recension de *Démocratie et procéduralisation du droit* de Philippe Coppens et Jacques Lenoble (2001) 42:2 C de D 337.
>
> Yves-Marie Morissette, recension de *L'administration de la preuve* de Léo Ducharme (2001) 46:4 RD McGill 1179.

6.7 COMMENTAIRES D'ARRÊT ET CHRONIQUES DE LÉGISLATION

Auteur, | « titre », | commentaire ou chronique | de | *intitulé* ou nom de la loi ou du projet de loi, | renseignements sur l'édition.

Indiquer le titre du commentaire d'arrêt ou de la chronique de législation entre guillemets, s'il y a lieu. Toutefois, si le titre indique déjà le nom de l'arrêt, omettre ces informations du reste de la référence.

Pour faire référence à **un commentaire d'arrêt**, mentionner **commentaire de** avant l'intitulé de l'arrêt.

> Léo Ducharme, « La proclamation de l'existence en droit québécois de la règle de common law de l'engagement implicite de confidentialité : *Lac d'amiante*, une décision judiciaire erronée », commentaire de *Lac d'amiante du Québec ltée c 2858-0702 Québec inc*, (2000) 79 R du B can 435.

Pour faire référence à **une chronique de législation**, la mention **chronique de** précède le titre de la loi.

> Jean-Pierre Colpron, « Les nouvelles règles visant à réduire les pertes en capital », chronique de l'art 1123 de la *Loi de l'impôt sur le revenu*, (1996) 18 Rev de plan fisc & success 177.

6.8 COMMENTAIRES, REMARQUES ET NOTES

Auteur, | « titre », | genre du texte, | renseignements sur l'édition.

Inscrire le genre du texte (**commentaire éditorial**, **note** ou **remarque**) avant les renseignements sur l'édition.

> Monroe Leigh, « The Yugoslav Tribunal: Use of Unnamed Witnesses Against Accused », **commentaire éditorial**, (1996) 90:2 AJIL 235.
>
> « What We Talk About When We Talk About Persons: The Language of Legal Fiction », **note**, (2001) 114:6 Harv L Rev 1745.

6.9 MANUSCRITS NON PUBLIÉS

6.9.1 Modèle de base

Auteur, | *titre* ou « titre », | date | [non publié, | archivé | lieu].

Faire référence au titre du manuscrit selon son genre. Pour les articles, placer le titre entre guillemets. Pour les monographies, inscrire le titre en italique. Faire suivre le titre du manuscrit de sa date de création. Indiquer que le manuscrit n'a pas été publié en mettant **[non publié, archivé]**, ainsi que l'endroit où le manuscrit se trouve.

> J Tremblay, « Nouveaux développements en droit du travail », mai 1997 [non publié, archivé à la Revue de droit de McGill].

6.9.2 Manuscrits à paraître

Auteur, | *titre* ou « titre », | renseignements sur l'édition | [à paraître en | date de publication prévue].

Faire référence au titre du manuscrit selon son genre. Pour les articles, placer le titre entre guillemets. Pour les monographies, inscrire le titre en italique. Inscrire les renseignements sur l'édition selon le genre du manuscrit, mais ne pas indiquer la date de publication. S'il s'agit d'une revue et que le numéro dans lequel le manuscrit sera publié est connu, indiquer ce numéro. Indiquer que le manuscrit n'a pas encore été publié en ajoutant [**à paraître**] et la date de publication prévue si disponible.

6.9.3 Thèses et dissertations

Auteur, | *titre*, | diplôme, | institution, | année | [non publiée].

Après avoir indiqué l'auteur et le titre du document, inscrire le diplôme dans le cadre duquel il a été écrit. Inclure la **discipline étudiée** (par ex. droit, science politique, économie), si l'on ne peut la déduire du diplôme ou du nom de l'institution. Après la mention de l'année, écrire **[non publiée]**. Faire référence aux thèses publiées sur support de microfiche (par ex. les

University Microfilms International) de la même manière que les références aux thèses sur support papier.

> Louise Potvin, *La personne et la protection de son image*, thèse de doctorat en droit, Université McGill, 1989 [non publiée].
>
> Val Napoleon, *Ayook: Gitksan Legal Order, Law and Legal Theory*, dissertation de doctorat, University of Victoria, 2009 [non publiée].

6.10 ALLOCUTIONS ET TEXTES PRÉSENTÉS DURANT DES CONFÉRENCES

Conférencier, | « titre » ou allocution, | événement, | présenté(e) à | lieu ou institution, | date | renseignements sur l'édition ou [non publié(e)].

Indiquer le titre de l'allocution, si possible. Si **aucun titre** n'est fourni, utiliser **allocution**. Inscrire l'événement dans le cadre duquel l'allocution a été prononcée ou le texte a été présenté. Indiquer le lieu ou l'institution où l'allocution a été faite.

Inclure les renseignements sur l'édition. Pour faire référence à une **allocution non publiée**, inscrire **[non publié(e)]** à la fin de la référence (section 6.9.1). Si l'allocution non publiée est disponible en ligne, inscrire l'adresse électronique sous **renseignements sur l'édition** (section 6.19). Pour faire référence à une **allocution publiée dans une collection**, respecter les règles de référence des ouvrages collectifs (section 6.3).

> Son excellence John Ralston Saul, allocution d'ouverture, Conférence du Conseil international d'études canadiennes, présentée à l'Université d'Ottawa, 18 mai 2000 [non publiée], en ligne : Le gouverneur général du Canada <www.gg.ca>.
>
> Le juge John H Gomery, « The Pros and Cons of Commissions of Inquiry » Série de conférences annuelles de la Revue de droit de McGill, présentée à la Faculté de droit de McGill, 15 février 2006 (2006) 51:4 RD McGill 783.

6.11 RECUEILS DE COURS

Professeur, | *titre*, | type de document, | faculté, | date ou année | référence précise.

Indiquer le type de document s'il n'est pas déjà inclus dans le titre. Les **recueils de cours** sont des compilations de textes pour les fins d'un cours particulier. Il est préférable d'indiquer la référence originale. Les **notes de cours** sont rédigées par le professeur pour un cours en particulier. Elles ne possèdent pas de référence originale.

> Lara Khoury et Geneviève Saumier, *Coursepack: Extra-contractual Obligations/ Torts*, Faculté de droit, Université McGill, 2003 à la p 20.
>
> Jean-Sébastien Brière, *Droit des brevets*, recueil de cours, Faculté de droit, Université de Sherbrooke, automne 2008 à la p 331.

6.12 MAGAZINES

Auteur, | « titre de l'article », | *titre du magazine* | volume : | numéro **ou** n° | (date) | 1re page de l'article | référence précise | source électronique.

Indiquer le nom de l'auteur suivi du titre de l'article entre guillemets. Indiquer le nom du magazine en italique. Placer tout autre renseignement (par ex. le lieu de publication) à la suite du nom du magazine, entre crochets et en italique. Indiquer le **volume et le numéro** en séparant ces informations par un deux-points (par ex. **10:30**). S'il n'y a pas de volume, n'indiquer que le numéro (par ex. **n° 20**). Indiquer la **date complète** entre parenthèses. Si la revue indique une période, n'indiquer que la **première journée de cette période**.

> Jacques Julliard, « Requiem pour un "peuple interdit" », *Le Nouvel Observateur* n° 1740 (12 mars 1998) 47 à la p 12.
>
> Julie Latour, « Garde partagée, avis partagés », *Magazine National [de l'Association du Barreau canadien]* (mars 2001), en ligne : <www.cba.org/abc/>.
>
> Me Jean Lozeau et Me Paul Ryan, « La faillite et la responsabilité fiscale des administrateurs et des tiers », *Le Monde Juridique* 12:6 17 à la p 19.

6.13 JOURNAUX, FILS DE PRESSE ET AUTRES SOURCES DE NOUVELLES

Auteur, | « titre de l'article », | *journal [lieu d'édition]* | (date) | page | source électronique.

Indiquer le nom de l'auteur, s'il y a lieu, suivi du titre de l'article entre guillemets. Indiquer le nom du journal, du fil de presse ou de toute autre source en italique. Tout autre renseignement, tel que le lieu de publication, se place entre crochets à la suite du nom du journal.

Journaux :

Indiquer le numéro du cahier si les pages sont numérotées par cahier. Pour les références précises, ne pas répéter le numéro de page si l'article ne paraît que sur une seule page.

Fils de Presse :

Un fil de presse est un service d'information transmettant les toutes dernières nouvelles par satellite ou tout autre système électronique. Remplacer le nom du journal par le nom du fil de presse. Pour plus de renseignements sur la référence aux sources électroniques, voir la section 6.19.

> Michel Venne, « Pour un accès gratuit aux lois sur Internet », *Le Devoir de Montréal* (28 mai 1997) A2.
>
> « Un organisme d'aide juridique est menacé de fermeture par Québec », *La Presse canadienne* (8 août 2001) (QL).

"Ruling on Baby with Three Mothers", *BBC News* (10 novembre 2005), en ligne : <news.bbc. co.uk> [perma.cc/EZ75-LSGB].

« Défaite des fabricants de tabac aux Etats-Unis », *La Presse [de Montréal]* (28 mai 1997) B10.

6.13.1 Éditoriaux et lettres à la rédaction

Auteur, | « titre de l'éditorial », | type de document, | *journal* | (date) | page | source électronique.

Indiquer **lettre à la rédaction** après le nom de l'auteur de la lettre et **éditorial** après le titre d'un éditorial. Mettre en italique le nom du journal, de la revue ou de toute autre source. Placer à la suite du titre, entre crochets et en italique, tout autre renseignement tel que le lieu de publication.

Jean Barrué, lettre à la rédaction, *Le Monde diplomatique* (avril 1997) 2.

Marie-Andrée Chouinard, « Coup dur », éditorial, *Le Devoir* (23 octobre 2009) A8.

6.14 COMMUNIQUÉS DE PRESSE

Organisme responsable, | genre du document, | numéro, | « titre » | (date) | source électronique.

Indiquer le genre du document tel qu'énoncé sur le document. Indiquer le **numéro du document** immédiatement après le genre du document, s'il y a lieu. Si possible, fournir la **date du document** entre parenthèses à la fin de la référence, mais avant la source électronique.

Organisation des Nations Unies, communiqué, CS/2284, « Le conseil demande le retrait immédiat des troupes israéliennes des villes palestiniennes dont Ramallah et la coopération des parties avec l'Envoyé spécial de Washington » (29 mars 2002), en ligne : *Couverture des réunions & communiqués de presse des Nations Unies* <www.un.org/press/fr> [perma.cc/74BJ-JQGB].

Cabinet du premier ministre du Québec, communiqué, « Journée internationale des femmes : "Nouvelles réalités, solidarités nouvelles" » (8 mars 2002), en ligne : *Site officiel du premier ministre du Québec* <www.premierministre.gouv.qc.ca/actualites/communiques>.

6.15 LETTRES ET ENTREVUES

Type de document | nom des personnes impliquées | (date) | renseignements supplémentaires (archives, sources électroniques ou imprimées).

Identifier une **lettre** ou une **entrevue** en indiquant **lettre de** ou **entrevue de**, suivi du nom des parties au début de la référence. Inclure le nom des parties, suivi de la date à laquelle la lettre a été rédigée ou à laquelle l'entevue s'est déroulée.

Si le titre d'une personne impliquée n'est pas mentionné dans le texte ou ne peut être déduit, fournir autant de renseignements que possible sur ce titre, précédés d'une virgule. Fournir le nom de l'intervieweur s'il n'est pas aussi l'auteur. Si la lettre ou l'entrevue est publiée, disponible en ligne ou archivée, inclure la référence.

Edward Beauvais par Douglas Sanderson (29 mai 1948) sur *This Week*, CBC Radio, Toronto, CBC Radio Archives.

PE Moore, Acting Superintendent of Medical Services, Indian Affairs Branch, à Ellen L Fairclough, Minister of Citizenship [aucune date] Hull, Affaires Indiennes et du Nord Canada (6-24-3, vol 2).

6.16 DOCUMENTS ARCHIVÉS

Titre du document | (autres renseignements), | lieu des archives, | nom des archives, | (numéro de classification).

Si un document se trouve dans des archives locales, fournir le plus de renseignements possible sur le document selon les règles de référence traditionnelles, suivis de l'information des archives.

Lettres patentes du roi François 1er nommant Jacques Cartier capitaine général de l'expédition destinée au Canada (17 octobre 1540, Saint-Prix), Ottawa, Archives nationales du Canada (MG 1-Série C11A).

Chief Andrew Paull à TA Crerar (22 juin 1944), Ottawa, Archives nationales du Canada (RG 10, vol 6826, file 496-3-2, pt 1).

6.17 PROPRIÉTÉ INTELLECTUELLE

6.17.1 Brevets

« Titre de l'invention », | Pays | Brevet n° | PCT Brevet n° | (date de dépôt), | référence précise.

Indiquer **le titre de l'invention** entre guillemets, suivi de **l'abréviation du pays** où le brevet a été émis ainsi que le numéro du brevet. Si le brevet a été délivré par le biais du **Traité de coopération en matière de brevets** (PCT), utiliser le modèle de référence **PCT Brevet n°** dans la référence. Si nécessaire, indiquer le numéro de brevet du pays et le numéro de brevet PCT séparés d'une virgule. Indiquer la date de dépôt entre parenthèses. Faire référence à l'abrégé (**abrégé**), au numéro de revendication (**rev**) ou à une figure (**fig**) en référence précise. S'il s'agit d'une **demande de brevet**, écrire **demande déposée le** avant la date de dépôt (par ex. **demande déposée le 30 août 2008**).

Doctrine et autres documents

« Épaulière pour violon », Can Brevet n° 2414383, PCT Brevet n° PCT/US2001/021243 (29 juin 2001), rev 10.

« Parallel network processor array », É-U Brevet n° 6854117 (31 octobre 2000), fig 9.

6.17.2 Marques de commerce

« Marque de commerce », | propriétaire inscrit, | pays | n° d'enregistrement | (date d'enregistrement), | état.

Indiquer **la marque de commerce** entre guillemets. Indiquer **le propriétaire inscrit** et **l'abréviation du pays** où la marque de commerce a été enregistrée. Écrire **le numéro d'enregistrement**. Le format du numéro varie selon le pays. Indiquer **la date d'enregistrement** entre parenthèses. Écrire **l'état actuel** de la marque de commerce dans le registre. Pour les marques de commerce des États-Unis, écrire **existante** pour *live* et **non existante** pour *dead.* Pour le Canada, écrire **enregistrée** ou **radiée**.

« Kellogg's Cinnamon Mini Buns à la cannelle », Kellogg Company, Can n° enr LMC424258 (4 mars 1994), radiée.

« Lego », Lego Juris A/S, É-U 78882203 (3 juin 2008), existante.

6.17.3 Droits d'auteur

« Titre de l'œuvre protégée » | (catégorie) | titulaire du droit d'auteur, | pays | n° d'enregistrement | (date d'enregistrement) | état.

Indiquer **le titre** de l'œuvre protégée entre guillemets. Au Canada, **la catégorie de l'œuvre** inclut les **œuvres littéraires**, **artistiques**, **dramatiques** et **musicales originales**; les **prestations d'interprètes**, **enregistrements sonores** et **signaux de communication**; ainsi que les **dispositifs mécaniques**. Indiquer **le titulaire du droit d'auteur** et **l'abréviation du pays** où le droit d'auteur a été enregistré. Écrire **le numéro d'enregistrement**. Le format du numéro varie selon le pays. Indiquer **la date d'enregistrement** entre parenthèses. Écrire **l'état actuel** (**enregistré** ou **radié**) du droit d'auteur dans le registre.

« Twilight » (musique) Mary Chapin Carpenter, É-U Pau002997899 (20 décembre 2005).

« Feel Happy » (enregistrement sonore) Warner Music Canada, Can 1035760 (24 janvier 2006) enregistré.

« Agrippa : Le livre noir » (littéraire) Éditions Michel Quintin, Can 1056747 (11 mars 2003) enregistré.

6.18 DOCUMENTS DE TRAVAIL

Auteur, | « titre » | (année) | institution | Document de travail | numéro/index.

Si le document de travail est disponible en ligne, indiquer son emplacement après le numéro/index (voir la section 1.6).

Doctrine et autres documents

Bernard Dafflon, « L'économie politique et la gestion territoriale des services environnementaux » (2013) Agence Française de Développement Document de travail 135.

Jacques Saint-Pierre, « Finance, stratégie et gouvernance » (2006) Faculté des sciences de l'administration de l'Université Laval Document de travail No 2006-021.

6.19 SOURCES ÉLECTRONIQUES

Cette section fournit des conseils pour les sources qui existent seulement ou principalement en ligne. Pour des conseils généraux sur la référence aux ressources électroniques, voir la section 1.6. Pour des conseils spécifiques par rapport à certaines sources disponibles à la fois en ligne en publication traditionnelle, voir la section appropriée pour le genre de source (par ex. jurisprudence (section 3.8), recueils encyclopédiques (section 6.4), journaux (section 6.16)).

6.19.1 Sites internet

Auteur, | « titre de la page ou de l'article » | (date de la page ou de l'article), | en ligne : | *nom du site internet* | <URL> | [URL archivée].

Richard Gold, « The Midas Conundrum: Why less can be more when it comes to intellectual property protection » (25 avril 2017), en ligne : *Centre for International Governance Innovation* www.cigionline.org/articles/midas-conundrum> [perma.cc/XAP7-VWDR].

« Tribunaux canadiens » (dernière modification le 21 juin 2017), en ligne : *Cour fédérale* <cas-cdc-www02.cas-satj.gc.ca> [perma.cc/WB8C-E55X].

Il est probable que plusieurs renseignements soient introuvables. Si tel est le cas, faire preuve de jugement et inclure les renseignements essentiels qui permettront aux lecteurs de retracer la source citée.

L'auteur est la personne qui a rédigé la source citée. Lorsqu'il est impossible d'identifier l'auteur, fournir le nom du propriétaire institutionnel du domaine. Omettre le nom de l'auteur si ce renseignement est évident dans le nom du site internet.

Le titre de la page ou de l'article permet aux lecteurs d'identifier la portion citée par rapport à la totalité du site internet. En l'absence d'une numérotation claire des pages sur le site internet, le titre est la référence la plus précise qui soit disponible.

Si possible, indiquer la date de publication de la page ou de l'article entre parenthèses (jour, mois et année). Sinon, indiquer la date de la dernière modification du site internet, introduite par **dernière modification le**. En dernier recours, indiquer la date de consultation, introduite par **dernière consultation le**.

Indiquer l'URL complète entre chevrons (<. . .>). Omettre les protocoles **http://** et **https://**, mais inclure tout protocole de forme différente. N'indiquer **www** que lorsque la source elle-même l'inclut.

6.19.1.1 Documents PDF

Utiliser le même format que pour les sites internet (6.19.1), mais fournir la référence précise après la date et ajouter **(pdf)** après les mots **en ligne**.

> Bernard Dafflon, « L'économie politique et la gestion territoriale des services environnementaux » (2013) à la p 37, en ligne **(pdf)** : *Université de Fribourg* <www.unifr.ch> [perma.cc/2V4H-CWAU].

6.19.1.2 Balados (podcasts)

Utiliser le même format que pour les sites internet (6.19.1), mais fournir la référence précise après la date et ajouter **(balado)** après les mots **en ligne**. Si possible, inscrire le nom de l'orateur à la place du nom de l'auteur.

> « Clerks! Part I » (26 octobre 2017) à 00h:03m:19s, en ligne **(balado)** : *Revue de droit de McGill* <lawjournal.mcgill.ca/fr/text/96> [perma.cc/C5W6-ANC4].

6.19.1.3 Vidéos et agrégateurs de vidéos en ligne

Les vidéos en ligne sont souvent copiées et mises sur d'autres comptes sans permission ou attribution. Si possible, citer le site internet original ou le compte qui a initialement mis la vidéo en ligne. Utiliser le même format que pour les sites internet (6.19.1), mais fournir la référence précise après la date et ajouter **(vidéo)** après les mots **en ligne**. Inclure le nom de l'auteur et le titre de la vidéo. Omettre le nom de l'auteur si ce renseignement est évident dans le nom du site internet.

> UCTelevision, « Russ Feingold — Legally Speaking » (27 juin 2013) à 00h:12m:15s, en ligne **(vidéo)** : *YouTube* <www.youtube.com> [perma.cc/AW5F-7QNQ].
>
> « Supreme Court Hearings: Supreme Court Reference Case on the Appointment of Justice Marc Nadon » (15 janvier 2014) à 02h:29m:30s, en ligne **(vidéo)** : *CPAC* <www.cpac.ca/en/programs/supreme-court-hearings/episodes/29928389> [perma.cc/J2EH-TFXL].

6.19.1.4 Blogues

6.19.1.4.1 Entrées de blogue

Utiliser le même format que pour les sites internet (6.19.1), mais ajouter **(blogue)** après les mots **en ligne**. Inclure l'auteur et le titre de l'entrée.

> Michael Geist, « Posner on Copyright: Restrictive Fair Use a Risk to Creativity » (2 octobre 2012), en ligne **(blogue)** : *Michael Geist* <www.michaelgeist.ca/content/view/6645/125> [perma.cc/9RQ9-BSEF].

6.19.1.4.2 Commentaires de blogue

Nom ou pseudonyme | (date et heure), | en ligne : | <URL>, | commentaire sur | référence complète du blogue.

Indiquer la référence du commentaire, suivie de **commentaire sur** et de la référence complète du blogue (voir la section 6.19.1.4.1). Certains sites offrent un lien direct vers les commentaires individuels. Faire alors référence à cette URL et non à celle de l'entrée principale du blogue. Indiquer la date et l'heure de publication de l'entrée ou du commentaire. Pour éviter toute confusion, utiliser le système horaire sur 24 heures.

> Gary P Rodriguez (16 février 2011 à 11:14), **commentaire sur** Daniel Poulin et Frédéric Pelletier, « Are We to Live with Useless Periods Forever? » (15 février 2011), en ligne (blogue) : *Slaw* <www.slaw.ca/2011/02/15/are-we-to-live-with-useless-periods-forever> [perma.cc/6TF9-58LZ].
>
> petes_PoV (6 octobre 2012 à 12:09), en ligne (blogue) : *Slashdot* <news.slashdot.org/comments.pl?sid=3167773&cid=41568655> [perma.cc/XR2Z-L2VQ], **commentaire sur** Timothy, « Gas Prices Jump: California Hardest Hit » (6 octobre 2012).

6.19.1.5 Réseaux sociaux

Auteur, | « première phrase de l'entrée » | (date de l'entrée), | autres renseignements, | en ligne : | *réseau social* | <URL>.

Si la première phrase est trop longue, tronquer la phrase convenablement et ajouter des points de suspension avant le guillemet fermant (par ex. « **Again our mighty Senators are blowing ou tax money. . .** »).

6.19.1.5.1 Entrées Facebook

Les autres renseignements comprennent le nom du groupe ou du profil individuel dont la page contient l'entrée citée, précédé par **publié sur**. Pour citer une page de groupe ou un profil individuel plutôt qu'une entrée spécifique, remplacer la première phrase par le nom du groupe ou du profil individuel, suivi de la date de création du groupe ou du profil si disponible.

> Barack Obama, « When I left office, I told you all that the single most important thing . . . » (5 octobre 2017), **publié sur** *Barack Obama*, en ligne : *Facebook* <www.facebook.com/barackobama> [perma.cc/9LXB-7URP].

6.19.1.5.2 Entrées Twitter

À la place de la première phrase, inclure le contenu complet du tweet entre guillemets. Indiquer la date et l'heure de la publication. Pour éviter toute confusion, utiliser le système horaire sur 24 heures.

> White House Archived, « Detailed, thorough timeline from Day 1: The Ongoing Administration-Wide Response to the BP Oil Spill http://bit.ly/aYOIA3 » (5 mai 2010 **à 9:00**), en ligne : *Twitter* <twitter.com/whitehouse/status/13433979066> [perma.cc/E2TK-E98U].

6.19.1.5.3 Entrées Reddit

Les autres renseignements comprennent le titre du fil sur lequel l'entrée citée est publiée, précédé par **publié sur**.

> Lawrence Lessig, « I spend as little time with lawmakers as possible » (2 juillet 2013), **publié sur** *I am Lawrence Lessig (academic, activist, now collaborator with DEMAND PROGRESS) AMA*, en ligne : *Reddit* <www.reddit.com/r/IAmA/comments/1hibzy/i_am_lawrence_lessig_academic_activist_now/caum9w2> [perma.cc/BXB6-7VNT].

6.19.2 Autres supports numériques

> Référence traditionelle, | type de support numérique : | *Titre du support*, | renseignements sur l'édition.

Fournir la référence traditionelle du document, incluant si possible l'auteur, le titre et la date. Indiquer le type de support numérique (par ex. **CD-ROM**, **DVD**, **BluRay**, **MiniDisc**) après la virgule. Si le titre du support est différent de celui dans la référence traditionnelle, indiquer le titre du disque en italique, suivi d'une virgule. Fournir les renseignements sur l'édition du support numérique.

> PW Hogg et ME Turpel, « Implementing Aboriginal Self-Government: Constitutional and Jurisdictional Issues », CD-ROM : *Pour sept générations : legs documentaire de la Commission royale sur les peuples autochtones*, Ottawa, Libraxus, 1997.
>
> *The Paper Chase*, 1973, DVD, Beverly Hills (Cal), 20th Century Fox Home Entertainment, 2003.

7 Sources étrangères F-113

7 SOURCES ÉTRANGÈRES

7.1 JURIDICTIONS DE COMMON LAW

7.1.1 Forme générale

Pour faire référence à une source d'un pays de common law qui n'est pas traité dans ce chapitre, utiliser le modèle suivant comme guide.

Intitulé | (année de décision), | référence principale | référence précise | référence parallèle, | (cour | indication géographique) | [*titre abrégé*].

Singh v Punjab, [1980] 2 Supreme Court Journal 475 à la p 524 (Inde) [*Singh*].
Hong Kong v Chan Hing Hung, [1998] 4 Hong Kong Court 487 à la p 488C (CFI Hong Kong) [*Chan*].
Alla Rahka v Mohamed Ahmed (1956), 29 LRK 6 (Kenya) [*Alla Rahka*].
Campbell v MGN Ltd, [2004] UKHL 22, [2004] 2 AC 457 (R-U) [*MGN*].

7.1.2 Intitulé, référence précise, titre abrégé, et historique judiciaire

Utiliser les règles régissant la jurisprudence canadienne pour l'intitulé (section 3.3), les références précises (section 3.8) et l'historique judiciaire (section 3.11). Pour le titre abrégé, voir la section 1.4.1.

7.1.3 Année

Généralement, ne fournir que l'année de la décision, ou bien l'omettre selon les règles de la section 3.4. Si nécessaire pour éviter une ambiguïté (par ex. lorsqu'on fait référence à une décision non publiée), indiquer la date entière au lieu de l'année seule.

7.1.4 Référence neutre, recueil imprimé, service électronique, ou décision non publiée

année et/ou volume | recueil impimé ou identifiant du tribunal | (série) | première page ou numéro de décision | (service électronique) | référence précise.

Favoriser une référence neutre à un recueil imprimé. Suivre les conventions de référence neutre adoptées par le pays, mais sinon, suivre les règles régissant les décisions canadiennes (année, volume, recueil imprimé, série, page). Favoriser un recueil imprimé à une base de données en ligne. Voir la section 3.6 pour les recueils imprimés.

Pour les bases de données en ligne, utiliser les références fournies par le service. À moins que le service soit assurément connu du lecteur, le rajouter entre parenthèses.

Pour les décisions non publiées qui n'ont aucun des éléments ci-haut, suivre la convention adoptée par la juridiction, s'il y a lieu, ou fournir des renseignements clairs, qui identifient le district judiciaire et le numéro de dossier (voir section 3.12). Indiquer la date entière (et non l'année seulement) entre parenthèses à la suite de l'intitulé.

Parmi les recueils imprimés, l'ordre décroissant de préférence est (1) les recueils imprimés officiels, (2) les recueils imprimés semi-officiels et (3) les recueils imprimés ayant la plus grande étendue géographique.

Référence neutre :

[2004] UKHL 22.

Recueil imprimé :

11 F Supp (2e) 858 at 860.

Service électronique :

[1995] FCJ no 206 (QL).

7.1.5 Indication géographique et cour

Le nom du pays et celui de la cour sont écrits au complet, sauf pour les exceptions suivantes : (1) les abréviations assurément connues du lecteur, (2) un nom distinctif et d'usage commun qui désigne un pays au lieu de son nom officiel (par ex. Pays-Bas au lieu de Royaume des Pays-Bas) et (3) la cour et/ou l'indication géographique si celles-ci ne sont pas évidentes d'après le reste de la référence

7.1.6 Juge

Utiliser des abréviations de titres seulement si celles-ci sont assurément connues du lecteur (par ex. l'on assume communément que JC désigne le juge en chef).

7.2 JURIDICTIONS DE DROIT CIVIL

7.2.1 Codes civils

Pour se référer à un code civil d'un ressort autre que ceux énumérés dans cette section, utiliser le modèle suivant. Ne pas mettre **Code civil** en italique.

Référence précise | Code civil | (indication géographique).

Art 46 Code civil (Allemagne).
Art 123 Code civil (Louisiane).

Cette section s'applique aux codes civils étrangers. Consulter la section 2.3 pour les codes canadiens. Consulter la section 7.5.1.2 pour les codes français.

Utiliser les directives suivantes pour faire référence à une source provenant d'une juridiction de droit civil qui n'est pas listée plus loin dans ce chapitre.

Cour et chambre, | ville, | date, | *intitulé,* | (année de publication), | recueil imprimé ou périodique | section | page et/ou numéro de décision | (annoté par l'auteur) | (pays).

Inclure tout élément qui s'applique. Inclure entre crochets une traduction française du nom de la cour ou de la chambre si nécessaire.

Tribunal de Commerce, Ostende, 12 octobre 1987 (1988), Revue de Droit

Corte Suprema de Justicia [Supreme Court], 15 novembre 1954, *Suàrez, Alfredo c Perez Estella*, 190 Revista Gaceta Jurídica 145, No 124-2008 (Chili).

Interm People's Court, Shanghai, 11 Mai 1988, *China National Technical Importer/ Exporter v Industry Res* (22 août 1988), China Law & Practice 26 (Chine).

Mahkamat al-Tamiez [Cour de Cassation Tamiez], 6 Mars 1974, année 5, 1 Al-Nashra al-Qadaiah 161, No 1428 (Iraq).

7.3 ROYAUME-UNI

Voir notamment le ***Oxford Standard for Citation of Legal Authorities*** (OSCOLA).

7.3.1 Législation

7.3.1.1 Lois

7.3.1.1.1 Royaume-Uni

Mettre **(R-U)** après le titre de la loi pour indiquer son origine. Lorsque le titre inclut l'année, ne pas mettre de virgule avant l'année. Lorsque le titre n'inclut pas l'année, l'indiquer après **(R-U)**, précédée d'une virgule.

Avant 1963 :

Titre | (R-U), | année, | année de règne | monarque, | chapitre, | référence précise.

Écrire l'année de règne en chiffres arabes (par ex. **1, 2, 3**). Inclure ensuite l'abréviation du monarque en chiffres romains (**Geo V**).

Statute of Westminster 1931 (R-U), **22 & 23 Geo** V, c 4, art 2.

Du 1er janvier 1963 à aujourd'hui :

Titre | (R-U), | année, | référence précise.

Northern Ireland Act 1998 (R-U), art 5.

7.3.1.1.2 Irlande du Nord

Pour se référer aux lois adoptées par l'ancien Parlement d'Irlande du Nord ou par l'Assemblée de l'Irlande du Nord, écrire **(IN)** au lieu de **(R-U)**.

National Insurance Act **(IN)**, 1946, art 7.

7.3.1.1.3 Écosse

Pour les lois adoptées par le Parlement écossais, écrire **(Écosse)** au lieu de **(R-U)** et fournir le numéro ASP (Acts of Scottish Parliament), précédé d'**ASP**.

Crofting Reform etc Act 2007 **(Écosse), ASP 7**.

7.3.1.1.4 Pays de Galles

Pour les *measures* adoptées par l'Assemblée nationale du pays de Galles, écrire **(Pays de Galles)** au lieu de **(R-U)** et faire référence aux Measures of the National Assembly for Wales (**NAWM** ou **MCCC**).

Learner Travel (Wales) Measure 2008 **(Pays de Galles)**, NAWM 2.

7.3.1.2 Projets de loi

Titre | (indication géographique), | session, | numéro du projet de loi, | référence précise | (renseignements supplémentaires).

Inclure **[HL]** (non italique) dans le titre pour les projets de loi qui proviennent de la Chambre des Lords. Voir l'**annexe A-4** pour les abréviations géographiques.

Harbours Bill [HL] (R-U), sess 2005—2006, Bill 40, art 2.

A Bill to amend the Game Preservation (Northern Ireland) Act 1928 (IN), sess 2001—2002, Bill 15/00, art 2 (Committee Stage Extension 29 octobre 2001).

Lorsque la session ne comprend pas l'année, écrire l'année entre parenthèses après la session.

Human Tissue (Scotland) Bill (Écosse), **2e sess (2005)**, Bill 42, art 6 (1re lecture 3 juin 2005).

7.3.1.3 Règlements et ordonnances

Titre | (indication géographique), | SR & O ou SI | année/numéro, | référence précise.

Pour les règlements et les ordonnances promulgués avant 1948, abréger **Statutory Rules & Orders** par **SR & O**. Après 1948, abréger **Statutory Instruments** par **SI**.

Penalties for Disorderly Behaviour (Amendment of Minimum Age) Order 2004 (R-U), SI 2004/3166.

Cheese Regulations 1970 (IN), SR & O 1970/14.

7.3.2 Jurisprudence

7.3.2.1 Modèle de base

Suivre le même modèle que pour la jurisprudence canadienne (section 3).

Référence neutre disponible :

Campbell v MGN Ltd, [2004] UKHL 22, [2004] 2 AC 457.

Référence neutre non disponible :

R v Woollin (1998), [1999] 1 AC 82 (HL (Eng)).

Consulter l'**annexe B-2** pour la liste des cours et de leurs abréviations et l'**annexe C-2** pour la liste des recueils de jurisprudence du Royaume-Uni et de leurs abréviations.

7.3.2.2 Référence neutre

Plusieurs tribunaux du Royaume-Uni ont officiellement adopté un système de référence neutre. Suivre les règles de la référence neutre au Canada (section 3.5) à l'exception de l'année, qui est placée entre crochets. Plusieurs anciennes décisions, principalement celles rendues par la House of Lords et par le Privy Council, ont une référence neutre rétroactive. Ces références neutres doivent être traitées comme si elles avaient été assignées par une cour. Les références neutres rétroactives sont disponibles sur **BAILII**.

7.3.2.3 Cours d'appel

Supreme Court of the United Kingdom	[année] UKSC numéro
House of Lords	[année] UKHL numéro
Privy Council	[année] UKPC numéro
England and Wales Court of Appeal (Division civile)	[année] EWCA Civ numéro
England and Wales Court of Appeal (Division criminelle)	[année] EWCA Crim numéro

Les références neutres pour les cours d'appel sont officielles **depuis le 11 janvier 2001**. La *Supreme Court of the United Kingdom* a assumé les fonctions judiciaires de la *House of Lords* le 1er octobre 2009.

Indiquer l'année de la décision entre crochets, suivie du code de désignation du tribunal et du numéro de la cause.

Campbell v MGN Limited, [2004] UKHL 22.
Fraser v HM Advocate, [2011] UKSC 24.
Copping v Surrey County Council, [2005] EWCA Civ 1604 au para 15.

7.3.2.4 High Court

[année] | cour | numéro | (division) | paragraphe.

Les références neutres pour la *High Court* sont officielles **depuis le 14 janvier 2002**, sauf pour *l'Administrative Court*, pour laquelle les références neutres sont officielles depuis le 11 janvier 2001. Pour les causes plaidées devant la *High Court*, la division de cette cour est placée entre parenthèses après le numéro de la cause. La *High Court* a trois divisions principales et plusieurs cours spécialisées.

Divisions et abréviations de la *High Court* :

Queen's Bench Division	**QB**
Administrative Court	Admin
Commercial Court	Comm
Admiralty Court	Admlty
Technology & Construction Court	TCC

Chancery Division	**Ch**
Patents Court	Pat
Companies Court	Comp

Family Division	**Fam**

[2005] EWHC 1974 (Admlty) au para 10.
[2005] EWHC 2995 (Comm).

7.3.2.5 Recueils

Les *Law Reports* sont **organisés en séries**. Se référer aux séries et non aux *Law Reports*. Puisqu'il n'y a pas de recueil distinct pour la Cour d'appel, inclure (**CA**) à la fin de chaque référence à une décision rendue par cette cour. Consulter l'**annexe C-2** pour les abréviations des *Law Reports*.

Beattie v E & F Beattie Ltd, [1938] Ch 708 (CA) 720 à la p 723.

Noter la distinction entre la collection récente de *Law Reports* et la collection de recueils de 1865 à 1875 du même nom (abrégée **LR**).

Rylands v Fletcher (1868), **LR** 3 HL 330.

Pour les décisions rendues avant 1865, faire référence aux *English Reports* (**ER**) plutôt qu'à un recueil nommé ou au moins fournir une référence parallèle. L'intégralité des *English Reports* est gratuitement accessible sur le site internet CommonLII.

Lord Byron v Johnston (1816), 2 Mer 28, **35 ER 851** (Ch).

7.3.2.6 Annuaires

Intitulé | (année), | annuaire | trimestre | année du règne | monarque, | numéro du feuillet (*folio*), | numéro du plaidoyer (*plea*).

Sources étrangères

Utiliser les abréviations de trimestres suivantes : **Mich** pour **Michaelmas**, **Hil** pour **Hilary**, **Pach** pour **Easter** et **Trin** pour **Trinity**. Indiquer l'année du règne en chiffres arabes (par ex. **1, 2, 3**). Indiquer le monarque en chiffres romains. Abréger **plea** par **pl** et **folio** par **fol**.

> *Doige's Case* (1422), YB Trin 20 Hen VI, fol 34, pl 4.

7.3.2.7 Réimpressions

Référence à l'annuaire, | reproduit dans, | traduit par | traducteur/directeur, | référence à la réimpression.

Pour une réimpression, fournir autant de renseignements que possible sur la première édition de l'annuaire. Se référer à la source dans laquelle se trouve la réimpression.

> *Randolph v Abbot of Hailes* (1313-14), YB 6&7 Edw II (Eyre of Kent), reproduit dans *Yearbooks of 6 Edward II* (1926), traduit par William Craddock, dir, 27 Selden Soc 32 à la p 33.

7.3.2.8 Écosse et Irlande du Nord

Lorsque le titre du recueil n'inclut pas l'indication géographique, indiquer Scot pour *Scotland* et **NI** pour *Northern Ireland*, entre parenthèses à la fin de la référence. Indiquer le nom de la cour, car chaque volume est divisé en parties selon la cour et chaque partie est paginée séparément. Voir l'**annexe B** pour les abréviations des tribunaux et l'**annexe C** pour les abréviations des recueils.

> *M'Courtney v HM Advocate*, [1977] JC 68 (HCJ Scot).
> *R v Crooks*, [1999] NI 226 (CA).

7.3.2.8.1 Référence neutre

Les règles concernant les références neutres sont les mêmes pour l'Écosse et l'Irlande du Nord. Suivre les règles sur les références neutres au Canada (section 3.5), à l'exception de l'année, qui est placée entre crochets.

7.3.2.8.1.1 Écosse

High Court of Justiciary	HCJT
Court of Criminal Appeal	HCJAC
Court of Session, Outer House	CSOH
Court of Session, Inner House	CSIH

> *Smith v Brown*, [2005] HCJT 2 (Scot).
> *Kinross v Dunsmuir*, [2005] HCJAC 3 au para 12 (Scot).
> *McBride v MacDuff*, [2005] CSOH 4 (Scot).

Sources étrangères

7.3.2.8.1.2 Irlande du Nord

Court of Appeal	NICA
Crown Court	NICC
County Court	NICty
Magistrates Court	NIMag
Queen's Bench Division	NIQB
Family Division	NIFam
Chancery Division	NICh

McDonnell v Henry, [2005] NICA 17.
Barkley v Whiteside, [2004] NIQB 12 au para 12.

7.3.2.9 *Juge*

Lord Justice	LJ
Lord Justices	LJJ
Master of the Rolls	MR
Lord Chancellor	LC
Vice Chancellor	VC
Baron	B
Chief Baron	CB

7.3.2.10 *Bases de données en ligne*

7.3.2.10.1 BAILII

Intitulé, | Identifiant donné par le service | (BAILII) | référence précise | (indication géographique | cour).

Ne pas confondre un identifiant BAILII et une référence neutre. Ajouter (**BAILII**) après l'identifiant afin d'éviter toute confusion.

London Borough of Harrow v Johnstone, [1997] UKHL 9 (**BAILII**) au para 6.

7.3.2.10.2 Service sans identifiant (Justis)

Intitulé	(année),	référence précise	(indication géographique | cour)	(disponible sur | nom du service éléctronique).

R v Woollin (1998), au para 23 (HL) (disponible sur Justis).

7.3.3 Documents gouvernementaux

Indiquer **R-U** au début de la référence.

7.3.3.1 Débats

R-U,	HL/HC	Deb	(date),	volume,	colonne	référence précise	(orateur).

Après R-U, indiquer la chambre. Abréger House of Commons par **HC** et House of Lords par **HL**. Indiquer l'orateur entre parenthèses à la fin de la référence si nécessaire.

R-U, HL Deb (3 mai 1983), vol 442, col 6 (Baroness Masham of Ilton).
R-U, HC Deb (27 mai 1774), vol 17, col 1357.

7.3.3.2 Command Papers

R-U,	organisme,	*titre*	(numéro du Command paper, | année)	référence précise	(président).

Indiquer le titre tel qu'il apparaît à la page titre du rapport. Indiquer le numéro du Command paper après le titre du document. Inscrire le nom du président entre parenthèses à la fin de la référence si ce renseignement est connu. L'abréviation appropriée du Command est essentielle pour identifier le document. Elle apparaît sur la page titre de chaque Command paper.

1833—1869	C (1re série)
1870—1899	C (2e série)
1900—1918	Cd
1919—1956	Cmd
1957—1986	Cmnd
1986—	Cm

R-U, HC, *Report of the Committee on the Law Relating to Rights of Light* (Cmnd 473, 1957-58) à la p 955 (CE Harman).

R-U, Department for Children, Schools and Families, *2008 Autumn Performance Report* (Cm 7507, 2008) à la p 54.

7.3.3.3 Documents non parlementaires

R-U, | organisme, | *titre*, | (type de document) | auteur, | renseignements sur l'édition.

Suivre les règles sur les documents non parlementaires canadiens, à la section 4.2.

Ne pas indiquer l'organisme s'il est déjà spécifié dans le titre.

R-U, Royal Commission on the Press, *Studies on the Press* (Working Paper n° 3) par Oliver Boyd-Barret, Colin Seymour-Ure et Jeremy Turnstall, Londres, Her Majesty's Stationery Office, 1978.

R-U, Law Commission, *Contempt of Court* (Consultation Paper n° 209) Londres, The Stationery Office, 2012.

7.4 ÉTATS-UNIS

Tous les éléments de référence à la législation des États-Unis sont en anglais, à l'exception des mentions telles que « codifié à ». En l'absence d'indications dans le present ouvrage, consulter ***The Bluebook: A Uniform System of Citation***.

7.4.1 Législation

7.4.1.1 Constitution fédérale et constitutions des États

Abréger **article** par **art**, **section** par **§** et **sections** par **§§**. Un paragraphe qui fait partie d'une section est une **clause**, abrégée **cl** (au singulier comme au pluriel).

US Const art II, § 2, cl 1.

Abréger **amendement** par **amend**.

Abréger **préambule** par **pmbl**. Indiquer les numéros d'article et de modification en chiffres romains majuscules. Les numéros de section et de clause sont indiqués en chiffres arabes (par ex. **1, 2, 3**).

US Const amend XVIII, § 1.

Voir l'**annexe A-2** pour la liste des abréviations des états.

Fla Const, Part V, § 3(b)(4).

7.4.1.2 Lois

Ordre hiérarchique des sources :

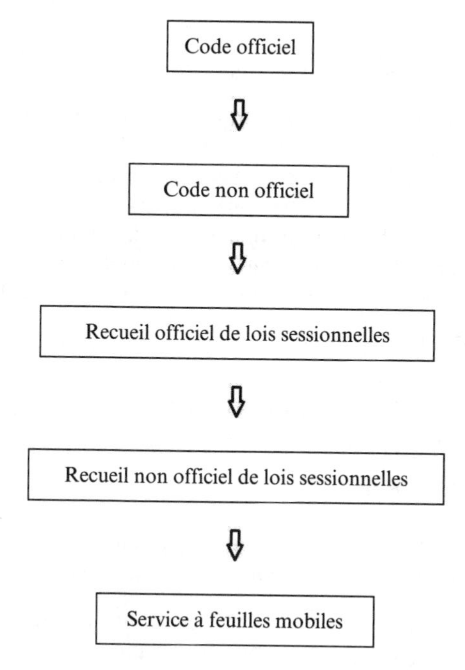

7.4.1.2.1 Codes

Aux États-Unis, un code constitue le regroupement et la codification par sujet des lois générales et permanentes des États-Unis. Un **code officiel** est un code des lois des États-Unis organisé en moins de 50 titres et rédigé sous la surveillance d'une autorité gouvernementale appropriée (par ex. le département de la Justice fédérale).

Le ***United States Code*** (USC) est le code officiel du gouvernement fédéral.

Pour déterminer si un code étatique est officiel ou non, consulter la liste des codes étatiques, disponible sur Findlaw (<statelaws.findlaw.com/state-codes.html>).

Un **code non officiel** est un code des lois des États-Unis préparé par une maison d'édition. Il existe deux codes non officiels pour les lois fédérales le ***United States Code Service*** (USCS) et le ***United States Code Annotated*** (USCA).

Titre, ∣ partie du code ∣ titre abrégé du code ∣ numéro du titre ∣ article ∣ (éditeur ∣ supplément ∣ année).

Ne pas se référer au titre original d'une loi codifiée. **N'indiquer le titre que pour des raisons particulières** (par ex. si la loi est normalement connue sous ce nom). Mettre le titre en italique.

Patient Protection and Affordable Care Act, 42 USC § 18001 (2010).

Si le code est **classé** par titres, par chapitres ou par volumes distincts et numérotés, indiquer le numéro de cette division. Dans le cas du code fédéral, indiquer la division avant l'abréviation du code.

Pa Stat Ann tit 63 § 4253 (West Supp 1986).

Ne pas mettre le titre abrégé du code en italique. Pour une référence à l'***Internal Revenue Code***, il est possible de remplacer **26 USC** par **IRC**.

IRC § 61 (1994).

À moins que le code ne soit publié par un éditeur officiel, indiquer le nom de l'éditeur avant l'année ou avant **Supp**, selon le cas. Pour indiquer un supplément inséré dans une pochette, écrire **Supp** avant la mention de l'année qui paraît sur la page titre du supplément.

Wis Stat Ann § 939645 (West Supp 1992).

Indiquer l'année de publication du code entre parenthèses à la fin de la référence. Pour un **recueil relié**, fournir l'année qui paraît sur la reliure. Pour un **supplément**, fournir l'année qui figure sur la page titre du supplément.

7.4.1.2.2 Lois sessionnelles

Les lois sessionnelles sont les lois promulguées par une session du Congrès, reliées et organisées par ordre chronologique. Les lois sessionnelles font le suivi d'une loi.

Titre ou date de promulgation, | numéro de la loi ou du chapitre, | partie, | référence au recueil des lois sessionnelles | première page de la loi | référence précise au recueil | (année) | (référence au code).

Indiquer le titre de la loi en italique. Si la loi n'a pas de titre, l'identifier par la date de sa promulgation (**Act of 25 April 1978**). S'il n'y a pas de date de promulgation, identifier la loi par sa date de mise en vigueur (**Act effective [date]**).

Indiquer le numéro de la loi (**public law number**), introduit par l'abréviation **Pub L No** ou par le numéro du chapitre précédé de **c**. Le numéro devant le trait d'union du *public law number* est le numéro de session; le numéro après le trait d'union est le numéro de référence. Pour se référer à une **partie particulière**, indiquer le numéro de la partie après le numéro de la loi ou le numéro du chapitre, selon le cas. Indiquer la référence précise au recueil.

Le **recueil officiel** des lois fédérales est le *Statutes at Large*, abrégé **Stat**. L'abréviation du recueil est précédée par le numéro de volume et suivie par la première page de la loi. Indiquer la **référence précise** au recueil de lois sessionnelles après la référence à la première page. Inclure une référence précise à la partie après le numéro de la loi ou du chapitre. Indiquer **l'année de publication** entre parenthèses à la fin de la référence, à moins que l'année ne fasse partie du titre de la loi. Si l'année du titre ne coïncide pas avec l'année de publication de la loi, les deux années doivent être indiquées. Voir l'exemple du *Coastal Zone Protection Act of 1996*.

Fournir les renseignements concernant la **codification de la loi** s'ils sont disponibles. Si une loi est divisée et classée sous plusieurs sections du code, fournir ce renseignement entre parenthèses à la fin de la référence ((**codifié tel que modifié dans plusieurs sections du 26 USC**) suivi du nom du code).

> *The Deficit Reduction Act of 1984*, Pub L No 98-369, 98 Stat 494 (codifié tel que modifié au 26 USC § 1-9504 (1988)).
>
> *Coastal Zone Protection Act of 1996*, Pub L No 104-150, § 7(2), 110 Stat 1380 à la p 1382 (1997).
>
> Act of 25 April 1978, c 515, § 3, 1978 Ala Acts 569 à la p 569 (codifié tel que modifié au Ala Code § 9-3-12 (1987)).

7.4.1.2.3 Recueil non officiel de lois sessionnelles

Titre, | numéro de la loi, | [volume] | recueil non officiel | référence précise, | référence au *Statutes at Large*.

Le recueil de lois sessionnelles fédérales le plus important est le ***United States Code Congressional and Administrative News***, abrégé **USCCAN**. Pour citer l'USCCAN, indiquer la référence aux ***Statutes at Large*** (**Stat**), recueils officiels dans lequel paraîtra la loi.

> *Veteran's Benefits Improvements Act of 1996*, Pub L No 104-275, [1996] **USCCAN** 3762, 110 **Stat** 3322.

7.4.1.3 Uniform Codes, Uniform Acts et Restatements

Titre | partie | (année d'adoption).

Les ***Uniform Codes*** et ***Uniform Acts*** sont des propositions législatives publiées par la *National Conference of Commissioners of Uniform State Laws*, qui visent l'adoption par tous les congrès d'états, les districts et les protectorats. Les ***Restatements*** sont des rapports sur l'état de la *common law* américaine qui portent sur tel sujet ou telle interprétation des lois publiques publiées par l'American Law Institute.

Indiquer le titre en italique, à moins qu'il ne s'agisse d'un code. Ne pas mettre de virgule après le titre d'un code ou d'un *Restatement*. Lorsqu'il existe plus d'un *Restatement*, indiquer son numéro entre parenthèses. Indiquer l'année d'adoption, de promulgation ou de la plus récente modification entre parenthèses à la fin de la référence.

> UCC § 2-012 (1995).
>
> *Uniform Adoption Act* § 10 (1971).
>
> *Restatement of Contracts* § 88 (1932).
>
> *Restatement (Second) of the Law of Property* § 15 (1977).

7.4.1.4 Projets de loi et résolutions

7.4.1.4.1 Projets de loi fédéraux

É-U, | Bill | chambre | numéro, | *titre*, | numéro du Congrès, | année, | référence précise | (état, si promulgué).

Abréger ***House of Representatives*** par **HR** et ***Senate*** par S.

> É-U, Bill HR 6, *Higher Education Amendments of 1988*, 105e Cong, 1997 (promulgué).
> É-U, Bill S 7, *Educational Excellence for All Learners Act of 2001*, 107e Cong, 2001, art 103.

7.4.1.4.2 Résolutions fédérales

É-U, | résolution | numéro, | *titre*, | numéro du Congrès, | année | (état, si promulgué).

> É-U, HR Con Res 6, *Expressing the Sense of the Congress Regarding the Need to Pass Legislation to Increase Penalties on Perpetrators of Hate Crimes*, 107e Cong, 2001.
> É-U, HR Res 31, *Designating Minority Membership on Certain Standing Committees of the House*, 104e Cong, 1995 (promulgué).

Abréviations employées pour les résolutions :

House Concurrent Resolutions	HR Con Res
House Resolutions	HR Res
House Joint Resolutions	HRJ Res
Senate Concurrent Resolutions	S Con Res
Senate Resolutions	S Res
Senate Joint Resolutions	SJ Res

7.4.1.4.3 Résolutions et lois étatiques

É-U, | catégorie du Bill ou de la résolution | numéro, | *titre*, | année ou numéro de la législature, | numéro ou désignation de la session législative, | état, | année, | référence précise | (état, si promulgué).

En plus des *Regular Sessions* (**Reg Sess**), les législateurs étatiques peuvent tenir des ***First, Second*** **et** ***Third Extraordinary Sessions***. Abréger ces expressions par **1st Extra Sess**, **2d Extra Sess** et **3d Extra Sess**. Abréger ***Special Sessions*** par **Spec Sess**. Voir la liste des abréviations des états à l'**annexe A-2**.

> É-U, AB 31, *An Act to Add Section 51885 to the Education Code, Relating to Educational Technology*, 1997-98, Reg Sess, Cal, 1996, art 1.
> É-U, SR 10, *Calling for the Establishment of a Delaware State Police Community Relations Task Force*, 141e Gen Assem, Reg Sess, Del, 2001 (promulgué).

7.4.1.5 Règles et règlements

7.4.1.5.1 Code of Federal Regulations

Le *Code of Federal Regulations* regroupe les règlements codifiés des États-Unis, classés selon les 50 mêmes titres que le *United States Code*.

Titre, | volume | recueil | référence précise | (année).

Indiquer le titre de la règle ou du règlement s'il est mieux connu ainsi. Pour les règles et les règlements fédéraux, se référer à la compilation officielle du gouvernement, si possible. Le *Code of Federal Regulations*, abrégé **CFR**, est la compilation officielle du gouvernement fédéral.

> *EPA Effluent Limitations Guidelines*, 40 CFR § 405.53 (1980).
> 47 CFR § 73.609 (1994).

7.4.1.5.2 Registre administratif

Les registres administratifs comprennent entre autres les règlements administratifs mis en application par les autorités gouvernementales.

Titre, | volume | Fed Reg | première page | (année) | (information sur la codification | référence précise).

Lorsque des règles ou des règlements n'ont pas encore été codifiés, se référer aux registres administratifs. Au niveau fédéral, se référer au ***Federal Register*** (**Fed Reg**). Indiquer le numéro du volume, l'abréviation du registre, le numéro de page et l'année. Si possible, indiquer à quel endroit la règle ou le règlement paraîtra dans le CFR ou autre compilation officielle à la fin de la référence.

> 44 Fed Reg 12437221 (1979) (sera codifié au 29 CFR § 552).
> *Outer Continental Shelf Air Regulations Consistency Update for California*, 70 Fed Reg 19472 (2009) (sera codifié au 40 CFR § 55).

7.4.2 Jurisprudence

7.4.2.1 Modèle de base

Intitulé, | vol | recueil | (série) | première page | référence précise | (indication géographique | cour | année) | (autre information).

Les références aux décisions administratives et à l'arbitrage suivent le même modèle de référence que les autres jugements. Pour l'arbitrage, fournir le nom de l'arbitre suivi d'une virgule et **Arb** entre parenthèses à la fin de la référence.

> *People v Kevorkian*, 527 NW (2d) 714 (Mich 1994).
> *Roche Holding Ltd*, 113 FTC 1086 aux pp 1087-90 (1990).
> *Headquarters Space & Missile*, 103 Lab Arb Rep (BNA) 1198 (1995)

7.4.2.2 Intitulé

Indiquer l'intitulé selon les règles de la section 3.3. Pour un État ou un pays, utiliser le nom couramment utilisé plutôt que la forme descriptive ou l'abréviation.

California v United States

Si une des parties est une ville dont le nom pourrait être confondu avec celui d'un État, indiquer les renseignements permettant de l'identifier entre parenthèses : **New York (City of)** ou **Washington (DC)**.

7.4.2.3 Référence neutre

Il n'existe **aucun standard uniforme aux États-Unis pour les références neutres**, toutefois certaines juridictions ont adopté ces références.

7.4.2.4 Recueil et série

Après l'intitulé, indiquer le numéro du volume, l'abréviation du recueil, le numéro de la série et la première page de l'arrêt. **Il y a toujours une espace entre l'abréviation du recueil et le numéro de la série.**

Lotus Development v Borland International, 140 F (3d) 70 (1er Cir 1998) [*Lotus*].

Avant 1875, les ***US Reports*** sont aussi numérotés en ordre consécutif selon chaque éditeur. Indiquer ce numéro ainsi que le nom de l'éditeur entre parenthèses après **US**.

Scott v Sanford, 60 US (19 How) 393 (1857).

Abréviations d'éditeurs :

Wallace	Wall
Black	Black
Howard	How
Peters	Pet
Wheaton	Wheat
Cranch	Cranch
Dallas	Dal

Pour la Cour suprême des États-Unis, faire référence aux recueils dans l'ordre de préférence suivant : **US** → **S Ct** → **L Ed (2d)** → **USLW**. Pour les cours fédérales, se référer à **F** ou **F Supp**. Pour les cours d'États, renvoyer au recueil régional plutôt qu'au recueil de l'État. Pour une liste plus étoffée des recueils et de leurs abréviations, voir l'**annexe C-2**.

7.4.2.5 Référence précise

Indiquer **à la p** avant la référence précise.

> *United States v McVeigh*, 153 F (3d) 1166 **à la p** 1170 (10e Cir 1998).

7.4.2.6 Cour

7.4.2.6.1 Cours fédérales

La **Cour suprême des États-Unis** ne nécessite pas d'abréviation, à moins de citer au ***United States Law Week*** (USLW). Pour citer à l'USLW, ajouter US ainsi que la date (jour, mois et année) entre parenthèses à la fin de la référence.

> *Roe v Wade*, 410 US 113 (1973).
>
> *AT&T v Iowa Utilities Board*, 66 USLW 3387 (US 17 novembre 1997).

Abréger les cours d'appel de chaque circuit en précisant le numéro du circuit.

> *Microsystems v Microsoft*, 188 F (3d) 1115 (9e Cir 1999).

Utiliser DC Cir pour désigner la **Cour d'appel du circuit du *District of Columbia*** et Fed Cir pour désigner la **Cour du circuit fédéral**.

Pour les cours de district, fournir l'abréviation du nom du district.

> *Yniguez v Mofford*, 730 F Supp 309 (D Ariz 1990).

7.4.2.6.2 Cours d'États

Indiquer le nom de la cour et l'indication géographique entre parenthèses, en utilisant les abréviations des **annexes A-2** et **B**.

> *Peevyhouse v Garland Coal & Mining*, 382 P (2d) 109 (**Okla Sup Ct** 1963).

Ne pas inclure le nom de l'État si celui-ci fait partie du titre du recueil.

> *Truman v Thomas*, 165 **Cal** Rptr 308 (**Sup Ct** 1980).

Ne pas inclure le nom de la cour s'il s'agit du plus haut tribunal de l'État.

> *Hinterlong v Baldwin*, 308 **Ill App** (3d) 441 (App Ct 1999).

7.4.2.7 Année de la décision

Fournir l'année de la décision entre parenthèses à la fin de la référence. S'il y a une abréviation d'un tribunal, inclure l'année au sein des mêmes parenthèses **(App Ct 1999)**.

7.4.2.8 Bases de données en ligne

7.4.2.8.1 Westlaw

Intitulé, | identifiant donné par le service | référence précise | (indication géographique | cour).

Si le seul identifiant est celui fourni par Westlaw, la decision est non publiée.

> *Fincher v Baker*, 1997 WL 675447 à la p 2 (Ala Civ App).

7.4.2.8.2 LexisNexis

Intitulé, | identifiant donné par le service | référence précise | (indication géographique | cour).

Si le seul identifiant est celui fourni par LexisNexis, la decision est non publiée.

> *Association for Molecular Pathology v Myriad Genetics*, 2013 US Lexis 4540 at 5 (USSC).

7.4.3 Documents gouvernementaux

Indiquer É-U au début de la référence.

7.4.3.1 Débats

É-U, | *Cong Rec*, | édition, | tome, | partie, | référence précise | (date) | (orateur).

Faire référence au ***Congressional Record*** (Cong Rec) pour les débats du Congrès qui ont eu lieu après 1873. Utiliser **l'édition quotidienne** seulement si le débat ne se trouve pas encore dans l'édition reliée.

> É-U, *Cong Rec*, t 125, 15, à la p 18691 (1979).
> É-U, *Cong Rec*, daily ed, t 143, 69, à la p H3176 (22 mai 1977) (Rep Portman).

7.4.3.2 Sessions de comités

7.4.3.2.1 Fédéral

É-U, | *titre*, | numéro du Congrès, | renseignements sur l'édition | référence précise | (orateur).

Toujours indiquer l'année de publication. Outre l'année, fournir le plus de renseignements possible sur l'édition.

> É-U, *Federal Property Campaign Fundraising Reform Act of 2000 : Hearing on HR 4845 Before the House Committee of the Judiciary*, 106e Cong, 2000 aux pp 2-3.
> É-U, *Assisted Suicide : Legal, Medical, Ethical and Social Issues : Hearing Before the Subcommittee on Health and Environment of the House Committee on Commerce*, 105e

Sources étrangères

Cong, Washington, DC, United States Government Printing Office, 1997 à la p 2 (Dr C Everett Koop).

7.4.3.2.2 État

É-U, | *titre*, | numéro du corps législatif ou année, | numéro ou désignation de la session législative, | État | (renseignements sur l'édition) | référence précise | (orateur).

Voir la liste des abréviations des États à l'**annexe A-2**. Toujours indiquer l'année de publication et fournir le plus de renseignements possible sur l'édition.

É-U, *Rico Litigation: Hearing on S 1197 Before the Senate Comm on Commerce and Econ Dev*, 41e légis, 1re sess rég 5, Ariz (1993) (affirmé par Barry Wong, analyste politique).

7.4.3.3 Rapports et documents

7.4.3.3.1 Fédéral

7.4.3.3.1.1 Documents et rapports numérotés

É-U, | organisme, | *titre* | (numéro), | renseignements sur l'édition | référence précise.

Indiquer l'organisme responsable, à moins qu'il ne soit mentionné dans le titre. Toujours indiquer l'année de publication et fournir le plus de renseignements possible sur l'édition.

É-U, *Secrecy: Report of the Commission on Protecting and Reducing Government Secrecy: Pursuant to Public Law 236, 103rd Congress* (S Doc n° 105-2), Washington, DC, US Government Printing Office, 1997 à la p 3.

É-U, Senate Committee on the Budget, 111e Cong, *Concurrent Resolution on the Budget FY 2010*, Washington, DC, US Government Printing Office, 2009 à la p 213.

Abréviations des numéros :

Documents	**Rapports**
HR Doc n°	HR Rep n°
HR Misc Doc n°	HR Conf Rep n°
S Doc n°	S Rep n°
S Exec Doc n°	

7.4.3.3.1.2 Documents non numérotés et *Committee Prints*

É-U, | organisme, | *titre*, | Committee Print, | renseignements sur l'édition | référence précise.

Indiquer le numéro du congrès avec l'organisme si pertinent. Toujours indiquer l'année de publication et fournir le plus de renseignements possible sur l'édition.

> É-U, Staff of House Committee on Veterans' Affairs, 105th Cong, *Persian Gulf Illnesses: An Overview*, Committee Print, 1998 à la p 15.
>
> É-U, National Commission on Children, *Beyond Rhetoric: A New American Agenda for Children and Families*, Washington (DC), The Commission, 1991 à la p 41.

7.4.3.3.2 État

É-U, | organisme, | *titre* | (numéro), | renseignements sur l'édition | référence précise.

Fournir le numéro du document, s'il y a lieu.

> É-U, California Energy Commission *Existing Renewable Resources Account*, vol 1 (500-01-014V1), 2001.

Toujours indiquer l'année de publication et fournir le plus de renseignements possible sur l'édition.

> É-U, Washington State Transport Commission, *Washington's Transportation Plan 2003–2022*, Washington State Department of Transportation, 2002.

7.5 FRANCE

7.5.1 Législation

7.5.1.1 Lois et autres instruments législatifs

Titre, | JO, | date de publication | (NC), | numéro de page ou de document, | référence parallèle.

Inclure le titre complet si l'instrument législatif n'est pas numéroté. S'il est numéroté, l'inclusion du titre est facultative.

Toujours faire référence au **Journal officiel de la République française** en premier lieu, abrégé **JO**. Le Journal officiel est disponible gratuitement en ligne sur le site internet de Légifrance (www.legifrance.gouv.fr). Inclure la date de publication et le numéro de page ou de document. Pour faire référence à la version imprimée du Journal officiel, fournir le numéro de page. Pour faire référence à la version électronique, fournir le numéro de document, précédé de **n°**. Pour les suppléments du JO, indiquer (NC) pour **numéro complémentaire** après la date de publication. Pour une liste des titres des anciens journaux officiels, voir la section 7.5.3.2.

> *Ordonnance n° 2001-766 du 29 août 2001*, JO, 31 août 2001, 13946, [2001] D 2564.
>
> *Décret du 5 décembre 1978 portant classement d'un site pittoresque*, JO, 6 décembre 1978 (NC), 9250.
>
> *Arrêté du 24 mai 2017 relatif à l'insaisissabilité de biens culturels*, JO, 17 juin 2017, n° 16.

Sources étrangères

7.5.1.2 Codes

***Code civil des Français* (1804–1807)**	art 9 **CcF**
***Code Napoléon* (1807–1814)**	art 9 **CN**
***Code civil* (1815–)**	art 2203 **C civ**
Code pénal	art 113-10 **C pén**
Code de propriété intellectuelle	art 123(8) **CPI**
Code de procédure civile	art 1435 **C proc civ**
Code de procédure pénale	art 144(2) **C proc pén**

Ne jamais fournir une référence complète pour se rapporter à un code. Pour faire référence aux codes mentionnés ci-dessus, utiliser le titre abrégé dès la première référence.

Pour faire référence à un code qui n'est pas dans la liste, écrire le nom du code au complet dans la première référence et créer un titre abrégé si nécessaire (par ex. **art 1** ***Code de la consommation*** **[C conso]**).

7.5.2.1 Modèle de base

Tribunal ou chambre | ville, | date, | *intitulé*, | [année de publication | semestre] | recueil | partie du recueil | numéro de page ou de document | référence précise, | numéro de la décision | (annotation).

Pour une liste des abréviations des noms de cours et de tribunaux français, consulter l'**annexe B-2**.

7.5.2.2 Cours

7.5.2.2.1 Tribunaux de première instance

Trib admin Rouen, 27 décembre 2007, [2008] JCP G II 10041 (note Colette Saujot).
Trib gr inst Paris, 10 septembre 1998, [1999 1er sem] Gaz Pal Jur 37.

7.5.2.2.2 Cour d'appel

CA Paris, 21 mai 2008, *K c E et Sté nationale de télévision France 2* [2008] JCP Jur 390, n° 06/07678.
CA Paris, 24 février 1998, [1998] D Jur 225 à la p 225.

7.5.2.2.3 Cour de cassation

Cass civ 1re, 14 décembre 1999, [1999] Bull civ I 222, n° 97-15.756.
Cass crim, 24 février 2009, [2009] D 951 à la p 951, n° 08-87.409.

7.5.2.2.4 Conseil d'État

Abréger **Conseil d'État** par CE.

> CE, 27 janvier 1984, *Ordre des avocats de la Polynésie française*, [1984] Rec 20.

7.5.2.2.5 Conseil constitutionnel

Abréger **Conseil constitutionnel** par **Cons const**.

> **Cons const**, 25 juin 1986, *Privatisations*, [1986] Rec 61, 86-207 DC.

7.5.2.3 Intitulé

L'intitulé des causes françaises n'est habituellement pas indiqué, sauf (1) pour se référer à une décision d'un tribunal administratif ou du Conseil d'État (mais pas dans tous les cas), (2) pour se référer à un jugement non publié ou à un jugement résumé dans la partie « Sommaire » d'un recueil, (3) pour éviter la confusion (par ex. lorsqu'un tribunal a rendu deux décisions un même jour) et (4) lorsque la cause est mieux connue sous le nom des parties que selon les renseignements habituels.

Mettre l'intitulé en italique, entre virgules, après la date à laquelle la décision a été rendue.

> Cass com, 22 janvier 1991, ***Ouest Abri***, [1991] D Jur 175.

7.5.2.4 Année et semestre

Indiquer l'année de publication entre crochets avant l'abréviation du recueil. Pour se référer à la version électronique de la **Gazette du Palais** (**Gaz Pal**), placer l'année de publication entre parenthèses avant le numéro du recueil.

> Cons const, 19 juin 2008, **[2008]** JCP G Jur 449, 2008-564 DC.
> Cass civ 1re, 15 février 2005, **(2006)** 337 Gaz Pal 46 (note S Lafargeas).

Pour faire référence à un numéro de la **Gazette du Palais** publié en 2000 ou avant, inclure le numéro de semestre après l'année de publication, mais avant le crochet fermant. Indiquer le numéro du semestre en nombres ordinaux, puis écrire **sem** pour **semestre**.

> CA Orléans, 23 octobre 1997, [1999 1er sem] Gaz Pal Jur 217, (note Benoît de Roquefeuil).

7.5.2.5 Recueil

Placer un seul espace entre chaque élément : **(1998 1re sem) Gaz Pal Jur 176**.

> Cass civ 3e, 23 juin 1999, (2000) JCP II 10333.

Voir l'**annexe C-2** pour une liste plus complète des abréviations des titres des recueils.

7.5.2.6 *Partie du recueil*

Lorsque la partie du recueil est numérotée, indiquer le numéro de la partie en chiffres romains après l'année de publication. Lorsque la partie du recueil n'est pas numérotée, indiquer l'abréviation du titre de la partie. Ne pas inclure la partie du recueil dans le cas du ***Recueil Lebon*** (**Rec**), de **l'*Actualité juridique de droit administratif*** (**AJDA**), de la ***Semaine juridique*** (**JCP**) après 24e numéro de 2009 ou du ***Dalloz*** (**D**) à partir de 2001.

Abréviation des titres des parties des recueils :

Chroniques	Chron
Doctrine	Doctr
Informations rapides	Inf
Jurisprudence	Jur
Legislation, Lois et décrets, Textes de lois, etc.	Lég
Panorama de jurisprudence	Pan
Sommaire	Somm

7.5.2.7 *Page et numéro de la décision*

Indiquer la première page de la décision après la partie du recueil ou son année de publication. Pour la ***Semaine juridique***, indiquer le numéro de la décision (par ex. **10000 bis**).

> Ass plén, 6 novembre 1998, [1999] JCP G II **10000 bis**.

Pour les ***Bulletin de la Cour de cassation***, mentionner le numéro de page et le numéro de la décision, séparés par une virgule et une espace.

> Cass civ 2e, 7 juin 2001, [2001] Bull civ II **75, nº 110**.

7.5.2.8 *Référence précise*

Étant donnée la brièveté de la plupart des jugements, les références précises sont rarement utilisées. Le cas échéant, indiquer la référence précise après le numéro de la première page, précédée de **à la p**.

> Trib gr inst Narbonne, 12 mars 1999, [1999 1er sem] Gaz Pal Jur 405 **à la p 406**.

7.5.2.9 *Notes*

Si la décision est suivie d'une note, d'un rapport ou d'une conclusion, ajouter cette information à la fin de la référence. Inscrire **note** entre parenthèses peu importe le type de document, suivi du nom de l'auteur.

> Cass civ 1re, 6 juillet 1999, [1999] JCP G II 10217 **(note Thierry Garé)**.

7.5.2.10 Décisions non publiées

Pour faire référence à une décision non publiée, indiquer le nom de la cour, la date de la décision, les mots **non publiée** et le numéro de la décision. Si possible, fournir les renseignements bibliographiques permettant de retracer une note à propos de la décision.

> Cass civ 1re, 4 février 2015, **non publiée**, nº 14-11.458, (2015) 113 R Lamy dr immatériel 16 (note Lionel Costes).

7.5.3 Documents gouvernementaux

Indiquer **France** au début de chaque référence à des documents gouvernementaux.

7.5.3.1 Débats

7.5.3.1.1 De 1787 à 1860

France, | *Archives parlementaires*, | série, | tome, | date, | référence précise | (orateur).

Abréger *Archives parlementaires : Recueil complet des débats législatifs et politiques des chambres françaises* par ***Archives parlementaires***. Indiquer la série après le titre. La première série couvre les années 1787—1799, alors que la deuxième série couvre les années 1800—1860. Les références précises se font aux **sections** et non pas aux articles. Le nom de l'orateur peut être ajouté, entre parenthèses à la fin de la référence.

> France, *Archives parlementaires*, 1re série, t 83, 5 janvier 1794, s 3.

7.5.3.1.2 De 1871 à aujourd'hui

France, | *journal*, | chambre, | Débats parlementaires, | division, | numéro et date, | référence précise | (orateur).

À partir de 1871, les débats parlementaires sont publiés dans le ***Journal officiel de la République française***, abrégé ***JO***. Indiquer la chambre, suivie de **Débats parlementaires.** Pour les débats parlementaires publiés entre 1871 et 1880 inclusivement, omettre la chambre et **Débats parlementaires.** Pour les débats parlementaires publiés entre 1943 et 1958 inclusivement, indiquer seulement **Débats de [nom de la chambre].**

La division ne doit être indiquée qu'à partir de 1980 pour l'Assemblée nationale et à partir de 1983 pour le Sénat. Dans le cas de l'Assemblée nationale, les débats parlementaires se scindent en deux : **Compte rendu intégral** et **Questions écrites remises à la Présidence de l'Assemblée nationale et réponses des ministres.** Il existe également deux divisions pour le Sénat : **Compte rendu intégral** et **Questions remises à la Présidence du Sénat et réponses des ministres aux questions écrites**.

Terminer par le numéro (s'il y a lieu) et la date de la séance, puis par la référence précise à la page consultée. Si nécessaire, ajouter le nom de l'orateur entre parenthèses à la fin de la référence.

France, *JO*, Assemblée nationale, Débats parlementaires, Compte rendu intégral, 1re séance du 23 janvier 2001, à la p 635 (Gilbert Maurel).

France, *JO*, Sénat, Débats parlementaires, Compte rendu intégral, séance du 3 avril 2001.

7.5.3.2 Anciens journaux officiels

France, | *titre*, | année ou date de publication, | tome ou volume | référence précise.

Les débats parlementaires, les documents parlementaires et les documents non parlementaires **précédant l'année 1871** sont généralement publiés à l'intérieur d'anciennes versions du *Journal officiel de la République française*.

1787–1810	*Gazette nationale, ou le Moniteur universel*
1811–1848	*Moniteur universel*
1848–1852	*Moniteur universel, Journal officiel de la République*
1852–1870	*Journal officiel de l'Empire français*

Le mode de référence peut varier selon l'organisation du journal. Généralement, la référence devrait au moins inclure le titre du journal, l'année de référence ou la date de publication, le tome ou le volume (s'il y a lieu), ainsi que le numéro de la page consultée.

France, *Journal officiel de l'Empire français*, 1868, t 1 à la p 14.

France, *Gazette nationale, ou le Moniteur universel*, 1er juillet 1791, t 9 à la p 3.

7.5.3.3 Documents parlementaires

7.5.3.3.1 Travaux et réunions parlementaires

France, | chambre, | organisme, | « titre des travaux », | Compte rendu ou *Bulletin* | (date) | (président).

Indiquer le titre des travaux, puis le numéro du compte rendu ou du bulletin correspondant. Les **Comptes rendus** sont utilisés pour les travaux de l'Assemblée nationale, alors que les ***Bulletins*** sont utilisés pour les travaux du Sénat. Contrairement au terme **Compte rendu**, le terme ***Bulletin*** est en italique. Terminer par la date, le président des travaux (facultatif), et la référence précise.

France, Assemblée nationale, Délégation aux droits des femmes, « Auditions sur le suivi de l'application des lois relatives à l'IVG et à la contraception », Compte rendu n° 4 (6 novembre 2001) (présidente : Martine Lignières-Cassou).

France, Sénat, Commission des affaires culturelles, « Auditions de M Jack Lang, ministre de l'éducation nationale », *Bulletin* du 11 juin 2001 (13 juin 2001)

7.5.3.3.2 Rapports d'information

France, | chambre, | organisme, | *titre du rapport,* | par auteur(s), | numéro du rapport | (date) | référence précise.

France, Sénat, Délégation pour l'Union européenne, *Le projet de traité établissant une Constitution pour l'Europe*, par Hubert Haenel, rapport n° 3 (1er octobre 2003) à la p 4.

France, Assemblée nationale, *Rapport d'information déposé en application de l'article 145 du Règlement par la mission d'information commune sur le prix des carburants dans les départements d'outre-mer*, par Jacques Le Guen et Jérôme Cahuzac, rapport n° 1885 (23 juillet 2009) à la p 63.

7.5.3.4 Documents non parlementaires

France, | organisme, | *titre,* | numéro, tome ou volume, | renseignements sur l'édition | référence précise | (renseignements additionnels).

La référence aux documents non parlementaires de France suit le même modèle de référence que les documents non parlementaires canadiens à la section 4.2.

France, *Commission d'enquête sur la sécurité du transport maritime des produits dangereux ou polluants*, Rapport n° 2535, t 1 (5 juillet 2000, président : Daniel Paul).

France, Conseil économique et social, *La conjoncture économique et sociale en 2005*, Avis et rapports du Conseil économique et social, *JO*, n° 2005-09 à la p I-4 (1er juin 2005, rapport présenté par Luc Guyau).

France, Ministère de la justice, *Bulletin officiel*, n° 82 à la p 3 (1er avril–30 juin 2001).

7.5.4 Doctrine

7.5.4.1 Modèle de base

Auteur, | « titre de l'article » | [année de publication] | recueil | partie | première page ou numéro du document | référence précise.

Indiquer le nom et le titre d'articles publiés dans les recueils généraux de France de la manière énoncée aux sections 6.1.2, 6.1.3, 7.5.2.4, 7.5.2.5 et 7.5.2.6. Consulter l'**annexe C-2** pour les abréviations des recueils français.

Jean-Christophe Galloux, « La loi du 6 mars 1998 relative à la sécurité et à la promotion d'activités sportives » [1998] JCP G I 1085.

Nicolas Molfessis, « La controverse doctrinale et l'exigence de transparence de la doctrine » [2003] RTD civ 161 à la p 161.

Hélène Popu et Jean-Philippe Tricoit, « Le partage des cendres » [2004] 19 Defrénois 1285.

Lorsque l'article n'a pas de pagination, inscrire le numéro de document (et le type de document, le cas échéant).

Alain Gauvin, « La question récurrente de la qualification juridique des dérivés de crédit » [2004] 3 R Dr bancaire & financier, étude 1000032 à la note 9 et texte correspondant.

Utiliser le même modèle pour faire référence à des commentaires publiés dans les recueils généraux français.

Xavier Labbée, « Esquisse d'une définition civiliste de l'espèce humaine » [1999] D Chron 437 à la p 440.

7.5.4.2 Notes

Auteur, | note sous | tribunal, | date de la décision, | [année de publication] | recueil | partie | première page ou numéro du document.

Les recueils français publient fréquemment des notes à la suite des résumés des décisions. Pour faire référence à une note, indiquer le nom de l'auteur, suivi des mots **note sous**. Faire référence à la décision conformément aux règles propres à la jurisprudence française, énoncées à la section 7.5.2.

Danielle Corrignan-Carsin, **note sous** Cass soc, 10 mai 1999, [1999] JCP G II 1425.

7.5.4.4 Recueils encyclopédiques

7.5.4.4.1 Modèle de base

Titre du répertoire, | édition, | identification de la rubrique | par | auteur de la rubrique, | référence précise.

Indiquer le titre complet du répertoire en italique. Lorsque **plus d'une édition** a été publiée, indiquer le numéro de l'édition.

Encyclopédie juridique Dalloz : répertoire de droit commercial, 2e éd, « Publicité foncière » par Luc Bihl, n° 256.
Juris-classeur civil, art 1354, fasc A par Roger Perrot.

7.5.4.4.2 Rubriques

Peu importe la méthode de classification des rubriques, toujours indiquer le numéro du fascicule après celui du volume. Ne pas indiquer la date de révision du fascicule.

Classées en ordre alphabétique :

Indiquer les mots-clés qui identifient la rubrique entre guillemets.

Encyclopédie juridique Dalloz : répertoire de droit civil, « Personnalité (droits de la) » par D Tallon, n° 153.

Si un numéro de fascicule est associé à une rubrique, ajouter **fasc**, suivi de l'indication alphanumérique appropriée.

Juris-classeur civil annexes, **« Associations », fasc 1-A** par Robert Brichet.

Classées selon les articles d'un code :

Indiquer le numéro de l'article sous lequel la rubrique est classée. Utiliser la même forme que celle du répertoire. Inclure le fascicule s'il y a lieu.

Juris-classeur civil, **art 1315—1326, fasc 20** par Daniel Veaux.

Classées par volume :

Indiquer le numéro du volume où se trouve la rubrique. Inclure le fascicule s'il y a lieu.

Juris-classeur commercial: banque et crédit, **vol 2, fasc 32** par Jean Stoufflet.

7.6 AUSTRALIE

7.6.1 Législation

Titre | (indication géographique), | année/numéro, | référence précise.

La présente section s'applique aux lois et à la législation déléguée (règlements). Écrire le titre abrégé officiel de la loi en italique. Inclure l'année dans le titre. Indiquer l'abréviation de l'indication géographique immédiatement après le titre. Pour les abréviations géographiques australiennes, consulter l'**annexe A-3**.

Loi :

Marine Pollution Act 1987 (NSW), 1987/299, art 53(1)(d).

Législation déléguée :

Admiralty Amendment Rules 2002 (No 1) (Cth), 2002/109, r 5(b).

7.6.2 Jurisprudence

7.6.2.1 Modèle de base

Suivre le même modèle que pour la jurisprudence canadienne, sauf pour l'année, qui doit être indiquée entre crochets (section 3).

Neilson v Overseas Projects Corporation of Victoria Ltd, [2005] HCA 54.

Lorsqu'il n'existe aucune référence neutre, **toujours fournir l'année du jugement** entre parenthèses après l'intitulé.

Standard Portland Cement Company Pty Ltd v Good (1983), 57 ALJR 151 (PC).

Donner l'année du recueil **seulement si l'année du jugement est différente**.

Thwaites v Ryan (1983), [1984] VR 65 (SC).

7.6.2.2 *Référence neutre*

Plusieurs tribunaux australiens ont adopté un système de référence neutre. Toutes les décisions disponibles sur AustLII ont une référence neutre. Suivre les règles sur les références neutres au Canada (section 3.5) à l'exception de l'année, qui est placée entre crochets.

7.6.2.3 *Recueil*

Consulter **l'annexe C-2** pour les abréviations des séries des *Law Reports*. Pour les décisions du ***Privy Council*** (PC) et de la ***High Court of Australia*** (HCA), faire référence aux **CLR**, sinon au **ALR**. Pour les autres décisions de cours générales, renvoyer de préférence au **FCR**, sinon au **FLR**. Pour les états et territoires australiens, privilégier le recueil étatique ou territorial officiel.

7.6.2.4 *Cour*

Consulter **l'annexe B-2** pour les abréviations des tribunaux australiens. Si l'indication géographique des tribunaux étatiques et territoriaux est évidente, n'indiquer que l'instance de la cour.

7.6.3 Documents gouvernementaux

Indiquer **Austl** au début de la référence.

7.6.3.1 *Débats*

Austl, | indication géographique, | chambre, | *Parliamentary Debates* | (date) | référence précise | (orateur).

Après **Austl**, inscrire l'indication géographique. Voir l'**annexe A-3** pour les abréviations australiennes. Toujours utiliser les *Parliamentary Debates* en tant que recueil.

> Austl, Commonwealth, House of Representatives, *Parliamentary Debates* (17 septembre 2001) à la p 30739 (M Howard, premier ministre).
>
> Austl, Victoria, Legislative Assembly, *Parliamentary Debates* (23 octobre 1968) à la p 1197.

7.6.3.2 *Rapports parlementaires*

Austl, | indication géographique, | *titre*, | numéro | (année) | référence précise.

Écrire **Parl Paper n°** avant le numéro.

> Austl, Commonwealth, *Department of Foreign Affairs Annual Report 1975*, Parl Paper n° 142 (1976) à la p 5.

Sources étrangères

7.6.3.3 *Rapports non parlementaires*

Austl, | indication géographique, | organisme, | *titre* | (type de document) | par auteur(s), | renseignements sur l'édition | référence précise.

Austl, Commonwealth, Royal Commission into Aboriginal Deaths in Custody, *Report of the Inquiry into the Death of Stanley John Gollan* par Commissioner Elliott Johnston, QC, Canberra, Australian Government Publishing Service, 1990 à la p 31.

Austl, Commonwealth, Law Reform Commission, *Annual Report 1998* (Rapport nº 49), Canberra, Australian Government Publishing Service, 1988.

7.6.3.4 *Documents des ministères*

Auteur, | indication géographique, | *titre*, | service du document, | numéro | (date) | référence précise.

Si des renseignements supplémentaires sont nécessaires pour identifier précisément l'indication géographique à l'intérieur de l'Australie, fournir l'indication géographique suivie de **Austl** entre parenthèses et avant la virgule précédant le titre.

Paul Keating, Commonwealth (Austl), *Opening of the Global Cultural Diversity Conference*, Ministerial Document Service, nº 172/94-95 (27 avril 1995) à la p 5977.

7.7.1 Législation

Titre | (N-Z), | année/numéro, | volume RS | première page.

La présente section s'applique aux lois et à la législation déléguée (règlements). Écrire le titre abrégé officiel de la loi en italique. Inclure l'année dans le titre. Indiquer l'abréviation de l'indication géographique immédiatement après le titre. S'il y a lieu, fournir le numéro du volume, suivi de **RS** (pour Reprint Series).

Loi :

Abolition of the Death Penalty Act 1989 (N-Z), 1989/119, 41 RS 1.

Législation déléguée :

High Court Amendment Rules (No 2) 1987 (N-Z), 1987/169, 40 RS 904.

Pour la législation déléguée, indiquer l'année de la Gazette et la page de la Gazette s'il y a lieu.

Ticketing of Meat Notice 1979 (N-Z), Gazette 1979, 2030.

7.7.2 Jurisprudence

7.7.2.1 Modèle de base

Suivre le même modèle que pour la jurisprudence canadienne, sauf pour l'année, qui doit être indiquée entre crochets (section 3).

> *R v Clarke*, [2005] NZSC 60.
> *Pfizer v Commissioner of Patents*, [2005] 1 NZLR 362 (HC).

7.7.2.2 Référence neutre

La Cour suprême de Nouvelle-Zélande a officiellement adopté un système de référence neutre pour les jugements qui ont été rendus en 2005 ou après. Suivre les règles de la référence neutre au Canada (section 3.5), à l'exception de l'année, qui est placée entre crochets.

7.7.2.3 Recueil

7.7.2.3.1 Law Reports

Les *Law Reports* sont divisés en séries. **Faire référence aux séries plutôt qu'aux *Law Reports*.** Puisqu'il n'y a pas de recueil particulier pour le ***Judicial Committee of the Privy Council*** (après 1932), la ***Court of Appeal*** ou la ***High Court***, inclure **PC**, **CA**, ou **HC** à la fin de chaque référence à une décision d'une de ces cours. Consulter **l'annexe C-2** pour les abréviations des séries des *Law Reports*.

7.7.2.4 Cour

N.B. Le ***Supreme Court Act 2003*** a créé la Cour suprême de Nouvelle-Zélande et a aboli les appels au *Privy Council*.

7.7.3 Documents gouvernementaux

Indiquer **N-Z** au début de la référence.

7.7.3.1 Débats

N-Z, | *Hansard*, | étape : | sujet | (numéro de la question) | date | (orateur).

Hansard fournit le type d'étape : ***Questions to Ministers***, ***Debate-General***, ***Report of [nom] Committee*** ou ***Miscellaneous***. Indiquer le titre du débat en tant que sujet (par ex. **Labour, Associate Minister–Accountability**). Ne pas répéter l'information si l'étape et le sujet sont les mêmes.

> N-Z, *Hansard*, Questions to Ministers : Biosecurity Risk-Motor Vehicle and Equipment Imports (n° 3) 1er mars 2000 (Ian Ewen-Street).

7.7.3.2 Documents parlementaires

N-Z, | « titre », | date, | session | (président) | préfixe et numéro.

Ne pas mettre d'espace entre le préfixe et le numéro.

N-Z, « Report of the Government Administration Committee, Inquiry into New Zealand's Adoption Laws », août 2001, 46e parlement (présidente : Dianne Yates)

N-Z, « Report of the Game Bird Habitat Trust Board for the year ended 31 August 1999 », février 2000, C.22.

7.8 AFRIQUE DU SUD

7.8.1 Législation

7.8.1.1 Lois

Titre, | (Afr du Sud), | numéro | de l'année, | référence précise.

Si l'indication géographique ne peut être aisément déduite du titre de la loi, inclure (**Afr du Sud**) après le titre.

Constitution of the Republic of South Africa 1996, nº 108 de 1996.

Consumer Protection Act (Afr du Sud), nº 68 de 2008, art 33.

7.8.1.2 Modifications et abrogations

Pour plus de détails, voir la section 2.1.11.

Constitution of the Republic of South Africa 1996, nº 108 de 1996 **mod par** *Constitution of the Republic of South Africa Amendment Act*, nº 3 de 1999.

7.8.1.3 Projets de loi

Numéro, | *titre*, | (Afr du Sud), | session, | parlement, | année, | référence précise.

B30-2005, *Precious Metals Bill* (Afr du Sud), 3e sess, 3e Parl, 2005.

B26-2005, *Nursing Bill* (Afr du Sud), 3e sess, 3e Parl, 2005, art 17.

7.8.2 Jurisprudence

Intitulé, | référence principale | référence précise | référence parallèle | (indication géographique | cour).

Les décisions récentes d'Afrique du Sud sont disponibles gratuitement sur la base de données en ligne **SAFLII**. Puisqu'il n'existe aucun identifiant propre à SAFLII, la référence principale doit être la référence neutre si elle est disponible. Suivre le même modèle que pour la jurisprudence canadienne, sauf pour l'année, qui doit être indiquée entre crochets (section 3).

La référence aux versions imprimées des décisions doit être faite aux ***South African Law Reports*** ou aux ***Butterworths Constitutional Law Reports*** autant que possible. Pour une liste des abréviations des recueils, voir l'**annexe C-2**. Si l'indication géographique et la cour ne sont pas évidentes dans le reste de la référence, fournir ces renseignements entre parenthèses à la fin de la référence. Pour les abréviations des cours sud-africaines, voir l'**annexe B-2**.

> *Messina Associated Carriers v Kleinhaus*, [2001] ZASCA 46 au para 10, [2001] 3 S Afr LR 868.

7.8.3 Documents gouvernementaux

7.8.3.1 Débats

Afr du Sud, | *Hansard*, | chambre, | date, | référence précise | (orateur).

> Afr du Sud, *Hansard*, Assemblée nationale, 9 février 2009, à la p 1 (MJ Ellis).

7.8.3.2 Rapports, documents de discussion et exposés

Titre, | commission, | numéro de projet | (date) | référence précise.

Inclure le nom de la commission s'il n'est pas mentionné dans le titre.

> *Truth and Reconciliation Commission of South Africa Report* (29 octobre 1998) au ch 1, para 91.
>
> *Report on Trafficking in Persons*, South African Law Reform Commission, projet n° 131 (août 2008) à la p 23.

7.9 UNION EUROPÉENNE

7.9.1 Règlements, directives, décisions, communications et informations

Les règlements, les directives, les décisions, les communications, les informations et les autres documents de l'Union européenne sont publiés dans le ***Journal officiel de l'Union européenne*** (JO). Celui-ci remplace le *Journal officiel des Communautés européennes* depuis le 1er février 2003.

Le JO est publié chaque jour ouvrable dans les langues officielles de l'Union européenne. Il comprend deux séries (la série L pour **la législation** et la série C pour **les communications et les informations**), ainsi qu'un supplément (la série S pour **les offres publiques**, disponible en format électronique depuis le 1er juillet 1998).

La législation des Communautés européennes comprend des règlements, des directives et des décisions. Ces documents sont publiés dans la série L (législation) du *Journal officiel de l'Union européenne*.

CE, | *titre*, | [année du journal] | JO, | série | numéro de volume/première page | référence précise.

Indiquer **CE** pour Communautés européennes, suivi du titre complet de l'instrument en italique. Le numéro de l'instrument est inclus dans le titre. Le **numéro des directives et des décisions** est composé de l'année et d'un numéro séquentiel (par ex. **98/85** ou **2004/29**). Pour faire référence à des règlements, inscrire le numéro séquentiel en premier, suivi de l'année (par ex. **2514/98**).

Pour faire référence au *Journal officiel de l'Union européenne*, indiquer **JO**, suivi de la série, du numéro de volume et de la première page de l'instrument, les deux derniers éléments étant séparés par une barre oblique (par ex. **L 15/14**).

Règlements :

> CE, *Règlement (CE) 218/2005 de la Commission du 10 février 2005 portant ouverture et mode de gestion d'un contingent tarifaire autonome pour l'ail à dater du 1er janvier 2005*, [2005] JO, L 39/5 à la p 6.

Directives :

> CE, *Directive 2004/29/CE de la Commission du 4 mars 2004 concernant la fixation des caractères et des conditions minimales pour l'examen des variétés de vigne*, [2004] JO, L 71/22.

Décisions :

> CE, *Décision 98/85/CE de la Commission du 16 janvier 1998 relative à certaines mesures de protection à l'égard des oiseaux vivants originaires de Hong Kong ou de la République populaire de Chine*, [1998] JO, L 15/45 à la p 45.

Communications et informations :

> CE, *Note explicative relative à l'annexe III de l'accord UE-Mexique (décision no 2/2000 du Conseil conjoint UE-Mexique)*, [2004] JO, C 40/2.

7.9.2 Jurisprudence

Intitulé, | numéro de la décision, | [année du recueil] | recueil | première page | référence précise.

Indiquer l'intitulé en utilisant la forme abrégée du nom des institutions (par ex. **Commission** et non **Commission des Communautés européennes**). Écrire le numéro de la décision. Un **C-** indique les décisions de la **Cour de Justice des Communautés européennes**, aussi connue sous le nom de Cour de Justice européenne (CJE). Un **T-** indique une décision du **Tribunal de première instance** (CJ (1re inst)).

Faire référence au recueil et indiquer la première page de la décision. Les décisions de la CJE et les décisions de la CJ (1re inst) sont reproduites dans la publication officielle de la Cour, le *Recueil de la jurisprudence de la Cour et du Tribunal de première instance*, couramment appelé ***Recueil de la Cour européenne*** (**Rec CE**). Les numéros de page sont précédés de **I-** s'il s'agit d'une **décision de la CJE** et de **II-** s'il s'agit d'une **décision de la CJ (1re inst)**.

Cour de Justice des Communautés européennes :

Commission c Luxembourg, C-26/99, [1999] Rec CE I-8987 à la p I-8995.

Tribunal de première instance :

Kesko c Commission, T-22/97, [1999] Rec CE II-3775 à la p II-3822.

7.9.3 Débats du Parlement européen

CE, | *date de la séance ou titre*, | [année] | JO, | annexe et numéro de volume/première page | référence précise.

Les débats du Parlement européen sont publiés dans l'annexe du *Journal officiel de l'Union européenne* (JO). Indiquer **CE**, suivi du titre du document ou de la date de la séance. Indiquer ensuite l'année de publication de la séance entre crochets, suivi de **JO**, du mot **annexe**, du numéro de volume et de la première page. Une barre oblique sépare le numéro du volume et la première page (par ex. **4-539/144**).

CE, *Séance du mercredi 5 mai 1999*, [1999] JO, annexe 4-539/144 à la p 152.

7.10 AUTRES TRADITIONS JURIDIQUES

7.10.1 Droit romain

Faire référence à la **division traditionnelle** (généralement un livre, un titre ou une partie) et non au numéro de page de l'édition ou de la traduction. Ne pas ajouter d'espace entre les numéros des différentes parties. Utiliser des chiffres arabes (par ex. **1, 2, 3**), suivis de points, pour indiquer les divisions, quelle que soit la forme utilisée dans l'édition ou dans la traduction.

L'abréviation **pr**, précédée d'une espace, signifie *principium* ou « début » et fait référence au document non numéroté avant la première section d'un titre. Indiquer l'édition ou la traduction utilisée entre parenthèses à la fin de la référence.

Pour faire référence au **Digeste de Justinien**, indiquer s'il y a lieu l'auteur du passage entre parenthèses à la fin de la référence.

Collection	**Abréviation**	**Exemple**
Lois des douze tables	XII Tab	XII Tab 8.2
Institutes de Gaius	G	G 3.220
Code de Théodose	Cod Th	Cod Th 8.14.1
Institutes de Justinien	Inst	Inst 4.4 pr (trad par Birks et McLeod)

Collection	Abréviation	Exemple
Digeste de Justinien	Dig	Dig 47.10.1 (Ulpian)
Codex de Justinien	Cod	Cod 6.42.16
Nouvelles	Nov	Nov 22.3

7.10.2 Droit canon

Faire référence à la **division traditionnelle** et non au numéro de page de l'édition ou de la traduction. Utiliser des chiffres arabes (par ex. **1, 2, 3**), suivis de points, pour indiquer les divisions, quelle que soit la forme utilisée dans l'édition ou dans la traduction. Indiquer l'édition ou la traduction utilisée entre parenthèses à la fin de la référence.

Collection	Abréviation	Exemple
Decretum de Gratien	-	**1re partie** : D 50 c 11 **2e partie** : C 30 q 4 c 5 **2e partie, *De poenitentia*** : De poen D 1 c 75 **3e partie** : De cons D 1 c 5
Décrétales de Grégoire IX (*Liber extra*)	X	X 5.38.12
Décrétales de Boniface VIII (*Liber sextus*)	VI	VI 5.2.16
Constitutions de Clément V (*Clementinae*)	Clem	Clem 3.7.2
Extravagantes de Jean XXII (*Extravagantes Johannis XXII*)	Extrav Jo XII	Extrav Jo XII 14.2
Extravagantes communes (Extravagantes communes)	Extrav Com	Extrav Com 3.2.9
Codex Iuris Canonici (1917)	1917 Code	1917 Code c 88, § 2
Codex Iuris Canonici (1983)	1983 Code	1983 Code c 221, § 1

7.10.3 Droit talmudique

Talmud, | *traité*, | référence précise.

Indiquer le Talmud de Babylone ou le Talmud de Jérusalem. Mettre le nom du traité en italique. Pour faire référence au Talmud de Babylone, indiquer la **pagination traditionnelle** (de l'édition Vilna) et non le numéro de page fourni par l'éditeur ou par le traducteur. Si une édition différente est utilisée (par ex. Warsaw), indiquer le nom de l'édition après la référence précise.

Pour faire référence à une édition ou à une traduction particulière, indiquer le nom de la maison d'édition entre parenthèses, suivi d'une référence précise (voir les sections 6.2.2.4.1 et 6.2.7 à 6.2.9). S'il y a une traduction, indiquer **[traduction par l'auteur]** dans le corps du texte à la fin de la citation, après les guillemets, mais avant l'appel de note (voir la section 6.2.2.4.2).

Utiliser des chiffres arabes (par ex. **1, 2, 3**) pour le numéro de feuille et les lettres **a** et **b** pour indiquer le numéro de page. Pour faire référence au **Talmud de Jérusalem**, fournir une référence précise correspondant au Mishna (**Mish**) et au Halacha (**Hal**) et non à la page. Indiquer une référence précise à une page si tous les renseignements sur l'édition peuvent être fournis entre parenthèses (voir les sections 6.2.7 à 6.2.9).

Talmud de Babylone, *Bava Metzia*, 11b.
Talmud de Jérusalem, *Sanhedrin*, Mish 1 Hal 5.

INDEX

Index

Index

Appendices

Annexes

TABLE OF CONTENTS / TABLE DES MATIÈRES

APPENDIX A / ANNEXE A

A. JURISDICTION ABBREVIATIONS ~ ABRÉVIATIONS DE JURIDICTIONS

(A-1) Abbreviations for Canada ~ Abréviations canadiennes

Jurisdiction / Indication géographique	**Statutes and Gazettes / Lois et gazettes**	**Regulations / Règlements**	**Courts and Journals / Cours et revues**	**Neutral Citation / Référence neutre**	**Law Reporters / Recueils de droit**
Alberta	A	Alta	Alta	AB	A or Alta
British Columbia / Colombie-Britannique	BC	BC	BC	BC	BC
Canada	C	C	C or Can	–	C or Can
Lower Canada / Bas-Canada	LC / B-C	LC / B-C	LC / B-C	–	LC / B-C
Manitoba	M	Man	Man	MB	Man
New Brunswick / Nouveau-Brunswick	NB / N-B	NB / N-B	NB / N-B	NB	NB / N-B
Newfoundland[1] *Terre-Neuve*[2]	N	Nfld	Nfld	NF	Nfld
Newfoundland & Labrador[3] / Terre-Neuve-et-Labrador[4]	NL	NL	NL	NL (NF — before 19 March 2002 / avant le 19 mars 2002)	Nfld
Northwest Territories / Territoires du Nord-Ouest	NWT / TN-O	NWT / TN-O	NWT / TN-O	NWT or NT	NWT / TN-O
Nova Scotia / Nouvelle-Écosse	NS	NS	NS	NS	NS
Nunavut	Nu	Nu	Nu	NU	Nu
Ontario	O	O or Ont	Ont	ON	O
Prince Edward Island / Île-du-Prince-Édouard	PEI	PEI	PEI	PE	PEI
Province of Canada	Prov C	Prov C	Prov C	–	–
Quebec / Québec	Q	Q	Q (Journals) or Qc (Courts)	QC	Q

---

1 **Gazette**: before 21 December 2001 / **Regulations**: before 13 December 2001 / **Most other purposes including statutes**: before 6 December 2001.

2 **Gazette**: avant le 21 décembre 2001 / **Règlements**: avant le 13 décembre 2001 / **Pour le reste (incluant les lois)** : avant le 6 décembre 2001.

3 **Gazette**: 21 December 2001 and after / **Regulations**: 13 December 2001 and after / **Most other purposes including statutes**: 6 December 2001 and after.

4 **Gazette**: depuis le 21 décembre 2001 / **Règlements**: depuis le 13 décembre 2001 / **Pour le reste (incluant les lois)** : depuis le 6 décembre 2001.

Jurisdiction / Indication géographique	**Statutes and Gazettes / Lois et gazettes**	**Regulations / Règlements**	**Courts and Journals / Cours et revues**	**Neutral Citation / Référence neutre**	**Law Reporters / Recueils de droit**
Saskatchewan	S	S or Sask	Sask	SK	Sask
Upper Canada / Haut-Canada	UC	UC	UC	–	UC
Yukon	Y	Y	Y	YK	Y

Canadian Postal Abbreviations / Abréviations postales canadiennes

Use the following list when referring to provinces in documents that are not mentioned in the previous table (e.g. "F Allard et al, eds, *Private Law Dictionary of Obligations and Bilingual Lexicons*, (Cowansville, QC: Yvon Blais, 2003)").

Utiliser la liste suivante pour faire référence à des documents qui ne sont pas mentionnés dans le tableau précédent (par ex. « Louis Beaudoin et Madeleine Mailhot, *Expressions juridiques en un clin d'œil*, Cowansville (QC), Yvon Blais, 1997 »).

Province or Territory / Province ou territoire	**Abbreviation / Abréviation**
Alberta	AB
British Columbia / Colombie-Britannique	BC
Manitoba	MB
New Brunswick / Nouveau-Brunswick	NB
Newfoundland and Labrador / Terre-Neuve-et-Labrador	NL
Northwest Territories / Territoires du Nord-Ouest	NT
Nova Scotia / Nouvelle-Écosse	NS
Nunavut	NU
Ontario	ON
Prince Edward Island / Île-du-Prince-Édouard	PE
Quebec / Québec	QC
Saskatchewan	SK
Yukon	YT

(A-2) Abbreviations for the United States ~ Abréviations américaines

Alabama	Ala	Minnesota	Minn
Alaska	Alaska	Mississippi	Miss
Arizona	Ariz	Missouri	Mo
Arkansas	Ark	Montana	Mont
California	Cal	Nebraska	Neb
Californie	Cal	Nevada	Nev
Caroline du Nord	NC	New Hampshire	NH
Caroline du Sud	SC	New Jersey	NJ
Colorado	Colo	New Mexico	N Mex
Connecticut	Conn	New York	NY
Dakota du Nord	N Dak	North Carolina	NC
Dakota du Sud	S Dak	North Dakota	N Dak
Delaware	Del	Nouveau Mexique	N Mex
District de Columbie	DC	Ohio	Ohio
District of Colombia	DC	Oklahoma	Okla
États-Unis	É-U	Oregon	Or
Florida	Fla	Pennsylvania	Pa
Floride	Fla	Pennsylvanie	Pa
Georgia	Ga	Rhode Island	RI
Géorgie	Ga	South Carolina	SC
Hawaii	Hawaii	South Dakota	S Dak
Idaho	Idaho	Tennessee	Tenn
Illinois	Ill	Texas	Tex
Indiana	Ind	United States	US
Iowa	Iowa	Utah	Utah
Kansas	Kan	Vermont	Vt
Kentucky	Ky	Virginia	Va
Louisiana	La	Virginie	Va
Louisiane	La	Virginie occidentale	W Va
Maine	Me	Washington	Wash
Maryland	Md	West Virginia	W Va
Massachussetts	Mass	Wisconsin	Wis
Michigan	Mich	Wyoming	Wyo

(A-3) Abbreviations for Australia ~ Abréviations australiennes

Jurisdiction / Indication géographique	Legislation and Courts / Législation et cours	Neutral citation / Référence neutre
Australia	Austl	–
Commonwealth	Cth	–
Australian Capital Territory / Territoire de la capitale australienne	ACT	–
New South Wales / Nouvelle-Galles du Sud	NSW	NSW
Northern Territory / Territoire du Nord	NT	NT
Queensland	Qld	Q
South Australia / Australie méridionale	SA	SA
Tasmania / Tasmanie	Tas	TAS
Victoria	Vic	V
Western Australia / Australie occidentale	WA	WA

(A-4) Other Jurisdictional Abbreviations ~ Abréviations d'autres juridictions

Afrique du sud	Afr du sud
Écosse	Écosse
États-Unis	É-U
European Union	EU
France	France
Hong Kong	HK
Ireland	I

Irelande du nord	IN
New Zealand	NZ
Northern Ireland	NI
Nouvelle-Zélande	N-Z
Royaume-Uni	R-U
Scotland	Scot
Singapore / Singapour	Sing
South Africa	S Afr
Union européenne	UE
United Kingdom	UK
United States	US

(A-5) Abbreviations in International Materials ~ Abréviations dans les documents internationaux

Abbreviation / Abréviation	**Meaning / Signification**
AC	Assemblée consultative (Conseil de l'Europe)
AG	Assemblée générale (NU)
AIEA	Agence internationale de l'énergie atomique (NU)
AP	Assemblée parlementaire (Conseil de l'Europe)
APEC	Asia Pacific Economic Cooperation
ATNIA	Australian Treaty National Interest Analysis
ATNIF	Australian Treaty not yet in force
ATS	Australian Treaty Series
AU	African Union
Bur	Bureau (NU)
C1	First Committee (UN) / Première commission (NU)

C2	Second Committee (UN) / Deuxième Commission (NU)
C3	Third Committee (UN) / Troisième Commission (NU)
CA	Consultative Assembly (Council of Europe)
Can TS	Canada Treaty Series
CCED	Conseil du commerce et du dévoloppement (NU)
CDH	Commission des droits de l'homme (NU)
CE	Communautés européennes
CES	Conseil économique et social (NU)
CIJ	Cour internationale de Justice
CJ (1re inst)	Tribunal de première instance (CE)
CJE	Cour de justice des Communautés européennes
CNUCED	Conférence des Nations Unies sur le commerce et le développement
CNUDCI	Commission des Nations Unies pour le droit commercial international
Comm Eur DH	Commission européenne des Droits de l'Homme
Comm Interam DH	Commission interaméricaine des Droits de l'Homme
Conseil de l'Europe	Conseil de l'Europe
Council of Europe	Council of Europe
Cour Eur DH	Cour européenne des Droits de l'Homme
Cour Interam DH	Cour interaméricaine des Droits de l'Homme
CPJI	Cour permanente de justice internationale
CS	Conseil de sécurité (NU)
CT	Conseil de tutelle (NU)
CTS	Consolidated Treaty Series
Dec	Decision
Déc	Décision
DJI	Documents juridiques internationaux
Doc	Document

Doc off	Document officiel
EC	European Communities
ECFI	European Court of First Instance
ECJ	Court of Justice of the European Communities
Emer	Emergency
ESC	Economic and Social Council (UN)
ETS	European Treaty Series
EU	European Union
Eur Comm HR	European Commission of Human Rights
Eur Ct HR	European Court of Human Rights
Extra	Extraordinaire
FMI	Fonds monétaire international (NU)
GA	General Assembly (GA)
GATT	Accord général sur les tarifs douaniers et le commerce General Agreement on Tariffs and Trade
GC	General Committee (UN)
HCDH	Haut-Commissariat aux droits de l'homme (NU)
HCR	Haut-Commissariat des Nations Unies pour les réfugiés
HRC	Human Rights Committee (UN)
IAEA	International Atomic Energy Agency (UN)
ICAO	International Civil Aviation Organization (NU)
ICJ	International Court of Justice
ICTR	International Criminal Tribunal for Rwanda (UN)
ICTY	International Criminal Tribunal for the Former Yugoslavia (UN)
ILM	International Legal Materials
ILO	International Labor Organization (UN)
IMF	International Monetary Fund (UN)

Inter-Am Comm HR	Inter-American Commission on Human Rights
Inter-Am Ct HR	Inter-American Court of Human Rights
LNTS	League of Nations Treaty Series
Mimeo	Mimeograph(ed)
Miméo	Miméographié
Mtg	Meeting
NATO	North Atlantic Treaty Organization
NU	Nations Unies
NUCED	Conférence des Nations Unies sur le commerce et le développement
OACI	Organisation de l'aviation civile internationale (NU)
OAS	Organization of American States
OASTS	Organization of American States Treaty Series
OÉA	Organisation des États américains
OHCHR	United Nations High Commissioner for Human Rights, Office of the (UN)
OIT	Organisation internationale du Travail
OMC	Organisation mondiale du commerce
OMPI	Organisation mondiale de la propriété intellectuelle
OR	Official Records
OTAN	Organisation du Traité de l'Atlantique Nord
PA	Parliamentary Assembly (Council of Europe)
PCIJ	Permanent Court of International Justice
Plen	Plenary
Plén	Pléniaire
Rec	Recommendation / Recommandation
Reg	Regulation
Res	Resolution
Rés	Résolution

RTF	Recueil des traités de la France
RTNU	Recueil des traités des Nations Unies
RTSN	Recueil des traités de la Société des Nations
RT Can	Recueil des traités du Canada
SC	Security Council
Sess	Session
Spec	Special
Spéc	Spécial
Supp	Supplement / Supplément
STE	Série des traités européens
TC	Trusteeship Council
TDB	Trade and Development Board (UN)
TI Agree	Treaties and other International Agreements of the United States of America 1776-1949
TIAS	United States Treaties and Other International Acts Series
TPIR	Tribunal pénal international pour le Rwanda (NU)
TPIY	Tribunal pénal international pour l'ex-Yougoslavie (NU)
UA	Union africaine
UE	Union européenne
UKFS	British and Foreign State Papers
UKTS	United Kingdom Treaty Series
UN	United Nations
UNCITRAL	United Nations Commission on International Trade Law
UNCTAD	United Nations Conference on Trade and Development
UNHCR	United Nations High Commissioner for Refugees
UNTS	United Nations Treaty Series
Urg	Urgence

USTA	United States Treaties and Other International Agreements
WBO	Banque mondiale World Bank Organization
WIPO	World Intellectual Property Organization
WTO	World Trade Organization

APPENDIX B / ANNEXE B

B. COURTS AND TRIBUNALS ~ COURS ET TRIBUNAUX

(B-1) General Rules ~ Règles générales

This appendix contains a list of abbrevations of courts and tribunals, both current and historical. Place the jurisdictional abbreviation before or after the court abbreviation according to the rules below.

Identify the **court** unless it is obvious from the reporter (**SCR**). See section 3. 9. Identify the **jurisdiction** unless it is obvious from the name of the court or the reporter (**TAQ**). For English abbreviations, the abbreviation for the province, territory, or state normally precedes the abbreviation for the court (**NBCA**; **Qc Sup Ct**). For French abbreviations, provide the abbreviation for the province after the abbreviation of the court for Ontario, New Brunswick and Quebec (**CA NB**; **CS Qc**), otherwise follow the English rule.

Identify the **country** if the province, territory or state is unfamiliar to the majority of readers and is not found in this *Guide*. Generally, courts located in a province, territory, or state are only identified using the abbreviation of that province, territory, or state. For example, it would be incorrect to write "NSWCA Austl" or "NSCA Can" because it is redundant.

Generally, federal, national, and unitary courts are identified by their country unless the country is obvious either from the reporter or from the abbreviation of the court itself. (The jurisdiction is obvious from the court's abbreviation when the name of the jurisdiction is contained in the abbreviation or when no other court shares the abbreviation.)

When citing from the Citizenship Appeals Court of Canada, the Court Martial Appeal Court, or the Exchequer Court of Canada, include the abbreviation **Can** (**Cit AC Can**). For any other Canadian federal court, the jurisdiction is obvious and **Can** should not be included.

The country abbreviation normally follows the court abbreviation (**DCNZ**), but there are exceptions, especially if the name of the jurisdiction is part of the name of the court (**NZCA**).

In **court acronyms**, there is no space in an abbreviation consisting solely of upper case letters. Leave a space when an abbreviation consists of both upper case letters and lower case letters (**BCCA**; **Ont Div Ct**; **NS Co Ct**; **Alta QB**).

Include the abbreviation of the **federal or provincial administrative agency or tribunal** in parentheses at the end of the citation if it is not evident from the title of the cited reporter. If an abbreviation cannot be found, use the full name. Use the abbreviation as it is provided by the administrative body. For further information, see section 3.14.

NB: In English, the abbreviation for "Supreme Court of Canada" is **SCC**, and the abbreviation for Superior Court is **Sup Ct**. In French, "Cour suprême du Canada" is abbreviated **CSC** and "Cour supérieure" is abbreviated **CS**. Also, note that the American abbreviations are **Super Ct** for "Superior Court" and **Sup Ct** for a state Supreme Court.

Cette annexe comprend une liste des abréviations des cours et des tribunaux, à la fois actuels et historiques. Mettre l'abréviation des indications géographiques avant ou après l'abréviation des cours en respectant les règles ci-dessous.

Identifier **la cour**, à moins que le recueil n'indique l'information (**RCS**). Voir section 3.9. Identifier **l'indication géographique**, à moins que cette information ne puisse être déduite du nom de la cour ou du recueil (**TAQ**).

Pour les abréviations en anglais, l'abréviation de la province, du territoire ou de l'État précède normalement l'abréviation de la cour (**NBCA** ; **Qc Sup Ct**). Pour les abréviations en français, fournir l'abréviation de la province après l'abréviation de la cour pour l'Ontario, le Nouveau-Brunswick et le Québec (**CA NB** ; **CS Qc**). Dans tous les autres cas, respecter la règle d'abréviation en anglais.

Identifier **le pays** si l'abréviation de la province, du territoire ou de l'État risque de ne pas être connue des lecteurs ou n'est pas fournie dans ce *Manuel*. Généralement, les cours siégeant dans une province, un territoire ou un État sont déjà identifiées par l'abréviation de la province, du territoire ou de l'État. Par exemple, il serait redondant d'écrire « NSWCA Austl » ou « NSCA Can ».

Les cours fédérale, nationale et unitaire sont identifiées par le nom du pays, à moins que celui-ci ne puisse être déduit du recueil ou de l'abréviation de la cour.

Lorsqu'on renvoie à la Cour d'appel de citoyenneté, la Cour d'appel de la cour martiale du Canada, ou la Cour de l'Échiquier, il faut inclure l'abréviation **Can** (**CA cit Can**). Pour toute autre cour fédérale, l'indication géographique **Can** est évidente et ne doit pas être incluse.

L'abréviation du pays suit l'abréviation de la cour (**DCNZ**), sauf si le nom de la juridiction fait partie du nom de la cour (par ex. NZCA).

Pour les **acronymes des cours**, il n'y a pas d'espace entre les lettres majuscules des abréviations. Toutefois, il y a un espace quand l'abréviation est formée de minuscules et/ou de majuscules (**CQ** ; **BCCA** ; **CQ crim & pén**).

Indiquer l'abréviation de **l'organe ou du tribunal administratif** entre parenthèses à la fin de la référence, s'il est impossible de le déduire du titre du recueil (utiliser le nom au complet si aucune abréviation n'est trouvée). Utiliser l'abréviation utilisée par l'organe administratif. Pour plus d'informations, voir la section 3.14.

N.B. En anglais, l'abréviation de « Supreme Court of Canada » est **SCC** et l'abréviation des cours supérieures est **Sup Ct**. En français, ces abréviations sont inversées : « Cour suprême du Canada » devient **CSC** et « Cour supérieure » devient **CS**. De plus, noter que les abréviations américaines sont **Super Ct** pour « Superior Court » et **Sup Ct** pour la Cour suprême des États-Unis.

(B-2) Abbreviations ~ Abréviations

Court or Tribunal / Cour ou tribunal	**Abbreviation / Abréviation**
Frequent abbreviations / Abréviations principales	
Cour d'appel	CA
Cour provinciale	CP
Cour supérieure	CS
Cour Suprême du Canada	CSC
Court of Appeal	CA
Court of Justice	Ct J
Federal Court of Appeal	FCA
High Court	HC
Provincial Court	Prov Ct
Superior Court	Sup Ct
Traffic Court	Traffic Ct
Youth Court	Youth Ct
Canadian Courts / Cours canadiennes	
Coroners Court	Cor Ct
Cour canadienne de l'impôt	CCI
Cour d'appel	CA
Cour d'appel de la cour martiale	CACM
Cour d'appel fédérale	CAF
Cour de comté	Cc
Cour de l'Ontario, division générale	Div gén Ont
Cour des divorces et des causes matrimoniales	C div & causes mat
Cour des juges de la Cour de comté siégeant au criminel	C j Cc crim
Cour des petites créances	C pet cré

Cour des successions	C succ
Cour divisionnaire	C div
Cour du Banc de la Reine	BR
Cour du Banc de la Reine (Division de la famille)	BR (div fam)
Cour du Banc de la Reine (Division de première instance)	BR (1re inst)
Cour du Québec	CQ
Cour du Québec, Chambre civile	CQ civ
Cour du Québec, Chambre civile (Division des petites créances)	CQ civ (div pet cré)
Cour du Québec, Chambre criminelle et pénale	CQ crim & pén
Cour du Québec, Chambre de la jeunesse	CQ jeun
Cour fédérale, première instance	CF (1re inst)
Cour municipale	CM
Cour provinciale	CP
Cour provinciale (Division civile)	CP Div civ
Cour provinciale (Division criminelle)	CP Div crim
Cour provinciale (Division de la famille)	CP Div fam
Cour supérieure	CS
Cour supérieure (Chambre administrative)	CS adm
Cour supérieure (Chambre civile)	CS civ
Cour supérieure (Chambre criminelle et pénale)	CS crim & pén
Cour supérieure (Chambre de la faillite et de l'insolvabilité)	CS fail & ins
Cour supérieure (Chambre de la famille)	CS fam
Cour supérieure (Division des petites créances)	CS pét cré
Cour suprême (Division d'appel)	C supr A
Cour suprême (Division de la famille)	C supr fam
Cour suprême (Division du Banc de la Reine)	C supr BR
Cour suprême du Canada	CSC

Court Martial Appeal Court	Ct Martial App Ct
Court of Appeal	CA
Court of Appeal in Equity	CA Eq
Court of Justice (General Division)	Ct J (Gen Div)
Court of Justice (General Division, Family Court)	Ct J (Gen Div Fam Ct)
Court of Justice (General Division, Small Claims Court)	Ct J (Gen Div Sm Cl Ct)
Court of Justice (Provincial Division)	Ct J (Prov Div)
Court of Justice (Provincial Division, Youth Court)	Ct J (Prov Div Youth Ct)
Court of Quebec	CQ
Court of Quebec (Civil Division)	CQ (Civ Div)
Court of Quebec (Civil Division, Small Claims)	CQ (Civ Div Sm Cl)
Court of Quebec (Criminal & Penal Division)	CQ (Crim & Pen Div)
Court of Quebec (Youth Division)	CQ (Youth Div)
Court of Queen's Bench	QB
Court of Queen's Bench (Family Division)	QB (Fam Div)
Court of Queen's Bench (Trial Division)	QB (TD)
Divisional Court	Div Ct
Divorce and Matrimonial Causes Court	Div & Mat Causes Ct
Federal Court (Trial Division)	FCTD
Federal Court of Appeal	FCA
High Court of Justice	H Ct J
Municipal Court	Mun Ct
Probate Court	Prob Ct
Provincial Court (Civil Division)	Prov Ct (Civ Div)
Provincial Court (Civil Division, Small Claims Court)	Prov Ct (Civ Div Sm Cl Ct)
Provincial Court (Criminal Division)	Prov Ct (Crim Div)
Provincial Court (Family Court)	Prov Ct (Fam Ct)

Provincial Court (Family Division)	Prov Ct (Fam Div)
Provincial Court (Juvenile Division)	Prov Ct (Juv Div)
Provincial Court (Small Claims Division)	Prov Ct (Sm Cl Div)
Provincial Court (Youth Court)	Prov Ct (Youth Ct)
Provincial Court (Youth Division)	Prov Ct (Youth Div)
Provincial Offences Court	Prov Off Ct
Small Claims Court	Sm Cl Ct
Superior Court (Administrative Division)	Sup Ct (Adm Div)
Superior Court (Bankruptcy and Insolvency Division)	Sup Ct (Bank & Ins Div)
Superior Court (Canada)	Sup Ct
Superior Court (Civil Division)	Sup Ct (Civ Div)
Superior Court (Criminal and Penal Division)	Sup Ct (Crim & Pen Div)
Superior Court (Family Division)	Sup Ct (Fam Div)
Superior Court (Small Claims Division)	Sup Ct (Sm Cl Div)
Supreme Court (Appellate Division) (Can provincial / Can Provinciale)	SC (AD)
Supreme Court (Family Division)	SC (Fam Div)
Supreme Court (Queen's Bench Division)	SC (QB Div)
Supreme Court (Trial Division)	SC (TD)
Supreme Court of Canada	SCC
Tax Court of Canada	TCC
Tax Review Board	T Rev B
Territorial Court	Terr Ct
Territorial Court (Youth Court)	Terr Ct Youth Ct
UK Courts / Cours du Royaume-Uni	
Chancery Court	Ch
Court of Justice (Scotland / Écosse)	Ct Just

Court of Sessions (Scotland / Écosse)	Ct Sess
High Court: Chancery Division (UK / R-U)	ChD
High Court: Family Division (UK / R-U)	FamD
High Court: Queen's Bench Division (UK / R-U)	QBD
High Court of Admiralty	HC Adm
High Court of Justice	HCJ
House of Lords (England / Angleterre)	HL (Eng)
House of Lords (Scotland / Écosse)	HL (Scot)
Judicial Committee of the Privy Council (Commonwealth)	PC
Stipendiary Magistrates' Court	Stip Mag Ct
United States Courts / Cours américaines	
Administrative Court	Admin Ct
Admiralty [Court, Division]	Adm
Alderman's Court	Alder Ct
Appeals Court	App Ct
Appellate Court	App Ct
Appellate Division	App Div
Bankruptcy [Court, Judge]	Bankr
Bankruptcy Appellate Panel	BAP
Board of Tax Appeals (US / É-U)	BTA
Borough Court	[name] Bor Ct
Chancery [Court, Division]	Ch
Children's Court	Child Ct
Circuit Court	Cir Ct
Circuit Court and Family Court	Cir Ct & Fam Ct
Circuit Court of Appeals (federal, US / fédéral, É-U)	Cir
Circuit Court of Appeals (state)	Cir Ct App

Citizenship Appeals Court (US / É-U)	Cit AC
City and Parish Courts	City & Parish Ct
City Court	[name] City Ct
Civil Appeals	Civ App
Civil Court	Civ Ct
Civil Court of Record	Civ Ct Rec
Civil District Court	Civ Dist Ct
Claims Court	Cl Ct
Commerce Court	Comm Ct
Common Pleas	CP
Commonwealth Court	Commw Ct
Conciliation Court	Concil Ct
Constitutional County Court	Const County Ct
County Court	Co Ct
County Court at Law	County Ct at Law
County Court Judges' Criminal Court	Co Ct J Crim Ct
County Judge's Court	County J Ct
County Recorder's Court	County Rec Ct
Court of [General, Special] Sessions	Ct [Gen, Spec] Sess
Court of Appeal[s] (state)	Ct App
Court of Appeals (federal)	Cir
Court of Chancery	Ct Ch
Court of Civil Appeals	Ct Civ App
Court of Claims	Ct Cl
Court of Common Pleas	Ct Com Pl
Court of Criminal Appeals	Ct Crim App
Court of Customs and Patent Appeals	CCPA

Court of Customs Appeals	Ct Cust App
Court of Errors	Ct Err
Court of Errors and Appeals	Ct Err & App
Court of Federal Claims	Ct Fed Cl
Court of First Instance	Ct First Inst
Court of International Trade	Ct Intl Trade
Court of Review	Ct Rev
Court of Special Appeals	Ct Spec App
Court of Tax Review	Ct T Rev
Criminal Appeals	Crim App
Criminal District Court	Crim Dist Ct
Customs Court	Cust Ct
District Court (US Federal / É-U fédéral)	D
District Court (US states / États des É-U)	Dist Ct
District Court of Appeal[s]	Dist Ct App
District Justice Court	Dist Just Ct
Domestic Relations Court	Dom Rel Ct
Emergency Court of Appeal[s]	Emer Ct App
Environmental Court	Env Ct
Equity [Court, Division]	Eq
Family Court	Fam Ct
General Sessions Court	Gen Sess Ct
High Court	High Ct
Housing Court	Housing Ct
Intermediate Court of Appeals	Intermed Ct App
Justice Court	J Ct
Justice of the Peace's Court	JP Ct

Juvenile and Family Court	Juv & Fam Ct
Juvenile Court	Juv Ct
Juvenile Delinquents' Court	Juv Del Ct
Land Court	Land Ct
Law Court	Law Ct
Magistrate Court	Magis Ct
Magistrate Division	Magis Div
Mayor's Court	Mayor's Ct
Municipal Court	[name] Mun Ct
Municipal Court not of Record	Mun Ct not Rec
Municipal Criminal Court of Record	Mun Crim Ct Rec
Orphans' Court	Orphans' Ct
Parish Court	[name] Parish Ct
Police Justice's Court	Police J Ct
Prerogative Court	Prerog Ct
Probate Court	Prob Ct
Recorder's Court	Rec Ct
Small Claims Court	Small Cl Ct
State Court	State Ct
Superior Court (US / É-U)	Super Ct
Supreme Court (federal)	US
Supreme Court (state, US / État, É-U)	Sup Ct
Supreme Court, Appellate Division (state, US / État, É-U)	Sup Ct App Div
Supreme Court of Appeals	Sup Ct App
Supreme Court of Errors	Sup Ct Err
Supreme Court of the United States	USSC
Supreme Judicial Court	Sup Jud Ct

Surrogate Court	Surr Ct
Tax Appeal Court	Tax App Ct
Tax Court	TC
Teen Court	Teen Ct
Town Court	Town Ct
Traffic Court	Traffic Ct
Tribal Court	[name] Tribal Ct
Unified Family Court	Unif Fam Ct
Water Court	Water Ct
Workers' Compensation Court	Workers' Comp Ct
Youth Court	Youth Ct
French Courts / Cours françaises	
Conseil constitutionnel (France)	Cons const
Conseil d'État (France)	Cons d'État
Cour de cassation : Assemblée plénière (France)	Cass Ass plén
Cour de cassation : Chambre commerciale (France)	Cass com
Cour de cassation : Chambre criminelle (France)	Cass crim
Cour de cassation : Chambre des requêtes (France)	Cass req
Cour de cassation : Chambre mixte (France)	Cass Ch mixte
Cour de cassation : Chambre sociale (France)	Cass soc
Cour de cassation : Chambres réunies (France)	Cass Ch réun
Cour de cassation : Deuxième chambre civile (France)	Cass civ 2e
Cour de cassation : Première chambre civile (France)	Cass civ 1e
Cour de cassation : Troisième chambre civile (France)	Cass civ 3e
Cour de magistrat	C mag
Cour de révision	C rév
Haute Cour de justice	HCJ

Justice de Paix (*before 1958 / avant 1958*) (France)	JP
Australian & New Zealand Courts / Cours d'Australie et de Nouvelle-Zélande	
Coroners Court	Cor Ct
District Court of Southern Australia	SADC
District Court of New Zealand	DCNZ
Environment Court	Env Ct
Family Court of New Zealand	Fam Ct NZ
Federal Court of Australia	FCA
High Court of Australia	HCA
Labour Court	Lab Ct
Magistrates' Court	Mag Ct
Magistrates' Court of New Zealand	Mag Ct NZ
Maori Appellate Court	Maori AC
Maori Land Court	Maori Land Ct
New Zealand Court of Appeal	NZCA
New Zealand Employment Court	NZ Empl Ct
New Zealand High Court	NZHC
New Zealand Supreme Court	NZSC
New Zealand Youth Court	NZYC
Privy Council	PC
Supreme Court of New South Wales	NSWSC
Supreme Court of New South Wales - Court of Appeal	NSWCA
Supreme Court of Queensland	QSC
Supreme Court of Queensland - Court of Appeal	QCA
Supreme Court of Southern Australia	SASC
Supreme Court of Tasmania	TASSC

Supreme Court of the Australian Capital Territory	ACTSC
Supreme Court of the Northern Territory	NTSC
Supreme Court of Victoria	VSC
Supreme Court of Victoria - Court of Appeal	VSCA
Supreme Court of Western Australia	WASC
Supreme Court of Western Australia - Court of Appeal	WASCA
Waitangi Tribunal	Waitangi Trib
South Africa Courts / Cours d'Afrique du Sud	
Constitutional Court of South Africa	S Afr Const Ct
Electoral Court of South Africa	S Afr Electoral Ct
High Court of South Africa	S Afr HC
Labour Court of Appeal of South Africa	S Afr Labour CA
Labour Court of South Africa	S Afr Labour Ct
Land Claims Court of South Africa	S Afr Land Claims Ct
Supreme Court of Appeal of South Africa	S Afr SC

(B-3) Neutral citation ~ Référence neutre

Below are the **dates of implementation** and the **abbreviations** of the neutral citation in Canadian courts. Before these dates, the neutral citation was not officially used and must not be cited for any given court.

Jurisdiction	Name of the court	Abbreviation	Implementation
Canada	Supreme Court of Canada	SCC	January 2000
	Federal Court	FC / FCT	February 2001
	Federal Court of Appeal	FCA	February 2001
	Tax Court of Canada	TCC	January 2003
	Court Martial Appeal Court of Canada	CMAC	October 2001
Alberta	Court of Appeal	ABCA	January 1998

	Court of Queen's Bench	ABQB	January 1998
	Provincial Court	ABPC	January 1998
British Columbia	Court of Appeal	BCCA	January 1999
	Supreme Court of British Columbia	BCSC	January 2000
	Provincial Court of British Columbia	BCPC	February 1999
Manitoba	Court of Appeal	MBCA	March 2000
	Court of Queen's Bench of Manitoba	MBQB	April 2000
	Provincial Court of Manitoba	MBPC	January 2007
New Brunswick	Court of Appeal of New Brunswick	NBCA	May 2001
	Court of Queen's Bench of New Brunswick	NBQB	January 2002
	Provincial Court	NBPC	December 2002
Newfoundland and Labrador	Supreme Court of Newfoundland and Labrador, Court of Appeal	NFCA NLCA	January 2001—2002 October 2002
	Supreme Court of Newfoundland and Labrador, Trial Division	NLSCTD NLTD	July 2003—2004 November 2004
Northwest Territories	Court of Appeal for the Northwest Territories	NWTCA	December 1999
	Supreme Court of the Northwest Territories	NWTSC	October 1999
	Territorial Court of the Northwest Territories	NWTTC	October 1999
Nova Scotia	Nova Scotia Court of Appeal	NSCA	September 1999
	Supreme Court of Nova Scotia	NSSC	December 2000
	Nova Scotia Family Court	NSFC	January 2006
	Provincial Court of Nova Scotia	NSPC	March 2001
Nunavut	Nunavut Court of Justice	NUCJ	January 2001
	Court of Appeal of Nunavut	NUCA	May 2006
Ontario	Ontario Court of Appeal	ONCA	January 2007
	Superior Court of Justice	ONSC	January 2010

	Ontario Court of Justice	ONCJ	January 2004
Prince Edward Island	Supreme Court, Appeal Division	PECA	January 2000
	Supreme Court, Trial Division	PESC	January 2000
Quebec	Court of Appeal of Québec	QCCA	January 2005
	Superior Court of Québec	QCCS	January 2006
	Court of Québec	QCCQ	January 2006
	Tribunal des professions du Québec	QCTP	January 1999
Saskatchewan	Court of Appeal for Saskatchewan	SKCA	January 2000
	Court of Queen's Bench	SKQB	January 1999
	Provincial Court	SKPC	January 2002
Yukon	Court of Appeal	YKCA	March 2000
	Supreme Court of the Yukon Territory	YKSC	March 2000
	Territorial Court of Yukon	YKTC	December 1999
	Small Claims Court	YKSM	May 2004

Le tableau ci-dessous expose les **dates d'entrée en vigueur** et les **abréviations** de la référence neutre pour les cours canadiennes. Avant ces dates, la référence neutre n'était pas officiellement en vigueur et ne peut être citée pour une cour.

Juridiction	**Nom de la cour**	**Abréviation**	**En vigueur**
Canada	Cour suprême du Canada	CSC	janvier 2000
	Cour fédérale	CF / CFPI	février 2001
	Cour d'appel fédérale	CAF	février 2001
	Cour canadienne de l'impôt	CCI	janvier 2003
	Cour d'appel de la cour martiale du Canada	CAMC	octobre 2001
Alberta	Court of Appeal	ABCA	janvier 1998
	Court of Queen's Bench	ABQB	janvier 1998
	Provincial Court	ABPC	janvier 1998
Colombie-	Court of Appeal	BCCA	janvier 1999

Britannique	Supreme Court of British Columbia	BCSC	janvier 2000
	Provincial Court of British Columbia	BCPC	février 1999
Île-du-Prince-Édouard	Supreme Court, Appeal Division	PECA	janvier 2000
	Supreme Court, Trial Division	PESC	janvier 2000
Manitoba	Cour d'appel	MBCA	mars 2000
	Cour du Banc de la Reine du Manitoba	MBQB	avril 2000
	Cour provinciale du Manitoba	MBPC	janvier 2007
Nouveau-Brunswick	Cour d'appel du Nouveau-Brunswick	NBCA	mai 2001
	Cour du banc de la Reine du Nouveau-Brunswick	NBQB	janvier 2002
	Cour provinciale	NBPC	décembre 2002
Nouvelle-Écosse	Nova Scotia Court of Appeal	NSCA	septembre 1999
	Supreme Court of Nova Scotia	NSSC	décembre 2000
	Nova Scotia Family Court	NSSC	janvier 2006
	Provincial Court of Nova Scotia	NSPC	mars 2001
Nunavut	Cour de justice du Nunavut	NUCJ	janvier 2001
	Cour d'appel du Nunavut	NUCA	mai 2006
Ontario	Cour d'appel de l'Ontario	ONCA	janvier 2007
	Cour supérieure de l'Ontario	ONSC	janvier 2010
	Cour de justice de l'Ontario	ONCJ	janvier 2004
Québec	Court of Appeal of Québec Cour d'appel du Québec	QCCA	janvier 2005
	Cour supérieure du Québec	QCCS	janvier 2006
	Cour du Québec	QCCQ	janvier 2006
	Tribunal des professions du Québec	QCTP	janvier 1999
Saskatchewan	Court of Appeal for Saskatchewan	SKCA	janvier 2000
	Court of Queen's Bench	SKQB	janvier 1999
	Provincial Court	SKPC	janvier 2002

Terre-Neuve-et-Labrador	Supreme Court of Newfoundland and Labrador, Court of Appeal	NFCA NLCA	janvier 2001—2002 octobre 2002
	Supreme Court of Newfoundland and Labrador, Trial Division	NLSCTD NLTD	juillet 2003—2004 novembre 2004
Territoires du Nord-Ouest	Cour d'appel des territoires du Nord-Ouest	NWTCA	décembre 1999
	Cour suprême des territoires du Nord-Ouest	NWTSC	octobre 1999
	Cour territoriale des territoires du Nord-Ouest	NWTTC	octobre 1999
Yukon	Cour d'appel	YKCA	mars 2000
	Cour suprême du territoire du Yukon	YKSC	mars 2000
	Cour territoriale du Yukon	YKTC	décembre 1999
	Cour des petites créances	YKSM	mai 2004

APPENDIX C / ANNEXE C

C. CASELAW REPORTERS ~ RECUEILS DE JURISPRUDENCE

(C-1) Canadian Official Reporters ~ Recueils officiels canadiens

Official reporters are published by the Queen's Printer. Whenever there is a discrepancy between two different versions of the same case, the version in the following reporters will be given precedence.

Ex CR	Canada Law Reports: Exchequer Court of Canada Reports of the Exchequer Court of Canada
FCR	Federal Court Reports
SCR	Canada Supreme Court Reports Canada Law Reports: Supreme Court of Canada Canada Supreme Court Reports

Les recueils officiels sont publiés par l'Imprimeur de la Reine. En cas de disparité entre un recueil officiel et un autre recueil, la version du recueil officiel a préséance.

RC de l'É	Recueils des arrêts de la Cour de l'Échiquier Rapports judiciaires du Canada : Cour de l'Échiquier
RCF	Recueils des arrêts de la Cour fédérale du Canada
RCS	Recueils des arrêts de la Cour suprême du Canada Rapports judiciaires du Canada : Cour suprême Recueils des arrêts de la Cour suprême du Canada

(C-2) All reporters and identifiers ~ Tous les recueils et les identifiants

For a more detailed list of *Law Reports*, consult the latest edition of ***Bieber's Dictionary of Legal Abbreviations***.

For the most part, selected reporters with recent jurisprudence have been included from all countries represented in this *Guide*, while selected reporters with both historical and recent jurisprudence have been included for Canada and the UK. If an English reporter is reprinted in whole or in part in the *English Reports*, the applicable volume(s) are indicated. French general reporters containing doctrine and jurisprudence may be found both in Appendix C and Appendix D.

Because reporters may cover a large time period during which many names have existed for a jurisdiction, the jurisdiction listed in the jurisdiction column is always the most recent name for the jurisdiction covered by the reporter.

Note that this list also contains online database identifiers. The online database service (e.g., QL, WL Can) is then indicated in parentheses. Canadian reporters and identifiers marked with an asterisk (*) are to be preferred.

Pour une liste plus détaillée des *Law Reports*, consulter la dernière édition du ***Bieber's Dictionary of Legal Abbreviations***.

La plupart des recueils de jurisprudence récents sont énumérés dans ce *Manuel*. Les recueils qui contiennent de la jurisprudence plus ancienne ne sont indiqués que pour le Canada et le Royaume-Uni. Si un recueil anglais est reproduit entièrement ou en partie dans les *English Reports*, indiquer le volume approprié. Les recueils généraux français contiennent de la doctrine et de la jurisprudence. Ils se trouvent donc à la fois dans l'annexe C et dans l'annexe D

Puisque les recueils peuvent couvrir une longue période de temps durant laquelle le nom de l'indication géographique a pu changer, la liste ci-dessous représente le nom le plus récent de l'indication géographique.

Noter que la liste suivante contient également des identifiants de bases de données en ligne. Le service de bases de données en ligne est indiqué entre parenthèses. Les recueils canadiens et les identifiants suivis d'un astérisque (*) doivent être privilégiés.

Abbreviation / Abréviation	Title of Reporter / Titre du recueil	Jurisdiction / Indication géographique
A	Atlantic Reporter	US / É-U
A (2d)	Atlantic Reporter (Second Series)	US / É-U
A (3d)	Atlantic Reporter (Third Series)	US / É-U
A & N	Alcock and Napier's Reports	I
A Crim R	Australian Criminal Reports	Austl
A Intl LC	American International Law Cases	US / É-U
A Intl LC (2d)	American International Law Cases (Second Series)	US / É-U
A Intl LC (3d)	American International Law Cases (Third Series)	US / É-U
A Intl LC (4th)	American International Law Cases (Fourth Series)	US / É-U
AALR	Australian Argus Law Reports	Austl
AAR	Administrative Appeals Reports	Austl
AAS	Arbitrage — Santé et services sociaux	Can (QC)
ABC	Australian Bankruptcy Cases	Austl
ABD	Canada, Public Service Commission, Appeals and Investigation Branch, Appeal Board Decisions	Can

AC	Law Reports, Appeal Cases	UK / R-U
ACA	Australian Corporate Affairs Reporter	Austl
ACF	Jugements de la Cour fédérale du Canada (QL)	Can
ACI	Jugements de la Cour canadienne de l'impôt (QL)	Can
ACLC	Australian Company Law Cases	Austl
ACLP	Australian Company Law and Practice	Austl
ACLR	Australian Company Law Reports	Austl
ACLR	Australian Construction Law Reporter	Austl
ACS	Jugements de la Cour suprême du Canada (QL)	Can
ACSR	Australian Corporations and Securities Reports	Austl
Act	Acton's Prize Cases (ER vol 12)	US / É-U
ACTR	Australian Capital Territory Reports	Austl (ACT)
ACWS	All Canada Weekly Summaries	Can
ACWS (2d)	All Canada Weekly Summaries (Second Series)	Can
ACWS (3d)	All Canada Weekly Summaries (Third Series)	Can
AD	South African Law Reports, Appellate Division	S Afr / Afr du Sud
Ad & El	Adolphus & Ellis's Reports (ER vols 110-113)	US / É-U
Adam	Adam's Justiciary Cases	Scot
Add	Addams's Reports (ER vol 162)	UK / R-U
ADIL	Annual Digest and Reports of Public International Law Cases	Intl
Admin LR	Administrative Law Reports	Can
Admin LR (2d)	Administrative Law Reports (Second Series)	Can
Admin LR (3d)	Administrative Law Reports (Third Series)	Can
Admin LR (4th)	Administrative Law Reports (Fourth Series)	Can
Admin LR (5th)	Administrative Law Reports (Fifth Series)	Can
ADR	Australian De Facto Relationships Law	Austl
AEBCN	Australian Business & Estate Planning Case Notes	Austl
AEBR	Australian Business & Assets Planning Reporter	Austl
AEUB	Alberta Energy and Utilities Board Decisions	Can (AB)
Afr LR (Comm)	African Law Reports: Commercial	Afr
Afr LR (Mal)	African Law Reports: Malawi Series	E Afr / Afr de l'est
Afr LR (SL)	African Law Reports: Sierra Leone Series	W Afr / Afr de l'ouest
AFTR	Australian Federal Tax Reporter	Austl
AIA	Affaires d'immigration en appel	Can
AIA (2e)	Affaires d'immigration en appel (nouvelle série)	Can

AILR	Australian Indigenous Law Reporter	Austl
AIN	Australian Industrial and Intellectual Property Cases	Austl
AJ	Alberta Judgments (QL)	Can (AB)
AJDA	Actualité juridique, droit administratif	France
AJDI	Actualité juridique, droit immobilier	France
AJDQ	Annuaire de jurisprudence et de doctrine du Québec	Can (QC)
AJPI	Actualité juridique, propriété immobilière	France
AJQ	Annuaire de jurisprudence du Québec	Can (QC)
Al	Aleyn's Select Cases (ER vol 82)	UK / R-U
Ala	Alabama Reports	US / É-U
Ala (NS)	Alabama Reports (New Series)	US / É-U
Alaska Fed	Alaska Federal Reports	US / É-U
Alaska R	Alaska Reports	US / É-U
ALD	Administrative Law Decisions	Austl
ALJR	Australian Law Journal Reports	Austl
All ER	All England Reports	UK / R-U
All ER (Comm)	All England Law Reports (Commercial Cases)	UK / R-U
All ER (EC)	All England Law Reports (European Cases)	UK / R-U
All ER Rep	All England Reports Reprints	UK / R-U
All ER Rep Ext	All England Reprints Extension Volumes	UK / R-U
ALLR	Australian Labour Law Reporter	Austl
ALMD	Australian Legal Monthly Digest	Austl
ALR	Administrative Law Reports in the British Journal of Administrative Law	UK / R-U
ALR	American Law Reports	US / É-U
ALR (2d)	American Law Reports (Second Series)	US / É-U
ALR (3d)	American Law Reports (Third Series)	US / É-U
ALR (4th)	American Law Reports (Fourth Series)	US / É-U
ALR (5th)	American Law Reports (Fifth Series)	US / É-U
ALR	Argus Law Reports	Austl
ALR	Australian Law Reports	Austl
Alta BAA	Alberta Board of Arbitration, Arbitrations under the Alberta Labour Act	Can (AB)
Alta BAAA	Alberta Board of Adjudication, Adjudications and Arbitrations under the Public Service Employee Relations Act	Can (AB)
Alta BIR	Alberta Board of Industrial Relations Decisions	Can (AB)

Alta ERCB	Alberta Energy Resources Conservation Board (Decisions Reports)	Can (AB)
Alta HRCR	Alberta Human Rights Commission, Reports of Boards of Inquiry	Can (AB)
Alta LR*	Alberta Law Reports	Can (AB)
Alta LR (2d)	Alberta Law Reports (Second Series)	Can (AB)
Alta LR (3d)	Alberta Law Reports (Third Series)	Can (AB)
Alta LR (4th)	Alberta Law Reports (Fourth Series)	Can (AB)
Alta LR (5th)	Alberta Law Reports (Fifth Series)	Can (AB)
Alta LRBD	Alberta Labour Relations Board Decisions	Can (AB)
Alta LRBR	Alberta Labour Relations Board Reports	Can (AB)
Alta OGCB	Alberta Oil and Gas Conservation Board Decisions	Can (AB)
Alta PSERB	Alberta Public Service Employee Relations Board Decisions	Can (AB)
Alta PSGAB	Alberta Public Services Grievance Appeal Board Adjudications and Arbitrations	Can (AB)
Alta PUB	Alberta Public Utilities Board Decisions	Can (AB)
Amb	Ambler's Reports, Chancery (ER vol 27)	UK / R-U
AMC	American Maritime Cases	US / É-U
AN-B	Jugements du Nouveau-Brunswick (QL)	Can (NB)
And	Anderson's Common Law Conveyancing and Equity (ER vol 123)	UK / R-U
Andr	Andrews' Reports (ER vol 95)	UK / R-U
Ann Conv Eur DH	Annuaire de la Convention européenne des droits de l'Homme	EU / UE
Anst	Anstruther's Reports (ER vol 145)	UK / R-U
ANWTYTR	Alberta, Northwest Territories & Yukon Tax Reporter	Can
App Cas	Appeal Cases	UK / R-U
App Div	New York Appellate Division Reports	UK / R-U
App Div (2d)	New York Appellate Division Reports (Second Series)	US / É-U
App Div (3d)	New York Appellate Division Reports (Third Series)	US / É-U
APR	Atlantic Provinces Reports	Can
AR*	Alberta Reports	Can (AB)
Arb Serv Rep	Arbitration Services Reporter	Can
Ariz	Arizona Reports	US / É-U
Ark	Arkansas Reports	US / É-U
Ark App	Arkansas Appellate Reports	US / É-U
Arn	Arnold's Reports	UK / R-U
Arn & H	Arnold and Hodges's Reports	UK / R-U

ASC Sum	Alberta Securities Commission Summaries	Can (AB)
ASLC	Australian Securities Law Cases	Austl
Asp MLC	Aspinall's Maritime Law Cases	UK / R-U
ATB	Canada Air Transport Board Decisions	Can
ATC	Australian Tax Cases	Austl
Atk	Atkyns's Reports, Chancery (ER vol 26)	UK / R-U
Av Cas	Aviation Cases	US / É-U
Av L Rep	Aviation Law Reporter	US / É-U
AWLD	Alberta Weekly Law Digest	Can (AB)
AZ	Azimut (SOQUIJ)	Can
B & Ad	Barnewall & Adolphus's Reports, King's Bench (ER vols 109-110)	UK / R-U
B & Ald	Barnewall & Alderson's Reports, King's Bench (ER vol 106)	UK / R-U
B & CR	Reports of Bankruptcy and Companies Winding-Up Cases	UK / R-U
B & Cress	Barnewall & Cresswell's Reports, King's Bench (ER vols 107-109)	UK / R-U
B & S	Best & Smith's Reports (ER vols 121-122)	UK / R-U
B Const LR	Butterworths Constitutional Law Reports	S Afr / Afr du sud
BA	Book of Awards (Arbtration Court, Court of Appeal)	NZ / N-Z
Ball & B	Ball and Beatty's Reports	I
Barn C	Barnardiston's Chancery Reports (ER vol 27)	UK / R-U
Barn KB	Barnardiston's King's Bench Reports (ER vol 94)	UK / R-U
Barnes	Barnes's Notes (ER vol 94)	UK / R-U
Batt	Batty's Reports	I
BC En Comm'n Dec	British Columbia Energy Commission Decisions	Can (BC)
BC Util Comm'n	British Columbia Utilities Commission Decisions	Can (BC)
BCAC	British Columbia Appeal Cases	Can (BC)
BCD	Bulletin des contributions directes, de la taxe sur la valeur ajoutée et des impôts indirects	France
BCHRC Dec	British Columbia Human Rights Commission Decisions	Can (BC)
BCJ	British Columbia and Yukon Judgments (QL)	Can (BC)
BCLR*	British Columbia Law Reports	Can (BC)
BCLR (2d)*	British Columbia Law Reports (Second Series)	Can (BC)
BCLR (3d)*	British Columbia Law Reports (Third Series)	Can (BC)
BCLR (4th)*	British Columbia Law Reports (Fourth Series)	Can (BC)
BCLR (5th)*	British Columbia Law Reports (Fifth Series)	Can (BC)
BCLRB Dec	British Columbia Labour Relations Board Decisions	Can (BC)

BCSCW Summ	British Columbia Securities Commission Weekly Summary	Can (BC)
BCWCR	British Columbia Workers' Compensation Reporter	Can (BC)
Bd Rwy Comm'rs Can	Board of Railway Commissioners for Canada — Judgments, Orders, Regulations, and Rulings	Can
Bd Trans Comm'rs Can	Board of Transport Commissioners for Canada — Judgments, Orders, Regulations, and Rulings	Can
BDM	Bulletin de droit municipal	Can (QC)
Beat	Beatty's Reports	I
Beaubien	Beaubien	Can (QC)
Beav	Beavan's Reports (ER vols 48-55)	UK / R-U
Bel	Bellewe's Reports (ER vol 72)	UK / R-U
Bell	Bell's Reports (ER vol 169)	UK / R-U
Ben & D	Benloe & Dalison's Reports (ER vol 123)	UK / R-U
Benl	Benloe's Reports (ER vol 73)	UK / R-U
BILC	British International Law Cases	UK / R-U
Bing	Bingham's Reports (ER vols 130-131)	UK / R-U
Bing NC	Bingham's New Cases (ER vols 131-133)	UK / R-U
BISD	Basic Instruments and Selected Documents	GATT
Bla H	H Blackstone Reports	UK / R-U
Bla W	W Blackstone Reports	UK / R-U
BLE	Bulletin du libre-échange	Can
Bli	Bligh's Reports, House of Lords (ER vol 4)	UK / R-U
Bli NS	Bligh's Repors (New Series) (ER vols 4-6)	UK / R-U
BLR	Business Law Reports	Can
BLR (2d)	Business Law Reports (Second Series)	Can
BLR (3d)	Business Law Reports (Third Series)	Can
BLR (4th)	Business Law Reports (Fourth Series)	Can
BLR (5th)	Business Law Reports (Fifth Series)	Can
Bos & Pul	Bosanquet & Puller's Reports (ER vols 126-127)	UK / R-U
Bos & Pul NR	Bosanquet & Puller's New Reports (ER vol 127)	UK / R-U
BR*	Recueils de jurisprudence du Québec : Cour du Banc de la Reine / du Roi	Can (QC)
BR*	Rapports judiciaires officiels de Québec : Cour du Banc de la Reine / du Roi	Can (QC)
BREF	Décisions du Bureau de révision de l'évaluation foncière	Can (QC)
Bridg	Sir John Bridgman's Reports	UK / R-U

Bridg Conv	Sir Orlando Bridgman's Conveyances	UK / R-U
Bridg J	Sir J Bridgman's Reports (ER vol 123)	UK / R-U
Bridg O	Sir O Bridgman's Reports (ER vol 124)	UK / R-U
Bro CC	Brown's Chancery Cases (by Belt) (ER vols 28-29)	UK / R-U
Bro PC	Brown's Parliamentary Cases (ER vols 1-3)	UK / R-U
Brod & Bing	Broderip & Bingham's Reports (ER vol 129)	UK / R-U
Brooke NC	Brooke's New Cases (ER vol 73)	UK / R-U
Brown & Lush	Browning & Lushington's Admiralty Reports (ER vol 167)	UK / R-U
Brownl	Brownlow & Goldesborough's Reports (ER vol 123)	UK / R-U
Bull civ	Bulletin des arrêts de la cour de cassation, Chambres civiles	France
Bull Concl fisc	Bulletin des conclusions fiscales	France
Bull Crim	Bulletin des arrêts de la cour de cassation, Chambre criminelle	France
Bull CVMQ	Bulletin — Commission des valeurs mobilières du Québec	Can (QC)
Bull OSC	Bulletin of the Ontario Securities Commission	Can (ON)
Bulst	Bulstrode's Reports, King's Bench (ER vols 80-81)	UK / R-U
Bunb	Bunbury's Reports, Exchequer (ER vol 145)	UK / R-U
Burr	Burrow's Reports (ER vols 97-98)	UK / R-U
Burrell	Burrell's Reports (ER vol 167)	UK / R-U
C & J	Crompton & Jervis's Reports (ER vols 148-149)	UK / R-U
C & M	Crompton & Meeson's Reports (ER vol 149)	UK / R-U
C & S	Clarke and Scully's Drainage Cases	Can (ON)
CA*	Recueils de jurisprudence du Québec : Cour d'appel	Can (QC)
CAC	Canada Citizenship Appeal Court, Reasons for Judgment	Can
CACM	Recueil des arrêts de la Cour d'appel des cours martiales du Canada	Can
CAEC	Commission d'appel des enregistrements commerciaux, Sommaires des décisions	Can (ON)
CAI	Décisions de la Commission d'accès à l'information	Can (QC)
Cal	California Reports	US / É-U
Cal (2d)	California Reports (Second Series)	US / É-U
Cal (3d)	California Reports (Third Series)	US / É-U
Cal (4th)	California Reports (Fourth Series)	US / É-U
CALP	Décisions de la Commission d'appel en matière de lésions professionnelles	Can (QC)
CALR	Criminal Appeals Law Reporter	Can
Calth	Calthrop's Reports (ER vol 80)	UK / R-U

Cam	Cameron's Privy Council Decisions	Can
Cameron PC	Cameron's Constitutional Decisions of the Privy Council	Can
Cameron SC	Cameron's Supreme Court Cases	Can
Camp	Campbell's Reports (ER vols 170-171)	UK / R-U
CanLII	CanLII (CanLII)	Can
Cape SCR	Supreme Court Reports (Cape)	S Afr / Afr du sud
CAQ	Causes en appel au Québec	Can (QC)
CAR	Commonwealth Arbitration Reports	Austl
Car & K	Carrington & Kirwan Reports (ER vols 174-175)	UK / R-U
Car & M	Carrington & Marshman Reports (ER vol 174)	UK / R-U
Car & P	Carrington & Payne (ER vols 171-173)	UK / R-U
CarswellAlta	Alberta Cases and Decisions (WL Can)	Can (AB)
CarswellBC	British Columbia Cases and Decisions (WL Can)	Can (BC)
CarswellMan	Manitoba Cases and Decisions (WL Can)	Can (MB)
CarswellNat	Federal Cases and Decisions (WL Can)	Can
CarswellNB	New Brunswick Cases and Decisions (WL Can)	Can (NB)
CarswellNfld	Newfoundland and Labrador Cases and Decisions (WL Can)	Can (NL)
CarswellNS	Nova Scotia Cases and Decisions (WL Can)	Can (NS)
CarswellNun	Nunavut Cases and Decisions (WL Can)	Can (NU)
CarswellNWT	Northwest Territories Cases and Decisions (WL Can)	Can (NT)
CarswellOnt	Ontario Cases and Decisions (WL Can)	Can (ON)
CarswellPEI	Prince Edward Island Cases and Decisions (WL Can)	Can (PE)
CarswellQue	Quebec Cases and Decisions (WL Can)	Can (QC)
CarswellSask	Saskatchewan Cases and Decisions (WL Can)	Can (SK)
CarswellYukon	Yukon Cases and Decisions (WL Can)	Can (YT)
Carey	Carey's Manitoba Reports	Can (MB)
Cart BNA	Cartwright's Cases on the British North America Act, 1867	Can
Carter	Carter's Reports, Common Pleas (ER vol 124)	UK / R-U
Carth	Carthew's Reports, King's Bench (ER vol 90)	UK / R-U
Cary	Cary's Chancery Reports (ER vol 21)	UK / R-U
CAS	Décisions de la Commission des affaires sociales	Can (QC)
Cas t Hard	Cases temp Hardwicke (ER vol 95)	UK / R-U
Cas t Talb	Cases temp Talbot (ER vol 25)	UK / R-U
CB	Common Bench Reports (ER vols 135-139)	UK / R-U
CB (NS)	Common Bench Reports (New Series) (ER vols 140-144)	UK / R-U

CBES*	Recueils de jurisprudence du Québec : Cour du bien-être social	Can (QC)
CBR	Copyright Board Reports	Can
CBR	Canadian Bankruptcy Reports	Can
CBR (3d)	Canadian Bankruptcy Reports (Third Series)	Can
CBR (4th)	Canadian Bankruptcy Reports (Fourth Series)	Can
CBR (5th)	Canadian Bankruptcy Reports (Fifth Series)	Can
CBR (NS)	Canadian Bankruptcy Reports (New Series)	Can
CCC	Cahiers du Conseil constitutionnel	France
CCC	Canadian Criminal Cases	Can
CCC (Nouv)	Nouveaux Cahiers du Conseil constitutionnel	France
CCC (2d)	Canadian Criminal Cases (Second Series)	Can
CCC (3d)	Canadian Criminal Cases (Third Series)	Can
CCC (NS)	Canadian Criminal Cases (New Series)	Can
CCEL	Canadian Cases on Employment Law	Can
CCEL (2d)	Canadian Cases on Employment Law (Second Series)	Can
CCEL (3d)	Canadian Cases on Employment Law (Third Series)	Can
CCEL (4th)	Canadian Cases on Employment Law (Fourth Series)	Can
CCL	Canadian Current Law	Can
CCL	Canadian Current Law: Jurisprudence / sommaires de la jurisprudence	Can
CCL	Canadian Current Law: Case Law Digests / sommaires de la jurisprudence	Can
CCL	Canadian Current Law: Case Digests / sommaires de la jurisprudence	Can
CCL Législation	Canadian Current Law: Annuaire de la législation	Can
CCL Legislation	Canadian Current Law: Legislation Annual	Can
CCLI	Canadian Cases on the Law of Insurance	Can
CCLI (2d)	Canadian Cases on the Law of Insurance (Second Series)	Can
CCLI (3d)	Canadian Cases on the Law of Insurance (Third Series)	Can
CCLI (4th)	Canadian Cases on the Law of Insurance (Fourth Series)	Can
CCLI (5th)	Canadian Cases on the Law of Insurance (Fifth Series)	Can
CCLR	Canadian Computer Law Reporter	Can
CCLS	Canadian Cases on the Law of Securities	Can
CCLT	Canadian Cases on the Law of Torts	Can
CCLT (2d)	Canadian Cases on the Law of Torts (Second Series)	Can
CCLT (3d)	Canadian Cases on the Law of Torts (Third Series)	Can

CCLT (4th)	Canadian Cases on the Law of Torts (Fourth Series)	Can
CCPB	Canadian Cases on Pensions and Benefits	Can
CCRI	Conseil canadien des relations industrielles, motifs de décision	Can
CCRTD	Conseil canadien des relations du travail, décisions	Can
CCRTDI	Conseil canadien des relations du travail, décisions et informations	Can
CDB-C	Collection de décisions du Bas-Canada	Can (QC)
CE	Commissaires enquêteurs	Can (QC)
CEB	Canadian Employment Benefits and Pension Guide Reports	Can
CEDH	Cour européenne des Droits de l'Homme	EU / UE
CEDH (Sér A)	Publications de la Cour européenne des Droits de l'Homme : Série A : Arrêts et décisions *(autre titre / other title: Recueil des arrêts et décisions de la cour européenne des droits de l'homme)*	EU / UE
CEDH (Sér B)	Publications de la Cour européenne des Droits de l'Homme : Série B : Mémoires, plaidoiries et documents	EU / UE
CEGSB	Crown Employees Grievance Settlement Board Decisions	Can (ON)
CELR	Canadian Environmental Law Reports	Can
CELR (3d)	Canadian Environmental Law Reports (Third Series)	Can
CELR (NS)	Canadian Environmental Law Reports (New Series)	Can
CER	Canadian Customs and Excise Reports	Can
CF*	Recueils des arrêts de la Cour fédérale du Canada	Can
CFLC	Canadian Family Law Cases	Can
CFP	Recueil des décisions des comités d'appel de la fonction publique	Can (QC)
Ch	Law Reports, Chancery	UK / R-U
Ch App	Law Reports, Chancery Appeal Cases	UK / R-U
Ch Ca	Cases in Chancery (ER vol 22)	UK / R-U
Ch CR	Chancery Chambers Reports	Can (ON)
Ch D	Law Reports, Chancery Division	UK / R-U
Ch R	Chancery Reports (ER vol 21)	UK / R-U
Chan Cas	Chancery Cases (ER vol 22)	UK / R-U
Chit	Chitty's Practice Reports, King's Bench	UK / R-U
Choyce Ca	Choyce Cases in Chancery (ER vol 21)	UK / R-U
CHRR	Canadian Human Rights Reporter	Can
CICB	Criminal Injuries Compensation Board Decisions	Can (ON)
CIJ Mémoires	Cour internationale de justice : Mémoires, plaidoiries et documents	Intl
CIJ Rec	Cour internationale de justice : Recueil des arrêts, avis consultatifs et ordonnances	Intl

CIPOO (M)	Commissaire à l'information et à la protection de la vie privée, Ontario, Ordres, Séries M	Can (ON)
CIPOO (P)	Commissaire à l'information et à la protection de la vie privée, Ontario, Ordres, Séries P	Can (ON)
CIPOS	Commissaire à l'information et à la protection de la vie privée, Ontario, Sommaires	Can (ON)
CIPR	Canadian Intellectual Property Reports	Can
CIRB	Canada Industrial Relations Board, Reasons for Decision	Can
CJCE	Recueil de la jurisprudence de la cour et du tribunal de première instance, Cour de justice des communautés européennes	EU / UE
Cl & F	Clark & Finnelly's Reports, House of Lords (ER vols 6-8)	UK / R-U
CLAS	Canadian Labour Arbitration Summaries	Can
CLD	Commercial Law Digest	Can
CLL	Canadian Current Law: Canadian Legal Literature	Can
CLLC	Canadian Labour Law Cases	Can
CLLR	Canadian Labour Law Reporter	Can
CLP	Décisions de la Commission des lésions professionnelles	Can (QC)
CLR	Commonwealth Law Reports	Austl
CLR	Construction Law Reports	Can
CLR (2d)	Construction Law Reports (Second Series)	Can
CLR (3d)	Construction Law Reports (Third Series)	Can
CLR (4th)	Construction Law Reports (Fourth Series)	Can
CLRBD	Canada Labour Relations Board Decisions	Can
CLRBDI	Canada Labour Relations Board Decisions and Information	Can
CLRBR	Canadian Labour Relations Board Reports	Can
CLRBR (2d)	Canadian Labour Relations Board Reports (Second Series)	Can
CLRBR (NS)	Canadian Labour Relations Board Reports (New Series)	Can
CM & R	Crompton, Meeson & Roscoe's Reports (ER vols 149-150)	UK / R-U
CMAR	Canada Court Martial Appeal Reports	Can
CMQ	Commission municipale du Québec	Can (QC)
CMR	Common Market Law Reports	EU / UE
CMR	Common Market Reporter	EU / UE
CNLC	Canadian Native Law Cases	Can
CNLR	Canadian Native Law Reporter	Can
Co Rep	Coke's Reports, King's Bench (ER vols 76-77)	UK / R-U
COHSC	Canadian Occupational Health and Safety Cases	Can

Coll	Collyer's Reports (ER vol 63)	UK / R-U
Colles	Colles's Reports, House of Lords (ER vol 1)	UK / R-U
Com	Comyns's Reports (ER vol 92)	UK / R-U
Comb	Comberbach's Reports (ER vol 90)	UK / R-U
Comm Eur DHDR	Décisions et rapports de la Commission européenne des Droits de l'Homme	EU / UE
Comm LR	Commercial Law Reports	Can
Comp Trib dec	Competition Tribunal, decisions	Can
Conc Bd Rpts	Conciliation Board Reports	Can
Cons sup N-F	Inventaire des jugements et déliberations du Conseil supérieur de la Nouvelle-France	Can / US
Cook Adm	Cook's Vice-Admiralty Reports	Can (QC)
Cooke CP	Cooke's Reports (Common Pleas) (ER vol 125)	UK / R-U
Coop Ch Ch	Cooper's Chancery Chambers Reports	Can (ON)
Coop G	Cooper's Cases in Chancery (ER vol 35)	UK / R-U
Coop Pr Ca	Cooper's Practice Cases, Chancery (ER vol 47)	UK / R-U
Coop t Br	Cooper, temp Brougham's Reports, Chancery (ER vol 47)	UK / R-U
Coop t Cott	Cooper, temp Cottenham's Reports, Chancery (ER vol 47)	UK / R-U
Cowp	Cowper's Reports (ER vol 98)	UK / R-U
Cox	Cox's Equity Reports (ER vols 29-30)	UK / R-U
CP*	Recueils de jurisprudence du Québec : Cour provinciale	Can (QC)
CPC	Carswell's Practice Cases	Can
CPC (2d)	Carswell's Practice Cases (Second Series)	Can
CPC (3rd)	Carswell's Practice Cases (Third Series)	Can
CPC (4th)	Carswell's Practice Cases (Fourth Series)	Can
CPC (5th)	Carswell's Practice Cases (Fifth Series)	Can
CPC (6th)	Carswell's Practice Cases (Sixth Series)	Can
CPC (7th)	Carswell's Practice Cases (Seventh Series)	Can
CPC (Olmstead)	Canadian Constitutional Decisions of the Judicial Committee of the Privy Council (Olmstead)	Can
CPC (Plaxton)	Canadian Constitutional Decisions of the Judicial Committee of the Privy Council (Plaxton)	Can
CPD	Law Reports, Common Pleas Division	UK / R-U
CPDR	Cape Provincial Division Reports	S Afr / Afr du sud
CPJI (Sér A)	Publications de la Cour permanente de justice internationale : Série A : Recueil des arrêts	Intl
CPJI (Sér A/B)	Publications de la Cour permamente de justice internationale : Série	Intl

	A/B : Arrêts, ordonnances et avis consultatifs	
CPJI (Sér B)	Publications de la Cour permamente de justice internationale : Série B : Recueil des avis consultatifs	Intl
CPJI (Sér C)	Publications de la Cour permanente de justice internationale : Série C : Plaidoiries, exposés oraux et documents	Intl
CPR	Canadian Patent Reporter	Can
CPR (2d)	Canadian Patent Reporter (Second Series)	Can
CPR (3d)	Canadian Patent Reporter (Third Series)	Can
CPR (4th)	Canadian Patent Reporter (Fourth Series)	Can
CPRB	Procurement Review Board of Canada, Decisions	Can
CPTA	Décisions de la Commission de protection du territoire agricole	Can (QC)
CR	Criminal Reports	Can
CR (3rd)	Criminal Reports (Third Series)	Can
CR (4th)	Criminal Reports (Fourth Series)	Can
CR (5th)	Criminal Reports (Fifth Series)	Can
CR (6th)	Criminal Reports (Sixth Series)	Can
CR (NS)	Criminal Reports (New Series)	Can
CRAC	Canadian Reports: Appeal Cases: appeals allowed or refused by the Judicial Committee of the Privy Council	Can
CRAT	Commercial Registration Appeal Tribunal — Summaries of Decisions	Can (ON)
CRC	Canadian Railway Cases	Can
CRD	Charter of Rights Decisions	Can
CRMPC	Commission de révision des marchés publics du Canada, décisions	Can
CRNZ	Criminal Reports of New Zealand	NZ / N-Z
CRR	Canadian Rights Reporter	Can
CRR (2d)	Canadian Rights Reporter (Second Series)	Can
CRT	Canadian Radio-Television and Telecommunications decisions and policy statements	Can
CRTC	Canadian Railway and Transport Cases	Can
CS*	Rapports judiciaires de Québec : Cour supérieure	Can (QC)
CS*	Recueils de jurisprudence du Québec : Cour supérieure	Can (QC)
CSD	Canadian Sentencing Digest	Can
CSP*	Recueils de jurisprudence du Québec : Cour des Sessions de la paix	Can (QC)
CSST	Jurisprudence en santé et sécurité du travail	Can (QC)
CSTR	Canadian Sales Tax Reports	Can
CT	Jurisprudence en droit du travail : Décisions des commissaires du	Can (QC)

	travail	
CT Cases	Canadian Transport Cases	Can
CTAB	Canada Tax Appeal Board Cases	Can
CTAB (NS)	Canada Tax Appeal Board Cases (New Series)	Can
CTBR	Canada Tariff Board Reports	Can
CTC	Canada Tax Cases	Can
CTC	Canadian Transport Cases	Can
CTC (NS)	Canada Tax Cases (New Series)	Can
CTCR	Canadian Transport Commission Reports	Can
CTR	Canadian Tax Reporter	Can
CTR	Cape Times Reports	S Afr / Afr du sud
CTR	Commission du tarif registre	Can
CTR	De Boo Commodity Tax Reports	Can
CTST	Canada Trade and Sales Tax Cases	Can
CTTT	Décisions du Commissaire du travail et du Tribunal du travail	Can (QC)
CTTTCRAA	Décisions du Commissaire du travail, du Tribunal du travail et de la Commission de reconnaissance des associations d'artistes	Can (QC)
Cun	Cunningham's Reports (ER vol 94)	UK / R-U
Curt	Curteis's Reports (ER vol 163)	UK / R-U
D	Recueil Dalloz / Recueil le Dalloz	France
D	Recueil Dalloz et Sirey	France
DA	Recueil analytique de jurisprudence et de législation (Dalloz)	France
Dan	Daniell's Reports (ER vol 159)	UK / R-U
Davis	Davis's Reports (Ireland) (ER vol 80)	I
DC	Recueil critique Dalloz	France
DCA	Canada, Commission de la fonction publique du Canada, décisions du comité d'appel	Can
DCA	Décisions de la cour d'appel / Queen's Bench Reports (Dorion)	Can (QC)
DCDRT	Décisions sur des conflits de droit dans les relations du travail	Can (QC)
DCL	Décisions de la Commission des loyers	Can (QC)
DCR	New Zealand District Court Reports	NZ / N-Z
DCRM	Commission de révision des marchés publics du Canada, décisions	Can
DDCP	Décisions disciplinaires concernant les corporations professionnelles	Can (QC)
DDOP	Décisions disciplinaires concernant les ordres professionnels	Can (QC)
De G & J	De Gex & Jones's Reports (ER vols 44-45)	UK / R-U

De G & Sm	De Gex & Smale's Reports (ER vols 63-64)	UK / R-U
De G F & J	De Gex, Fisher & Jones's Reports (ER vol 45)	UK / R-U
De G J & S	De Gex, Jones & Smith's Reports (ER vol 46)	UK / R-U
De G M & G	De Gex, Macnaghten & Gordon's Reports (ER vols 42-44)	UK / R-U
Dea & Sw	Deane & Swabey's Reports (ER vol 164)	UK / R-U
Dears	Dearsly's Crown Cases (ER vol 169)	UK / R-U
Dears & B	Dearsly and Bell's Crown Cases (ER vol 169)	UK / R-U
Déc B-C	Décisions des Tribunaux du Bas-Canada	Can (QC)
Déc trib Mont	Précis des décisions des tribunaux du district de Montréal	Can (QC)
DELD	Dismissal and Employment Law Digest	Can
DELEA	Digest of Environmental Law and Environmental Assessment	Can
Den	Denison's Crown Cases (ER vols 1-2)	UK / R-U
Dés OAL	Décisions des orateurs de l'Assemblée législative de la province de Québec (Desjardins)	Can (QC)
DFQE	Droit fiscal québécois express	Can (QC)
DH	Recueil hebdomadaire Dalloz	France
Dick	Dickens's Reports (ER vol 21)	UK / R-U
DJC	Documentation juridique au Canada	Can
DJG	Dalloz jurisprudence général	France
DLQ	Droits et libertés au Québec	Can (QC)
DLR*	Dominion Law Reports	Can
DLR (2d)*	Dominion Law Reports (Second Series)	Can
DLR (3d)*	Dominion Law Reports (Third Series)	Can
DLR (4th)*	Dominion Law Reports (Fourth Series)	Can
DOAL	Décisions des orateurs, assemblée législative	Can (NB)
Dods	Dodson's Reports (ER vol 165)	UK / R-U
Donn	Donnelly's Reports (ER vol 47)	UK / R-U
Doug	Douglas's Reports (ER vol 99)	UK / R-U
Dow	Dow's Reports (ER vol 3)	UK / R-U
Dow & Cl	Dow & Clark's Reports (ER vol 6)	UK / R-U
Dowl & Ry	Dowling & Ryland's Reports (ER vol 171)	UK / R-U
DP	Recueil périodique et critique de jurisprudence (Dalloz)	France
Drap	Draper's King's Bench Reports	Can (ON)
Drew	Drewry's Reports (ER vols 61-62)	UK / R-U
Drew & Sm	Drewry & Smale's Reports (ER vol 62)	UK / R-U

DRL	Décisions de la Régie du logement	Can (QC)
DTC	Dominion Tax Cases	Can
DTE	Droit du travail express	Can (QC)
Dy	Dyer's Reports, King's Bench (ER vol 73)	UK / R-U
E & A	Grant's Upper Canada Error and Appeal Reports	Can (ON)
E Afr CAR	Eastern Africa Court of Appeals Reports	Afr
E Afr LR	Eastern Africa Law Reports	Afr
East	East's Reports (ER vols 102-104)	UK / R-U
ECHR	European Court of Human Rights	EU / UE
ECHR (Ser A)	Publications of the European Court of Human Rights: Series A: Judgments and Decisions	EU / UE
ECHR (Ser B)	Publications of the European Court of Human Rights: Series B Pleadings, Oral Arguments and Documents	EU / UE
ECR	European Court Reports: Reports of Cases before the Court	EU / UE
Eden	Eden's Reports, Chancery (ER vol 28)	UK / R-U
Edw	Edwards's Admiralty Reports (ER vol 165)	UK / R-U
E Distr LDR	Eastern Districts' Local Division Reports	S Afr / Afr du sud
E Distr R	Eastern Districts' Reports	S Afr / Afr du sud
EHRR	European Human Rights Reports	EU / UE
El & Bl	Ellis & Blackburn's Reports (ER vols 118-120)	UK / R-U
El & El	Ellis & Ellis's Reports, King's Bench (ER vols 120-121)	UK / R-U
El Bl & El	Ellis, Blackburn & Ellis's Reports (ER vol 120)	UK / R-U
ELLR	Employment and Labour Law Reporter	Can
ELR	Eastern Law Reporter	Can
ELR	Environmental Law Reporter of New South Wales	Austl
EMLR	Entertainment and Media Law Reports	UK / R-U
Eq Ca Abr	Equity Cases Abridged, Chancery (ER vols 21-22)	UK / R-U
ER	English Reports	UK / R-U
ERNZ	Employment Reports of New Zealand	NZ / N-Z
Esp	Espinasse's Reports	UK / R-U
ETR	Estates and Trusts Reports	Can
ETR (2d)	Estates and Trusts Reports (Second Series)	Can
ETR (3d)	Estates and Trusts Reports (Third Series)	Can
EULR	European Union Law Reporter	EU / UE
Eur Comm'n HRCD	Collection of Decisions of the European Commission of Human Rights	EU / UE

Eur Comm'n HRDR	European Commission of Human Rights: Decisions and Reports	EU / UE
Ex CR*	Exchequer Court of Canada Reports	Can
Ex CR*	Canada Law Reports: Exchequer Court	Can
Ex D	Law Reports, Exchequer Division	UK / R-U
Exch Rep	Exchequer Reports	UK / R-U
EYB	Éditions Yvon Blais (Référence)	Can
F	Session Cases (Fraser) (Fifth Series)	Scot / Écosse
F	Federal Reporter	US / É-U
F (2d)	Federal Reporter (Second Series)	US / É-U
F (3d)	Federal Reporter (Third Series)	US / É-U
F & F	Foster and Finalson's Reports (ER vol 168)	UK / R-U
F Cas	Federal Cases	US / É-U
F Supp	Federal Supplement	US / É-U
F Supp (2d)	Federal Supplement (Second Series)	US / É-U
Fam	Law Reports, Family Division	UK / R-U
Fam LR	Family Law Reports	Austl
Farm Products App Trib Dec	Farm Products Appeal Tribunal Decisions	Can (ON)
FC*	Canada Federal Court Reports	Can
FCAD	Federal Court of Appeal Decisions	Can
FCJ	Federal Court Judgments (QL)	Can
FCR	Federal Court Reports	Austl
FCR*	Federal Court Reports	Can
Fitz-G	Fitz-Gibbons' Reports (ER vol 94)	UK / R-U
FLD	Family Law Digest	Can
FLR	Federal Law Reports	Austl
FLRAC	Family Law Reform Act Cases	Can (ON)
FLRR	Family Law Reform Reporter	Can
Foord	Foord's Reports	S Afr / Afr du Sud
Forrest	Forrest's Reports (ER vol 145)	UK / R-U
Fort	Fortescue's Reports (ER vol 92)	UK / R-U
Fost	Foster's Reports (ER vol 168)	UK / R-U
Fox Pat C	Fox's Patent, Trade mark, Design, and Copyright Cases	Can
FPR	Fisheries Pollution Reports	Can
FTLR	Financial Times Law Reports	UK / R-U

FTLR	Free Trade Law Reports	Can
FTR	Federal Trial Reports	Can
FTU	Free Trade Update	Can
Gaz LR	Gazette Law Reports	NZ / N-Z
Gaz Pal	Gazette du Palais	France
Ghana LR	Ghana Law Reports (West Africa)	W Afr / Afr de l'ouest
Giff	Giffard's Reports (ER vols 65-66)	UK / R-U
Gilb Cas	Gilbert's Cases in Law & Equity (ER vol 93)	UK / R-U
Gilb Rep	Gilbert's Reports, Chancery (ER vol 25)	UK / R-U
GLR	Gazette Law Reports	NZ / N-Z
Godbolt	Godbolt's Reports (ER vol 78)	UK / R-U
Good Pat	Goodeve's Abstract of Patent Cases	UK / R-U
Gould	Gouldsborough's Reports (ER vol 75)	UK / R-U
Gow	Gow's Reports (ER vol 171)	UK / R-U
Gr	Grant's Upper Canada Chancery Reports	Can (ON)
Greg R	Gregorowski's Reports (Orange Free State)	S Afr / Afr du sud
Griq WR	Griqualand West Reports (Cape of Good Hope)	S Afr / Afr du sud
GSTR	Canadian Goods and Services Tax Reporter / Reports / Monitor	Can
GTC	Canadian GST & Commodity Tax Cases	Can
H & C	Hurlstone & Coltman's Reports (ER vols 158-159)	UK / R-U
H & M	Hemming & Miller's Reports (ER vol 71)	UK / R-U
H & N	Hurlstone & Norman's Reports (ER vols 156-158)	UK / R-U
H & Tw	Hall & Twells' Reports (ER vol 47)	UK / R-U
H & W	Haszard & Warburton's Reports	Can (PE)
Hag Adm	Haggard's Admiralty Reports (ER vol 166)	UK / R-U
Hag Con	Haggard's Consistory Reports (ER vol 161)	UK / R-U
Hag Ecc	Haggard's Ecclesiastical Reports (ER vol 162)	UK / R-U
Hague Ct Rep	Hague Court Reports (1916)	Intl
Hague Ct Rep (2d)	Hague Court Reports (Second Series) (1932)	Intl
Hardr	Hardres' Reports (ER vol 145)	UK / R-U
Hare	Hare's Reports (ER vols 66-68)	UK / R-U
Harr & Hodg	Harrison and Hodgins Municipal Report	Can (ON)
Hay & M	Hay & Marriott's Reports (ER vol 165)	UK / R-U
Her Tr Nor	Heresy Trials in the Diocese of Norwich	UK / R-U
Het	Hetley's Reports (ER vol 124)	UK / R-U

HL Cas	Clark's House of Lords Cases (ER vols 9-11)	UK / R-U
HL Cas	House of Lords Cases	UK / R-U
Hob	Hobart's Reports (ER vol 80)	UK / R-U
Hodg	Hodgins Election Cases	Can (ON)
Hodges	Hodges' Reports	UK / R-U
Holt	Holt's Reports (ER vol 171)	UK / R-U
Holt, Eq	Holt's Equity Reports (ER vol 71)	UK / R-U
Holt, KB	Holt's King's Bench Cases (ER vol 90)	UK / R-U
Hut	Hutton's Reports (ER vol 123)	UK / R-U
IAA	Industrial Arbitration Awards	NZ / N-Z
IAR	Industrial Arbitration Reports	Austl (NSW)
IBDD	Instruments de base et documents divers	GATT
I Ch R	Irish Chancery Reports	I
ICC	Indian Claims Commission Decisions	US / É-U
ICJ Pleadings	International Court of Justice: Pleadings, Oral Arguments, Documents	Intl
ICJ Rep	International Court of Justice: Reports of Judgments, Advisory Opinions, and Orders	Intl
ICLR	Irish Common Law Reports	I
ICR	Industrial Cases Reports	UK / R-U
ICR	Industrial Court Reports	UK / R-U
ICSID	International Centre for Settlement of Investment Disputes (World Bank)	Intl
ILR	Insurance Law Reporter	Can
ILR	Canadian Insurance Law Reporter	Can
ILR	International Law Reports	Intl
ILR	Irish Law Reports	I
ILRM	Irish Law Reports Monthly	I
ILTR	Irish Law Times Reports	I
IMA	Institute of Municipal Assessors of Ontario, Court Decisions	Can (ON)
Imm ABD	Immigration Appeal Board Decisions	Can
Imm AC	Immigration Appeal Cases	Can
Imm AC (2d)	Immigration Appeal Cases (Second Series)	Can
Imm LR	Immigration Law Reporter	Can
Imm LR (2d)	Immigration Law Reporter (Second Series)	Can
Imm LR (3d)	Immigration Law Reporter (Third Series)	Can

Imm LR (4th)	Immigration Law Reporter (Fourth Series)	Can
Inter-Am Ct HR (Ser A)	Inter-American Court of Human Rights, Series A: Judgments and Opinions	Intl
Inter-Am Ct HR (Ser B)	Inter-American Court of Human Rights, Series B: Pleadings, Oral Arguments, and Documents	Intl
Inter-Am Ct HR (Ser C)	Inter-American Court of Human Rights, Series C: Decisions and Judgments	Intl
IR	Irish Law Reports	I
IR Eq	Irish Reports, Equity Series	I
IRCL	Irish Reports, Common Law Series	I
J & H	Johnson & Hemming's Reports (ER vol 70)	UK / R-U
Jac	Jacob's Reports (ER vol 37)	UK / R-U
Jac & W	Jacob & Walker's Reports (ER vol 37)	UK / R-U
J-cl Admin	Juris-classeur Administratif	France
J-cl BC	Juris-classeur Banque et crédit	France
J-cl Brev	Juris-classeur Brevets d'invention	France
J-cl C-C	Juris-classeur Concurrence-consommation	France
J-cl C-D	Juris-classeur Contrats-distribution	France
J-cl Civ	Juris-classeur Civil	France
J-cl Civ Annexe	Juris-classeur Civil annexe	France
J-cl Coll terr	Juris-classeur Collectivités territoriales	France
J-cl Com gén	Juris-classeur Commercial général	France
J-cl Constr	Juris-classeur Construction	France
J-cl Coprop	Juris-classeur Copropriété	France
J-cl Div	Juris-classeur Divorce	France
J-cl Dr comp	Juris-classeur Droit comparé	France
J-cl Dr de l'enfant	Juris-classeur Droit de l'enfant	France
J-cl Dr Intl	Juris-classeur Droit International	France
J-cl Env	Juris-classeur Environnement	France
J-cl Eur	Juris-classeur Europe	France
J-cl F com	Juris-classeur Fonds de commerce	France
J-cl Fisc	Juris-classeur Fiscal	France
J-cl Fisc imm	Juris-classeur Fiscalité immobilière	France
J-cl Fisc intl	Juris-classeur Fiscal international	France
J-cl Foncier	Juris-classeur Foncier	France
J-cl Impôt	Juris-classeur Impôt sur la fortune	France

J-cl MDM	Juris-classeur Marques, dessins et modèles	France
J-cl Not Form	Juris-classeur Notarial formulaire	France
J-cl Pén	Juris-classeur Pénal	France
J-cl Proc	Juris-classeur Procédure	France
J-cl Proc coll	Juris-classeur Procédures collectives	France
J-cl Proc fisc	Juris-classeur Procédures fiscales	France
J-cl Proc pén	Juris-classeur Procédure pénale	France
J-cl Prop litt art	Juris-classeur Propriété littéraire et artistique	France
J-cl Rép prat Dr priv	Juris-classeur Répertoire pratique de droit privé	France
J-cl Resp civ Ass	Juris-classeur Responsabilité civile et Assurances	France
J-cl Séc Soc	Juris-classeur sécurité sociale	France
J-cl Sociétés	Juris-classeur Sociétés	France
J-cl Trav	Juris-classeur Travail	France
JCP	Semaine Juridique	France
JE	Jurisprudence Express	Can (QC)
Jenk	Jenkins's Reports (ER vol 145)	UK / R-U
JL	Jurisprudence Logement	Can (QC)
JM	Décisions du juge des mines du Québec	Can (QC)
JM	Justice municipale	Can (QC)
Johns	Johnson's Reports (ER vol 70)	UK / R-U
Jones T	Jones, T, Reports (ER vol 84)	UK / R-U
Jones W	Jones, W, Reports (ER vol 82)	UK / R-U
JQ	Jugements du Québec (QL)	Can (QC)
Jug et dél NF	Jugements et délibrérations du Conseil souverain de la Nouvelle-France	Can (QC)
Jug et dél Q	Jugements et délibrérations du Conseil supérieur de Québec	Can (QC)
K & J	Kay & Johnson's Reports (ER vols 69-70)	UK / R-U
Kay	Kay's Reports (ER vol 69)	UK / R-U
KB	Law Reports, King's Bench	UK / R-U
Keble	Keble's Reports (ER vols 83-84)	UK / R-U
Keen	Keen's Reports (ER vol 48)	UK / R-U
Keilway	Keilway's Reports (ER vol 72)	UK / R-U
Kel J / Kel	Kelyng, Sir John's Reports (ER vol 84)	UK / R-U
Kel W	Kelynge, William's Reports (ER vol 25)	UK / R-U
Keny	Kenyon's Reports (ER vol 96)	UK / R-U

Kenya LR	Kenya Law Reports	Kenya
KLR	Kenya Law Reports	Kenya
Kn	Knapp's Privy Council Appeal Cases (ER vol 12)	UK / R-U
L Ed	United States Supreme Court, Lawyers' Edition	US / É-U
L Ed (2d)	United States Supreme Court, Lawyers' Edition (Second Series)	US / É-U
LAC	Labour Arbitration Cases	Can (ON)
LAC (2d)	Labour Arbitration Cases (Second Series)	Can (ON)
LAC (3d)	Labour Arbitration Cases (Third Series)	Can (ON)
LAC (4th)	Labour Arbitration Cases (Fourth Series)	Can (ON)
Lane	Lane's Reports (ER vol 145)	UK / R-U
Lap Sp Dec	Laperrière's Speakers' Decisions	Can
LAR	Labor Arbitration Reports	US / É-U
Latch	Latch's Reports, King's Bench (ER vol 82)	UK / R-U
LC Jur	Lower Canada Jurist	Can (QC)
LCBD	Land Compensation Board Decisions	Can (ON)
LCR	Land Compensation Reports	Can
LCR	Lower Canada Reports	Can (QC)
Le & Ca	Leigh & Cave's Reports (ER vol 169)	UK / R-U
Leach	Leach's Cases on Crown Law (ER vol 168)	UK / R-U
Lee	Lee's Ecclesiastical Reports (ER vol 161)	UK / R-U
Leo	Leonard's Reports (ER vol 74)	UK / R-U
Lev	Levinz's Reports (ER vol 83)	UK / R-U
Lewin	Lewin's Crown Cases on the Northern Circuit (ER vol 168)	UK / R-U
Ley	Ley's Reports (ER vol 80)	UK / R-U
Lilly	Lilly's Assize Cases	UK / R-U
Lit	Littleton's Reports (ER vol 120)	UK / R-U
Ll LR	Lloyd's List Law Reports	UK / R-U
Lloyd's Rep	Lloyd's Law Reports	UK / R-U
Lloyd's Rep	Lloyd's List Law Reports	UK / R-U
Lloyd's Rep Med	Lloyd's Law Reports (Medical)	UK / R-U
LN	Legal News	Can (QC)
LR A & E	Law Reports, Admiralty and Ecclesiastical Cases (ER vols 1-4)	UK / R-U
LR A & E	Law Reports, Admiralty and Ecclesiastical Cases	UK / R-U
LR CCR	Law Reports, Crown Cases Reserved	UK / R-U
LR Ch App	Law Reports, Chancery Appeals	UK / R-U

LR CP	Law Reports, Common Pleas	UK / R-U
LR Eq	Law Reports, Equity Cases	UK / R-U
LR Ex	Law Reports, Exchequer	UK / R-U
LR Ir	Law Reports, Ireland	I
LR P & D	Law Reports, Probate and Divorce	UK / R-U
LR QB	Law Reports, Queen's Bench	UK / R-U
LR RP	Law Reports, Restrictive Practices	UK / R-U
LR Sc & Div	Law Reports, House of Lords Scotch and Divorce Appeal Cases	UK / R-U
LRHL	Law Reports, English and Irish Appeals	I / UK / R-U
LRPC	Law Reports, Privy Council	UK / R-U
Lush	Lushington's Reports (ER vol 167)	UK / R-U
Lut	Lutwyche's Reports (ER vol 125)	UK / R-U
M & M	Moody & Malkin (ER vol 173)	UK / R-U
M & Rob	Moody & Robinson (ER vol 174)	UK / R-U
M & S	Maule & Selwyn's Reports (ER vol 105)	UK / R-U
M & W	Meeson & Welsby's Reports (ER vols 150-153)	UK / R-U
M'Cle	M'Cleland's Reports (ER vol 148)	UK / R-U
M'Cle & Yo	M'Cleland & Younge's Reports (ER vol 148)	UK / R-U
Mac & G	M'Naghten & Gordon's Reports (ER vols 41-42)	UK / R-U
Macl & R	Maclean & Robinson's Reports (ER vol 9)	UK / R-U
MACMLC	Digest of the Selected Judgements of the Maori Appellate Court and Maori Land Court	NZ / N-Z
Madd	Maddock's Reports (ER vol 56)	UK / R-U
Man & G	Manning & Granger's Reports (ER vols 133-135)	UK / R-U
Man LR	Manitoba Law Reports (Queen's Bench)	Can (MB)
Man MTBD	Manitoba Motor Transport Board Decisions	Can (MB)
Man R*	Manitoba Reports	Can (MB)
Man R (2d)*	Manitoba Reports (Second Series)	Can (MB)
Man R temp Wood	Manitoba Reports temp Wood (ed Armour)	Can (MB)
Maori L Rev	Maori Law Review	NZ / N-Z
March, NR	March's New Cases (ER vol 82)	UK / R-U
MC	Malayan Cases	Sing
MCC	Mining Commissioner's Cases	Can (ON)
MCD	Magistrates' Court Decisions	NZ /N-Z
MCR	Montreal Condensed Reports / Précis des décisions des tribunaux	Can (QC)

	du district de Montréal	
MCR	Magistrates' Court Reports	NZ / N-Z
Mer	Merivale's Reports (ER vols 35-36)	UK / R-U
MHRC Dec	Manitoba Human Rights Commission Decisions	Can (MB)
MJ	Manitoba Judgments (QL)	Can (MB)
MLB Dec	Manitoba Labour Board Decisions	Can (MB)
MLR (KB)	Montreal Law Reports, King's Bench	Can (QC)
MLR (QB)	Montreal Law Reports, Queen's Bench	Can (QC)
MLR (SC)	Montreal Law Reports, Superior Court	Can (QC)
MMC	Martin's Mining Cases	Can (BC)
Mod	Modern Reports (ER vols 86-88)	UK / R-U
Moo Ind App	Moore's Reports, Indian Appeals, Privy Council (ER vols 18-20)	UK / R-U
Moo KB	Moore's Reports, King's Bench (ER vol 72)	UK / R-U
Moo PC	Moore's Reports, Privy Council (ER vols 12-15)	UK / R-U
Moo PCNS	Moore's Reports, Privy Council, (New Series) (ER vols 15-17)	UK / R-U
Mood	Moody's Reports (ER vols 168-169)	UK / R-U
Mos	Mosely's Reports (ER vol 25)	UK / R-U
MPLR	Municipal and Planning Law Reports	Can
MPLR (2d)	Municipal and Planning Law Reports (Second Series)	Can
MPLR (3d)	Municipal and Planning Law Reports (Third Series)	Can
MPLR (4th)	Municipal and Planning Law Reports (Fourth Series)	Can
MPLR (5th)	Municipal and Planning Law Reports (Fifth Series)	Can
MPR	Maritime Provinces Reports	Can
MVR	Motor Vehicle Reports	Can
MVR (2d)	Motor Vehicle Reports (Second Series)	Can
MVR (3d)	Motor Vehicle Reports (Third Series)	Can
MVR (4th)	Motor Vehicle Reports (Fourth Series)	Can
MVR (5th)	Motor Vehicle Reports (Fifth Series)	Can
MVR (6th)	Motor Vehicle Reports (Sixth Series)	Can
My & Cr	Mylne & Craig's Reports (ER vols 40-41)	UK / R-U
My & K	Mylne & Keen's Reports (ER vols 39-40)	UK / R-U
NACD	Native Appeal Court Selected Decisions (Natal and Transvaal)	S Afr / Afr du sud
NACR	Native Appeal Court Reports	S Afr / Afr du sud
NB Eq	New Brunswick Equity Reports (Trueman)	Can (NB)
NB Eq Cas	New Brunswick Equity Cases (Trueman)	Can (NB)

NBESTD	New Brunswick Employment Standards Tribunal Decisions	Can (NB)
NBHRC Dec	New Brunswick Human Rights Commission Decisions	Can (NB)
NBJ	New Brunswick Judgments (QL)	Can (NB)
NBLEBD	New Brunswick Labour and Employment Board Decisions	Can (NB)
NBLLC	New Brunswick Labour Law Cases	Can (NB)
NBPPABD	New Brunswick Provincial Planning Appeal Board Decisions	Can (NB)
NBR*	New Brunswick Reports	Can (NB)
NBR (2d)*	New Brunswick Reports (Second Series)	Can (NB)
NE	Northeastern Reporter	US / É-U
NE (2d)	Northeastern Reporter (Second Series)	US / É-U
NEBD	National Energy Board, Reasons for Decision	Can
Nels	Nelson's Reports, Chancery (ER vol 21)	UK / R-U
Nfld & PEIR*	Newfoundland and Prince Edward Island Reports	Can (NL/PE)
Nfld LR*	Newfoundland Law Reports	Can (NL)
Nfld Sel Cas	Newfoundland Selected Cases	Can (NL)
NHRC Dec	Newfoundland Human Rights Commission Decisions	Can (NL)
NI	Northern Ireland Law Reports	NI / IN
NJ	Newfoundland and Labrador Judgments (QL)	Can (NL)
NLR	Nigeria Law Reports	Nigeria
NLR	Nyasaland Law Reports (Malawi)	Malawi
NLR (NS)	Natal Law Reports (New Series)	S Afr / Afr du sud
NLR (OS)	Natal Law Reports (Old Series)	S Afr / Afr du sud
Noy	Noy's Reports (ER vol 74)	UK / R-U
NPDR	Natal Provincial Division Reports	S Afr / Afr du sud
NR	National Reporter	Can
NSBCPU Dec	Nova Scotia Board of Commissioners of Public Utilities Decisions	Can (NS)
NSCGA Dec	Nova Scotia Compendium of Grievance Arbitration Decisions	Can (NS)
NSHRC Dec	Nova Scotia Human Rights Commissions Decisions	Can (NS)
NSJ	Nova Scotia Judgments (QL)	Can (NS)
NSR*	Nova Scotia Reports	Can
NSR (2d)*	Nova Scotia Reports (Second Series)	Can (NS)
NSRUD	Nova Scotia Reported and Unreported Decisions	Can (NS)
NSW St R	New South Wales State Reports	Austl (NSW)
NSWLR	New South Wales Law Reports	Austl (NSW)
NSWR	New South Wales Reports	Austl (NSW)

NSWSCR	New South Wales Supreme Court Reports	Austl (NSW)
NSWWN	New South Wales Weekly Notes	Austl (NSW)
NTAR	National Transportation Agency of Canada Reports	Can
NTJ	Northern Territory Judgments	Austl (NT)
NTLR	Northern Territory Law Reports	Austl (NT)
NTR	Northern Territory Reports	Austl (NT)
Nu J	Nunavut Judgments (QL)	Can (NU)
NW	Northwestern Reporter	US / É-U
NW (2d)	Northwestern Reporter (Second Series)	US / É-U
NWTJ	Northwest Territories Judgments (QL)	Can (NT)
NWTR*	Northwest Territories Reports	Can (NT)
NWTSCR	Northwest Territories Supreme Court Reports	Can (NT)
NY	New York Reports	US / É-U
NY (2d)	New York Reports (Second Series)	US / É-U
NY (3d)	New York Reports (Third Series)	US / É-U
NYS (2d)	New York Supplement (Second Series)	US / É-U
NZAC	Judgments of the Arbitration Court of New Zealand	NZ /N-Z
NZAR	New Zealand Administrative Reports	NZ / N-Z
NZBLC	New Zealand Business Law Cases	NZ / N-Z
NZFLR	New Zealand Family Law Reports	NZ / N-Z
NZILR	New Zealand Industral Law Reports	NZ / N-Z
NZIPR	New Zealand Intellectual Property Reports	NZ / N-Z
NZLR	New Zealand Law Reports	NZ / N-Z
NZPCC	New Zealand Privy Council Cases	NZ / N-Z
NZTC	New Zealand Tax Cases	NZ / N-Z
OAC	Ontario Appeal Cases	Can (ON)
OAR*	Ontario Appeal Reports	Can (ON)
OELD	Ontario Environmental Law Digest	Can (ON)
OFLR	Ontario Family Law Reporter	Can (ON)
OHRC Dec	Ontario Human Rights Commission Decisions	Can (ON)
OHRC Transcr	Ontario Human Rights Commission, Trancripts of Selected Hearings	Can (ON)
OHRCBI	Ontario Human Rights Commission, Board of Inquiry	Can (ON)
OIC Arb	Ontario Insurance Commission, Arbitration Cases	Can (ON)
OJ	Ontario Judgments (QL)	Can (ON)

Olmsted PC	Olmsted's Privy Council Decisions	Can
OLR*	Ontario Law Reports	Can (ON)
OLRB Rep	Ontario Labour Relations Board Reports	Can (ON)
OMB Dec	Ontario Municipal Board Decisions	Can (ON)
OMB Index	Ontario Municipal Board Index to Applications Disposed of	Can (ON)
OMBR	Ontario Municipal Board Reports	Can (ON)
ONED	Office national de l'énergie, décisions	Can
Ont D Crim	Ontario Decisions — Criminal	Can (ON)
Ont D Crim Conv	Ontario Decisions — Criminal Convictions Cases	Can (ON)
Ont D Crim Sent	Ontario Decisions — Criminal Sentence Cases	Can (ON)
Ont Elec	Ontario Election Cases	Can (ON)
Ont En Bd Dec	Ontario Energy Board Decisions	Can (ON)
Ont Envtl Assessment Bd Dec	Ontario Environmental Assessment Board Decisions	Can (ON)
Ont Health Disciplines Bd Dec	Ontario Health Disciplines Board Decisions	Can (ON)
Ont Pol R	Ontario Police Reports	Can (ON)
OPR	Ontario Practice Reports	Can (ON)
OR*	Ontario Reports	Can (ON)
OR (2d)*	Ontario Reports (Second Series)	Can (ON)
OR (3d)*	Ontario Reports (Third Series)	Can (ON)
Orange Free State Prov Div R	Orange Free State Provincial Division Reports	S Afr / Afr du sud
OSC Bull	Ontario Securities Commission Bulletin	Can (ON)
OSCWS	Ontario Securities Commission Weekly Summary	Can (ON)
Ow	Owen's Reports (ER vol 74)	UK / R-U
OWCAT Dec	Ontario Workers' Compensation Appeals Tribunal Decisions	Can (ON)
OWN	Ontario Weekly Notes	Can (ON)
OWR	Ontario Weekly Reporter	Can (ON)
P	Law Reports, Probate, Divorce, and Admiralty Division	UK / R-U
P	Pacific Reporter	US / É-U
P (2d)	Pacific Reporter (Second Series)	US / É-U
P (3d)	Pacific Reporter (Third Series)	US / É-U
P Wms	Peere Williams's Reports (ER vol 24)	UK / R-U
Palm	Palmer's Reports (ER vol 81)	UK / R-U
Park	Parker's Reports (ER vol 145)	UK / R-U

Patr Elec Cas	Patrick's Election Cases (Upper Canada / Canada West)	Can (ON)
PCIJ (Ser A)	Publications of the Permanent Court of International Justice: Series A, Collection of Judgments	EU / UE
PCIJ (Ser A/B)	Publications of the Permanent Court of International Justice: Series A/B, Judgments, Orders and Advisory Opinions	EU / UE
PCIJ (Ser B)	Publications of the Permanent Court of International Justice: Series B, Collection of Advisory Opinions	EU / UE
PCIJ (Ser C)	Publications of the Permanent Court of International Justice, Series C, Pleadings, Oral Statements and Documents	EU / UE
PD	Law Reports, Probate, Divorce, and Admiralty Division	UK / R-U
Peake	Peake's Reports (ER vol 170)	UK / R-U
Peake Add Cas	Peake's Reports (Additional Cases) (ER vol 170)	UK / R-U
PEI	Prince Edward Island Supreme Court Reports	Can (PE)
PEIJ	Prince Edward Island Judgments (QL)	Can (PE)
PER	Pay Equity Reports	Can (ON)
Per CS	Extraits ou précédents des arrêts tirés des registres du Conseil supérieur de Québec (Perrault)	Can (QC)
Perr P	Extraits ou précédents des arrêts tirés des registres de la prévosté de Québec (Perrault)	Can (QC)
Peters	Peters' Prince Edward Island Reports	Can (PE)
PFP	Pandectes françaises périodiques	France
Ph	Phillips' Reports (ER vol 41)	UK / R-U
Phill Ecc	Phillimore's Ecclesiastical Reports (ER vol 161)	UK / R-U
Pl Com	Plowden's Commentaries (ER vol 75)	UK / R-U
PNGCB Alta	Petroleum and Natural Gas Conservation Board of Alberta	Can (AB)
Pollex	Pollexfen's Reports (ER vol 86)	UK / R-U
Pop	Popham's Reports (ER vol 79)	UK / R-U
PPR	Planning and Property Reports	Can (ON)
PPSAC	Personal Property Security Act Cases	Can
PPSAC (2d)	Personal Property Security Act Cases (Second Series)	Can
PPSAC (3d)	Personal Property Security Act Cases (Third Series)	Can
PRBC	Procurement Review Board of Canada Decisions	Can
PRBR	Pension Review Board Reports	Can
Prec Ch	Precedents in Chancery (T Finch) (ER vol 24)	UK / R-U
Price	Price's Reports (ER vols 145-147)	UK / R-U
Pyke	Pyke's Reports	Can (QC)
Q St R	Queensland State Reports	Austl (Qld)

QAC	Québec Appeal Cases	Can (QC)
QB	Queen's Bench Reports (ER vols 113-118)	UK / R-U
QBD	Law Reports, Queen's Bench Division	UK / R-U
Qc Comm dp déc	Québec Commission des droits de la personne, décisions des tribunaux	Can (QC)
QJ	Quebec Judgments (QL)	Can (QC)
Qld Lawyer Reps	Queensland Lawyer Reports	Austl (Qld)
QLR	Quebec Law Reports	Can (QC)
QPR	Québec Practice Reports	Can (QC)
QR	Queensland Reports	Austl (Qld)
RAC	Ramsay, Appeal Cases	Can (QC)
RAT	Recueil d'arrêts sur les transports	Can
Raym Ld	Raymond, Lord Reports (ER vols 91-92)	UK / R-U
Raym T	Raymond, Sir T Reports (ER vol 83)	UK / R-U
RC de l'É*	Recueil des arrêts de la Cour de l'Échiquier	Can
RC de l'É*	Rapports judiciaires du Canada : Cour de l'Échiquier	Can
RCCT	Recueil des décisions de la Commission canadienne des transports	Can
RCDA	Recueil des décisions de la Commission du droit d'auteur	Can
RCDA	Recueil de jurisprudence canadienne en droit des assurances	Can
RCDA (2e)	Recueil de jurisprudence canadienne en droit des assurances (deuxième série)	Can
RCDA (3e)	Recueil de jurisprudence canadienne en droit des assurances (troisième série)	Can
RCDA (4e)	Recueil de jurisprudence canadienne en droit des assurances (quatrième série)	Can
RCDA (5e)	Recueil de jurisprudence canadienne en droit des assurances (cinquième série)	Can
RCDE	Recueil de jurisprudence canadienne en droit de l'environnement	Can
RCDE (3e)	Recueil de jurisprudence canadienne en droit de l'environnement (troisième série)	Can
RCDE (ns)	Recueil de jurisprudence canadienne en droit de l'environnement (nouvelle série)	Can
RCDF	Recueil de jurisprudence canadienne en droit de la faillite	
RCDF (2e)	Recueil de jurisprudence canadienne en droit de la faillite (nouvelle série)	Can
RCDF (3e)	Recueil de jurisprudence canadienne en droit de la faillite (troisième série)	Can
RCDF (4e)	Recueil de jurisprudence canadienne en droit de la faillite (quatrième série)	Can

RCDF (5e)	Recueil de jurisprudence canadienne en droit de la faillite (cinquième série)	Can
RCDSST	Recueil de jurisprudence canadienne en droit de la santé et de sécurité au travail	Can
RCDT	Recueil de jurisprudence canadienne en droit du travail	Can
RCDT (2e)	Recueil de jurisprudence canadienne en droit du travail (deuxième série)	Can
RCDT (3e)	Recueil de jurisprudence canadienne en droit du travail (troisième série)	Can
RCDT (4e)	Recueil de jurisprudence canadienne en droit du travail (quatrième série)	Can
RCDVM	Recueil de jurisprudence canadienne en droit des valeurs mobilières	Can
RCE	Recueil des arrêts du Conseil d'Etat statuant au contentieux et du Tribunal des conflits, des arrêts des cours administratives d'appel et des jugements des tribunaux administratifs	France
RCF*	Recueil des décisions des Cours fédérales	Can
RCRAS	Recueil de jurisprudence canadienne en matière de retraite et d'avantages sociaux	Can
RCRC	Recueil de jurisprudence canadienne en responsabilité civile	Can
RCRC (2e)	Recueil de jurisprudence canadienne en responsabilité civile (deuxième série)	Can
RCRC (3e)	Recueil de jurisprudence canadienne en responsabilité civile (troisième série)	Can
RCRC (4e)	Recueil de jurisprudence canadienne en responsabilité civile (quatrième série)	Can
RCRP	Recueil des arrêts du Conseil de révision des pensions	Can
RCS*	Rapports judiciaires du Canada : cour suprême	Can
RCS*	Recueils des arrêts de la Cour suprême du Canada	Can
RCT	Rapports de la Commission du tarif	Can
RDCC	Recueil des décisions du Conseil constitutionnel	France
RDCFQ	Recueil des décisions, Commission de la fonction publique et Comité d'appel de la fonction publique	Can (QC)
RDF	Recueil de droit de la famille	Can
RDFQ	Recueil de droit fiscal québécois	Can (QC)
RDI	Recueil de droit immobilier	Can (QC)
RDJ	Revue de droit judiciaire	Can (QC)
RDJC	Recueil de droit judiciaire de Carswell	Can
RDJC (2e)	Recueil de droit judiciaire de Carswell (deuxième série)	Can
RDJC (3e)	Recueil de droit judiciaire de Carswell (troisième série)	Can

RDJC (4e)	Recueil de droit judiciaire de Carswell (quatrième série)	Can
RDJC (5e)	Recueil de droit judiciaire de Carswell (cinquième série)	Can
RDJC (6e)	Recueil de droit judiciaire de Carswell (sixième série)	Can
RDJC (7e)	Recueil de droit judiciaire de Carswell (septième série)	Can
RDP	Revue de droit pénal	Can (QC)
RDT	Revue de droit du travail	Can (QC)
Rec	Recueil des arrêts du Conseil d'Etat statuant au contentieux et du Tribunal des conflits, des arrêts des cours administratives d'appel et des jugements des tribunaux administratifs	France
RECJ	Records of the Early Courts of Justice of Upper Canada	Can (ON)
Recueil Lebon	Recueil des arrêts du Conseil d'Etat statuant au contentieux et du Tribunal des conflits, des arrêts des cours administratives d'appel et des jugements des tribunaux administratifs	France
RED	Ritchie's Equity Decisions	Can (NB)
Rép admin	Encyclopédie juridique Dalloz : Répertoire de contentieux administratif	France
Rep Ch	Reports in Chancery (ER vol 21)	UK / R-U
Rép civ	Encyclopédie juridique Dalloz : Répertoire de droit civil	France
Rép com	Encyclopédie juridique Dalloz : Répertoire de droit commercial	France
Rép commun	Encyclopédie juridique Dalloz : Répertoire de droit communautaire	France
Rép pén & proc pén	Encyclopédie juridique Dalloz : Répertoire de droit pénal et de procédure pénale	France
Rép proc civ	Encyclopédie juridique Dalloz : Répertoire de procédure civile	France
Rép soc	Encyclopédie juridique Dalloz : Répertoire des sociétés	France
Rep t Finch	Reports, temp Finch (Nelson's folio Reports) (ER vol 23)	UK / R-U
Rép tr	Encyclopédie juridique Dalloz : Répertoire de droit du travail	France
Rev serv arb	Revue des services d'arbitrage	Can
RFL	Reports of Family Law	Can
RFL (2d)	Reports of Family Law (Second Series)	Can
RFL (3d)	Reports of Family Law (Third Series)	Can
RFL (4th)	Reports of Family Law (Fourth Series)	Can
RFL (5th)	Reports of Family Law (Fifth Series)	Can
RFL (6th)	Reports of Family Law (Sixth Series)	Can
RFL (7th)	Reports of Family Law (Seventh Series)	Can
Rhod & NL R	Rhodesia & Nyasaland Law Reports	E Afr / Afr de l'Est
Rhod LR	Rhodesian Law Reports	Zimb
RIAA	Report of International Arbitral Awards	Intl

Ridg t Hard	Ridgeway, temp Hardwicke's Reports (ER vol 27)	UK / R-U
Ritch Eq Rep	Ritchie's Equity Reports	Can (NS)
RJ imm	Recueil de jurisprudence en droit de l'immigration	Can
RJ imm (2e)	Recueil de jurisprudence en droit de l'immigration (deuxième série)	Can
RJ imm (3e)	Recueil de jurisprudence en droit de l'immigration (troisième série)	Can
RJ imm (4e)	Recueil de jurisprudence en droit de l'immigration (quatrième série)	Can
RJC	Revue de jurisprudence commerciale	France
RJC	Recueil de jurisprudence en droit criminel	Can
RJC (3e)	Recueil de jurisprudence en droit criminel (troisième série)	Can
RJC (4e)	Recueil de jurisprudence en droit criminel (quatrième série)	Can
RJC (5e)	Recueil de jurisprudence en droit criminel (cinquième série)	Can
RJC (6e)	Recueil de jurisprudence en droit criminel (sixième série)	Can
RJC (ns)	Recueil de jurisprudence en droit criminel (nouvelle série)	Can
RJDA	Recueil de jurisprudence en droit des affaires	Can
RJDA (2e)	Recueil de jurisprudence en droit des affaires (deuxième série)	Can
RJDA (3e)	Recueil de jurisprudence en droit des affaires (troisième série)	Can
RJDA (4e)	Recueil de jurisprudence en droit des affaires (quatrième série)	Can
RJDA (5e)	Recueil de jurisprudence en droit des affaires (cinqième série)	Can
RJDC	Recueil de jurisprudence en droit de la construction	Can
RJDC (2e)	Recueil de jurisprudence en droit de la construction (deuxième série)	Can
RJDC (3e)	Recueil de jurisprudence en droit de la construction (troisième série)	Can
RJDC (4e)	Recueil de jurisprudence en droit de la construction (quatrième série)	Can
RJDI	Recueil de jurisprudence en droit immobilier	Can
RJDI (2e)	Recueil de jurisprudence en droit immobilier (deuxième série)	Can
RJDI (3e)	Recueil de jurisprudence en droit immobilier (troisième série)	Can
RJDI (4e)	Recueil de jurisprudence en droit immobilier (quatrième série)	Can
RJDI (5e)	Recueil de jurisprudence en droit immobilier (cinqième série)	Can
RJDM	Recueil de jurisprudence en droit municipal	Can
RJDM (2e)	Recueil de jurisprudence en droit municipal (deuxième série)	Can
RJDM (3e)	Recueil de jurisprudence en droit municipal (troisième série)	Can
RJDM (4e)	Recueil de jurisprudence en droit municipal (quatrième série)	Can
RJDM (5e)	Recueil de jurisprudence en droit municipal (cinquième série)	Can
RJDT	Recueil de jurisprudence en droit du travail	Can (QC)
RJF	Revue de jurisprudence fiscale	France

RJF	Recueil de jurisprudence en droit de la famille	Can
RJF (2e)	Recueil de jurisprudence en droit de la famille (deuxième série)	Can
RJF (3e)	Recueil de jurisprudence en droit de la famille (troisième série)	Can
RJF (4e)	Recueil de jurisprudence en droit de la famille (quatrième série)	Can
RJF (5e)	Recueil de jurisprudence en droit de la famille (cinquième série)	Can
RJF (6e)	Recueil de jurisprudence en droit de la famille (sixième série)	Can
RJF (7e)	Recueil de jurisprudence en droit de la famille (septième série)	Can
RJO (3e)	Recueil de jurisprudence de l'Ontario (troisième série) (1882-1991 : voir *Ontario Reports*)	Can (ON)
RJQ*	Recueils de jurisprudence du Québec	Can (QC)
RJS	Revue de jurisprudence sociale	France
RL	Revue légale	Can (QC)
RL (ns)	Revue légale (nouvelle série)	Can (QC)
RNB (2d)*	Recueil des arrêts du Nouveau Brunswick (deuxième série) (1825-1928 : voir *New Brunswick Reports*)	Can (NB)
Rob / Rob Chr	Robinson, C's Reports (ER vol 165)	UK / R-U
Rob Ecc	Robertson's Ecclesiastical Reports (ER vol 163)	UK / R-U
Rolle	Rolle's Reports (ER vol 81)	UK / R-U
RONTC	Recueil des décisions de l'office national des transports du Canada	Can
Roscoe	Roscoe's Reports	S Afr / Afr du sud
RPC	Reports of Patent Cases	UK / R-U
RPC	Reports of Patent, Design and Trademark Cases	UK / R-U
RPEI	Reports of cases determined in the Supreme Court, Court of Chancery, and Court of Vice-Admiralty of Prince Edward Island	Can (PE)
RPQ	Rapports de pratique de Québec	Can (QC)
RPR	Real Property Reports	Can
RPR (2d)	Real Property Reports (Second Series)	Can
RPR (3d)	Real Property Reports (Third Series)	Can
RPTA	Recueil en matière de protection du territoire agricole	Can (QC)
RR	Revised Reports	UK / R-U
RRA	Recueil en responsabilité et assurance	Can (QC)
RS	Recueil Sirey	France
RSA	Recueil de sentences arbitrales	Intl
RSA	Recueil de sentences arbitrales	Can (QC)
RSE	Recueil des sentences de l'éducation	Can (QC)
RSF	Recueil de jurisprudence en droit des successions et des fiducies	Can

RSF (2e)	Recueil de jurisprudence en droit des successions et des fiducies (deuxième série)	Can
RSF (3e)	Recueil de jurisprudence en droit des successions et des fiducies (troisième série)	Can
RSP	Recueil des ordonnances de la régie des services publics	Can (QC)
RTC	Décisions et énoncés de politique sur la radiodiffusion et les télécommunications canadiennes	Can
Russ	Russell's Reports (ER vol 38)	UK / R-U
Russ & M	Russell & Mylne's Reports (ER vol 39)	UK / R-U
Russ & Ry	Russell & Ryan's Crown Cases (ER vol 168)	UK / R-U
Russ ER	Russell's Election Reports	Can (NS)
S Afr LR	South African Law Reports	S Afr / Afr du sud
S Ct	Supreme Court Reporter	US / É-U
SAFP	Sentences arbitrales de la fonction publique	Can (QC)
SAG	Sentences arbitrales de griefs	Can (QC)
Salk	Salkeld's Reports (ER vol 91)	UK / R-U
SALR	South Australia Law Reports	Austl
SARB Dec	Social Assistance Review Board Selected Decisions	Can (ON)
SARB Sum	Social Assistance Review Board Summaries of Decisions	Can (ON)
Sarbah	Sarbah's Fanti Law Reports	Ghana
Sask C Comp B	Saskatchewan Crimes Compensation Board, Awards	Can (SK)
Sask Human Rights Comm'n Dec	Saskatchewan Human Rights Commission Decisions	Can (SK)
Sask LR*	Saskatchewan Law Reports	Can (SK)
Sask LRBD	Saskatchewan Labour Relations Board Decisions	Can (SK)
Sask LRBDC	Saskatchewan Labour Relations Board, Decisions and Court Cases	Can (SK)
Sask LRBR	Saskatchewan Labour Relations Board, Report of Meetings	Can (SK)
Sask R*	Saskatchewan Reports	Can
Sask SC Bull	Saskatchewan Securities Commission Monthly Bulletin	Can (SK)
SASR	South Australia State Reports	Austl (SA)
Sav	Savile's Reports (ER vol 123)	UK / R-U
Say	Sayer's Reports (ER vol 96)	UK / R-U
SCC Cam	Canada Supreme Court Cases (Cameron) (Published / publié 1918)	Can
SCC Cam (2d)	Canada Supreme Court Reports (Cameron) (Published / publié 1925)	Can
SCC Coutl	Canada Supreme Court Cases (Coutlée)	Can
SCCB	Supreme Court of Canada Bulletin of Proceedings	Can

SCCD	Supreme Court of Canada Decisions	Can
SCCR	Supreme Court of Canada Reports Service	Can
SCJ	Supreme Court of Canada Judgments (QL)	Can
Scot LR	Scottish Law Reporter	Scot / Écosse
SCR*	Canada Law Reports: Supreme Court of Canada	Can
SCR*	Canada Supreme Court Reports	Can
SE	South Eastern Reporter	US / É-U
SE (2d)	South Eastern Reporter (Second Series)	US / É-U
Searle	Searle's Reports	S Afr / Afr du sud
SEC Dec	Securities and Exchange Commission Decisions	US / É-U
Sel Ca t King	Select Cases, temp King (ER vol 25)	UK / R-U
Sem Jur	Semaine Juridique	France
Sess Cas	Session Cases	UK / R-U
Sess Cas	Session Cases	Scot / Écosse
Sess Cas D	Session Cases (Second Series) (Dunlop)	Scot / Écosse
Sess Cas F	Session Cases (Fifth Series) (Fraser)	Scot / Écosse
Sess Cas M	Session Cases (Third Series) (Macpherson)	Scot / Écosse
Sess Cas R	Session Cases (Fourth Series) (Rettie)	Scot / Écosse
Sess Cas S	Session Cases (Shaw & Balantine)	Scot / Écosse
Show KB	Shower's Reports, King's Bench (ER vol 89)	UK / R-U
Show PC	Shower's Reports, Privy Council (ER vol 1)	UK / R-U
Sid	Siderfin's Reports, King's Bench (ER vol 82)	UK / R-U
Sim	Simons's Reports (ER vols 57-60)	UK / R-U
Sim (NS)	Simons's New Reports (ER vol 61)	UK / R-U
Sim & St	Simons & Stuart's Reports (ER vol 57)	UK / R-U
SJ	Saskatchewan Judgments (QL)	Can (SK)
SLLR	Sierra Leone Law Reports	Sierra Leone
SLR	Singapore Law Reports	Sing
SLR (R)	Singapore Law Reports (Reissue)	Sing
SLT	Scots Law Times	Scot / Écosse
Skin	Skinner's Reports (ER vol 90)	UK / R-U
Sm & G	Smale & Giffard's Reports (ER vol 65)	UK / R-U
Sm & S	Smith and Sager's Drainage Cases	Can (ON)
SNB & B	Sarawak, North Borneo and Brunei Supreme Court Reports	Malay
So	Southern Reporter	US / É-U

So (2d)	Southern Reporter (Second Series)	US / É-U
So (3d)	Southern Reporter (Third Series)	US / É-U
SOLR	Sexual Offences Law Reporter	Can
Sp Ecc & Ad	Spinks's Ecclesiastical & Admiralty Reports (ER vol 164)	UK / R-U
Sp PC	Spinks' Prize Court Cases (ER vol 164)	UK / R-U
SRLA	Speakers' Rulings, Legislative Assembly	Can (NB)
SSC	Sarawak Supreme Court Reports	Malay
SSLR	Straits Settlements Law Reports	Sing
St-MSD	Saint-Maurice's Speakers' Decisions	Can (QC)
Stark	Starkie's Reports (ER vol 171)	UK / R-U
Stewart	Stewart's Vice-Admiralty Reports	Can (NS)
Stockton	Stockton's Vice-Admiralty Reports	Can (NB)
Str	Strange's Reports (ER vol 93)	UK / R-U
STR	Canadian Sales Tax Reporter	Can
Stu Adm	Stuart's Vice-Admiralty Reports (Lower Canada)	Can (QC)
Stu KB	Stuart's Reports (Lower Canada)	Can (QC)
Sty	Style's Reports (ER vol 82)	UK / R-U
Sudan LR	Sudan Law Reports	Sudan
SW	South Western Reporter	US / É-U
SW (2d)	South Western Reporter (Second Series)	US / É-U
SW (3d)	South Western Reporter (Third Series)	US / ÉU
Sw & Tr	Swabey & Tristram's Reports (ER vol 164)	UK / R-U
Swab	Swabey's Reports (ER vol 166)	UK / R-U
Swans	Swanston's Reports (ER vol 36)	UK / R-U
TA	Décisions du Tribunal d'arbitrage	Can (QC)
TAAT	Tribunal d'appel des accidents du travail	Can (ON)
Talb	Talbot's Cases temp (ER vol 25)	UK / R-U
Taml	Tamlyn's Reports (ER vol 48)	UK / R-U
TAQ	Décisions du Tribunal administratif du Québec	Can (QC)
Tas LR	Tasmanian Law Reports	Austl (Tas)
Tas R	Tasmania Reports	Austl (Tas)
Tas SR	Tasmania State Reports	Austl (Tas)
Taun	Taunton's Reports (ER vols 127-129)	UK / R-U
Tax ABC	Tax Appeal Board Cases	Can
Tax ABC (NS)	Tax Appeal Board Cases (New Series)	Can

TBR	Tariff Board Reports	Can
TBRD	Taxation Board of Review Decisions	Austl
TBRD (NS)	Taxation Board Review Decisions (New Series)	Austl
TCD	Tribunal de la concurrence, décisions	Can
TCJ	Tax Court of Canada Judgments (QL)	Can
TCT	Canadian Trade and Commodity Tax Cases	Can
TE	Recueils de jurisprudence du tribunal de l'expropriation	Can (QC)
Terr LR*	Territories Law Reports	Can (NT)
TJ*	Recueils de jurisprudence du Québec : Tribunal de la jeunesse	Can (QC)
TLLR	Tenant and Landlord Law Repors	Can (ON)
TLR	Times Law Reports	UK / R-U
TMR	Trademark Reporter	US / É-U
Toth	Tothill's Reports (ER vol 21)	UK / R-U
TPEI	Tucker's Select Cases of Prince Edward Island	Can (PE)
TR	Term Reports (ER vols 99-101)	UK / R-U
TSPAAT	Tribunal d'appel de la sécurité professionnelle et de l'assurance contre les accidents du travail	Can (ON)
TT	Tribunal du travail	Can (QC)
TTC	Hunter's Torrens Title Cases	Austl, Can, NZ N-Z, UK R-U
TTR	Trade and Tariff Reports	Can
TTR (2d)	Trade and Tarrif Reports (Second Series)	Can
Turn & R	Turner & Russell's Reports, Chancery (ER vol 37)	UK / R-U
UC Ch	Grant's Upper Canada Chancery Reports	Can (ON)
UC Chamb Rep	Upper Canada Chambers Reports	Can (ON)
UCCP	Upper Canada Common Pleas Reports	Can (ON)
UCE & A	Upper Canada Error and Appeal Reports (Grant)	Can (ON)
UCKB	Upper Canada King's Bench Report (Old Series)	Can (ON)
UCQB	Upper Canada Queen's Bench Reports (New Series)	Can (ON)
UCQB (OS)	Upper Canada Queen's Bench Reports (Old Series)	Can (ON)
Uganda LR	Uganda Law Reports	Uganda
US	United States Reports	US / É-U
US App DC	United States Court of Appeals Reports	US / É-U
USLW	United States Law Week	US / É-U
Vaugh	Vaughan's Reports (ER vol 124)	UK / R-U

Vent	Ventris' Reports (ER vol 86)	UK / R-U
Vern	Vernon's Reports (ER vol 23)	UK / R-U
Ves & Bea	Vesey & Beames' Reports (ER vol 35)	UK / R-U
Ves Jr	Vesey Junior's Reports (ER vols 30-34)	UK / R-U
Ves Sr	Vesey Senior's Reports (ER vols 27-28)	UK / R-U
VLR	Victorian Law Reports	Austl (Vic)
VR	Victorian Reports	Austl (Vic)
W Rob	W Robinson's Reports (ER vol 166)	UK / R-U
WAC	Western Appeal Cases	Can
WALR	Western Australia Law Reports	Austl (WA)
WAR	Western Australia Reports	Austl (WA)
WAR (NS)	Western Australia Reports (New Series)	Austl (WA)
WCAT Dec	Workers' Compensation Appeal Tribunal Decisions	Can (NL)
WCATR	Workers' Compensation Appeals Tribunal Reporter	Can (ON)
WCB	Weekly Criminal Bulletin	Can
WCB (2d)	Weekly Criminal Bulletin (Second Series)	Can
WDCP	Weekly Digest of Civil Procedure	Can
WDCP (2d)	Weekly Digest of Civil Procedure (Second Series)	Can
WDFL	Weekly Digest of Family Law	Can
Welsb H & G	Welsby, Hurlstone & Gordon's Exchequer Reports (ER vols 154-156)	UK / R-U
West	West's Reports (ER vol 9)	UK / R-U
West's Alaska (2d)	West's Alaska Digest (Second Series)	US / É-U
West, t Hard	West, temp Hardwicke Reports (ER vol 25)	UK / R-U
Wight	Wightwick's Reports (ER vol 145)	UK / R-U
Will Woll & H	Willmore, Wollaston & Hodges's Reports	UK / R-U
Willes	Willes's Reports (ER vol 125)	UK / R-U
Wilm	Wilmot's Reports (ER vol 97)	UK / R-U
Wils Ch	Wilson's Reports, Chancery (ER vol 37)	UK / R-U
Wils Ex	Wilson's Reports, Exchequer (ER vol 159)	UK / R-U
Wils KB	Wilson's Reports, King's Bench (ER vol 95)	UK / R-U
Winch	Winch's Reports (ER vol 124)	UK / R-U
WLAC	Western Labour Arbitration Cases	Can
WLR	Weekly Law Reports	UK / R-U
WLR	Western Law Reporter	Can

WLRBD	Canadian Wartime Labour Relations Board Decisions	Can
WLTR	Western Law Times and Reports	Can
Wms Saund	Williams' & Saunders's Reports (ER vol 85)	UK / R-U
WSIATR	Workplace Safety and Insurance Appeals Tribunal Reporter	Can (ON)
WWR*	Western Weekly Reports	Can
WWR (NS)*	Western Weekly Reports (New Series)	Can
Wyatt W & A'B	Wyatt, Webb & A'Beckett's Reports (Supreme Court of Victoria)	Austl
Y & C CC	Younge & Collyer's Chancery Cases (ER vols 62-63)	UK / R-U
Y & C Ex	Younge & Collyer's Reports (ER vol 160)	UK / R-U
Y & J	Younge & Jervis's Reports (ER vol 148)	UK / R-U
YAD	Young's Admiralty Decisions	Can (NS)
YB Eur Conv HR	Yearbook of the European Convention on Human Rights	EU / UE
YJ	British Columbia and Yukon Judgments (QL)	Can (YT)
Yel	Yelverton's Reports (ER vol 80)	UK / R-U
You	Younge's Reports (ER vol 159)	UK / R-U
YR*	Yukon Reports	Can (YT)

APPENDIX D / ANNEXE D

D. PERIODICALS AND YEARBOOKS ~ PÉRIODIQUES ET ANNUAIRES

Abbreviations ~ Abréviations

Name of Periodical or Yearbook / Nom du périodique ou de l'annuaire	**Abbreviation / Abréviations**
Actualité et droit international	Actu & dr int
Actualités du droit	Actu du dr
Actualités juridiques, droit administratif	Actu jur dr admin
Adelaide Law Review	Adel L Rev
Adelphia Law Journal	Adelphia LJ
Administrative and Regulatory Law News	Admin & Reg L News
Administrative Law Journal of the American University *(formerly / anciennement Administrative Law Journal)*	Admin LJ Am U
Administrative Law Review	Admin L Rev
Advocate (Idaho)	Advocate (Idaho)
Advocate (Vancouver)	Advocate
Advocates' Journal	Adv J
Advocates' Quarterly	Adv Q
African-American Law and Policy Report	Afr-Am L & Pol'y Rep
Air & Space Law	Air & Space L
Air & Space Lawyer	Air & Space Lawyer
Air Force Law Review	AFL Rev
Akron Law Review	Akron L Rev
Akron Tax Journal	Akron Tax J
Alabama Law Review	Ala L Rev
Alaska Law Review	Alaska L Rev
Albany Law Environmental Outlook	Alb L Envtl Outlook
Albany Law Journal of Science & Technology	Alb LJ Sci & Tech
Albany Law Review	Alb L Rev
Alberta Law Quarterly	Alta L Q
Alberta Law Review	Alta L Rev
Alternatives Journal	Alt J
American Association of Law Libraries Spectrum	AALL Spec

American Bankruptcy Institute Journal	Am Bankr Inst J
American Bankruptcy Institute Law Review	Am Bankr Inst L Rev
American Bankruptcy Law Journal	Am Bank LJ
American Bar Association Antitrust Law Journal	ABA Antitrust LJ
American Bar Association Criminal Justice	ABA Criminal Justice
American Bar Association Entertainment & Sports Lawyer	ABA Ent & Sports Lawyer
American Bar Association Family Advocate	ABA Fam Advocate
American Bar Association Family Law Quarterly	ABA Fam LQ
American Bar Association Journal	ABA J
American Bar Association Law Practice Management	ABA LPM
American Bar Association Section of Intellectual Property Law	ABAIPL
American Bar Association Tort and Insurance Law Journal	ABA Tort & Ins LJ
American Business Law Journal	Am Bus LJ
American Criminal Law Review	Am Crim L Rev
American Indian Law Review	Am Indian L Rev
American Intellectual Property Law Association Quarterly Journal	AIPLA QJ
American Journal of Comparative Law	Am J Comp L
American Journal of Criminal Law	Am J Crim L
American Journal of International Arbitration	Am J Intl Arb
American Journal of International Law	AJIL / Am J Intl L
American Journal of Jurisprudence	Am J Juris
American Journal of Law & Medicine	Am J L & Med
American Journal of Legal History	Am J Leg Hist
American Journal of Tax Policy	Am J Tax Pol'y
American Journal of Trial Advocacy	Am J Trial Advoc
American Law and Economics Review	Am L & Econ Rev
American Review of International Arbitration	Am Rev Intl Arb
American University International Law Review (*formerly / anciennement American University Journal of International Law & Policy*)	Am U Intl L Rev
American University Journal of Gender, Social Policy and the Law (*formerly / anciennement American University Journal of Gender and the Law*)	Am UJ Gender Soc Pol'y & L
American University Journal of International Law and Policy	Am U J Intl L & Pol'y
American University Law Review	Am U L Rev
Analyse de politiques (*Canadian Public Policy*)	Analyse de pol
Anglo-American Law Review	Anglo-Am L Rev

Animal Law	Animal L
Annales de droit aérien et spacial	Ann dr aér & spat
Annales de droit de Louvain	Ann dr Louv
Annales de l'Université des sciences sociales de Toulouse	Ann de l'UssT
Annales de la propriété industrielle artistique et littéraire	Ann pr ind art & lit
Annals of Air and Space Law	Ann Air & Sp L
Annals of Health Law	Ann Health L
Annuaire canadien de droit international	ACDI
Annuaire canadien des droits de la personne	ACDP
Annuaire de droit aérien et spatial	Ann dr aér & spat
Annuaire de droit maritime et aérien	Ann dr marit & aér
Annuaire de droit maritime et aéro-spatial	Ann dr marit & aéro-spat
Annuaire de l'Institut de droit international	Ann inst dr int
Annuaire de la Convention européenne des droits de l'Homme	Ann Conv eur DH
Annuaire de la Haye de droit international	Ann Haye dr int
Annuaire de la Société des Nations	Ann SN
Annuaire français de droit international	AFDI
Annuaire français des droits de l'Homme	Ann fr DH
Annuaire français du transport aérien	Ann fr transp aér
Annuaire de la Société française de droit aérien et spatial	Ann S fr dr aér & spat
Annuaire de législation étrangère	Ann lég étrang
Annuaire de législation française	Ann lég fr
Annuaire des collectivités locales	Ann coll loc
Annuaire de philosophie de droit	Ann phil dr
Annuaire des Nations Unies	Ann NU
Annuaire international de justice constitutionnelle	Ann int j const
Annuaire suisse de droit international	Ann suisse dr int
Annual Survey of American Law	Ann Surv Am L
Annual Survey of Australian Law	Ann Surv Austl L
Annual Survey of Commonwealth Law	Ann Surv Commonwealth L
Annual Survey of English Law	Ann Surv Engl L
Annual Survey of International & Comparative Law	Ann Surv Intl & Comp L
Annual Survey of South African Law	Ann Surv S Afr L
Antitrust Law and Economics Review	Antitrust L & Econ Rev
Antitrust Law Journal	Antitrust LJ

Appeal: Review of Current Law and Law Reform	Appeal
Arab Law Quarterly	Arab LQ
Arbitration International	Arb Intl
Arizona Journal of International and Comparative Law	Ariz J Intl & Comp L
Arizona Law Review	Ariz L Rev
Arizona State Law Journal	Ariz St LJ
Arkansas Law Review	Ark L Rev
Art, Antiquity, and the Law	Art Ant & L
Artificial Intelligence and Law	AI & L
Asia-Pacific Journal of Environmental Law	Asia Pac J Envtl L
Asia-Pacific Journal of Human Rights and the Law	Asia Pac J HR & L
Asia-Pacific Journal of International Law	Asia Pac J Intl L
Asia-Pacific Law Review	Asia Pac L Rev
Asian Law Journal	Asian LJ
Asian-Pacific American Law Journal *(formerly / anciennement Asian American Pacific Islands Law Journal)*	Asian Pac Am LJ
Asian-Pacific Law & Policy Journal	Asian Pac L & Pol'y J
Auckland University Law Review	Auckland UL Rev
Australian and New Zealand Journal of Criminology	Austl & NZ J Crim
Australian Bar Review	Austl Bar Rev
Australian Business Law Review	Austl Bus L Rev
Australian Competition and Consumer Law Journal	Austl Competition & Cons LJ
Austalian Insurance Law Journal	Austl Ins LJ
Australian Journal of Contract Law	Austl J Contract L
Australian Journal of Corporate Law	Austl J Corp L
Australian Journal of Family Law	Austl J Fam L
Australian Journal of Human Rights	Austl J H R
Australian Journal of Labour Law	Austl J Lab L
Australian Journal of Legal History	Austl J Leg Hist
Australian Law Journal	Austl LJ
Australian Property Law Journal	Austl Prop LJ
Australian Torts Law Journal	Austl Torts LJ
Austrian Journal of Public and International Law	Aus J Pub & Intl L
Austrian Review of International and European Law	Aus Rev Intl & Eur L
Baltimore Law Review	Baltimore L Rev

Banking and Finance Law Review	BFLR
Banking and Financial Services Policy Report: A Journal on Trends in Regulation and Supervision (*formerly / anciennement Banking Policy Report*)	Banking & Fin Serv Pol'y Rep
Banking Law Journal	Banking LJ
Banque et droit	B & dr
Baylor Law Review	Baylor L Rev
Behavioural Sciences and the Law	Behav Sci & L
Bench and Bar	B Bar
Berkeley Journal of African-American Law and Policy (*formerly / anciennement African-American Law and Policy Report*)	Berkeley J Afr-Am L & Pol'y
Berkeley Journal of Employment and Labour Law	BJELL
Berkeley Journal of Gender Law and Justice (*formerly / anciennement Berkeley Women's Law Journal*)	Berkeley Women's LJ / Berkeley J Gender L & Just
Berkeley Journal of Health Care Law	Berkeley J Health Care L
Berkeley Journal of International Law	BJIL
Berkeley Technology Law Journal	BTLJ
Berkeley Women's Law Journal	Berkeley Women's LJ
Biotechnology Law Report	Biotech L Rep
Boston Bar Journal	Boston Bar J
Boston College Environmental Affairs Law Review	Boston College Envtl Aff L Rev
Boston College International and Comparative Law Review	Boston College Intl & Comp L Rev
Boston College Journal of Law & Social Justice (*formerly / anciennement Boston College Third World Law Journal*)	Boston College JL & Soc Just
Boston College Law Review	Boston College L Rev
Boston College Third World Law Journal	Boston College Third World LJ
Boston University International Law Journal	BU ILJ
Boston University Journal of Science and Technology Law	BUJ Sci & Tech L
Boston University Journal of Tax Law	BUJ Tax L
Boston University Law Review	BUL Rev
Boston University Public Interest Law Journal	BU PILJ
Brandeis Law Journal	Brandeis LJ
Brigham Young University Education and Law Journal	BYU Educ & LJ
Brigham Young University Law Review	BYUL Rev
British Columbia Law Notes	BCLN
British Institute of International and Comparative Law	Brit Inst Intl & Comp L
British Journal of Criminology	Brit J Crim

British Medical Journal	Brit Med J
British Tax Review	Brit Tax Rev
British Yearbook of International Law	Brit YB Intl L
Brooklyn Journal of International Law	Brook J Intl L
Brooklyn Law Review	Brook L Rev
Buffalo Criminal Law Review	Buff Crim L Rev
Buffalo Environmental Law Journal	Buff Envtl LJ
Buffalo Human Rights Law Review	Buff HRL Rev
Buffalo Law Review	Buff L Rev
Buffalo Public Interest Law Journal	Buff Pub Int LJ
Buffalo Women's Law Journal	Buff Women's LJ
Bulletin canadien VIH-SIDA et droit	Bull can VIH-SIDA & D
Bulletin of International Legal Developments (*formerly / anciennement Bulletin of Legal Developments*)	Bull Intl Leg Dev
Business Law Review	Bus L Rev
Business Lawyer	Bus Lawyer
BYU Journal of Public Law	BYUJ Pub L
Cahiers de droit	C de D
Cahiers de droit de l'entreprise	C de D entr
Cahiers de droit européen	C de D eur
Cahiers de l'Institut québécois d'administration judiciaire	CIQAJ
Cahiers de propriété intellectuelle	CPI
California Bankruptcy Journal	Cal Bankr J
California Criminal Law Review	Cal Crim L Rev
California Law Review	Cal L Rev
California Regulatory Law Reporter	Cal Reg L Rep
California State Bar Journal	Cal St Bar J
California Western International Law Journal	Cal W Int' LJ
California Western Law Review	Cal WL Rev
Cambridge Law Journal	Cambridge LJ
Cambridge Yearbook of European Legal Studies	Cambridge YB Eur Leg Stud
Campbell Law Review	Campbell L Rev
Canada-United States Law Journal	Can-USLJ
Canadian Bar Association Papers	CBA Papers
Canada Law Journal	Can LJ

Canadian Bar Association Year Book	CBAYB
Canadian Bar Journal	Can Bar J
Canadian Bar Review	Can Bar Rev
Canadian Bioethics Report	Can Bioethics R
Canadian Business Law Journal	Can Bus LJ
Canadian Business Review	Can Bus Rev
Canadian Class Action Review	Can Class Action Rev
Canadian Communications Law Review	Can Comm L Rev
Canadian Community Law Journal	Can Community LJ
Canadian Competition Law Review (*formerly / anciennement Canadian Competition Policy Record)*	Can Competition L Rev
Canadian Competition Policy Record	Can Competition Pol'y Rec
Canadian Competition Record *(formerly / anciennement Canadian Competition Policy Record)*	Can Competition Rec
Canadian Council on International Law (Proceedings)	Can Council Intl L Proc
Canadian Criminal Law Review	Can Crim L Rev
Canadian Criminology Forum	Can Crim Forum
Canadian Current Tax	Can Curr Tax
Canadian Environmental Law News	Can Envtl L News
Canadian Family Law Quarterly	Can Fam LQ
Canadian HIV/AIDS Policy and Law Review	Can HIV/AIDS Pol'y & L Rev
Canadian Human Rights Advocate	Can HR Advoc
Canadian Human Rights Yearbook	Can Hum Rts YB
Canadian Intellectual Property Review	CIPR
Canadian International Lawyer	Can Intl Lawyer
Canadian Journal of Administrative Law and Practice	Can J Admin L & Prac
Canadian Journal of Criminology	Can J Crim
Canadian Journal of Criminology and Corrections	Can J Crim & Corr
Canadian Journal of Criminology and Criminal Justice (*formerly / anciennement Canadian Journal of Corrections, Canadian Journal of Criminology and Criminal Justice and Corrections*)	Can J Corr
Canadian Journal of Family Law	Can J Fam L
Canadian Journal of Insurance Law	Can J Ins L
Canadian Journal of International Business Law and Policy	Can J Intl Bus L & Pol'y
Canadian Journal of Law and Jurisprudence	Can JL & Jur
Canadian Journal of Law and Society	CJLS

Canadian Journal of Law and Technology	CJLT
Canadian Journal of Women and the Law	CJWL
Canadian Labour and Employment Law Journal	CLELJ
Canadian Law Library Review (*formerly / anciennement Canadian Law Libraries*)	Can L Libr Rev
Canadian Law Review	Can L Rev
Canadian Law Times	Can LT
Canadian Lawyer	Can Lawyer
Canadian Legal Studies	Can Legal Stud
Canadian Medical Association Journal	CMAJ
Canadian Municipal Journal	Can Mun J
Canadian Native Law Bulletin	Can NL Bull
Canadian Public Policy	Can Pub Pol'y
Canadian Tax Foundation (Conference Report / Rapport de conférence)	Can Tax Found
Canadian Tax Highlights	Can Tax Highlights
Canadian Tax Journal	Can Tax J
Canadian Tax News	Can Tax N
Canadian Taxation: A Journal of Tax Policy	Can Tax'n
Canadian Yearbook of International Law	Can YB Intl Law
Capital University Law Review	Capital UL Rev
Cardozo Arts and Entertainment Law Journal	Cardozo Arts & Ent LJ
Cardozo Electronic Law Bulletin	Cardozo EL Bull
Cardozo Journal of International and Comparative Law *(formerly / anciennement New Europe Law Review)*	Cardozo J Intl & Comp L
Cardozo Journal of Law and Gender (*formerly / anciennement Cardozo Women's Law Journal*)	Cardozo J L & Gender
Cardozo Law Review	Cardozo L Rev
Cardozo Studies in Law and Literature	Cardozo Stud L & Lit
Caribbean Law Review	Caribbean L Rev
Carolina Law Journal	Carolina LJ
Case Western Reserve Journal of International Law	Case W Res J Intl L
Case Western Reserve Law Review	Case W Res L Rev
Catholic University Law Review	Cath U L Rev
Chapman Law Review	Chapman L Rev
Chicago Journal of International Law	Chicago J Intl L
Chicago Lawyer	Chicago Lawyer

Chicago-Kent Law Review	Chicagio-Kent L Rev
Chicano-Latino Law Review *(formerly / anciennement Chicano Law Review)*	Chicano-Latino L Rev
Children's Legal Rights Journal	Child Leg Rts J
China Law Reporter	China L Rep
Chinese Yearbook of International Law and Affairs	Chinese YB Intl L & Aff
Chitty's Law Journal	Chitty's LJ
Civil Justice Quarterly	CJQ
Civil Liberties Review	Civ Lib Rev
Cleveland State Law Review	Clev St L Rev
Cleveland-Marshall Law Review	Clev-Marshall L Rev
Clinical Law Review	Clinical L Rev
Coastal Management	Coastal Mgmt
Colorado Journal of International Environmental Law & Policy	Colo J Intl Envtl L & Pol'y
Colorado Lawyer	Colo Lawyer
Columbia Business Law Review	Colum Bus L Rev
Columbia Human Rights Law Review	Colum HRLR
Columbia Journal of Asian Law *(formerly / anciennement Journal of Chinese Law)*	Colum J Asian Law
Columbia Journal of East European Law	Colum J E Eur L
Columbia Journal of Environmental Law	Colum J Envtl L
Columbia Journal of European Law	Colum J Eur L
Columbia Journal of Gender and Law	Colum J Gender & L
Columbia Journal of Law and Social Problems	Colum JL & Soc Probs
Columbia Journal of Law and the Arts	Colum J L & Arts
Columbia Journal of Transnational Law	Colum J Transnat'l L
Columbia Law Review	Colum L Rev
Columbia Science and Technology Law Review	Colum Sci & Tech L Rev
Commercial Law Journal	Com LJ
Commercial Leasing Law and Strategy	Com Leasing L & Strategy
Common Law World Review	Comm L World Rev
Common Market Law Review	CML Rev
Commonwealth Law Bulletin	Commonwealth L Bull
Commonwealth Legal Education	Commonwealth Leg Educ
Communication Law & Policy	Comm L & Pol'y
Communications Lawyer	Comm Lawyer

Comparative and International Law Journal of Southern Africa	Comp & Intl LJS Afr
Comparative Juridical Review	Comp Jurid Rev
Comparative Labor Law and Policy Journal *(formerly / anciennement Comparative Labor Law Journal)*	Comp Lab L & Pol'y J
Computer Law and Security Report	Computer L & Sec Report
Computer Law Review and Technology Journal	Computer L Rev & Tech J
Computer Lawyer	Computer Lawyer
Congressional Digest	Cong Dig
Connecticut Bar Journal	Conn Bar J
Connecticut Insurance Law Journal	Conn Ins LJ
Connecticut Journal of International Law	Conn J Intl L
Connecticut Public Interest Law Journal	Conn Pub Int LJ
Connecticut Probate Law Journal	Conn Prob LJ
Connecticut Law Review	Conn L Rev
Constitutional Commentary	Const Commentary
Constitutional Forum Constitutionnel	Const Forum Const
Construction Law Journal	Construction LJ
Construction Lawyer	Construction Lawyer
Consumer Finance Law Quarterly Report	Cons Fin LQ Rep
Cooley Law Review	Cooley L Rev
Copyright Bulletin	Copyright Bull
Cornell International Law Journal	Cornell Intl LJ
Cornell Journal of Law & Public Policy	Cornell JL & Pub Pol'y
Cornell Law Review	Cornell L Rev
Corporate Taxation	Corp Tax'n
Cours de perfectionnement du notariat	CP du N
Creighton Law Review	Creighton L Rev
Crime, Law and Social Change	Crime L & Soc Change
Criminal Law Forum	Crim LF
Criminal Law Quarterly	Crim LQ
Criminal Law Review	Crim L Rev
Criminologie	Criminol
Critical Criminology	Crit Criminol
Croatian Arbitration Yearbook	Croatian Arb YB
Croatian Critical Law Review	Croat Crit L Rev

Cumberland Law Review	Cumb L Rev
Current Law Yearbook	Current LYB
Current Legal Problems	Current Leg Probs
Currents: International Trade Law Journal	Currents: Intl Trade LJ
Dalhousie Journal of Legal Studies	Dal J Leg Stud
Dalhousie Law Journal	Dal LJ
Defense Counsel Journal	Def Couns J
Delaware Journal of Corporate Law	Del J Corp L
Delaware Law Review	Del L Rev
Denver Journal of International Law & Policy	Denv J Intl L & Pol'y
Denver University Law Review *(formerly / anciennement Denver Law Journal)*	Denv UL Rev
Department of State Bulletin	Dep't St Bull
DePaul Business & Commercial Law Journal (*formerly / anciennement DePaul Business Law Journal*)	DePaul Bus & Comm LJ
DePaul Journal of Health Care Law	DePaul J Health Care L
DePaul Law Review	DePaul L Rev
DePaul-LCA Journal of Art and Entertainment Law and Policy	DePaul-LCA J Art & Ent L & Pol'y
Dickinson Journal of Environmental Law & Policy	Dick J Envtl L & Pol'y
Dickinson Journal of International Law	Dick J Intl L
Dickinson Law Review	Dick L Rev
Dispute Resolution Journal *(formerly / anciennement Arbitration Journal)*	Disp Resol J
District of Columbia Law Review	DCL Rev
Drake Journal of Agricultural Law	Drake J Agric L
Drake Law Review	Drake L Rev
Droit africain du travail	DAT
Droit des sociétés	Dr soc
Droit et cultures	Dr et cult
Droit et patrimoine	Dr et pat
Droit et société	Dr et soc
Droit européen des transports	Dr eur transp
Droit maritime français	Dr marit fr
Droit social	Dr social
Duke Environmental Law & Policy Forum	Duke Envtl L & Pol'y F
Duke Journal of Comparative & International Law	Duke J Comp & Intl L
Duke Journal of Gender Law & Policy	Duke J Gender L & Pol'y

Duke Law and Technology Review	Duke L & Tech Rev
Duke Law Journal	Duke LJ
Duquesne Business Law Journal	Duq Bus LJ
Duquesne Law Review	Duq L Rev
East European Business Law	E Eur Bus L
East European Constitutional Review	E Eur Const Rev
East European Human Rights Review	E Eur HR Rev
Ecology Law Quarterly	Ecology LQ
Edinburgh Law Review	Ed L Rev
Education & Law Journal	Educ & LJ
Elder Law Journal	Elder LJ
Election Law Journal	Election LJ
Electronic Journal of Comparative Law	Electronic J Comp L
Emory Bankruptcy Developments Journal	Emory Bankr Dev J
Emory International Law Review *(formerly / anciennement Emory Journal of International Dispute Resolution)*	Emory Intl L Rev
Emory Law Journal	Emory LJ
Employee Rights & Employment Policy Journal	Employee Rts & Employment Pol'y J
Energy Law Journal	Energy LJ
Entertainment & Sports Lawyer	Ent & Sports Lawyer
Entertainment Law & Finance	Ent L & Fin
Environmental Law	Envtl L
Environmental Law and Management	Envtl L & Mgmt
Environmental Law and Policy Journal	Envtl L & Pol'y J
Environmental Law Journal	Envtl LJ
Environmental Lawyer	Envtl Lawyer
Environmental Policy and Law	Envtl Pol'y & L
Environs: Environmental Law and Policy Journal	Environs
Estates, Trusts and Pensions Journal (*formerly / anciennement Estates and Trusts Journal*)	Est Tr & Pensions J
Estates and Trusts Journal (*formerly / anciennement Estates and Trusts Quarterly*)	Est & Tr J
Estates and Trusts Quarterly	E & TQ
Estates Trusts & Pensions Journal	ETPJ
Études internationales	Études int

European Business Law Review	Eur Bus L Rev
European Competition Law Review	Eur Competition L Rev
European Environmental Law Review	Eur Envtl L Rev
European Human Rights Law Review	Eur HRL Rev
European Intellectual Property Review	Eur IP Rev
European Journal for Education Law and Policy	Eur J Educ L & Pol'y
European Journal of Crime, Criminal Law, and Criminal Justice	Eur J Crime, Crim L & Crim J
European Journal of Criminal Policy & Research	Eur J Crim Pol'y & Research
European Journal of Health Law	Eur J Health L
European Journal of International Law	Eur J Intl L
European Journal of Law & Economics	Eur J L & Econ
European Journal of Law Reform	Eur J L Reform
European Journal of Migration and Law	Eur J Migr & L
European Journal of Social Security	Eur J Soc Sec
European Law Journal	Eur LJ
European Law Review	Eur L Rev
European Legal Forum	Eur Leg F
European Review of Private Law	Eur R Priv L
European Transport Law	Eur Transp L
Family Court Review *(formerly / anciennement Family & Conciliation Courts Review)*	Fam Ct Rev
Family Law Quarterly	Fam LQ
Family Law Review	Fam L Rev
Federal Bar News and Journal	Fed B News & J
Federal Circuit Bar Journal	Fed Cir BJ
Federal Communications Law Journal	Fed Comm LJ
Federal Courts Law Review	Fed Cts L Rev
Feminist Legal Studies	Fem Leg Stud
Florida Bar Journal	Fla BJ
Florida Coastal Law Review	Fla Coastal L Rev
Florida Journal of International Law	Fla J Intl L
Florida Law Review *(formerly / anciennement University of Florida Law Review)*	Fla L Rev
Florida State Journal of Transnational Law & Policy	Fla St J Transnat'l L & Pol'y
Florida State University Journal of Land Use & Environmental Law	Fla St UJ Land Use & Envtl L

Florida State University Law Review	Fla St UL Rev
Florida Tax Review	Fla Tax Rev
Food & Drug Law Journal	Food & Drug LJ
Fordham Environmental Law Review	Fordham Envtl LJ
Fordham Finance, Securities & Tax Law Forum	Fordham Fin Sec & Tax LF
Fordham Intellectual Property, Media & Entertainment Law Journal	Fordham IP Media & Ent LJ
Fordham International Law Journal	Fordham Intl LJ
Fordham Journal of Corporate and Finance Law (*formerly / anciennement Fordham Finance, Securities and Tax Law Forum*)	Fordham J Corp & Fin L
Fordham Law Review	Fordham L Rev
Fordham Urban Law Journal	Fordham Urb LJ
FORUM du droit international	FORUM
George Mason Law Review	Geo Mason L Rev
George Mason University Civil Rights Law Journal	Geo Mason U Civ Rts LJ
George Washington International Law Review *(formerly / anciennement George Washington Journal of International Law and Economics)*	Geo Wash Intl L Rev
George Washington Law Review	Geo Wash L Rev
Georgetown Immigration Law Journal	Geo Immigr LJ
Georgetown International Environmental Law Review	Geo Intl Envtl L Rev
Georgetown Journal of Gender and the Law	Geo J Gender & L
Georgetown Journal of International Law	Geo J Intl L
Georgetown Journal of Legal Ethics	Geo J Leg Ethics
Georgetown Journal on Poverty Law & Policy *(formerly / anciennement Georgetown Journal on Fighting Poverty)*	Geo J on Poverty L & Pol'y
Georgetown Law Journal	Geo LJ
Georgetown Public Policy Review	Geo Pub Pol'y Rev
Georgia Journal of International and Comparative Law	Ga J Intl & Comp L
Georgia Law Review	Ga L Rev
Georgia State University Law Review	Ga St U L Rev
Global Business Law Review	Global Bus L Rev
Golden Gate University Law Review	Golden Gate UL Rev
Gonzaga Law Review	Gonz L Rev
Great Plains Natural Resources Journal	Great Plains Nat Resources J
Griffith Law Review	Griffith L Rev
Hague Yearbook of International Law	Hague YB Intl L
Hamline Journal of Public Law and Policy	Hamline J Pub L & Pol'y

Hamline Law Review	Hamline L Rev
Harvard BlackLetter Law Journal	Harv BlackLetter LJ
Harvard Civil Rights-Civil Liberties Law Review	Harv CR-CLL Rev
Harvard Environmental Law Review	Harv Envtl L Rev
Harvard Human Rights Journal *(formerly / anciennement Harvard Human Rights Yearbook)*	Harv Hum Rts J
Harvard International Law Journal	Harv Intl LJ
Harvard Journal of Law & Technology	Harv JL & Tech
Harvard Journal of Law and Gender	Harv JL & Gender
Harvard Journal of Law and Public Policy	Harv JL & Pub Pol'y
Harvard Journal on Legislation	Harv J on Legis
Harvard Law Review	Harv L Rev
Harvard Negotiation Law Review	Harv Negot L Rev
Harvard Women's Law Journal	Harv Women's LJ
Hastings Communications & Entertainment Law Journal	Hastings Comm & Ent LJ
Hastings Constitutional Law Quarterly	Hastings Const LQ
Hastings International and Comparative Law Review	Hastings Intl & Comp L Rev
Hastings Law Journal	Hastings LJ
Hastings West-Northwest Journal of Environmental Law and Policy	Hastings W-Nw J Envtl L & Pol'y
Hastings Women's Law Journal	Hastings Women's LJ
Hawaii Bar Journal	Haw Bar J
Hawaill Law Review	Haw L Rev
Health and Human Rights	Health & Hum Rts
Health Law in Canada	Health L Can
Health Law Journal	Health LJ
Heidelberg Journal of International Law	Heidelberg J Intl L
High Technology Law Journal	High Tech LJ
Hitotsubashi Journal of Law and Politics	HJLP
Hofstra Labor & Employment Law Journal	Hofstra Lab & Empl LJ
Hofstra Law Review	Hofstra L Rev
Hofstra Property Law Journal	Hofstra Prop LJ
Holdsworth Law Review	Hold LR
Hong Kong Law Journal	Hong Kong LJ
Houston Journal of International Law	Hous J Intl L
Houston Law Review	Hous L Rev

Howard Journal of Criminal Justice	How J Crim Justice
Howard Law Journal	How LJ
Howard Scroll: The Social Justice Law Review	How Scroll
Human Rights in Development	Hum Rts Dev
Human Rights Internet Reporter	HRIR
Human Rights Journal	Hum Rts J
Human Rights Law Journal	HRLJ
Human Rights Quarterly	Hum Rts Q
Human Rights Tribune	Hum Rts Trib
ICSID Review	ICSID Rev
Idaho Law Review	Idaho L Rev
IDEA: The Journal of Law and Technology	IDEA
Illinois Bar Journal	Ill BJ
Illinois Law Quarterly	Ill LQ
ILSA Journal of International & Comparative Law	ILSA J Intl & Comp L
Immigration and Nationality Law Review	Immig & Nat'lity L Rev
Indiana International and Comparative Law Review	Ind Intl & Comp L Rev
Indiana Journal of Global Legal Studies	Ind J Global Leg Stud
Indiana Law Journal	Ind LJ
Indiana Law Review	Ind L Rev
Indigenous Law Journal	Indigenous LJ
Industrial & Labor Relations Review	Indus & Lab Rel Rev
Industrial Law Journal	Indus LJ
Industrial Relations Law Journal	Indus Rel LJ
Information and Communications Technology Law	Inf & Comm Tech L
Information Bulletin on Legal Affairs (Council of Europe)	Inf Bull
Insolvency Bulletin	Insol Bull
Intellectual and Comparative Law Quarterly	ICLQ
Intellectual Property & Technlology Forum	IP & Tech F
Intellectual Property & Technology Law Review	IP & Tech L Rev
Intellectual Property Journal	IPJ
Intellectual Property Law Bulletin	IPL Bull
Intellectual Property Law Newsletter	IPL News
International and Comparative Corporate Law Journal	Intl & Comp Corp LJ
International and Comparative Law Quarterly (*formerly / anciennement British*	ICLQ

Institute of International and Comparative Law)	
International and Comparative Law Review	Intl & Comp L Rev
International Arbitration Law Review	Intl Arb L Rev
International Business Law Journal	IBLJ
International Business Lawyer	Intl Bus Lawyer
International Commercial Litigation	Intl Com Lit
International Commission of Jurists Review	Intl Commission Jur Rev
International Community Law Review (*formerly / anciennement International Law FORUM du droit international*)	Intl Community L Rev
International Company and Commercial Law Review	Intl Co & Com L Rev
International Criminal Law Review	Intl Crim L Rev
International Financial Law Review	Intl Fin L Rev
International Insights	Intl Insights
International Insurance Law Review	Intl Ins L Rev
International Journal	Intl J
International Journal for Jurisprudence and Legal Philosophy	Intl J Juris & Leg Phil
International Journal for the Semiotics of Law	Intl J Sem L
International Journal of Children's Rights	Intl J Child Rts
International Journal of Communications Law & Policy	Intl J Comm L & Pol'y
International Journal of Comparative Labour Law and Industrial Relations	Intl J Comp Lab L & Ind Rel
International Journal of Conflict Management	Intl J Confl Mgmt
International Journal of Cultural Property	Intl J Cult Prop
International Journal of Franchising and Distribution Law	Intl J Franch & Distrib L
International Journal of Human Rights	Intl JHR
International Journal of Offender Therapy and Comparative Criminology	Intl J Off Ther & Comp Crim
International Journal of Law and Information Technology	Intl JL & IT
International Journal of Law and Psychiatry	Intl J L & Psychiatry
International Journal of Law Policy and the Family	Intl JL Pol'y & Fam
International Journal of Legal Information	Intl J Leg Info
International Journal of Marine and Coastal Law	Intl J Mar & Coast L
International Journal of the Sociology of Law	Intl J Soc L
International Journal of Refugee Law	Intl J Refugee L
International Lawyer	Intl Lawyer
International Legal Materials	ILM
International Legal Perspectives	Intl Leg Persp

International Legal Practitioner	Intl Leg Practitioner
International Legal Theory	Intl Leg Theory
International Maritime and Commercial Law Yearbook	Intl Mar & Com L YB
International Review of Criminal Policy	Intl Rev Crim Pol'y
International Review of Industrial Property and Copyright Law	Intl Rev Ind Prop & C'right L
International Review of Law & Economics	Intl Rev L & Econ
International Review of Law Computers & Technology	Intl Rev L Comp & Tech
International Review of the Red Cross	Intl Rev Red Cross
International Tax and Business Lawyer	Intl Tax & Bus Lawyer
International Trade Law & Regulation	Intl Trade L Reg
International Trade Law and Practice	Intl Trade L & Pract
International Trade Law Quarterly	ITLQ
Iowa Law Review	Iowa L Rev
Irish Jurist	Ir Jur
Islamic Law & Society	Islamic L & Soc
Israel Law Review	Israel LR
Issues in Law & Medicine	Issues L & Med
Jersey Law Review	Jersey L Rev
Jewish Law Report	Jewish LR
John Marshall Journal of Computer and Information Law	John Marshall J Computer & Info L
John Marshall Law Quarterly	John Marshall LQ
John Marshall Law Review	John Marshall L Rev
Journal de droit européen	JDE
Journal des juges provinciaux	J juges prov
Journal des notaires et des avocats	J not et av
Journal des tribunaux	J Tribun
Journal du Barreau	J du B
Journal du droit des jeunes	J dr jeunes
Journal du droit international	JDI
Journal of Affordable Housing and Community Development Law	J Aff Housing & Community Dev L
Journal of African Law	J Afr L
Journal of Agricultural Law	J Agric L
Journal of Air Law	J Air L
Journal of Air Law and Commerce	J Air L & Com
Journal of Animal Law	J Animal L

Journal of Animal Law and Ethics	J Animal L & Ethics
Journal of Appellate Practice & Process	J App Pr & Pro
Journal of Art & Entertainment Law	J Art & Ent L
Journal of BioLaw & Business	J BioLaw & Bus
Journal of Business Law	J Bus L
Journal of Catholic Legal Studies (*formerly / anciennement The Catholic Lawyer*)	J Cath Leg Stud
Journal of Chinese Law	J Chinese L
Journal of College and University Law	JC & UL
Journal of Commonwealth Law and Legal Education	J Commonwealth L & Leg Educ
Journal of Comparative Business and Capital Market Law	J Comp Bus & Cap Mkt L
Journal of Conflict and Security Law (*formerly / anciennement Journal of Armed Conflict Law*)	J Confl & Sec L
Journal of Conflict Resolution	J Confl Resolution
Journal of Constitutional Law in Eastern and Central Europe	J Const LE & Cent Eur
Journal of Contemporary Health Law & Policy	J Contemp Health L & Pol'y
Journal of Contemporary Law	J Contemp L
Journal of Contemporary Legal Issues	J Contemp Leg Issues
Journal of Corporate Taxation	J Corp Tax'n
Journal of Corporation Law	J Corp L
Journal of Criminal Justice Education	J Crim J Educ
Journal of Criminal Law	J Crim L
Journal of Criminal Law & Criminology	J Crim L & Criminology
Journal of Dispute Resolution	J Disp Resol
Journal of Empirical Legal Studies	J Empirical Leg Stud
Journal of Energy, Natural Resources & Environmental Law	J Energy Nat Resources & Envtl L
Journal of Energy Law & Policy	J Energy L & Pol'y
Journal of Environmental Law	J Envtl L
Journal of Environmental Law & Litigation	J Envtl L & Litig
Journal of Environmental Law & Practice	J Envtl L & Prac
Journal of European Integration	J Eur Integration
Journal of Family Law	J Fam L
Journal of Gender, Race & Justice	J Gender Race & Just
Journal of Health and Hospital Law	J Health & Hosp L
Journal of Health Care Law and Policy	J Health Care L & Pol'y

Journal of Health Politics, Policy and Law	J Health Pol Pol'y & L
Journal of Information, Law and Technology	J Inf L & Tech
Journal of Intellectual Property	J Intell Prop
Journal of Intellectual Property Law	J Intell Prop L
Journal of International Arbitration	J Intl Arb
Journal of International Banking Law and Regulation	J Intl Banking L & Reg
Journal of International Economic Law	J Intl Econ L
Journal of International Financial Markets, Institutions and Money	J Intl Fin Markets Inst & Money
Journal of International Law & Business	J Intl L & Bus
Journal of International Legal Studies	J Intl Leg Stud
Journal of International Taxation	J Intl Tax
Journal of International Wildlife Law and Policy	J Intl Wildlife L & Pol'y
Journal of Juvenile Law	J Juvenile L
Journal of Land, Resources and Environmental Law (*formerly / anciennement Journal of Energy, Natural Resources and Environmental Law*)	J Land Resources & Envtl L
Journal of Land Use and Environmental Law	J Land Use & Envtl L
Journal of Law, Information & Science	J L Info & Sci
Journal of Law, Medicine and Ethics	JL Med & Ethics
Journal of Law and Commerce	JL & Com
Journal of Law and Economics	JL & Econ
Journal of Law and Education	JL & Educ
Journal of Law and Equality	JL & Equality
Journal of Law and Family Studies	JL & Fam Stud
Journal of Law and Health	JL & Health
Journal of Law, Economics and Organization	JL Econ & Org
Journal of Law and Policy	JL & Pol'y
Journal of Law and Politics	JL & Pol
Journal of Law and Religion	JL & Religion
Journal of Law and Social Policy	J L & Soc Pol'y
Journal of Law and Society	JL & Soc'y
Journal of Law in Society	JL in Soc'y
Journal of Legal Advocacy and Practice	J Leg Advoc & Prac
Journal of Legal Economics	J Leg Econ
Journal of Legal Education	J Leg Educ
Journal of Legal History	J Leg Hist

Journal of Legal Medicine	J Leg Med
Journal of Legal Pluralism and Unofficial Law (*formerly / anciennement Journal of Legal Pluralism*)	J Leg Pluralism & Unofficial L
Journal of Legal Studies	J Leg Stud
Journal of Legislation	J Legis
Journal of Legislation and Public Policy	J Legis & Pub Pol'y
Journal of Maritime Law & Commerce	J Mar L & Com
Journal of Medicine and Law	J Med & L
Journal of Mineral Law & Policy	J Min L & Pol'y
Journal of Multistate Taxation and Incentives	J Multistate Tax'n & Incentives
Journal of Natural Resources & Environmental Law (*formerly / anciennement Journal of Mineral Law & Policy*)	J Nat Resources & Envtl L
Journal of Parliamentary and Political Law	JPPL
Journal of Personal Injury Law	J Pers Inj L
Journal of Pharmacy and Law	J Pharmacy & L
Journal of Planning and Environmental Law	J Plan & Envtl L
Journal of Politics and Law	J Politics & L
Journal of Private International Law	J Priv Intl L
Journal of Products Liability	J Prod Liab
Journal of Proprietary Rights	J Proprietary Rts
Journal of Public Policy, Administration and the Law	J Pub Pol'y Admin & L
Journal of Science & Technology Law	J Sci & Tech L
Journal of Small & Emerging Business Law	J Small & Emerging Bus L
Journal of Social Welfare and Family Law (*formerly / anciennement Journal of Social Welfare Law*)	J Soc Welfare & Fam L
Journal of Social Welfare Law	J Soc Welfare L
Journal of South Pacific Law	J South Pac L
Journal of Southern Legal History	J South Leg Hist
Journal of Space Law	J Space L
Journal of Taxation	J Tax'n
Journal of Technology Law & Policy	J Tech L & Pol'y
Journal of the History of International Law	J Hist Intl L
Journal of the Indian Law Institute	J Indian L Inst
Journal of the Institute for the Study of Legal Ethics	J Inst for Study Leg Ethics
Journal of the Law Society of Scotland	JL Soc Scotland
Journal of the Legal Profession	J Leg Prof

Journal of the Patent & Trademark Office Society	J Pat & Trademark Off Soc'y
Journal of the Suffolk Academy of Law	J Suffolk Academy L
Journal of Transnational Law & Policy	J Transnat'l L & Pol'y
Journal of World Trade	J World Trade
Journal of World Trade Law, Economics and Policy	J World Trade L Econ & Pol'y
Juridical Review	Jurid Rev
Kansas Journal of Law & Public Policy	Kan JL & Pub Pol'y
Kansas Law Review	Kan L Rev
Kentucky Children's Rights Journal	Ky Children's Rts J
Kentucky Law Journal	Ky LJ
Korean Journal of International and Comparative Law	Korean J Intl & Comp L
La Raza Law Journal	La Raza LJ
Labor Law Journal	Lab LJ
Labor Lawyer	Lab Lawyer
Land and Water Law Review	Land & Water L Rev
Law & Policy	Law & Pol'y
Law and Business Review of the Americas (*formerly / anciennement NAFTA Law and Business Review of the Americas*)	L & Bus Rev Americas
Law and Contemporary Problems	Law & Contemp Probs
Law and History Review	L & Hist Rev
Law and Inequality	Law & Ineq
Law and Philosophy	Law & Phil
Law and Policy in International Business	Law & Pol'y Intl Bus
Law and Politics Book Review	Law & Pol Book Rev
Law and Practice of International Courts and Tribunals	Law & Prac Intl Cts & Trib
Law and Psychology Review	Law & Psychol Rev
Law and Sexuality: A Review of Lesbian and Gay Legal Issues	Law & Sexuality
Law and Social Inquiry	Law & Soc Inquiry
Law and Society Review	Law & Soc'y Rev
Law Librarian	Law Libr'n
Law Library Journal	Law Libr J
Law Office Management and Administration Report	Law Off Mgmt & Admin Rep
Law Office Technology Review	Law Off Tech Rev
Law Practice Management (formerly / anciennement Legal Economics)	Law Prac Mgmt

Law Quarterly Review	Law Q Rev
Law Review of Michigan State University Detroit College of Law	Law Rev Mich St U Det CL
Law Society Gazette (Law Society of Upper Canada)	L Soc'y Gaz
Law Society's Gazette and Guardian Gazette	L Soc'y Gaz & Guardian Gaz
Law, Technology and Insurance	Law Tech & Ins
Lawyers Journal (*formerly / anciennement Pittsburgh Legal Journal*)	Lawyers J
Legal Ethics (*formerly / anciennement Ethics*)	Leg Ethics
Legal History (*formerly / anciennement Australian Journal of Legal History*)	LH
Legal History Review	Leg Hist Rev
Legal Information Management	Leg Info Mgmt
Legal Issues of Economic / European Integration	LIEI
Legal Medical Quarterly	L Med Q
Legal Reference Services Quarterly	Leg Ref Serv Q
Legal Studies	LS
Legal Theory	Leg Theory
Leiden Journal of International Law	Leiden J Intl L
Lex Electronica : Revue du droit des technologies de l'information	Lex Electronica
Lloyd's Maritime and Commercial Law Quarterly	LMCLQ
Los Angeles Lawyer	LA Lawyer
Louisiana Bar Journal	La BJ
Louisiana Law Review	La L Rev
Lower Canada Jurist	LC Jurist
Lower Canada Law Journal	LCLJ
Loyola Consumer Protection Journal	Loy Con Prot J
Loyola Law Review (New Orleans)	Loy L Rev
Loyola of Los Angeles Entertainment Law Journal	Loy LA Ent LR
Loyola of Los Angeles International & Comparative Law Journal	Loy LA Intl & Comp LJ
Loyola of Los Angeles Law Review	Loy LA L Rev
Loyola Poverty Law Journal	Loy Poverty LJ
Loyola University of Chicago Law Journal	Loy U Chicago LJ
Maastricht Journal of European and Comparative Law	MJECL
Macquarie Jornal of International and Comparative Environmental Law	Macq J Intl & Comp Envtl L
Maine Law Review	Me L Rev
Malaya Law Review	Mal L Rev
Malayan Law Journal	MLJ

Manitoba Bar News	Man Bar N
Manitoba Law Journal	Man LJ
Maori Law Review	Maori L Rev
Marquette Intellectual Property Law Review	Marq Intell Prop L Rev
Marquette Law Review	Marq L Rev
Marquette Sports Law Review	Marq Sports L Rev
Maryland Journal of Contemporary Legal Issues	Md J Contemp Leg Issues
Maryland Journal of International Law (*formerly / anciennement Maryland Journal of International Law and Trade*)	Md J Intl L
Maryland Law Review	Md L Rev
Massachusetts Law Review	Mass L Rev
McGeorge Law Review *(formerly / anciennement Pacific Law Journal)*	McGeorge L Rev
McGill International Journal of Sustainable Development Law and Policy	JSDLP
McGill Journal of Law and Health (*formerly / anciennement McGill Health Law Publication*)	McGill JL & Health
McGill Law Journal	McGill LJ
Media Law & Policy	Media L & Pol'y
Medical Law Review	Med L Rev
Medicine & Law	Med & L
Medicine, Science and the Law	Med Sci Law
Medico-Legal Journal	Med Leg J
Melbourne University Law Review	Melbourne UL Rev
Mercer Law Review	Mercer L Rev
Michigan Bar Journal	Mich Bar J
Michigan Business Law Journal	Mich Bus LJ
Michigan Journal of Gender & Law	Mich J Gender & L
Michigan Journal of International Law	Mich J Intl L
Michigan Journal of Law Reform	Mich JL Reform
Michigan Journal of Race & Law	Mich J Race & L
Michigan Law & Policy Review	Mich L & Pol'y Rev
Michigan Law Journal	Mich LJ
Michigan Law Review	Mich L Rev
Michigan State University — DCL Journal of International Law and Practice (*formerly / anciennement Michigan State University — DCL Journal of International Law*)	MSU-DCL J Intl L & Prac
Michigan Telecommunications & Technology Law Review	Mich Telecomm & Tech L Rev

Military Law Review	Mil L Rev
Minnesota Journal of International Law (*formerly / anciennement Minnesota Journal of Global Trade*)	Minn J Intl L
Minnesota Journal of Law, Science, and Technology (*formerly / anciennement Minnesota Intellectual Property Review*)	Minn J L Sci & Tech
Minnesota Law Review	Minn L Rev
Mississippi College Law Review	Miss CL Rev
Mississippi Law Journal	Miss LJ
Mississippi Law Review	Miss L Rev
Missouri Environmental Law and Policy Review	Mo Envtl L & Pol'y Rev
Missouri Law Review	Mo L Rev
Modern Law Review	Mod L Rev
Monash University Law Review	Monash UL Rev
Monde Juridique	Monde Jur
Money Laundering Law Report	Money Laundering L Rep
Montana Law Review	Mont L Rev
Montana Lawyer	Mont Lawyer
Monthly Labor Review	Monthly Lab Rev
Murdoch University Electronic Journal of Law	Murdoch UEJL
NAFTA Law & Business Review of the Americas	NAFTA L & Bus Rev Am
National Banking Law Review	Nat'l Banking L Rev
National Black Law Journal	Nat'l Black LJ
National Insolvency Review	Nat'l Insolv Rev
National Institute of Justice Journal	Nat'l Inst Just J
National Journal of Constitutional Law	NJCL
National Journal of Sexual Orientation Law	Nat'l J Sex Orient L
National Law Journal	Nat'l LJ
National Law Review	Nat'l L Rev
National Real Property Law Review	Nat'l Real PLR
National Tax Journal	Nat'l Tax J
Natural Resources & Environment	Nat Resources & Env't
Natural Resources Journal	Nat Resources J
Naval Law Review	Naval L Rev
Nebraska Law Review	Neb L Rev
Neptunus: Maritime and Oceanic Law Review	Neptunus

Netherlands International Law Review	Nethl Intl L Rev
Netherlands Quarterly of Human Rights	Nethl QHR
New England International and Comparative Law Annual	New Eng J of Intl & Comp L Ann
New England Journal of International and Comparative Law (*formerly / anciennement New England International and Comparative Law Annual*)	New Eng J of Intl & Comp L
New England Journal of Medicine	New Eng J Med
New England Journal on Criminal & Civil Confinement	New Eng J Crim & Civ Confinement
New England Law Review	New Eng L Rev
New Europe Law Review	New Eur L Rev
New Jersey Lawyer	NJ Lawyer
New Law Journal	New LJ
New Mexico Law Review	NML Rev
New York City Law Review	NY City L Rev
New York International Law Review	NY Intl L Rev
New York Law Journal	NYLJ
New York Law Review	NYL Rev
New York Law School Journal of Human Rights	NYL Sch J Hum Rts
New York Law School Law Review	NYL Sch L Rev
New York State Bar Journal	NY St BJ
New York University Clinical Law Review	NYU Clin L Rev
New York University East European Constitutional Review	E Eur Const Rev
New York University Environmental Law Journal	NYU Envtl LJ
New York University International Journal of Constitutional Law	NYU Intl J Cont L
New York University Journal of International Law & Politics	NYUJ Intl L & Pol
New York University Journal of Legislation & Public Policy	NYUJ Legis & Pub Pol'y
New York University Law Review	NYUL Rev
New York University Review of Law & Social Change	NYU Rev L & Soc Change
New Zealand Law Journal	NZLJ
New Zealand Law Review	NZLR
New Zealand Universities Law Review	NZULR
Non-Profit Law Yearbook	Non-Profit L Yearbook
Non-State Actors and International Law	Non-State Actors & Intl L
Nordic Journal of International Law	Nordic J Intl L
North Carolina Central Law Review (*formerly / anciennement North Carolina Central Law Journal*)	NC Cent L Rev

North Carolina Journal of International Law & Commercial Regulation	NCJ Intl L & Com Reg
North Carolina Law Review	NCL Rev
North Dakota Law Review	NDL Rev
Northern Illinois University Law Review	N Ill UL Rev
Northern Ireland Legal Quarterly	N Ir Leg Q
Northern Kentucky Law Review	N Ky L Rev
Northwestern Journal of International Law & Business	Nw J Intl L & Bus
Northwestern University Law Review	Nw UL Rev
Notre Dame Journal of International and Comparative Law	Notre Dame J Intl & Comp L
Notre Dame Journal of Law Ethics and Public Policy	Notre Dame JL Ethics & Pub Pol'y
Notre Dame Law Review	Notre Dame L Rev
Nova Law Review	Nova L Rev
Ocean & Coastal Law Journal *(formerly / anciennement Territorial Sea Journal)*	Ocean & Coastal LJ
Ocean Development & International Law	Ocean Dev & Intl L
OECD Journal of Competition Law and Policy	OECD J Competition L & Pol'y
Ohio Northern University Law Review	Ohio NUL Rev
Ohio State Journal on Dispute Resolution	Ohio St J Disp Resol
Ohio State Law Journal	Ohio St LJ
Oklahoma City University Law Review	Okla City UL Rev
Oklahoma Law Review	Okla L Rev
Oregon Law Review	Or L Rev
Osaka University Law Review	Osaka UL Rev
Osgoode Hall Law Journal	Osgoode Hall LJ
Otago Law Review	Otago L Rev
Ottawa Law Review	Ottawa L Rev
Oxford Journal of Legal Studies	Oxford J Leg Stud
Oxford University Commonwealth Law Journal	OUCLJ
Pace Environmental Law Review	Pace Envtl L Rev
Pace International Law Review (*formerly / anciennement Pace Yearbook of International Law*)	Pace Intl L Rev Pace YB Intl L
Pace Law Review	Pace L Rev
Pacific Law Journal	Pac LJ
Pacific Rim Law and Policy Journal	Pac Rim L & Pol'y J
Panstwo i Prawo	Panstwo i Prawo

Patent Law Annual	Pat L Ann
Penn State Law Review	Penn St L Rev
Pepperdine Law Review	Pepp L Rev
Philippine Law Journal	Philippine LJ
Pittsburgh Legal Journal	Pittsburgh Leg J
Polish Contemporary Law	Polish Contemp L
Polish Yearbook of International Law	Polish YB Intl L
Potomac Law Review	Potomac L Rev
Probate and Property	Prob & Prop
Probate Law Journal	Prob LJ
Products Liability Law Journal	Prod Liab LJ
Provincial Judges Journal	Prov Judges J
Psychology, Public Policy & Law	Psychol Pub Pol'y & L
Public Contract Law Journal	Pub Cont LJ
Public Interest Law Review	Pub Int L Rev
Public Land & Resources Law Review	Pub Land & Resources L Rev
Public Land Law Review	Pub Land L Rev
Queen's Law Journal	Queen's LJ
Quinnipiac Health Law Journal	Quinnipiac Health LJ
Quinnipiac Law Review (*formerly / anciennement Bridgeport Law Review*)	Quinnipac L Rev
Quinnipiac Probate Law Journal (*formerly / anciennement Connecticut Probate Law Journal*)	Quinnipiac Prob LJ
Real Estate Law Journal	Real Est LJ
Real Property, Probate & Trust Journal	Real Prop Prob & Tr J
Recueil des Cours	Rec des Cours
Regent University Law Review	Regent UL Rev
Relations Industrielles (Industrial Relations)	RI
Responsabilité civile et assurances	Resp civ et assur
Restitution Law Review	RLR
Review of Banking and Financial Law *(formerly / anciennement Annual Review of Banking Law)*	Rev Banking & Fin L
Review of Central and East European Law	Rev Cent & E Eur L
Review of Constitutional Studies	Rev Const Stud
Review of European Community and International Environmental Law	RECIEL
Review of Litigation	Rev Litig

Revue administrative	Rev admin
Revue algérienne des sciences juridiques, économiques et politiques	Rev ASJEP
Revue belge de droit constitutionnel	RBDC
Revue belge de droit international	Rev b dr Intern
Revue canadienne de criminologie et de justice pénale	Rev can dr crim
Revue canadienne de droit administratif et de pratique	RCDAP
Revue canadienne de droit communautaire	Rev can dr commun
Revue canadienne de droit de commerce	Rev can dr comm
Revue canadienne du droit de la concurrence	Rev Can dr con
Revue canadienne de droit familial	Rev Can dr fam
Revue canadienne de droit international	RCDI
Revue canadienne de droit pénal	RCDP
Revue canadienne de propriété intellectuelle	RCPI
Revue canadienne des bibliothèques de droit	Rev can bibl dr
Revue canadienne des recours collectifs	Rev can recours coll
Revue canadienne droit et société	RCDS
Revue canadienne du droit d'auteur	RCDA
Revue critique	Rev crit
Revue critique de droit international privé	Rev crit dr int privé
Revue critique de jurisprudence belge	RCJB
Revue critique de législation et de jurisprudence du Canada	RCLJ
Revue d'études constitutionnelles	R études const
Revue d'études juridiques	REJ
Revue d'histoire du droit	Rev hist dr
Revue d'histoire du droit international	Rev hist dr int
Revue d'intégration européenne	RIE
Revue de droit d'Ottawa	RD Ottawa
Revue de droit de l'ULB	Rev dr ULB
Revue de droit de l'Université de Sherbrooke	RDUS
Revue de droit de l'Université du Nouveau-Brunswick	RD UN-B
Revue de droit de McGill	RD McGill
Revue de droit des affaires internationales	RDAI
Revue de droit et santé de McGill (*anciennement / formerly Publication en droit de la santé de McGill*)	RD & santé McGill
Revue de droit immobilier	RD imm

Revue de droit international de sciences diplomatiques et politiques	RDISDP
Revue de droit international et de droit comparé	Rev DI & DC
Revue de droit parlementaire et politique	RDPP
Revue de droit social	RDS
Revue de droit uniforme	Rev dr unif
Revue de jurisprudence	R de J
Revue de l'arbitrage	Rev arb
Revue de la common law en français	RCLF
Revue de la Recherche Juridique	RRJ
Revue de législation et de jurisprudence	R de L
Revue de planification fiscale et financière (*anciennement / formerly Revue de planification fiscale et successorale*)	RPFF
Revue des Juristes de l'Ontario	Rev juristes de l'Ont
Revue des sociétés	Rev sociétés
Revue du Barreau	R du B
Revue du Barreau canadien	R du B can
Revue du droit	R du D
Revue du droit de l'Union Européenne	RDUE
Revue du droit public et de la science politique en France et à l'étranger	RDP
Revue du Notariat	R du N
Revue égyptienne de droit international	Rev EDI
Revue européenne de droit privé	RED privé
Revue européenne de droit public	RED public
Revue européenne de philosophie et de droit	REPD
Revue Femmes et Droit	RFD
Revue fiscale canadienne	Rev fiscale can
Revue française de droit administratif	Rev fr dr admin
Revue française de droit aérien et spatial	Rev fr dr aérien
Revue française de droit constitutionnel	Rev fr dr constl
Revue générale de droit	RGD
Revue générale de droit international public	RGDIP
Revue générale du droit des assurances	RGDA
Revue hellénique de droit international	RHDI
Revue historique de droit français et étranger	RHD
Revue interdisciplinaire d'études juridiques	RIEJ

Revue internationale de droit comparé	RIDC
Revue internationale de droit économique	RIDE
Revue internationale de droit et politique de développement durable de McGill	RDPDD
Revue internationale de droit pénal	Rev IDP
Revue internationale de la Croix-Rouge	RICR
Revue internationale de la propriété industrielle et artistique	RIPIA
Revue internationale de politique criminelle	Rev IPC
Revue internationale de sémiotique juridique	RISJ
Revue internationale du droit d'auteur	RIDA
Revue juridique de l'environnement	RJE
Revue juridique des étudiants et étudiantes de l'Université Laval	RJEUL
Revue juridique La femme et le droit	Rev jur femme dr
Revue juridique Thémis	RJT
Revue juridique Thémis de l'Université de l'Université de Montréal (anciennement / formerly Revue juridique Thémis)	RJTUM
Revue nationale de droit constitutionnel	RNDC
Revue québécoise de droit international	RQDI
Revue suisse de droit international et de droit européen	RSDIE
Revue suisse de jurisprudence	RSJ
Revue trimestrielle de droit civil	RTD civ
Revue trimestrielle de droit commercial et de droit économique	RTDcom
Revue trimestrielle de droit européen	RTD eur
Revue universelle des droits de l'homme	RUDH
Richmond Journal of Global Law & Business	Rich J Global L & Bus
Richmond Journal of Law & Technology	Rich JL & Tech
Richmond Journal of Law and the Public Interest	Rich JL & Pub Int
Roger Williams University Law Review	Roger Williams U L Rev
Rutgers Computer & Technology Law Journal	Rutgers Computer & Tech LJ
Rutgers Journal of Law and Religion	Rutgers JL & Religion
Rutgers Law Journal (*formerly / anciennement Rutgers-Camden Law Journal*)	Rutgers LJ
Rutgers Law Review	Rutgers L Rev
Rutgers Race and the Law Review	Rutgers Race & L Rev
Rutgers-Camden Law Journal	Rutgers-Camden LJ
Saint John's Journal of Legal Commentary	St John's J Leg Comment
Saint John's Law Review	St John's L Rev

Saint Louis University Law Journal	Saint Louis ULJ
Saint Louis University Public Law Review	St Louis U Pub L Rev
Saint Louis-Warsaw Transatlantic Law Journal	St Louis-Warsaw Transatlantic LJ
Saint Mary's Law Journal	St Mary's LJ
Saint Thomas Law Review	St Thomas L Rev
San Diego Law Review	San Diego L Rev
San Joaquin Agricultural Law Review	San Joaquin Agric L Rev
Santa Clara Computer & High Technology Law Journal	Santa Clara Comp & High Tech LJ
Santa Clara Law Review	Santa Clara L Rev
Saskatchewan Bar Review	Sask Bar Rev
Saskatchewan Law Review	Sask L Rev
Scandinavian Studies in Law	Scand Stud L
Scottish Current Law Yearbook	Scot Curr LYB
Seattle University Law Review *(formerly / anciennement University of Puget Sound Law Review)*	Seattle UL Rev
Securities Regulation Law Journal	Sec Reg LJ
Seton Hall Constitutional Law Journal	Seton Hall Const LJ
Seton Hall Journal of Sports and Entertainment Law	Seton Hall J Sports & Ent L
Seton Hall Law Review	Seton Hall L Rev
Seton Hall Legislative Journal	Seton Hall Legis J
Sherbrooke Law Review	Sherbrooke L Rev
Singapore Academy of Law Annual Review	SAL Ann Rev
Singapore Academy of Law Journal	Sing Ac LJ
Singapore Journal of International and Comparative Law	Sing JICL
Singapore Journal of Legal Studies	Sing JLS
Singapore Law Review	Sing L Rev
Singapore Year Book of International Law	SYBIL
SMU Law Review	SMU L Rev
Social and Legal Studies	Soc & Leg Stud
South African Journal on Human Rights	SAJHR
South African Law Journal	SALJ
South African Yearbook of International Law	SAYBIL
South Carolina Environmental Law Journal	SC Envtl LJ
South Carolina Law Review	SCL Rev
South Dakota Law Review	SDL Rev

South Texas Law Review *(formerly / anciennement South Texas Law Journal)*	S Tex L Rev
Southern California Interdisciplinary Law Journal	S Cal Interdisciplinary LJ
Southern California Law Review	S Cal L Rev
Southern California Review of Law and Women's Studies	S Cal Rev L & Women's Stud
Southern California Sports & Entertainment Law Journal	S Cal Sports & Ent LJ
Southern Illinois University Law Journal	S Ill ULJ
Southern University Law Review	SUL Rev
Southwestern Journal of International Law (*formerly / anciennement Southwestern Journal of Law and Trade in the Americas*)	Sw J Intl L
Southwestern Law Review	Sw L Rev
Space Policy	Space Pol'y
Special Lectures of the Law Society of Upper Canada	Spec Lect LSUC
Sports Lawyers Journal	Sports Lawyer J
Stanford Environmental Law Journal	Stan Envtl LJ
Stanford Journal of Animal Law and Policy	Stan J Animal L & Pol'y
Stanford Journal of International Law	Stan J Intl L
Stanford Journal of Law, Business & Finance	Stan JL Bus & Fin
Stanford Journal of Legal Studies	Stan J Legal Stud
Stanford Law & Policy Review	Stan L & Pol'y Rev
Stanford Law Review	Stan L Rev
Stanford Technology Law Review	Stan Tech L Rev
Statute Law Review	Stat L Rev
Stetson Law Review	Stetson L Rev
Suffolk Journal of Trial and Appellate Advocacy	Suffolk J Trial & Appellate Advoc
Suffolk Transnational Law Review *(formerly / anciennement Suffolk Transnational Law Journal)*	Suffolk Transnat'l L Rev
Suffolk University Law Review	Suffolk UL Rev
Supreme Court Economic Review	Sup Ct Econ Rev
Supreme Court Law Review	SCLR
Supreme Court Review	Sup Ct Rev
Supreme Court Economic Review	Sup Ct Econ Rev
Sydney Law Review	Sydney L Rev
Syracuse Journal of International Law & Commerce	Syracuse J Intl L & Com
Syracuse Law Review	Syracuse L Rev
Syracuse University Law and Technology Journal	Syracuse UL & TJ

Tax Law Review	Tax L Rev
Telecommunications & Space Journal	Telecom & Space J
Temple Environmental Law & Technology Journal	Temp Envtl L & Tech J
Temple International & Comparative Law Journal	Temp Intl & Comp LJ
Temple Law Review *(formerly / anciennement Temple Law Quarterly)*	Temp L Rev
Temple Political & Civil Rights Law Review	Temp Pol & Civ Rts L Rev
Tennessee Law Review	Tenn L Rev
Texas Bar Journal	Tex BJ
Texas Hispanic Journal of Law and Policy *(formerly / anciennement Hispanic Law Journal)*	Tex Hispanic J L & Pol'y
Texas Intellectual Property Law Journal	Tex Intell Prop LJ
Texas International Law Journal	Tex Intl LJ
Texas Journal of Business Law	Tex J Bus L
Texas Journal of Women & the Law	Tex J Women & L
Texas Journal on Civil Liberties and Civil Rights	Tex J on CL & CR
Texas Law Review	Tex L Rev
Texas Review of Law & Politics	Tex Rev L & Pol
Texas Tech Law Review	Tex Tech L Rev
Texas Wesleyan Law Review	Tex Wesleyan L Rev
Theoretical Inquiries in Law	Theor Inq L
Third World Legal Studies	Third World Legal Stud
Thomas Jefferson Law Review	Thomas Jefferson L Rev
Thomas M Cooley Journal of Practical & Clinical Law	TM Cooley J Prac & Clinical L
Thomas M Cooley Law Review	TM Cooley L Rev
Thurgood Marshall Law Review	T Marshall L Rev
Tilburg Law Review	Tilburg L Rev
Toledo Journal of Great Lakes' Law, Science & Policy	Tol J Great Lakes' L Sci & Pol'y
Tolley's Communications Law	Tolley's Comm L
Tort Trial and Insurance Practice Law Journal (***formerly / anciennement Tort & Insurance Law Journal***)	Tort Trial & Ins Prac LJ
Touro Environmental Law Journal	Touro Envtl LJ
Touro International Law Review	Touro Intl L Rev
Touro Law Review	Touro L Rev
Trade Law Topics	Trade L Topics
Transnational Law & Contemporary Problems	Transnat'l L & Contemp Probs

Transportation Law Journal	Transp LJ
Travaux de l'Association Henri Capitant des amis de la culture juridique française	Travaux de l'assoc Henri Capitant
Tribal Law Journal	Tribal LJ
Tribune des droits humains	Trib dr hum
Trust Law International	Trust L Intl
Trusts & Estates	Trusts & Est
Tulane Environmental Law Journal	Tul Envtl LJ
Tulane European & Civil Law Forum	Tul Eur & Civ LF
Tulane Journal of International & Comparative Law	Tul J Intl & Comp L
Tulane Journal of Law and Sexuality	Tul JL & Sexuality
Tulane Law Review	Tul L Rev
Tulane Maritime Law Journal	Tul Mar LJ
Tulsa Journal of Comparative & International Law	Tulsa J Comp & Intl L
Tulsa Law Journal	Tulsa LJ
UC Davis Journal of International Law & Policy	UC Davis J Intl L & Pol'y
UC Davis Law Review	UC Davis L Rev
UCLA Asian Pacific American Law Journal	UCLA Asian Pac Am LJ
UCLA Entertainment Law Review	UCLA Ent L Rev
UCLA Journal of Environmental Law & Policy	UCLA J Envtl L & Pol'y
UCLA Journal of International Law and Foreign Affairs	UCLA J Intl L & Foreign Aff
UCLA Journal of Law and Technology	UCLA JL & T
UCLA Law Review	UCLA L Rev
UCLA Pacific Basin Law Journal	UCLA Pac Basin LJ
UCLA Women's Law Journal	UCLA Women's LJ
UMKC Law Review	UMKC L Rev
UNCTAD Law Review: Journal on Law, Trade and Development	UNCTAD L Rev
Uniform Commercial Code Law Journal	Unif Comm Code L J
Uniform Law Conference of Canada (Proceedings)	Unif L Conf Proc
Uniform Law Review	Unif L Rev
United States-Mexico Law Journal	US-Mex LJ
University of Arkansas at Little Rock Law Review	U Ark Little Rock L Rev
University of Baltimore Intellectual Property Law Journal	U Balt Intell Prop LJ
University of Baltimore Journal of Environmental Law	U Balt J Envtl L
University of Baltimore Law Forum	U Balt LF

University of Baltimore Law Review	U Balt L Rev
University of British Columbia Law Review	UBC L Rev
University of California at Davis Law Review	UC Davis L Rev
University of Chicago Law Review	U Chicago L Rev
University of Chicago Law School Roundtable	U Chicago L Sch Roundtable
University of Chicago Legal Forum	U Chicago Legal F
University of Cincinnati Law Review	U Cin L Rev
University of Colorado Law Review	U Colo L Rev
University of Dayton Law Review	U Dayton L Rev
University of Detroit Mercy Law Review	U Det Mercy L Rev
University of Florida Journal of Law & Public Policy	U Fla JL & Pub Pol'y
University of Ghana Law Journal	UGLJ
University of Hawaii Law Review	U Haw L Rev
University of Illinois Law Review	U Ill L Rev
University of Kansas Law Review	U Kan L Rev
University of Louisville Law Review (*formerly /anciennement Brandeis Law Journal*)	U Louisville L Rev
University of Malaya Law Review	U Mal L Rev
University of Memphis Law Review	U Mem L Rev
University of Miami Business Law Review	U Miami Bus L Rev
University of Miami Entertainment & Sports Law Review	U Miami Ent & Sports L Rev
University of Miami Inter-American Law Review	U Miami Inter-Am L Rev
University of Miami International & Comparative Law Review *(formerly / anciennement University of Miami Yearbook of International Law)*	U Miami Intl & Comp L Rev
University of Miami Law Review	U Miami L Rev
University of Michigan Journal of Law Reform	U Mich JL Ref
University of New Brunswick Law Journal	UNBLJ
University of New South Wales Law Journal	UNSWLJ
University of Pennsylvania Journal of Constitutional Law	U Pa J Const L
University of Pennsylvania Journal of International Law (*formerly / anciennement* ***University of Pennsylvania Journal of International Economic Law***)	U Pa J Intl L
University of Pennsylvania Journal of Labor and Employment Law	U Pa J Lab & Employment L
University of Pennsylvania Law Review	U Pa L Rev
University of Pittsburgh Law Review	U Pitt L Rev
University of Queensland Law Jounal	UQLJ

University of Richmond Law Review	U Rich L Rev
University of San Francisco Journal of Law and Social Challenges	USF JL & Soc Challenges
University of San Francisco Law Review	USF L Rev
University of San Francisco Maritime Law Journal	USF Mar LJ
University of Tasmania Law Review	U Tasm L Rev
University of the District of Columbia Law Review *(formerly / anciennement District of Columbia Law Review)*	UDC L Rev
University of Toledo Law Review	U Tol L Rev
University of Toronto Faculty of Law Review	UT Fac L Rev
University of Toronto Law Journal	UTLJ
University of Western Australia Law Review	UWA L Rev
University of Western Ontario Law Review	UWO L Rev
Upper Canada Law Journal	UCLJ
Utah Bar Journal	Utah BJ
Valparaiso University Law Review	Val U L Rev
Vanderbilt Journal of Entertainment Law & Practice	Vand J Ent L & Prac
Vanderbilt Journal of Transnational Law	Vand J Transnat'l L
Vanderbilt Law Review	Vand L Rev
Vermont Bar Journal	Vt BJ
Vermont Journal of Environmental Law (*formerly / anciennement Res Communes: Vermont's Journal of the Environment*)	VJEL
Victoria University of Wellington Law Review	VUWLR
Vietnam Law & Legal Forum	Vietnam L & Legal Forum
Villanova Environmental Law Journal	Vill Envtl LJ
Villanova Law Review	Vill L Rev
Villanova Sports and Entertainment Law Journal	Vill Sports & Ent LJ
Virginia Environmental Law Journal	Va Envtl LJ
Virginia Journal of International Law	Va J Intl L
Virginia Journal of Law & Technology	Va JL & Tech
Virginia Journal of Social Policy & Law	Va J Soc Pol'y & L
Virginia Journal of Sports and the Law	Va J Sports & L
Virginia Law Review	Va L Rev
Virginia Tax Review	Va Tax Rev
Waikato Law Review: Taumauri	Waikato L Rev
Wake Forest Law Review	Wake Forest L Rev

Waseda Bulletin of Comparative Law	Waseda Bull Comp L
Washburn Law Journal	Washburn LJ
Washington & Lee Law Review	Wash & Lee L Rev
Washington & Lee Race & Ethnic Ancestry Law Journal *(formerly / anciennement Race & Ethnic Ancestry Law Journal)*	Wash & Lee Race & Ethnic Ancestry LJ
Washington Law Review	Wash L Rev
Washington University Journal of Law & Policy	Wash UJL & Pol'y
Washington University Journal of Urban and Contemporary Law	Wash UJ Urb & Contemp L
Washington University Law Quarterly	Wash ULQ
Wayne Law Review	Wayne L Rev
Web Journal of Current Legal Issues	Web JCLI
West Virginia Journal of Law & Technology	W Va J L & T
West Virginia Law Review	W Va L Rev
West Virginia Lawyer	W Va Law
Western Law Review (Canada)	West LR
Western Law Review (San Francisco)	West L Rev
Western New England Law Review	W New Eng L Rev
Western Ontario Law Review	West Ont L Rev
Western State University Law Review	W St U L Rev
Widener Journal of Public Law	Widener J Pub L
Widener Law Symposium Journal	Widener L Symp J
Willamette Journal of International Law & Dispute Resolution	Willamette J Intl & Disp Resol
Willamette Law Review	Willamette L Rev
William & Mary Bill of Rights Journal	Wm & Mary Bill Rts J
William & Mary Environmental Law & Policy Review	Wm & Mary Envtl L & Pol'y Rev
William & Mary Journal of Women and the Law	Wm & Mary J Women & L
William & Mary Law Review	Wm & Mary L Rev
William Mitchell Law Review	Wm Mitchell L Rev
Windsor Review of Legal and Social Issues	Windsor Rev Legal Soc Issues
Windsor Yearbook of Access to Justice	Windsor YB Access Just
Wisconsin Environmental Law Journal	Wis Envtl LJ
Wisconsin International Law Journal	Wis Intl LJ
Wisconsin Law Review	Wis L Rev
Wisconsin Women's Law Journal	Wis Women's LJ
Women's Rights Law Reporter	Women's Rts L Rep

World Arbitration and Mediation Report	World Arb & Mediation Rep
World Arbitration and Mediation Review (*formerly / anciennement World Arbitration and Mediation Report*)	World Arb & Mediation Rev
World Trade and Arbitration Materials	WTAM
Wyoming Law Review *(formerly / anciennement Land and Water Law Review)*	Wyo L Rev
Yale Human Rights and Development Law Journal	Yale Human Rts & Dev LJ
Yale Journal of International Law	Yale J Intl L
Yale Journal of Law & Feminism	Yale JL & Feminism
Yale Journal of Law & the Humanities	Yale JL & Human
Yale Journal on Regulation	Yale J Reg
Yale Law & Policy Review	Yale L & Pol'y Rev
Yale Law Journal	Yale LJ
Yearbook: Commercial Arbitration	YB Comm Arb
Yearbook of Air and Space Law	YB Air & Sp L
Yearbook of Copyright and Media Law	YB Copyright & Media L
Yearbook of European Environment Law	YB Eur Env L
Yearbook of European Law	YB Eur L
Yearbook of International Environmental Law	YB Intl Env L
Yearbook of International Humanitarian Law	YB Intl Human L
Yearbook of International Law	YB Intl L
Yearbook of Maritime Law	YB Marit L
Yearbook of the Canadian Bar Association	YB CBA
Yearbook of the European Convention on Human Rights	YB Eur Conv HR
Yearbook of the Institute of International Law	YB Inst Intl L
Yearbook of the International Court of Justice	YBICJ
Yearbook of the United Nations	YBUN
Yearbook on Human Rights	YBHR

Appendices / Annexes

APPENDIX E / ANNEXE E

E. ONLINE DATABASES ~ BASES DE DONNÉES EN LIGNE

Abreviations ~ Abréviations

Australasian Legal Information Institute	AustLII
Azimut	Azimut
British and Irish Legal Information Institute	BAILII
Butterworths Services	Butterworths
Canadian Legal Information Institute / Institut canadien d'information juridique	CanLII
Commonwealth Legal Information Institute	CommonLII
Hong Kong Legal Information Institute	HKLII
Inforoute Notariale	Inforoute
Justis	Justis
KluwerArbitration	Kluwer
La Référence	Référence
Lawnet (Singapore)	Lawnet
Legal Information Institute	LII
Legifrance	Legifrance
LexisNexis	Lexis
LexUM	LexUM
New Zealand Legal Information Institute	NZLII
Pacific Islands Legal Information Institute	PacLII
Qualisult Systems	Qualisult
LexisNexis Quicklaw	QL
Répertoire électronique de jurisprudence du Barreau	REJB
Société québécoise d'information juridique	SOQUIJ
Southern African Legal Information Institute	SAFLII

Taxnet Pro	Taxnet Pro
Westlaw (US)	WL
Westlaw International	WL Int
Westlaw (UK)	WL UK
WestlawNext Canada	WL Can
World Legal Information Institute	WorldLII